VICTORIAN AMERICA

Victorian America

Transformations in Everyday Life, 1876–1915

THOMAS J. SCHLERETH

 HarperPerennial
A Division of HarperCollins*Publishers*

VICTORIAN AMERICA. Copyright © 1991 by Thomas J. Schlereth. All rights reserved. Printed in the United States of America. No part of this book may be used or reproduced in any manner whatsoever without written permission except in the case of brief quotations embodied in critical articles and reviews. For information address HarperCollins Publishers, Inc., 10 East 53rd Street, New York, NY 10022.

HarperCollins books may be purchased for educational, business, or sales promotional use. For information, please call or write: Special Markets Department, HarperCollins Publishers, Inc., 10 East 53rd Street, New York, NY 10022. Telephone: (212) 207-7528; Fax: (212) 207-7222.

First HarperPerennial edition published 1992.

The Library of Congress has catalogued the hardcover edition as follows:
Schlereth, Thomas J.
   Victorian America : transformations in everyday life, 1876–1915 /
Thomas J. Schlereth.
      p.   cm.—(Everyday life in America ; 4)
   Includes bibliographical references and index.
   ISBN 0-06-016218-X
   1. United States—Social life and customs—1865–1918. I. Title.
II. Series.
E168.S35   1991   89-46555
973.8—dc20

ISBN 0-06-092160-9 (pbk.)

   05 RRD H 20 19

For

Louis Valentine Schlereth
Magdalen Anne Roos
Jacob Joseph Dorsch
Ida May Schremmer
Gertrude Dolores Dorsch
John Albert Schlereth

Their times began in these times

CONTENTS

INTRODUCTION

"He who has lived, alive, during the past fifty years," wrote Louis Sullivan in his *Kindergarten Chats* (1924), "has viewed an extraordinary drama." If one were born in 1856, as was Sullivan, one would have lived through an era marked by the assassination of three American presidents, the impeachment of a fourth, and a stolen election by a fifth. In the years between the Civil War and World War I, the nation admitted twelve new states, which doubled its geography, making it by 1912 the largest continental republic in the world. Americans voted on ten different constitutional amendments, seven of which were law by 1920. The country's population, number of foreign born, suicides, industrial laborers, divorces, gross national product, and white-collar workers all doubled.

To categorize such political, economic, and demographic changes, historians have often used (and juxtaposed) two of the labels that period gave itself, based on Mark Twain and Charles Dudley Warner's satire, *The Gilded Age* (1873), or Herbert Croly's manifesto, *Progressive Democracy* (1913). Other interpreters, then as now, rejected these periodizations as too limited in their political plots of corruption versus reform. Thus, some historians have found the times to be confident, gay, good, or vulnerable, while others have seen them as an age of excess, energy, and enterprise; finally, for still others, the metaphor of color—brown, mauve, or white—explains America's essence between 1876 and 1915.[1]

In the following chapters, I write of Victorian America, arguing that the period ended not at the English monarch's death in 1901 but with the outbreak of World War I in 1914.[2] While Anglo-Saxon Protestants dominated Victorian America, other religious, racial, and ethnic groups made inroads on its cultural hegemony. American Indians, Hispanic Americans, recent immigrants from Eastern Europe and Asia, and most black Americans, however, felt its social control even though few entered its social ranks.

In researching everyday life in Victorian America, I repeatedly observed how many workplaces, housing preferences, consumer choices, recreational pursuits, eating habits, and demographic patterns underwent transition or transformation. Other historians have noticed the transitional quality of the times as well, many seeing the 1890s as a crucial turning point.[3] In monitoring such cultural transformations, I restrict my survey largely to changes in common phenomena: technologies, social institutions, metropolitan newspapers, vital statistics, mass-circulation magazines, photography, and advertising, to name a few.[4]

Although my analysis is a brief, synoptic study, I support it with several interpretive moorings. For example, I argue that migration, movement, and mobility accelerated enormously in Victorian America and, accordingly, devote my first chapter to their impact. Here I also watch the growing metropolitan character of everyday life, recognizing that by 1915 the Bureau of the Census used the concept of a metropolitan district to identify twenty-five central cities with populations of 200,000 or more.[5]

New communication media account, in part, for the new expanded urbanism. Novel cultural forms, such as the motion picture, developed; others, like the metropolitan daily newspaper, were repeatedly reshaped. Without the telegraph and telephone as its central nervous system, the early twentieth-century metropolis would have been stunted by congestion and slowed to the pedestrian pace of messengers and postmen. Without the typewriter, the business machine, and the elevator, it is hard to imagine an office in the urban skyscraper or the central business district.

Economic historians who are attentive to these factors sometimes call this an age of modernization. While they quarrel about precisely when in the nineteenth century modernization began and exactly when in the twentieth century it had reached its zenith, most acknowledge 1870 to 1920 as a critical phase. For instance, Richard Brown, who claims earlier precedents for modernization in America, suggests that its characteristics include industrial production, a commercial agriculture, technological innovation, the accumulation of capital, an urban consciousness, bureaucratic organization, occupational specialization, and widespread education.[6]

The hierarchical and organizational control prompted by the rapid incorporation of America touched the daily life of factory workers as well as office managers.[7] The quantification and standardization of everyday experience by time clocks, entrance examinations, governmental questionnaires, and life insurance policies changed work habits, educational goals, and life expectations. Victorians delighted in quoting statistics, and I use such data, when appropriate, to demarcate some of everyday life's commonalities. So, too, the abundance of mass-produced, mass-distributed material goods, largely products of the metropolis and its advertising media, altered ideas regarding status and wealth in a society that aspired to be a people of plenty.[8]

Individuals who primarily did manual labor, worked for a daily wage, and lived at a low-income level populate all my chapters. So do people who were employed in white-collar positions, who earned a weekly or monthly salary, and lived at a middle-income level. I pay particular attention to the middle class because it increasingly controlled the country's political, social, and cultural agendas.[9] It promoted the consumerism I outline in Chapter 4, the forms of striving summarized in Chapter 7, and the cultural trends displayed at the American world's fairs from 1876 to 1915.

Who made up this "new" middle class? In part, those who always had—doctors, lawyers, ministers, skilled craftsmen, small businessmen, bankers, newspaper editors, and settled farmers. By 1915 white-collar managers, technicians, sales- and servicepeople, factory supervisors, and civil servants swelled its ranks.[10] This middle-class constituency, with its range of modest to substantial incomes, had its dissenters and deserters. Not everyone wanted to get in or got into its ranks. People on the periphery—rural tenants;

most black, Hispanic, Indian, and Asian Americans; and the urban proletariat—having no middle place, were kept in their place.

The growing middle classness of American everyday life happened only gropingly and incompletely. Depressions from 1873 to 1877 and 1893 to 1897 slowed its development. The decade 1879 to 1889 was probably the most violent in American history in terms of civil disorders and labor-capital conflicts. In 1886, "the year of the Great Upheaval," for example, the bloody Haymarket Massacre occurred in Chicago, 700,000 workers went on strike, anti-Chinese rioting erupted in Seattle, and the U.S. military continued its war against the Chiricahua Apache chief Geronimo. Socialism made its greatest advances in the era as a viable political alternative in American politics. Yet new economic opportunities appeared after 1900 when more nonfarm jobs and an increase in real incomes promised a brighter future for a large number of people, particularly urban dwellers. These Americans, noted Walter Nugent, shifted their aspirations from "land hunger to home-ownership-hunger, money-hunger, or durable-goods-hunger."[11] In shorthand terms, they became consumers; they sought goods more than land. In the process, many were either further entrenched within or assimilated into a reshaped and expanded urban and suburban middle class.

Historians have paid most attention to this class's leaders—its academics, engineers, managers, and various reformers—a group often lumped under the label "Progressives." But this minority was not enough. Followers had to come from the white-collar world of office, bureau, and business to forge a new middle-class consensus that admitted newcomers while testing their ethnic, economic, and educational qualifications. The Victorian middle-class coalition imposed its will, often with repressive methods or class confrontations. While its attitudes exerted a pervasive influence in certain areas (for example, consumerism) on the everyday life of the working class, in other cultural sectors (for example, new forms of recreation), the working-class culture changed middle-class habits.

Readers will also find here the nineteenth century's intrigue (and my own) with the material world. We need to "investigate the objects that were prominent parts of Victorian everyday life,"

Kenneth Ames wrote, "precisely because the Victorians themselves were fascinated with material culture. By studying the things that surrounded them we can not only better comprehend their physical environment but come closer to their psychological environment as well."[12] I agree. I maintain that between 1876 and 1915, Americans experienced a fundamental transformation in the number, variety, complexity, and use of the artifacts that they increasingly came to rely on to do their work, to cope with the physical world, and to regulate their social relations. This materialism, in addition to its statistical manifestations (the increased accessibility of goods for all incomes), had important cultural ramifications. Many of the period's writers, among them Mark Twain and Thorstein Veblen, recognized how material differences increasingly defined life's accomplishments and possibilities as their contemporaries embraced what Louis Mumford would later call "the goods' life."[13]

World's expositions, quintessential Victorian artifacts, displayed this material world in unprecedented scale and scope. Between 1876 and 1916 nearly 100 million people visited a dozen major international expositions held in the United States. I use several fairs to summarize changes and continuities in American everyday experience.[14] For example, Americans attending expositions at Philadelphia and San Francisco witnessed changes along a diverse cultural spectrum. In 1876 they favored soda water, patent medicines, and took multicourse noon meals; by 1915 they preferred white flour, cold-cereal breakfasts, and fast-food lunches. In the Centennial's Machinery Hall, individual leather makers crafted horse saddles, completing one every two days; at the Panama-Pacific Exposition, industrial laborers working on an assembly line built a new Ford every half hour. In 1893 electricity contended with steam as the dominant energy source only to be challenged by oil in 1915. Queen Anne houses yielded to California bungalows as the nation's residential ideal. Perhaps most significant of these changes was a transformed middle-class culture, expanded by increasing bureaucratization, fueled by consumer abundance, promulgated by communications technology, and motivated to hold power without property and to maintain hegemony with education and expertise.

Unfortunately this volume will not convey the staggering visual impact of the expanded pictorial and polychromatic culture that flooded everyday life between the advent of photography in the 1840s to the beginning of talking pictures in the 1920s. Series format and design prevents giving the era's graphic evidence its visual due. As a compromise I adapt a technique from Vachel Lindsay. Writing in *The Motion Picture as Art* (1915), Lindsay recognized that America was becoming a world of visual images, of signs and symbols—in his words, a "hieroglyphic civilization." Since the creation, manipulation, and consumption of images is an important premise in Victorian America, I have selected and arranged two types of graphics. Before each chapter, readers will find two separate, often contrasting, images. I have juxaposed such graphics to highlight the period's cultural tensions and paradoxes. Within each chapter, I have also included a visual portfolio to document important cultural changes, contrasts, and contradictions that are relevant to the chapter's topic. In doing so, I follow an interpretive framework of the era first suggested by a contemporary British author, James F. Muirhead, in his travel account, *The Land of Contrasts: A Briton's View of His American Kin* (1898), and one later expanded by other historians of Victorian America.[15]

For the historian there are no banal things.
. . . The humble objects of which we speak
have shaken our modes of living to its very
roots. Modest things of daily life, they
accumulate into forces acting upon whoever
moves within the objects of our civilization.

—SIEGFRIED GIEDION

To make a start
out of particulars
and make them general, rolling
up the sum, by defective means.

—WILLIAM CARLOS WILLIAMS

VICTORIAN AMERICA

FIGURE P.1.   View of grounds and buildings, International Centennial Exposition, Fairmont Park, Philadelphia, Pennsylvania (1876). Lithograph courtesy of the Library of Congress, Division of Prints and Photographs.

FIGURE P.2.   Advertisement for Abendroth Brothers Range Company, International Centennial Exposition, Philadelphia, Pennsylvania. Chromolithograph courtesy of the New-York Historical Society.

PROLOGUE:

AMERICANS AT THE 1876

CENTENNIAL EXPOSITION

AT DAWN on May 10, 1876, the tower bell in Philadelphia's
Independence Hall began to ring. The city's chimes and church
bells, including the Liberty Bell, expanded the clamor. All proclaimed the opening of the Centennial Exhibition celebrating a
century of American Independence. Before its conclusion in mid-
November, 9,910,966 people passed through its automatic, self-
registering turnstiles.

Philadelphia's multiple-building plan (figure P.1) reflected the
enormous expansion of the nineteenth century's material universe. In the Machinery Hall, the Corliss Engine, an apt symbol for
the age, commanded public attention as the world's largest steam
engine. People lined up to watch this mechanical behemoth go
into action, twice a day, as it energized the seventy-five miles of
belts and shafts driving shining rows of machinery—lathes and
saws, drills and looms, presses and pumps—that increasingly characterized the American workplace.

Several of the fair's buildings were analogues to everyday life
institutions: the manufacturing hall resembled the new department stores, such as Wanamakers in Philadelphia; the machinery
building paralleled the rise of industrial factories; while the agriculture palace recalled county or state fairs. The horticultural hall
represented the Victorian love of exotic gardens enshrined in glass
conservatories. New metropolitan museums of art drew part of
their inspiration from exposition art galleries. The Centennial's
layout of intersecting grand avenues anticipated the Progressive's

fascination with city planning, particularly as evidenced at the 1893 Chicago fair or 1915 San Francisco fair. Finally, the suburban quality of the smaller state pavilions, including their eclectic architectural styles, mirrored current American residential patterns.

The exposition's directors first sought to have the fair open weekday evenings and Sunday. Sabbatarians lobbied successfully to keep the Centennial Exhibition closed on Sundays, and the fear of a possible fire from gas lighting of the exhibit halls at night meant a daily 6 P.M. curfew. In 1876, the first time Congress entertained a prohibition amendment to the Constitution, prohibitionists banned the sale of beer and spirits from many fairs' concessions.

Laborers usually had to take time off from their typical six-day work week to attend the Centennial. In a few instances, companies such as the Yale Lock Company and the Baltimore Cotton Mill owners paid their workers' way. Such excursions paralleled the use of the annual company picnic to maintain factory loyalty and employee morale. In the immediate aftermath of the Molly Maguire troubles in the Pennsylvania coal fields, the Reading Coal and Iron Company arranged for 1,100 miners, wives, and children to receive a free railroad trip to the fair.[1]

The Centennial's Bureau of Transportation anticipated much modern transport planning by providing several ways to get to the fair: horse-drawn streetcar, carriage, steamboat, and railroad. While scores of locomotives and passenger cars displayed at various places confirmed railroads as the dominant form of long-distance land transport in 1876, a separate Carriage Building, with its several hundred vehicles, affirmed the principal means of transport for everyday travel.

An elevated monorail carrying up to sixty people shuttled across the Belmont Ravine. One could travel vertically as well as horizontally: Outdoors at the Belmont Hill Tower an elevator carried forty people 185 feet up to an observation platform for a bird's-eye view; indoors, elevator companies exhibited their steam and hydraulic mechanisms for hoisting and lowering goods and people. One could also arrange personal transport. Relaxing in a rented

(60 cents an hour) rolling chair, pushed by a porter, Walt Whitman took in the fair site and its sights.

Geologist William Blake, typifying the Victorian fascination with systems of order and control, proposed that the material universe of the Centennial be organized in ten departments which could be divided and subdivided into one hundred groups and one thousand classes. While Blake's major departments were later modified to seven, his concept of decimal notation prevailed. More important, it influenced how Americans would find books in their public libraries. Melville Dewey used Blake's system as the basis for his decimal system of arranging books, first published as a pamphlet in June 1876.[2]

Classification schemes also codified the exposition's competitions. Awards served as advertisements that were emblazoned on company letterheads, product labels, and salesmen's trade cards. Who won what award counted. General Francis A. Walker, the chief of the Centennial's Bureau of Awards, said that Americans had "a strong passion for statistics." The Centennial's management affirmed his claim. Because of its records, we know how many persons were admitted at each of 106 gates during each hour on every day and the meteorological data for every hour of every day. Also documented are the age of the oldest person who received medical treatment (96 years) and the youngest (2 weeks), plus the number of arrests made by the Centennial's guards (675) for offenses ranging from larceny (160) to fornication (1).[3]

We do not know exactly how many people saw which exhibits — among the estimated 31,000 that displayed both the commonplaces of their culture (reed organs, bone corsets, kitchen ranges [figure P.2], ingrain carpets, sewing machines) and the recent innovations (ready-made shoes, linoleum floor coverings, canned foods, dry yeast) that would influence everyday life. A shrewd observer could point to artifacts that signed the times and others that signaled the future. For example, several displays foreshadowed the coming communications revolution, Alexander Graham Bell's telephone and Christopher B. Sholes's Remington typewriter being only two of the most famous harbingers of things to come.

The U.S. Government Building and The Woman's Pavilion represented the slow but steady expansion of the nation-state and the continual debate over women's rights. The federal Patent Office, celebrating its fortieth anniversary at the Centennial, displayed over 5,000 patent models that had accompanied patent applications, unaware that between 1876 and 1915 it would grant 816,854 patents. The Smithsonian Institution, in conjunction with the Department of the Interior, mounted an immense array of Indian "curiosities"—everything from tepees to pottery, beaded moccasins to totem poles—designed to portray the Native American and his culture. Unfortunately, the exhibition, premised on the assumption that Indians were expendable in the wake of American expansion, depicted them as relics of an earlier evolutionary stage. William Dean Howells, an observer for the *Atlantic Monthly,* reinforced this stereotype: "The red man, as he appears in effigy and in photograph in this collection, is a hideous demon, whose malign traits can hardly inspire any emotion softer than abhorrence."

The Woman's Pavilion owed its existence to a characteristic American institution: the private voluntary association whose purpose is some civic or common cause. The building's exhibits included a working steam engine run by Emma Allison. More than seventy-five women displayed their recently patented inventions. Implements used in laundering, ironing, food preparation, and cooking represented the traditional sphere of homemaking. Others hinted at the economic fact that by 1876 women constituted close to 20 percent of the American labor force outside the home. Female workers ran the pavilion's telegraph office, spooling machine, Jacquard loom, cylinder printing press, and sewing and knitting machines.

To more radical suffragists like Elizabeth Cady Stanton and Susan B. Anthony, the Woman's Building did not say or do enough for the equal rights struggle: on July Fourth, they and others staged a counterdemonstration by reading a "Women's Declaration of Independence" at the other end of the official celebration in downtown Philadelphia. To moderate advocates of women's rights, such as Elizabeth Harbert and Elizabeth Gillispie, the Woman's Building provided a beginning: it served as a gathering of women whose political awareness had been heightened at least in a symbolic way.

New food and beverage preferences surfaced at the 1876 exposition. Americans ate bananas (separately packaged in tin foil and costing 10 cents) in large numbers for the first time. Hot popcorn, known to Native Americans and rural folk for centuries, became a favorite snack food for urbanites who, after the fair, demanded it when attending baseball games, vaudeville shows, and nickelodeons. Cigars, as evidenced by the six separate concession stands devoted to their sale, continued their popularity, although plug chewing had numerous advocates. Ice cream soda fountains were everywhere.

The Philadelphia Centennial opened in the trough of the depression of 1873 and closed shortly before the massive railroad strikes of 1877, the first outburst of nationwide industrial labor conflict. It, like the period it inaugurated, was riddled with paradox. Ostensibly it commemorated 1776, yet only a few colonial relics were exhibited: Washington's false teeth, a few colonial army uniforms, and the contents of a "New England Kitchen of 1776." In 1876 Americans looked forward, not to their past. In that year, they participated in the most disputed presidential election ever, heard Ulysses S. Grant apologize for the scandals of his administration, and witnessed the first national convention of the Greenback party. They also took in the National League's first baseball season and made John Habberton's pulp novel, *Helen's Babies,* the year's best-seller, while banning Mark Twain's *The Adventures of Tom Sawyer* at the Brooklyn and Denver public libraries.

FIGURE 1.1. Medical examination station, U.S. Immigration Service, Ellis Island, New York City (1912). Photograph courtesy of the National Archives Trust.

FIGURE 1.2. Indian reservation barracks, Bureau of Indian Affairs (ca. 1890s). Stereograph courtesy of the Library of Congress, Division of Prints and Photographs.

1   MOVING

Migration and movement, mobility and motion characterized identity in Victorian America. A country in transition was also
in transit. Everyone seemed en route: emigrating and immigrating, removing or being removed, resettling and relocating, in
many directions—east to west, south to north, rural to urban,
urban to suburban. In American slang, "going places" came to
mean a geographic as well as a social destination. Movement so
touched this American era that it deserves to be treated first in any
survey of its everyday life.

An overseas diaspora marked the personal history of a quarter
of Americans living in 1915. These "new" immigrants figure
prominently in the national image of the period, an age of unprecedented immigration and one immortalized in two national
symbols: the Statue of Liberty (1886) and Ellis Island (1892). Immigration entailed both departure and destination. The rupture of
traditional everyday life—relocation from familiar surroundings,
separation from kinfolk, the experience of becoming a foreigner
and ceasing to belong—took a toll that will never be completely
knowable.

America also experienced continual internal migration, causing
Norwegian novelist, Knut Hamsun, to note, "Everyday is moving
day.... The population is only half-settled."[1] Treks westward took
every conceivable form: Arizona land runs, Yukon gold rushes,
California dreams. Flights out of the South took blacks to northern
cities and whites to the Southwest plains. Midwesterners, in a

revolt from the village, poured into Milwaukee and Minneapolis, Cleveland and Chicago.

Movement increased on the margin as well as in the mainstream. Vagrants, squatters, and regiments of unemployed workers, took to the roads; some (for instance, Coxey's Army in 1893–94) marched on Washington (figure 1.9) to dramatize their plight. Paradoxically, as homeless, landless, and jobless Americans roamed city streets in the 1890s, other citizens took to traveling about on annual vacations.

Some Americans were moved against their will or prevented from moving. American Indian nations were systematically removed to (usually western) reservations. Nativists, a half million strong in the American Protective Association in 1894, clamored that some foreigners ought to be excluded or restricted in their movements, particularly if they were Orientals, Jews, or Catholics. Jim Crow laws sought to keep blacks in their place.

Immigrants and Emigrants

ARRIVALS: EUROPE, ASIA, THE AMERICAS

Immigration officials, nativists, and social reformers often turned to statistics to demonstrate the massive influx of newcomers. For example, the U.S. Department of Labor mounted an "electrical diagram" at the 1915 Panama-Pacific Exposition that furnished spectators with extensive data on the "races of alien arrivals; occupations of those persons admitted; causes of exclusion; and arrests and deportations by classes."[2] The display noted that before the Civil War, the banner year for new immigrants was 1854, when 427,833 people arrived. A new peak was reached in 1882, when 788,992 entered. However, in the early twentieth century the annual influx passed the million mark six times, and in 1907 the figure rose to 1,285,349.

Many who came after the 1880s were labeled "new immigrants" because they differed from those who previously emigrated largely from northern and western Europe. The outflow of Italians, Greeks, Slovaks, Poles, Russians, Austro-Hungarians, as well as people from the Orient (first the Chinese, then the Japanese and the Filipinos) and from Mexico diversified everyday American life. These new immigrants differed in religious background, for many were Greek Orthodox, Buddhist, or Roman Catholic, entering a basically Protestant society; a large segment were Russian and Polish Jews. The new immigrants spoke numerous languages and were generally poorer and less educated and more differentiated in color and culture than were the earlier immigrants.

In focusing only upon national statistics and ethnic diversity, historians often lose sight of emigrating and immigrating as personal historical acts. Why did individuals or families decide to go or to stay? How did they journey? Did they feel uprooted or transplanted? How did their everyday lives change?

In summarizing the European experience, John Bodnar suggests a combination of factors that prompted people to leave: the commercialization of agriculture, the decline of craft work, changes in landownership patterns, expansion of the population, and major shifts in the financial and market conditions of capitalism. To be sure, the familiar imponderables—wanderlust, adventure, family problems—played their part, but most of those who moved did so because they were "pragmatically adjusting their goals and behavior throughout the nineteenth century to meet the changing economic realities in Europe as well as opportunities in America."

Most emigrant streams Bodnar identifies followed one of two courses. Skilled artisans and independent farmers, threatened by the factory production of cheap goods and by the commercialization of agriculture, left first. Hoping to avoid the "further decline in social and economic status, they usually possessed modest financial resources, left in family units, and were less likely to return." As a pioneer wave, they "exercised leadership and influence in American ethnic communities." A second group, larger in size and poorer in status, "consisted of marginal land owners who hoped to earn enough to return and increase their holdings," the children of such owners, and those with no real property. This second group was comprised more of individuals than of family groupings and, at least initially, their intent often was to come to America to earn money that would allow them to improve their life once they returned to Europe. Whatever their plans, most immigrants set out well prepared for their journeys. Through kinship networks, labor agents, and other intermediaries, as well as emigrants' guides and maps, most had amassed a wealth of detailed information, before departing, concerning exactly where they wanted to go and how to get there.[3]

Emigrants first journeyed to a major seaport, such as Liverpool, Hamburg, Le Havre, Bremen, or Antwerp. Once they were there, numerous decisions had to be made: which baggage runners, boardinghouse keepers, and provisioners to trust; which border officials, emigration officers, and government bureaucrats to placate; and which tickets, sailing routes, and accommodations to purchase. Unlike earlier in the century, travel costs were lower: By 1900, a steerage ticket from Naples to New York cost $15. In the 1870s America's export of bulky raw materials—timber, cotton, tobacco, grain—prompted the cheap fares. The linens, china, and wines brought back on the return voyage left ample space for passengers who were willing to endure travel in steerage class. By 1900, large steamships that were specifically designed for the immigrant trade, such as the Hamburg-America's *Imperator,* carried 700 first-, 600 second-, and 1,000 third-class passengers, as well as 1,800 in steerage. The average transatlantic emigrant passage took fewer than ten days from northwest European ports and slightly longer from Adriatic ones.

At some stage before emigrating, the immigrants reviewed their material possessions. We still do not know enough about how they decided what things to bring and what to abandon. Certain items were standard: birth certificates, passports, inspection cards, exit visas, tickets—public artifacts validating their private existence. Others, for example, such as feather bedding, were deemed vital to their personal comfort and cultural heritage. Still others were objects of memory (diaries and correspondence), of status (linens and tableware), and of identity (heirlooms and photos). To prove they were not paupers, they carried a small reserve of cash, the average sum being $31.39 between 1899 and 1910.[4]

When the emigrants stepped ashore and became immigrants, another cycle of person processing began. They encountered the uniformed federal authorities at one of seventy embarkation stations, such as those in Baltimore, New Orleans, or San Francisco. The rites of passage (figure 1.1) through America's most famous and busiest immigrant station, New York's Ellis Island, etched its impact upon everyday American life in immigrant novels and autobiographies, vaudeville humor, the photography of Lewis Hine, and the oral traditions of the 12 million people who moved through its halls beginning in 1892. Immigration inspectors conducted a battery of tests (for example, for tuberculosis, glaucoma, and insanity) on the new arrivals. Most got through in a few hours; about 20 percent were detained for further questioning and observation, and 1 percent were deported. Those who were barred from entry under the 1891 immigration legislation were the severely retarded or mentally ill, paupers, felons, polygamists, contract laborers, and people with contagious diseases.

Legislation excluded others, particularly peoples whose race or culture seemed alien to white Americans. Thus, for the first time in the nation's history, an 1882 federal law checked the immigration of a specific ethnic group by banning the entry of the Chinese for ten years (the courts had already ruled the Chinese ineligible for naturalization). Resentment of the Chinese mounted, particularly on the West Coast, so that by 1902 the exclusionists in Congress had secured the prohibition of the Chinese indefinitely. Only when they remained behind the colorful lion-gates of urban chinatowns did the Chinese find a measure of security. The saying "not a Chinaman's chance" reflected their plight throughout Victorian America (figure 4.7).

Nativist and racist violence erupted over immigration. Anti-immigrant forces organized their hatred into powerful institutions like the Immigrant Restriction League and the Ku Klux Klan. Beginning in 1882, a fifty-cent head tax was imposed upon any immigrant entering the country by water. Legislation making literacy a requirement for entry into the United States passed Congress in 1896, 1903, and 1915, only to be vetoed by the president.

Not everyone who emigrated to America stayed to be an immigrant in America. Roughly a fourth to a third who came left again. Many planned to do so from the beginning, moving seasonally just to work and returning home annually to their families. Among Pittsburgh's steelworkers from 1908 to 1910 (including a bad, middling, and prosperous year), forty-four southern and eastern Europeans departed the country for every hundred who arrived.[5] Between 1899 and 1924, about half the Italians, Hungarians, and Slovaks; about 12 percent of the Irish; and about 23 percent of the Scandinavians likewise recrossed the Atlantic after working in America. Mexicans and Canadians, moving through America's side doors, came only intending to return home. Others, like many Greeks (between one-fifth and one-fourth of Greece's work force was in the United States by 1909), stayed semipermanently to send money home. These sojourners traveled back and forth to visit kin, display their affluence, deliver goods or money, find a bride, or escort other family members to the United States.[6] Still others returned home or went elsewhere because everyday life in America repulsed or rejected them. Assimilation proved too difficult, racial or ethnic prejudice too strong, and economic opportunities too meager.

RESETTLING AND MIGRATING

Massive expansion into the trans-Mississippi West is only the best-known story of continual movement within the United States; internal migration also took place to and from regions, cities, and suburbs. There were, of course, exceptions—people for whom, despite a half century of railroad building, everyday life was static and stationary. The old New England family, poor but proud, as photographed by Chansonetta Emmons in the 1890s; certain southern aristocrats still clinging to their ancestral halls with no use for the "go-getter" mentality of "New South" Atlanta; and Old New Yorkers and Old Philadelphians, incarnations of tradition celebrated in nostalgic novels and dutiful autobiographies, bemoaned the "Great Restlessness." Others disagreed, arguing that not being able and willing to move implied stagnation. "Mobility," noted Howard Mumford Jones, "which had been a mark of a westering society from the beginning, became an absolute virtue in an industrial democracy wherein mechanism put a special premium on speed and movement and a special disadvantage on standing still."[7]

Even the era's policy on Indian reservations (figure 1.2) operated on this premise. Forced to migrate to new areas that were not then desired by the ever-moving white settlers or removed (ostensibly for their betterment) to land intentionally set aside for them, Native Americans soon discovered that white settlers and their demands for resources—land, water, minerals—quickly engulfed the tribes even in their new locations and insisted that they be moved yet again. James Earle Fraser's poignant sculpture, *The End of the Trail,* displayed in 1915 at the Panama-Pacific Exposition, aptly symbolized the eradication of many of America's first immigrants, done, in part, in the cause of movement.

Forced migrations relocated other dispossessed Americans. Beginning in 1854, the New York Children's Aid Society arranged "orphan trains" that took ninety thousand abandoned and orphaned children from eastern cities to new lives in the western states. Upon arrival in a western community, farm families and townspeople looked over the young passengers and chose which ones to adopt.

Orphan trains represented but a small part of two aspects of the demographic history of the late nineteenth century. First, an enormous and persistent outflow of the native-born population (over 2.5 million from 1870 to 1900) took place from the East to the West (figure 1.3), a trend balanced by a massive influx of foreign-born persons into the East. Second, this pattern was altered in the 1890s, when the West attracted far more total immigrants than did the East.[8]

What did this movement westward mean for everyday life? For many, it entailed almost continual transience. Frontier historians calculate that nineteenth-century westerners moved on an average of four to five times as adults. Richard Garland, father of novelist Hamlin Garland, aptly represents, in William L. Barney's estimate, an entire generation of northern farmers. Born into a Maine farm family, Garland clerked for Amos Lawrence in Boston, "went west with his parents on the Erie Canal in 1840, worked as a lumberjack in the forests of the upper Midwest, cleared a 160-acre farm in Wisconsin, marched off to fight for the Union, returned home, sold the farm, and moved to Minnesota, to Iowa, and finally to South Dakota."[9] Not without reason did his son title one of his writings, *Main Travelled Roads* (1891).

Homesteading immigrants populated the western migration in

ever-increasing numbers by the 1890s. Here the case of Mary Ida
Schremmer and her family is instructive. The Schremmers, who
came from Jacobsdorf, Germany, in 1888, booked train passage
out of Baltimore to join fellow Germans along the Platte in Nebraska. Mary Ida vividly remembered the five-day journey across
the United States in the "zulu" railroad cars, constructed of two
sections containing double berths made of wooden slats astride a
narrow aisle. Travelers padded the slats with their own blankets
and clothing. The zulu cars contained a cooking stove on which
the passengers prepared their food en route. At journey's end, the
new Nebraskans disembarked on the prairie, and railroad employees disinfected the cars. Once in Nebraska, the travelers could stay
for three or four days, rent free, at Immigrant Houses located in
Omaha and Lincoln, until they had located the land they wanted
to acquire, either through purchase or homesteading. The
Schremmers staked a claim, built a sod house, and eked out a
marginal subsistence for a few years before, in a fashion typical of
another important demographic trend of the 1890s, they abandoned rural life, moved to a German enclave in Pittsburgh, Pennsylvania, and became part of the urban working class by the turn
of the century.

Several spectacular migrations captured the national imagination of Victorian America. The Klondike Gold Run of 1897, the
sudden settlement of Oregon's Christmas Valley in 1902, and the
real estate boom in southern California, 1900–15, were all striking
examples of Americans on the move. None of them, however,
equaled the famous Oklahoma "land runs" of 1889–93.

"OKLAHOMA—THE LAST CHANCE!" proclaimed handbills an-
nouncing Congress's decision to allow white settlement on a fer-
tile tract of "unassigned lands" in Oklahoma's Indian Territory
beginning on April 22, 1889. Government surveyors divided 2
million acres into quarter sections for homesteads and reserved
larger tracts for town sites. Two federal offices, artifacts of the era's
penchant for "doing a land-office business," were hastily constructed at Guthrie Station (where the Santa Fe Railroad crossed
the Cimarron) and at the Kingfisher stage stop. Thousands of land-
hungry settlers massed for the stampede. Contractors stockpiled
lumber and prefabricated buildings to erect towns overnight.

Merchants vied for freight space to ship goods to the boom communities. Every known mode of transport was lined up for the race for Oklahoma: horses, mules, ponies, wagons, prairie schooners, carriages, bicycles, and trains (which could travel only at a speed equal to that of a horse).

Three days before the opening, home seekers gathered on the perimeters of the promised land. At twelve o'clock on April 22, the starting flag dropped, a bugle sounded, and cavalry guns signaled the opening of the final frontier (figure 1.7). Within hours, the "Magic City of Guthrie" was a seething, barely believable reality. By sunset, practically every homestead and all the town lots in the virgin cities of Kingfisher, Stillwater, Oklahoma City, El Reno, and Norman were taken. Ten thousand people crowded into five hundred makeshift homes. "Tents of all colors, blankets of every shade, flags and streamers of every hue, coats, and in fact anything and everything that could be hoisted to the breeze, served both as shelter and as signs of habitation on lots."[10] Even westerners admitted they had never seen anything like it. Survivors who made the run were apt to recall in later years, like one of Edna Ferber's fictional characters, Yancey Cravat, in the novel *Cimarron:* "Creation! Hell! That took six days. This was done in one. It was history made in a hour—and I helped make it."

Other Oklahoma Indian reservations were overrun and claimed, the most turbulent in September 1893, when a hundred thousand people stamped into the Cherokee outlet. As desperate land-hungry men, many ruined in the drought and depression of 1893, competed for the dwindling public domain, violence flared. One successful settler stumbled over the body of a man with a slit throat and crushed skull, hidden in a hollow soon after the opening. Another party of pioneers boasted of frightening blacks from a claim with threats of lynching. Their neighbors endorsed the act with cries of "That's right; we don't want any niggers in this country."[11]

Southern blacks and whites resettled in the West as part of another crucial geographic reorientation of the American people originating in the post–Civil War South, a region that experienced a continual outflow of population. Departing whites were hard-pressed farmers, tired of tenant farming or sharecropping, and whose makeshift signs, GONE TO TEXAS or GONE TO OKLAHOMA, announced their hopes for a new life by moving to a new place. In the first large-scale migration of blacks out of the South, six thousand freedmen, known as the "exodusters," left the lower Mississippi Valley for Kansas in 1879. Increasingly, however, blacks sought nonagricultural jobs in the North, thus initiating the "Great Migration" from field to factory for thousands, changing forever the everyday lives of the black migrants and the racial status quo in much of the North. For example, from 1910 to 1920, 10.4 percent of the black population of Alabama and Mississippi left the region.[12] Blacks usually moved in stages, first migrating to southern towns or large cities, such as Birmingham, Savannah, or Memphis. There they worked as domestics, construction laborers, or railroad hands before moving again to a northern city. The blacks traveled in the summer when train fares were cheaper or, if lucky, on tickets provided to black porters who received free excursion passes as company gratuities. Many black porters and waiters later assumed leadership roles in their communities; they also founded, after a bitter struggle, the first black unions.

Rural white folk also migrated to American cities. As Frederick Jackson Turner noted, of the one thousand counties in the United States that decreased in population between 1910 and 1920, almost all were rural, and the two thousand that increased in population were urban and industrial (figure 1.6). Later historians concurred about this demographic shift. One found a turnover of almost 78 percent in the five small towns of Grant County, Wisconsin, from 1880 to 1895; another estimated that between 1860 and 1900, "for every city laborer who took up farming, 20 farmers flocked to the city." Finally, as Walter Nugent recognized, as early as the 1870s a "metropolitan mode" of life developed in sections of New England, the Middle Atlantic states, and parts of the Midwest. This shift involved more than a movement of people from farm to city; as I shall show later, it also involved a reorientation of values and a rearrangement of many patterns of everyday life.[13]

Some demographers estimate that the mobility rates were as high on the urban frontier as on the western one. Movement took place within the cities, out to their suburban perimeters, and to other cities. Slums and ghettos entrapped many, but others moved out and on to different economic opportunities, home ownership, or another town. For example, the most striking characteristic of a study of 1,775 men in Omaha between 1880 and 1920 was that only about 3 percent had lived in the same place for as long as two decades. These residential movements parallel similar patterns for other cities as different as Newburyport, St. Paul, Rochester, Toledo, Poughkeepsie, Des Moines, and Seattle.[14]

During the nineteenth century, a fairly substantial "floating proletariat" drifted in and out of American cities. At work in fields, on the railroads, or in isolated mining or lumbering sites, these unmarried, unskilled hired men, day laborers, and migrant workers spilled back into cities during the winter months in search of temporary work while living in cheap lodging houses. Individuals in ethnic communities often acted as employment agents for such laborers. Whether as the Italian *banchiere,* the Mexican *enganchador,* or the Japanese *kieyaku-nin,* these immigrants sent compatriots to construction jobs, agricultural work, and railroad-section sites by the thousands. Acting as money changers and moneylenders, letter writers, and legal advisers, they did it all, for a fee.[15]

The mobility and numbers of "a new, more aggressive type of homeless man emerged—the tramp" during the depression of the 1870s. The dramatic increase in and continual presence of this "underclass" alarmed many (also mobile) middle-class Americans who argued for the stronger antivagrancy laws and "tramp acts" passed by city councils in the 1880s. While stereotyped as immigrants and radicals in novels like John Hay's *The Bread-Winners* (1883), tramps who rode the railroads were frequently native- and urban-born, young, and literate. Such books as Josiah Flynt's *Tramping with Tramps* (1899) and Jack London's *The Road* (1907) chronicled their lives, at once parodies of and reactions to the dominant culture's apotheosis of mobility.[16]

Certain working-class families moved with a frequency almost equal to that of the single laborers. Black and white sharecroppers migrated continuously, their debts transferred among landlords, which made it difficult to escape indebtedness. Miners' families in western and northeastern Pennsylvania, West Virginia, and the

Midwest led, in one miner's words, "a gypsy's life," a third of them
moving every two years in search of work.[17]

Beginning in the 1870s, the fear of being overwhelmed by the
growing disorder, uprootedness, and complexity of urban life fostered an escapist mentality among some Americans, "pushing"
them to new suburbs. Others, refusing to share residential space
with recent immigrants and minority groups, sought social and
cultural homogeneity in suburban living. For still others, the move
to the suburbs meant, for the first time in their lives, owning their
own homes. The suburban impulse also resulted from "pull" factors. A rural ideal, symbolized in part by the country's western
frontiers, enticed mobile Americans toward the outskirts of growing metropolitan areas. A long-standing cultural tradition espoused the virtues of a small, pastoral community of single-family,
detached houses as the embodiment of the national character.[18]
As Chapter 3 shows, railroad suburbs developed outside almost
every large American city by the 1880s. But the high cost of both
housing in and train fares to and from these outlying areas (together with extra commuting time) meant that only the affluent
could afford them. Only with the advent of the electric streetcar
did a move to the suburbs become a more frequent possibility for
workers and their families.

MOVING AND TOURING

In New York City, May 1, the traditional end of residential leases,
meant a chaotic yearly change of place. One observer, Samuel
Woodworth, thought it almost indescribable: "May Day in New
York must be seen, and heard, and felt, and tasted, in order to be
known and appreciated. . . . About one-third of a population of two
hundred thousand souls change their residence annually."[19] Several express companies—American Express, Wells Fargo, and
American Messenger Service (later United Parcel Service)—
moved an increasing cache of American possessions. As they prospered, some went into such sidelines as banking, writing money
orders, and eventually traveler's checks.

Americans seemed to delight especially in moving items of
great size. House movers, for example, enjoyed regular work in
most large cities (figure 1.5). Rather than tear down houses, home

owners or their realtors often had them moved. George Pullman, later famous for his mobile empire of palace cars, acquired his initial capital from moving buildings, first in Albion, New York, to make way for the expansion of the Erie Canal, and second in Chicago, where he raised the block-long Tremont Hotel without disrupting its dinner service.

Modern transport—steamships, railroads, electric interurbans—coupled with expanded leisure time and discretionary income—meant that an annual vacation, usually taken in the summer, became a middle-class ideal. Often a businessman would send his wife and children to a resort for all or part of a summer, joining them only on the weekends by train.[20] Workers, unable to take off from their jobs for long periods, commonly made one-day excursions to the seashore and amusement resorts like Atlantic City and Coney Island.

Railroads brought tourists to spectacular scenic landscapes like the Grand Tetons, wonders that were once remote and accessible only to the hearty or wealthy. The Chicago, Burlington, and Quincy, for example, conducted escorted group tours and gave away guidebooks, souvenirs, and postcards to promote trips. During the 1880s, a new tourist sleeping car, a spartan version of the standard Pullman coach, could be booked at an economical rate. Railroad corporations, securing government leases, turned public parks into private profit by constructing resort hotels, such as Old Faithful Inn at Yellowstone (built by the Northern Pacific) and the Glacier Hotel in Glacier National Park (built by the Great Northern). Fred Harvey collaborated with the Atchison, Topeka & Santa Fe Railroad to build fifteen hotels and tourist restaurants (ninety "Harvey Houses" by 1917) throughout the Southwest, including El Tavor on the south rim of the Grand Canyon.

Automobiles eventually led to the decline of railroad resort hotels, but, in turn, promoted the rise of auto camping and tourist homes. Motor cars, once democratized through mass production and mass distribution, spawned an unprecedented cult of personal movement. Automobiling provided new freedom of action and direct contact with landscape unknown to passengers of trains and ships (figure 1.10).

Mobility Modes

HORSE AND MULE

To travel locally in 1915 rural America, one walked or rode a horse or a mule. Such animals were central to a community's geography. Movement between towns, between farms, and between towns and farms depended almost entirely upon the saddle horse, the four-wheel buggy, or the two-mule wagon. Commercial drays carried railroad freight, moved households for local citizens, and made deliveries for stores that lacked their own wagons. Peddlers' wagons delivered ice, coal, and foodstuffs.

Small-town Main Streets, designed to accommodate turning teams, were lined with hitching rails and mounting blocks. Courthouse squares had at least one water trough. Feed and sale barns, livery stables, blacksmith, wagon, and harness shops, and residential horse-and-carriage stables filled the everyday landscape. So did manure swarming with flies. (One estimate calculated that New York's horse population deposited 2.5 million pounds of manure and 60,000 gallons of urine on the city's streets each day.) Horse-drawn transport dictated the pace (roughly ten to fifteen miles an hour) of much daily life; it determined the circuits of salesmen, the layout of school districts and cemeteries, and many nineteenth-century recreational patterns.

The livery stable served as the hub of this horse-powered universe. There drummers rented horses and carriages to haul sample cases into the hinterland. Fancy buggies and sleighs could be booked for picnics, fairs, and elopements. The funeral parlor's hearse, the doctor's rig, the town water cart, and hotel hacks were usually stored there. The western livery stable often sold or traded saddles and harnesses and offered hay, grain, wood, kerosene, and coal in retail or wholesale lots. It provided covert arenas for boxing bouts, gambling, and cock fights, and, in a community gone dry because of local prohibition, it often doubled as a saloon.

A male-dominated environment, perfect for the loafing and gossiping of retirees, hired men, and stable hands, livery stables fascinated small boys—a fact that such diverse interpreters of Midwestern life as Louis Bromfield, Sherwood Anderson, and William Allen White all noted. There Anderson and White learned the mores of drinking and Bromfield the facts of life. In the latter's opinion, "small boys who learned of sex in such places gained a more wholesome attitude than those who listened to whispered stories in YMCA locker rooms."[21]

By 1900 over 2.4 million mules provided tractive power for the nation's farms; in the lower South, lower Midwest, and the West, they plowed and harrowed the land, snaked logs from the woods, hauled split wood to tobacco-curing barns, and pulled the circular sweeps of cane-grinding mills. In the mines of Pennsylvania, West Virginia, and Southern Illinois, they trucked in timbers for ceiling supports and pulled out cars loaded with ore or coal (figure 2.6). They took people to town, to church, and to the grave. Many southern farmers preferred working mules rather than horses even though horses could be bought more cheaply. In their view, mules lived longer, resisted diseases and withstood heat better, ate less, were more surefooted in the crops, and were smarter and more easily trained.

Mule trains and muleskinners influenced American speech and humor. The mule's notorious flatulence ("A farting mule is a good mule") pervaded many Southern folktales. Josh Billings called the animal "a singular stubborn fact" and recommended: "To break a mule—begin at his head." At the turn of the century, Fink's Mules, billed as the World's Equine Joy Fest, were among vaudeville's most famous animal acts.

The great epizootics of the nineteenth century emphasize how vital horses and mules were to everyday life. The animal counterparts to epidemics that afflict people, the epizootic of 1872 claimed almost a quarter of the nation's horses (over 4 million) and brought the country to a virtual standstill for three months before the winter killed the mosquitoes that transmitted its virus. By that time the financial losses suffered helped bring on the Panic of 1873. In many cities, teams of men pulled carts and wagons as homes went without fuel deliveries, fires blazed unfought, and garbage remained uncollected.

TRAIN AND TROLLEY

The development of railroads from 1876 to 1915 looms as an epic chapter in an epic time. The major contours of this revolution, in which men grabbed for mastery of space as well as of time, are monumental: four U.S. transcontinental lines by the 1890s, trains arriving and departing Chicago (the "Freight-Handler of the World") every four minutes by 1900, and the American landscape covered by more trackage than any other country by 1920. Railroads (figure 1.4) became the nation's largest industry, surpassing all others as a buyer of iron, steel, and coal; as a user of capital; and as the country's largest employer (1.7 million workers in 1910). The railroad industry, with its monopolies, stock manipulations, rate conspiracies, and government subsidies, also represented the new business order and its unprecedented corporate power. In Alan Trachtenberg's words, it served as "the most conspicuous machine of the age," the era's "symbol of mechanization and of economic and political change."[22]

Railroads reshaped the American-built environment and reoriented American behavior. "In a quarter of a century," claimed the *Omaha Daily Republican* in 1883, "they have made the people of the country homogeneous, breaking through the peculiarities and provincialisms which marked separate and unmingling sections." The iron horse simultaneously exploited the landscape of natural resources, made velocity of transport and economy of scale necessary parts of industrial production, and carried consumer goods to households; it dispatched immigrants to unsettled places, drew emigrants away from farms and villages to cities; and sent men and guns to battle. It standardized time and travel, seeking to annihilate distance and space by allowing movement at any time and in any season or type of weather. In its grand terminals and stations, architects re-created historic Roman temples and public baths, French châteaus and Italian bell towers—edifices that common folk used as stages for many of everyday life's high emotions: meeting and parting, waiting and worrying, planning new starts or coming home.

Passenger terminals, like the luxury express trains that hurled people over grade crossings and past small-town depots, spotlight

FIGURE 1.3. Thomas Hovenden, *Breaking Home Ties* (1890), oil on canvas. Courtesy of the Philadelphia Museum of Art, given by Ellen Harrison McMichael in memory of C. Emory McMichael.

FIGURE 1.4. Advertisement for Great American Tea Company: "Ten Minutes for Refreshments" (ca. 1880). Chromolithograph courtesy of the Library of Congress, Division of Prints and Photographs.

FIGURE 1.5. S. W. Matteson, *Re-arranging San Francisco* (1900). Photograph courtesy of the Milwaukee Public Museum.

FIGURE 1.6. S. W. Matteson, *Household Goods Crossing Montana* (1888). Photograph courtesy of the Milwaukee Public Museum.

FIGURE 1.7.   William Prettyman, *Opening of the Cherokee Outlet*, Oklahoma Territory (September 16, 1893). Photograph courtesy of the Archives and Manuscripts Division, Oklahoma Historical Society.

FIGURE 1.8.   William Sontag, *The Bowery at Night* (1895), oil on canvas. Courtesy of the Museum of the City of New York.

FIGURE 1.9. Underwood and Underwood, *On to Washington! Marshall Browne and Coxey's Army* (1894). Stereograph courtesy of the Library of Congress, Division of Prints and Photographs.

FIGURE 1.10. Wayside Inn, Sudbury, Massachusetts (ca. 1905). Photograph courtesy of the Henry Ford Museum and Greenfield Village.

the romance of railroading (The Twentieth-Century Limited sped between Chicago and New York in twenty hours by 1915). Equally important to everyday life were the slow freight trains chugging through industrial zones, the morning and evening commuter locals shuttling back and forth between suburban stations and urban terminals, and the incessant comings and goings of the classification or switching yards. Moreover, in addition to its being a transportation pathway equipped with a mammoth physical plant of tracks, signals, crossings, bridges, and junctions, plus telegraph and telephone lines, the railroad nurtured factory complexes, coal piles, warehouses, and generating stations, forming along its right-of-way what John Stilgoe aptly called "the metropolitan corridor" of the American landscape.[23]

As the era's most visible example of modern technology's first major invasion of daily life, railroads also mirrored the culture's contradictions. Before and after the Supreme Court's 1896 decision in *Plessy vs. Ferguson,* blacks rode in separate cars and used only "Colored" entrances, barbershops, rest rooms, and water fountains at most southern depots. Over a third of the labor-capital confrontations from 1870 to 1920 involved the railroads, beginning with the first nationwide strikes of 1877. In 1894 the American Railway Union, led by Eugene V. Debs, boycotted all Pullman railroad cars in sympathy for Pullman workers who were protesting wage cuts, thereby setting off a national political, economic, and constitutional crisis. While they were efficient movers of men and materials, railroads also caused injury and death. "Two hundred thousand have been killed or injured by the railroads of the United States in the past twenty years," wrote one observer in 1921. "Thirty thousand of them were children, and more than 125,000 of them wage earners."[24]

Horse-drawn omnibuses and horse-drawn streetcars (moving on a fixed rail) emerged as the first public transit early in nineteenth-century America. Although only slightly faster than walking, they encouraged urban expansion and home construction to a distance of three to five miles from a downtown area. By the 1870s, middle-class families moved to horsecar suburbs like Roxbury outside Boston, Germantown in Philadelphia, and Highland Park outside Oakland.

More Americans rode the horsecar than its competitor, the cable car. Developed in San Francisco in 1882 by William Smith Hallidie, a Scottish immigrant who had done well in the wire-rope business, the cable car saw installations in several American cities—Chicago, New York, Philadelphia, and, of course, San Francisco, where it still operates. Although the cable car was cleaner (no manure), quieter (the gear machinery was underground), and more powerful (able to carry larger cars with more people up steeper inclines), it demanded a high capital investment to build and maintain.

Electrical engineer Frank Julian Sprague changed all this in 1887 with his development of the electric streetcar in a citywide transport system for Richmond, Virginia. Sprague's cars got their power (and their name) from a small, four-wheel carriage connected to the cars by a flexible overhead cable. This carriage, called a "troller," was pulled or trolled along the wires. In the history of American technology, the electric trolley became one of the most rapidly accepted innovations in transport. The auto, by comparison, which developed at about the same time, took longer. By 1890, forty-one cities had electric streetcar lines; five years later, 850 lines were in operation. In the 1910s, the trolley effectively tripled the size of the metropolis (figure 1.8); one could now speak of a "streetcar city" instead of the antebellum "walking city."[25]

Trolleys raised the potential speed of city travel to twenty miles per hour, moving even faster in sparsely populated areas. Most important, trolleys were cheap. Instead of a zoned fare (used by the steam railroads serving the affluent suburbs), most trolleys charged a flat fee, with free transfers, on most routes. By the 1890s, trolley companies achieved sufficient operating efficiency so that the average fare dropped from a dime to a nickel.

Trolleys fostered Sunday country outings, traveling concerts, and group picnics. Amusement parks, summer resorts, and baseball fields developed adjacent to their lines. The Brooklyn Dodgers, for example, were so named not because of their agility on the playing field but in tribute to their fans, who had to avoid speeding cars in the maze of trolley lines crisscrossing the city.

Interurban trolleys or trains, first introduced to connect the cities of Granville and Newark, Ohio, gave a special flair to moving through Victorian America. These heavy, individually powered cars ran more frequently than did mainline trains. Famous interurbans, like the Muncie Meteor to Indianapolis, reached speeds of eighty miles an hour. By 1915, it was possible, with frequent changes of line, to move by interurban from New York to Boston for a fare under four dollars or to travel from Freeport, Illinois, to Ithaca, New York, a distance of over one thousand miles.[26] Armed with a tube of nickels for fares and a Kodak camera for recording their trip's adventures, newlyweds Clinton and Louise Lucas took a 1904 wedding trip from Delaware to Maine that they later wrote up as *A Trolley Honeymoon* (1904).

AUTO AND CANAL

In addition to advances in mechanized transport—incline railways to hilltop suburbs like Price Hill in Cincinnati or Mt. Washington in Pittsburgh, elevated railroads, such as New York's Third or Sixth Avenue Els, or subway systems pioneered by Boston (1897) and New York (1904)—the end of the Gilded Age was the beginning of the Automotive Age. Initially seen as a rich man's toy when autos were exhibited at the 1893 World's Fair, by 1916 a Ford Model T sold for $360. In that year, U.S. manufacturers produced over 1.7 million cars and 181,348 commercial vehicles; 4.8 million motor vehicles were registered with 25,500 garages and 13,500 repair shops to service them.

Prior to World War I, the horseless carriage coexisted with the horse. Many locales required motorists to stop their cars when approaching horse-drawn vehicles so as not to frighten the animals. Debate over the two modes of personal mobility colored the local talk of saloons, livery stables, county fairs, and dinner tables. Skeptics insisted that animal power proved more expedient on water-logged and mud-slick roads. Proponents argued that the motor car would be cheaper, more efficient, faster, more reliable, and cleaner.

Probably no car had more effect on the daily lives of Americans than did the Ford Model T, first introduced to the public in 1908 at a cost of $850. As its maker always insisted, you could have any color you wished, as long as it was black. The Model T, a no-

nonsense car with nothing fancy about it, had no bumpers, no speedometer, no temperature gauge, no spare tire. Shortly after purchase, owners ordered from the Sears, Roebuck catalog or a parts dealer the "accessories," such as shock absorbers, an accelerator, gas and oil gauges, and bigger rear brakes. Outfitted with a left-hand drive (soon standard with all American manufacturers), its twenty-two-horsepower engine could do thirty-five miles per hour if you dared let her rip.

The self-propelled vehicle altered commuting and communicating routines. It created a new built environment of auto showrooms, gasoline stations, motels, fast-food franchises, and surface highways. It fostered driving schools (YMCAs offered such instruction by 1904), necessitated personal liability insurance (over twenty-five thousand drivers in New York City had such coverage by 1916), and stimulated a new era in American cartography (thousands of road maps were distributed by oil companies by the 1920s). It gave new meaning to the American fascination with being on the move. With the massive highway system it ultimately created, it eventually transformed the American house (with its built-in garage), as well as the urban and rural landscapes.

Victorian Americans also supported a massive change in landscape outside their borders, when the U.S. government took over, from the French, the construction of a transoceanic canal across the Isthmus of Panama. To build its "Big Ditch," thereby cutting 7,873 miles and three weeks from the water trip between San Francisco and New York, President Theodore Roosevelt purchased the French rights for $40 million, despite the opposition of Colombia, the country that owned the land. Roosevelt, who grew exasperated when negotiations with Colombia did not move as quickly as he wished, aided a New York–planned "local revolution" led by two of the French Panama Company's members. To ensure its success, Roosevelt stationed American cruisers off Colón the evening before the revolt began and landed U.S. troops the next day. Three hours into the revolution, the United States recognized the new nation, Panama, that seceded from Colombia (1903).

In 1904, the American government began building the then-largest transport corridor in the world, a project that cost a total of twenty-two thousand lives and some $367 million, in addition to the $287 million lost by the French in the 1880s. Countless books and newspaper and magazine articles, describing and illustrating the canal's progress, made it an icon of imperial technology and a popular vacation site.[27] In 1913, for example, twenty thousand American tourists took in its engineering marvels. The canal had other implications. William Gorgas cleared the area of yellow fever (also called Panama fever) and promoted urban sanitation procedures that helped control infectious diseases in southern cities, such as New Orleans and Mobile. The canal's pioneering construction techniques were later applied to the development of American highways. The "Path Between the Seas" was only the most colossal monument to the civil engineering of movement in Victorian America; other feats included the Brooklyn Bridge (built from 1868 to 1883), the New York State Barge Canal (1909), the Indianapolis Speedway (1912), and hundreds of Central and Union railroad stations.

Enumerating Moves

THE PUBLIC CENSUS, 1870–1920

Americans knew a great many statistics about the Panama Canal project because they were as fascinated with counting as with moving. For example, the federal census (beginning in 1850) compared a citizen's place of residence with his or her place of birth, establishing one fix on migration. The culture quantified many dimensions of everyday life, housing a massive record of information in a new architecture for statistical storage: gigantic city halls, pretentious county courthouses, and colossal federal bureaucracies, as well as private settlement houses and the social science departments of universities.

Not everyone reveled in the growing apotheosis of arithmetic. Eugene R. White, writing in the 1901 *Atlantic Monthly,* thought that the contemporary "Plague of Statistics" had gone too far. He complained: "We group disasters as merchants corner markets. Do we plead the cause of temperance? Here statistics prevail, and they may be had patiently plotted out even to the number of drunkards to the square rod in Cuyahoga County, Ohio, or the arrests for inebriety in Kokomo, Indiana, for 1900. We go about reforming and purifying the world, with a committee report at elbow and a statistical compilation in each hand."

The more than two hundred schedules of the encyclopedic censuses of 1880 and 1890 that asked thirteen thousand questions exceeded the capability of the personnel and machinery to collect, collate, and disgorge the answers. These two censuses, for example, attempted to find data on travel, losses from fires, garbage disposal, cemeteries, rail traffic, prisons, occupations, polygamy, and unemployment.

Despite its statistical indigestion, the 1890 census looms as both a demographic and technological watershed. According to it, the United States no longer had a moving frontier; settled areas extended throughout almost the entire nation. Although several states had been recently formed from the northwestern territories (Montana, the Dakotas, and Washington in 1889) and the western mountain regions (Wyoming and Idaho in 1890), the country was now one-third urban. The 1890 census also assumed landmark status because of its new methods of tabulation. Herman Hollerith, a young engineer working for the Bureau of the Census, developed a mechanism, based upon the principle of the Jacquard loom, that punched and sorted cards on which information had been entered in code form. The "Hollerith cards" immediately sped up the processing of census returns and set in motion a sequence of data processing that, in part, led to the modern computer.

The findings of the 1920 census prove instructive when compared with similar numbers gathered in 1870. The 1920 census (population over 106 million), in addition to representing a 279 percent increase over 1870 (population over 38 million), also confirmed another demographic trend: America, despite its great westward expansion (much of which came about from the establishment of new western cities), had become an urban-suburban nation. This urbanization reflected a transformation in the economic base, as well as the increased size and number of American cities. Before the Civil War, cities grew because of the expansion of those mercantile activities—trading, retailing, warehousing—that had always been the basis of urban commercial life. After the war, however, growth also resulted from manufacturing for non-local markets, an activity that had existed in small towns located near sources of water power and had little impact on large cities until steam and electric power became widespread, respectively, in the 1870s and the 1910s.

The unprecedented growth of the middle classes likewise emerges from the federal census statistics from 1870 to 1920. In addition to the old middle class of farmers and small entrepreneurs, a managerial, professional, and commercial cohort grew steadily. In 1860, the Bureau of the Census found that about 750,000 persons were engaged in "professional service" and other managerial and "commercial" positions. By 1890, the number in similar occupations had risen to 2,160,000, while in 1910 it more than doubled again to 4,420,000. These "new" middle classes, composed of salaried professionals, managers, salespeople, and office workers, tended to be based in cities. They played a large role in the era's politics, consumer and leisure revolutions, and the expansion of educational opportunities.[28]

As Nell Irvin Painter reminds us, however, "just as ethnic and racial divisions make it misleading (though convenient) to speak of a single American working class, there was no single middle class either." Plurality pervaded both class designations, since "there were working *classes* and middle *classes* [italics added], not only agricultural and industrial, but also of many ethnicities and races." Furthermore, the term *middle classes* should be seen as "a fluid category that includes individual (or family) self-definition, tastes, and attitudes."[29]

INVENTING STANDARD TIME

Decisions about time itself changed in postbellum America. Modern time, with its kinship to movement, came into being for the first time. Time no longer conformed to the natural rhythms of the sun and seasons, but to the mechanical pace of the pocket watch, the factory whistle, or the railroad-station clock.

In 1876 time was not yet a commodity that was measured, adjusted, and distributed throughout the country. In rural areas, the sunrise, high noon, and sunset determined the routines of farm and craft. People measured time's passing in the results of harvests and the pages of almanacs. Towns and cities used the sun overhead at noon to set their public clocks. Since the sun appears to move across the sky from east to west, a city a few miles east of another would mark noon first and would remain a few minutes ahead of its western neighbor throughout the day. Communities that were miles apart were also minutes apart. Sacramento, California, for example, was 3 hours, 9 minutes, and 51 seconds earlier than New York City, but 3 minutes and 56 seconds later than San Francisco. Railroads (figure 1.4) complicated things further. Buffalo's main terminal had three separate clocks, one for each railroad using the station and a fourth set to Buffalo "city time."

People could also choose from various public sources of time: clocks on churches or town halls, time guns at military installations, timepieces in jewelers' windows, or whistles and bells in factories—the last attesting to time's new role in determining industrial work routines and wages (see chapter 2). Time balls like those atop Boston's Equitable Life Assurance headquarters or New York's Western Union building were popular public displays of time. Typically placed on a pole atop a tall structure, the large metal globes usually rose and fell once every day at noon, as observing city dwellers stopped to check their watches. The ritual survives in the midnight inauguration of New Year's Day in New York's Times Square.

After a decade's discussion among railroad executives, scientists, civil engineers, and meteorologists, an association of railroad managers, without benefit of federal law or public demand, set a date for standardizing time. On Sunday, November 18, 1883, at noon, Standard Railway Time went into effect with the fall of Western Union's New York time ball. Everyday life that day had two noons, local time and standard time. As the *Indianapolis Daily Sentinel* noted that day, a new time had begun: "The sun is no longer to boss the job. People—55,000,000 people—must now eat, sleep and work, as well as travel by railroad time."

Standard Railway Time replaced a profusion of local times with five standard zones—Intercolonial, Eastern, Central, Mountain, and Pacific—each of which had a uniform time within its boundaries. Not everyone liked the "new" time. States like Georgia and Ohio and cities such as Pittsburgh and Louisville rejected it for years. Between 1883 and 1915, standard time came to trial before the Supreme Courts of various states (many hotbeds of rural radicalism and Populist protest) at least fifteen times. Opposition also came in defense of regional pride and religious literalism—"Kentucky's sun" and "God's Time." Others complained that clock time conflicted with seasonal variations in the available sunlight, thereby disrupting everyday routines.[30]

Ultimately the dissident voices were stilled. Standard Railway Time became federal law with the Standard Time Act of 1918, the same year the United States first experimented with nationwide daylight savings time. Created to serve American commercial and scientific interests in the last century, standard time symbolized more than convenient timekeeping. It dramatized industrial capitalism's acute awareness that time was money and its obsession with punctuality, order, and regularity. In brief, it typified the growing quantification, regimentation, homogeneity, and standardization that had crept into many aspects of everyday life by 1915.

FIGURE 2.1. Detroit Publishing Company, Labor Day crowd, Main Street, Buffalo, New York (ca. 1900). Photograph courtesy of the Library of Congress, Division of Prints and Photographs.

FIGURE 2.2. Robert Koehler, *The Strike* (1886), oil on canvas. Courtesy of Lee Baxandall, Green Mountain Editions, Oshkosh, Wisconsin.

2

A<small>LTHOUGH</small> work experiences differed widely in Victorian America, several trends are evident. Women and children entered the American work force in large numbers. Marginal, part-time, and seasonal workers also increased. Tenant farmers, sharecroppers, hired hands, and migrant workers toiled in agriculture, while their urban counterparts—railroad laborers, construction workers, and day men—worked day to day in temporary jobs. Office work absorbed more and more women within the business bureaucracies that began expanding in the 1880s. The corporate revolution prompted the need for managers (supervisors, division heads, and office chiefs) and monitors (bookkeepers, accountants, and lawyers). Finally, service work—both the labor of household servants and that of service professionals, such as teachers, nurses, and social workers—increased.

Daily interaction between workers and managers shifted dramatically during the concluding decades of the nineteenth century. How people defined work and capital, craftsmanship and ownership, wealth and income, business and labor, changed. Two statistics indicate one aspect of the almost continual upheaval: the rate of business failures—over 15,000 in 1893 alone—and the unprecedented incidence of strikes (figure 2.2)—almost 37,000 (involving over 7 million workers) recorded between 1881 and 1905.[1]

With escalating polarization, both workers and managers contended—violently and repeatedly—over every aspect of the spreading wage-factory system of production: work hours, work day, the pace, safety, machinery, conditions, security, and wages. They fought each other with lockouts and boycotts, with new "labor-saving" machinery and industrial sabotage, with wage cuts and work slowdowns, and with scab labor and organized unions.

Worker-management confrontations took place in agriculture (for example, the strike by the Industrial Workers of the World—the IWW—at the Durst Ranch in Wheatland, California, in 1913) and mining (thirty-nine men, women, and children killed in the "Ludlow Massacre" during the United Mine Workers' strike in Colorado in 1914), but especially within a new working class that was emerging in the economy's expanding manufacturing sector—an industrial labor force that, by 1900, comprised over a third of the nation's population and a third of which was immigrant.

This ever-growing urban, alien (in the eyes of many native-born Americans), largely unskilled work force lived close to the poverty line, an indicator that moved from $506 per year in 1877 to $544 in 1893 to $660 in 1909. Through these decades, about 40 percent of these workers lived slightly above the poverty level and another 40 percent lived below it, with a fourth of the latter number, despite wages from wives and children, often almost destitute.[2]

Finally, it must be remembered that chronic unemployment characterized many unskilled workers' day-to-day experiences, particularly during the hard times—1873–79, 1882–85, 1893–97, 1907–08—that came with cruel regularity. In addition to these major depressions and recessions, an estimated 23 to 30 percent of the industrial labor force was out of work for some time every year during the period.[3]

Agrarian Life

MIDDLING FARMERS

Farm workers suffered a strange paradox in postbellum America. Never had there been a greater expansion of agriculture than in the final three decades of the nineteenth century. Between 1870 and 1900 more acres (431 million) of virgin land came under new cultivation than in all the country's history (408 million previously). Crop production yielded equally impressive statistics. By 1900, American farmers were producing up to 150 percent more of the staples—cotton, wheat, and corn—than they had in 1870.

Despite the plentitude, farmers were not a people of plenty. Beginning with the depression of 1873, agricultural prices began a quarter-century-long slide that did not improve until the 1910s. Wheat prices declined by three-quarters while corn dropped by two-thirds. Poverty seemed endemic for many tenant farmers and sharecroppers. Violent nature—drought, soil erosion, plagues of grasshoppers, floods, and boll weevils—ravaged the countryside. Although agricultural employment increased (60 percent) between 1860 and 1890, it did not keep pace with the growth of nonfarm jobs (300 percent). The 1870 census, for the first time in American history, counted farmers as a minority work force, constituting 47.4 percent of the nation's gainfully employed. By 1920, that figure had dropped to 27 percent.

Farmers also saw their political power and status decline. No longer the Jeffersonian yeomen of the earth, their everyday lives faced several tensions: traditional agricultural practices versus modern mechanized methods; single-family farming versus commercial agriculture; laissez-faire economics versus political action and class protest. Farmers organized for the first time, creating the Patrons of Husbandry (the Grange), the northern and southern Farmer's Alliances, and, finally, the People's party in 1892. These organizations emphasized cooperation and improved farm life; they also lobbied against unfair railroad rates, high interest rates, bank foreclosures, and high property taxes.

Seasonal cycles conditioned the routines of settled rural communities as geographically separate as Chelsea, Vermont; Salem, North Carolina; and Henry County, Iowa. These farmers relied primarily on family members for labor. They participated in some aspects of the commercialized economy while retaining certain traditional agricultural practices. They lived neither in rural backwaters nor on primitive frontiers. They were families, as one of their Indiana number put it, of "middling mind," proponents of a mixed agriculture and middle-class values. The parameters and pace of their everyday existence are succinctly depicted in the thousands of lithographed illustrations that appeared in the county historical atlases that were published in the 1880s.

Many contemporary writers portrayed rural New England in the late nineteenth century as a series of decaying townships haunted by the specter of deserted farms and dilapidated schools and churches. To their eyes, the region presented a picture of incurable blight that was directly attributable to the loss of population to the West and the cities. Supposedly only the graveyard flourished. Chelsea, Vermont, as studied by Hal Baron, reveals another picture, one in which economic activity had, compared to its peak in the 1830s, slowed but not stopped.

Despite a declining population throughout the latter half of the nineteenth century, the township always contained about two hundred working farms, whose size, location, and value changed little. Wool, butter, and maple sugar remained these farms' principal products in more or less fixed proportions. Economic opportunities were ultimately limited by the finite supply of land. Once settled, the number of sites of family farms in such a region eventually reached its maximum. The purchase of new farm machinery to implement improved farming techniques was a onetime change that altered methods of farm production, but it did not mark the beginning of an ever-expanding agricultural economy.

Chelsea's residents coped with these realities by maintaining strong family and community ties. Fathers usually passed the family land to their youngest sons because these sons came of age when their fathers were ready to retire or reduce their activities. The sequenced transference of ownership to the youngest rather than to the oldest son was necessary because the average New England farm generally was not a large enough or profitable enough operation to support the father's still full household together with that of his elder offspring. Thus, the youngest son would enter a partnership with his father, becoming co-owner of the family farm with full rights of inheritance.

The youngest son took on a host of familial responsibilities as a result of these arrangements. It became his duty to continue farming the land in concert with his father. He also frequently assumed all his father's debts and liabilities, with the expectation that he would never sell his part of the farm while his parents were alive. Part of these duties included responsibility for the care not only of his parents, but of any unmarried sisters who might continue to live at home. If his father died and these sisters married, he would be the one to provide their dowries. This arrangement between fathers and youngest sons was an attempt to insure economic security for two generations and, in the process, to promote continuity within the community.[4]

Older sons from such farm families had to find their own economic opportunities. Some tried local nonagricultural options; others simply moved, usually to neighboring townships where, provided with enough money from their fathers for down payments on farms, they continued their agrarian careers. They tended to marry local women. In the 1880 census, for instance, approximately three-quarters of the married men in their thirties had taken wives from the immediate community; six, in fact, married the girl next door. Geographic proximity to extended families, by virtue of marriage, was common. In all cases, kinship facilitated the exchange of labor, machinery, and financial assistance, surviving via ties within the generations as well as between them. These families' everyday lives, though interconnected with larger national markets and an expanding capitalist economy, were lived in a community where neither boom nor bust prevailed. They were content, by and large, to stay down on the farm.

Families in rural North Carolina shared certain parallel experiences although with different crops. These southerners knew a year-round life of family labor: an annual cycle of planting, harvesting, and marketing, of corn shucking, tobacco curing, and cotton ginning. Work routines had changed little since the early nineteenth century.

Flue-cured, or bright-leaf tobacco, grown primarily in Virginia, the Carolinas, and Georgia, had to be tended constantly. In winter, as seedlings germinated in plant beds, a tobacco grower cut wood to be used in his curing barns in July and August. After breaking and harrowing the land with his mules, he transplanted his seedlings into fertilized "hills," about four thousand to an acre. In late summer, when the plant's bottom leaves yellowed, men trimmed three or four ripe leaves from each stalk, putting them in a mule-drawn sled; a trucker drove a loaded sled to the scaffold, where women and children handed the tobacco bundle to a stringer (usually a woman) who tied it securely to a four-foot stick. A stick boy took a full stick to a rack. Workers took morning and afternoon breaks for soft drinks and snacks like moon pies, eating a main meal at noon.

After racking came barning, the transfer of some thousand to fifteen hundred tobacco-filled sticks (figure 2.3) into an average, five-room, sixteen-foot-square, twenty-foot-high North Carolina tobacco barn. Young and old participated in the day and night, week-long alchemy of curing the greenish yellow weed into gold leaf. The farmer first fired up the barn to 100 degrees for a day or so and then fixed the tobacco's color by increasing the heat (another day at 140 degrees); a final escalation (to 180 degrees) dried the stems. After barning, the family graded and tied the crop for market.

Competition for the crop began in the countryside with the midsummer appearance of auctioneers' broadsides on barns and country stores promising high profits and a "down-home" welcome at tobacco warehouses like Pepper's in Winston-Salem or Parrish's in Durham. Once the farmer unloaded his tobacco into the warehouse, he would fraternize with other farmers, go drinking, or take in the amusements—patent-medicine ballyhoos, shooting galleries, and other entertainments. After a night on the town, he might sleep in his wagon or a hotel or in one of the warehouse's segregated camp rooms.

"The next morning, in a cavernous building festooned with flags on the outside and bustle everywhere within, he carefully piled up his leaves for the buyers to eye and appraise." The monetary value of a year's toil would be decided in a few seconds. The auctioneer, a man among men in the male warehouse culture, dominated the floor's buying and controlled its sale. "Jovial and exuberant, he rarely missed a telltale wink, nod, salute or out-stuck tongue, among the herd of bidders. In 1870 an auctioneer could dispatch several pile of leaves a minute; by 1920 he closed a sale every nine seconds. The farmer had his cash in hand ten minutes after the final bid."[5]

On the Iowa prairies, family farms created the nineteenth century's corn-and-hog belt. The diary of John Savage details a typical annual routine in that region. The Savage family began farming in Henry County with 75 acres in 1856 and added 40 acres of brushland in 1867. They rented additional cropland and pasturage until 1879, when, through the purchase of a neighboring 150-acre farm, they had more land than they could farm themselves. At this point, they became landlords to their own tenant farmer.

In January and February, the Savage family butchered the hogs for home consumption, cut rails and firewood, and moved fodder from the fields into their barnyard. During March, they often grubbed and cleared brushland and began spring lambing. April meant spraying their apple orchard with a solution of lye and lime, as well as sowing oats. Planting continued in May with potatoes, sorghum, and early corn. June saw the shearing of sheep and the plowing of fields for corn. It was also the month in which the family members worked off their road tax. By July they were haying and harvesting wheat and oats. In July and August, the winter-wheat fields were manured and plowed; seed corn was also picked at this time. Fall planting came next, as well as the fattening of hogs, the grinding of sorghum, and the threshing of wheat. October meant picking corn and apples and digging potatoes. If December's weather held, they continued clearing new land as well as splitting fence rails.

The Savages may be considered typical middle-class, even progressive, farmers. They subscribed to five journals, including the *Rural New Yorker*. John Savage, who also taught school part time, joined the Grange in 1873 and supervised its cooperative store. His wife, Tacy, although she made her own soap, did not have to spin or weave her own cloth. In these years, moreover, she had a sewing machine, did her laundry in a mechanized washing machine, and, by the late 1870s, could listen to her daughter play a ninety-dollar reed parlor organ.[6]

TENANTS AND HIRED HANDS

In 1880 the federal census, for the first time, reported tenancy rates, that is, the percentage of American farmers who did not own the land they worked. A quarter of the farms in the nation then were operated by tenants. By the century's end, the national incidence was 35 percent.

In the South, sharecropping and tenancy grew out of plantation agriculture. In the Corn Belt, tenancy (39 percent in Illinois) rose rapidly as land prices escalated beyond the reach of average agrarians. Throughout the country, particularly during the depression of 1893–97, farm foreclosures led to land-lease arrangements.

Farm-lease contracts took various forms, but two types generally circumscribed families who tilled soil owned by others. Cash renter agreements were more common in the Midwest, whereas share contracts, or sharecropping, dominated the South. In the first arrangement, a tenant farmer rented land from a landlord at an agreed-upon cash amount (or cash equivalent in corn or cotton), usually payable at the end of the harvest season. The tenant furnished his own equipment, horses or mules, and labor for farming the acreage for which he had contracted. He might rent a residence from his landlord, but frequently he occupied a mortgaged home of his own. He usually could determine what he would grow and where and when he sold his crop.

Sharecropping, on the other hand, sorely limited a farmer's options. The landowner furnished, in addition to the land, all the necessary equipment and supplies—tools, seed, fertilizer, farm animals, and usually housing. The sharecropper provided labor. In return for using the land, equipment, and housing, the propertyless sharecropper turned over from one-fourth to one-half his crop. The landlord often attached "a crop lien" agreement that gave him first claim on the remainder of the tenant's harvest. Finally, he (or the merchant of the local country store) frequently advanced the sharecropper additional credit for food and clothing throughout the year, using the sharecropper's portion of the crop as collateral. Towering interest rates, higher prices for goods bought on credit ("the two-price system" of many Southern country stores), and sometimes outright cheating frequently produced debts that matched or exceeded the income from the sale of the sharecropper's part of the crop.

Whatever the lease agreement, most sharecroppers, many of whom were black, shared a common way of life. They lived an existence largely without cash, since no actual money ever changed hands in many contracts. Cotton growers often paid their ginning costs by agreeing to let the gin operator have the cotton seed and its oil. As renters of practically everything, their material world was sparse—usually a one-room log or frame homestead, in which the family cooked, ate, and slept. D. W. Brooks, who knew tenant life on northeastern Georgia farms as a boy, once said that many such farmers were both astronomers and agronomists. They could, he noted, observe the stars through the roofs of their leaky dogtrot or shotgun houses and study the soil through the holes in the floor. Personal possessions were scant—a pine table, a few chairs, a rickety cupboard that held a miscellany of dishes and pans, mattresses filled with corn shucks, a Bible, and perhaps a few pictures cut from magazines or newspapers.[7]

Tenancy forced many farmers to purchase some of their food. Lease contracts often demanded the use of all available acreage for the cash crop, sometimes requiring that cotton be planted right up to the sharecropper's cabin door. Many landlords required tenants to pay extra rent to keep pastureland for stock or space for a vegetable garden. Such practices meant, ironically, that many Southern farmers who rented land relied heavily upon store-bought food, especially the region's three Ms: (corn)meal, molasses, and (hog) meat.

Tenant life also spawned "feast-and-famine" cycles: times of abundance (albeit limited to when the crop came in) and periods of belt-tightening and habitual mobility. Since, by tradition, tenant contracts ran for one year only (and tenants had no assurance that their leases would be renewed), tenants' lives took on an episodic quality, prone to constant uncertainty. Approximately one-third of all tenants moved each year. To "get by," many worked at two or three additional jobs. For example, the twelve black tenant farmers on the Waverly Plantation in Mississippi in 1888, in addition to maintaining their fields, also worked part time at local sawmills, brickyards, and charcoal kilns.[8]

Numerous hired men and migrant farm workers labored for a weekly or monthly wage throughout the nineteenth century. Before the Civil War, these hired hands were considered fledgling yeomen, apprenticed on the land as they supposedly made their way upward to become farm owners. Usually American born, the antebellum hired man was often kin to or at least known to his employer. He worked beside his boss, ate at the same table, often slept under the same roof, and (if he stayed on) came to be considered family.

In Victorian America, however, his status and origins changed. His prospects for a farm of his own diminished. As a German or Irish immigrant, he was now seen as a transient, a worker who was not related and foreign. Moreover, as agriculture became more commercialized, farmers thought of his labor as simply another factor in their costs. Some farmers responded to these changed conditions by segregating their hired hands in workers' barracks outside the family residence.[9]

Parallel with the changing attitude toward the single hired man came the expanding use of seasonal migrant workers—men, women, and children—for planting and picking beans, peas, tomatoes, blueberries, and cranberries on large commercial truck farms in New Jersey and Maryland or harvesting citrus fruits, grapes, nuts, and produce in California. The extensive hand labor of these early agribusinesses required numerous workers to plant, cultivate, weed, and harvest crops: broccoli in winter, asparagus in spring, almonds in summer, grapes in autumn. While the large commercial farmers would hire white laborers (unemployed "bummers" and "bindlestiffs"), they preferred cheap foreign workers whom they looked upon as a separate and inferior caste. Consequently, by 1880, one-third of California's farm workers were Chinese immigrants. These energetic laborers, willing to accept living and working conditions and wages that whites rejected, worked under a labor-contract system. One of their countrymen typically functioned not only as the agent through which their labor was sold, but as their immediate supervisor ("Chinese boss" or "head boy").

In some respects, the great California orchards and produce farms resembled the plantations of the antebellum South. Both were highly commercial forms of agriculture, requiring substantial capital investments and large labor gangs. Of course there was a significant difference. Whereas the southern planter maintained his slaves year round, the California commercial farmer employed only a seasonal workforce. He provided no permanent accommodations while his crews worked for him and dismissed them at harvest's end.[10]

When the supply of Chinese farm workers diminished because of the Chinese Exclusion Act of 1882, California's capitalist growers continually recruited other foreign laborers (Portuguese, Italians, Japanese) for their factories in the fields. By 1909, nearly half (45 percent) California's total farm labor force was Japanese. The Japanese entered the fields by underbidding their competition (including the Chinese), hiring themselves out through *keiyakunin* (contractors), who arranged wage agreements and working conditions that included eating, boarding, and recreational associations. As Kevin Starr relates, "once they eliminated the competition, the Japanese behaved just like union labor: controlling their numbers to keep wages high, negotiating one grower against another, organizing quick strikes when they felt exploited."[11] They also rented land wherever they could and eventually bought their own farms. One San Joaquin farmer, George Shima, who arrived in California in 1889 as a young laborer, controlled 85 percent of the state's potato crop by 1913, earning him the undisputed title of the state's "Potato King."

Most nomadic farm workers, however, worked someone else's land throughout their lifetimes, moving from harvest to harvest, living in shacks or tents, and taking their children into the fields in forfeit of their education. Receiving no pension or unemployment benefits, they enabled enormous wealth to be accumulated, but their share in that largess remained meager.

COMMERCIAL AGRICULTURE

In several regions of the country, the self-sufficient, diversified farm, by 1900, slowly gave way to a more specialized, commercial agriculture. California's endless tracts of row crops, orchard trees, and grape vines—planted, cultivated, and irrigated with mechanized precision—were examples of a pattern that also characterized the sugar-beet industry in Colorado, wheat farming in Oregon (figure 2.4), or hop growing in Washington. This trend toward larger acreages, mechanization, and crop specialization first captured the American public's imagination in the 1870s with the famous "bonanza farms" of the Red River valley.

The significance of these huge agricultural enterprises—often owned by eastern capitalists or western speculators who hired professional managers to oversee their forty-thousand-acre farms—lay not in their numbers but in the fact that they so boldly signaled American agriculture's future. Countless articles about the bonanza farming of wheat appeared in newspapers and farm journals, and farm-implement manufacturers boasted in their advertisements that certain bonanza enterprises used only their equipment.[12]

Oliver Dalrymple, native Philadelphian, lawyer, public official—a failure as a grain speculator but a success as a southern Minnesota wheat farmer—typifies the manager of the bonanza farm. With 34 million acres in the Red River Valley (one wheat field alone was larger than Manhattan), Dalrymple divided his farms into administrative units of 5,000 acres a piece. Each division had its own "headquarters," consisting of a house for the superintendent, boardinghouses for the workers, stables, granaries, and blacksmith and machine shops. During the growing season, 250 men worked a bonanza tract with the help of 400 or more horses and mules.

Bonanza farming, like large-scale mining and timbering, resembled military life. Almost totally a masculine enterprise, its echelons of managers, men, and machines marched across the landscape like regiments in formation. One observer described it as "the army system applied to agriculture." A manager "marshals his men, arrays his instruments of war, and with mechanical precision the whole force moves forward to conquer and exact rich tribute from the land."[13]

The military simile made sense to a generation of Civil War veterans. But bonanza farming also invited comparison with the pace and precision of factory work, particularly in its obsession with time saving. To market grain quickly, the bonanza farmer threshed wheat directly in the field. Instant communication seemed an essential component of efficiency, so Dalrymple connected all his farms by telephone, years before this new technology was widely used even in urban areas.

Bonanza farming also took place in California's Central Valley, providing the setting for Frank Norris's novel, *The Octopus* (1901), and in parts of Nebraska and Kansas. The phenomenon advertised these regions, exciting the imaginations of restless settlers who, hoping to reap small bonanzas of their own, migrated westward. The highly mechanized bonanza operations encouraged implement use among smaller farmers. The value of farm equipment rose from $271 million to $3,595 million between 1870 and 1920 and consisted of riding plows with multiple shares; grain drills that planted, fertilized, and covered seed; and ponderous combines—pulled by as many as forty horses—that could reap, thresh, and bag grain in a simultaneous operation. Grain elevators and giant silos, new landmarks of the new commercial farming, resulted from agriculture's increasing control by finance capitalists and the new commodities exchanges in distant cities. Together, mechanization, "cash-crop" farming, and stock trading in commodities entangled independent, local farmers in an international network of storing, shipping, and selling.

PACKING AND CANNING

Industrial capitalism, in addition to commercializing the countryside, drastically changed the circumstances of many agricultural products once they left the fields. New food-processing enterprises altered everyday ways of cooking and eating, and large-scale transformations in the cotton and tobacco industries changed the ways people dressed and behaved.

Gail Borden, living on the Texas frontier in antebellum America and weary of the monotonous diets of overland travelers, began experimenting with ways to preserve and make portable one of the bulkiest and most perishable foods: milk. In 1856, he took out a patent for evaporating milk in a vacuum and preserving it in a can. Condensing foodstuffs for American tables became Borden's mania: "I mean to put a potato into a pillbox, a pumpkin into a tablespoon, the biggest sort of watermelon into a saucer."[14]

Others followed Borden's example in processing flour and meat. Neighborhood or regional millers, before the 1880s, ground grain into flour, returning some to the farmers and selling the rest to bakers and housewives. Similarly, most butcher shops, frequently serving as their own slaughterhouses, sold meat raised locally. Railroads and companies, such as Swift and Armour, General Mills and Pillsbury, changed this traditional purveying. Reaching westward, where wheat and livestock could be grown on a commercial scale, these corporations funneled grain and cattle into Minneapolis–St. Paul, Chicago, and St. Louis, where gigantic plants converted the raw materials into national brands.

Pittsburgh's H. J. Heinz revolutionized another aspect of the food industry by employing mass-production techniques to sell preserved foods traditionally "put up" or "canned" at home. A combination of commercial farming, new canning methods, and masterful advertising campaigns made his company the country's largest general food processor by 1900. By then, although famous for "57 varieties," the firm manufactured more than two hundred food products, including such items as baked beans and tomato ketchup, previously regional foods that the company's distribution and marketing networks turned into national favorites.

Lillian Weizmann bottled pickles at the Heinz Pittsburgh plant, beginning in 1901 at age fourteen and becoming a departmental forewoman by 1918. She worked from 7:00 A.M. to 5:40 P.M., but on Saturday her shift ended at 4:40. Her day began in the worker's dressing room, where she changed her shirtwaist and skirt for a freshly laundered uniform, white apron, and mopcap—each of which she purchased and laundered. She worked, as did hundreds of others, at long tables with five women to a side. Her task: deftly inserting pickles, one at a time, into bottles. Most days she packed an average of 150 bottles for a daily wage of approximately $1.50.[15]

In tobacco-processing plants in Durham, North Carolina, other women workers transformed agricultural produce into consumer products. Here traditional hand-labor tasks done by blacks, both men and women, coexisted with innovative machinery usually operated by whites. The production and sale of tobacco products expanded dramatically in Victorian America. In 1870, 7 million pounds of leaf were sold; by 1920, that figure had tripled; the production of cigarettes, an innovation of the era, went from a half billion in 1880 to 124 billion in 1919. This growth resulted partially from the aggressive advertising of the W. T. Blackwell firm and the Duke family dynasty. Blackwell, who made Bull Durham tobacco, spent $300,000 a year to distribute posters and paint signs of a virile bull. The firm offered and paid rewards for new mechanical inventions to increase production and cut labor costs. By 1883 its sale of 5 million pounds of smoking tobacco was the nation's largest. The company's motto typified the brazenness that built its empire: "Let buffalo gore buffalo, and the pasture go to the strongest."

In the 1880s, James Buchanan "Buck" Duke decided to take on Bull Durham by mass-producing cigarettes, a product that would, within a generation, change Americans' tobacco-using habits. While common in Europe, cigarettes entered American life in a big way only in the 1860s. They were an attractive alternative to chewing tobacco, cigars, snuff, or pipes, providing quick stimulation that was well suited to America's fast-paced urban life. They were clean, convenient, and potent. Using skilled Jewish immigrants, Duke began his manufacturing operation at a rate of one craftsman hand rolling four cigarettes a minute. By 1884, he decided to mechanize, leasing two machines invented by an eighteen-year-old Virginian named James Bonsack that, once perfected, could roll cigarettes by the hundreds per minute. The machinery was ultimately developed to the point that it automatically took in the tobacco, made the cigarettes, and packaged, labeled, and placed them in cartons.

Young white women from the Piedmont tended Duke's machines. Despite the work's monotony, the machinery's pace, and standing in place all day, the work provided jobs for many sharecroppers' daughters. Duke's "cigarette girls" rolled about fifteen thousand cigarettes during a sixty-five-hour week, earning fifty cents a thousand. Tobacco factory work also meant more jobs for blacks, but these jobs were not the better ones. Black women prepared the tobacco leaves for the machines in the factory's segregated leaf department. With handkerchiefs tied over their noses to keep from inhaling the dust and fumes, they removed the stems from the leaves and graded the tobacco. These black women received half the wages the white women earned "on the cigarette side." Black men, working in gangs hauling hogsheads of tobacco to the machine floors likewise received less than half the pay of white men.[16]

Mass merchandising, as well as mass production, made cigarettes fixtures of everyday life. Duke, who bested his chief competitors—R. J. Reynolds and Blackwell—until federal antitrust

action in 1911 forced him to disband his corporation of 150 companies, made wide use of gift coupons and colorful trading cards as
promotions. Sales mounted as purchasers bought again and again
to acquire their prizes and to complete their collections of cards
of scantily clad women, baseball players, presidents, and prize-
fighters. Packet coupons were redeemable for photo albums for
the family, pennants for college boys, or silk stockings for ladies.

Industrial Laboring

SITES AND SHOPS

Workers, earning their living by what they extracted from or out
of the earth, increased fivefold in Victorian America. The timber
and coal, ores and oil they wrenched from America's remaining
wild terrain fueled its industrial complexes. Lumberjacks, miners,
and oil riggers worked in harsh, isolated, almost totally masculine,
and transitory environments. Work camps organized their days
and nights.

In the white pine forests of Michigan and Wisconsin, thousands
of "jacks" worked every winter in the 1880s. By the next decade,
the last frontier of giant fir, cedar, and redwood in the Pacific
Northwest fell before the ax. The timber went into cabinets for
sewing machines, inexpensive parlor and bedroom suites, and prefabricated balloon-frame housing.

For a dollar a day, payable in the spring when the seasonal
onslaught on the virgin forest temporarily stopped, lumbermen
felled trees, sawed them into lengths that sawmills could handle,
and hitched them behind horses, oxen, or locomotives that towed
the lumber over an iced "skid road." Camps worked two-week
stints before a day's holiday (usually a Saturday) could be spent in
a neighboring sawmill town's "skid row" of bars and brothels.

Many miners lived similar routines. In the half-century after the
famous "Forty-Niner" treks to California, there were other
"rushes"—to Leadville, Colorado, in 1877; to Goldfield, Nevada, in
1901; and to the Yukon in Alaska in 1897—where a speculative
mining economy fostered a risk-all attitude to discover a "glory
lode." Some of the mining camps, such as Coeur D'Alene, Idaho,

and Butte, Montana, quickly evolved into small cities. Here other workers labored in huge crushing and smelting plants processing ores.

Although sometimes started by a single prospector, most western mining operations were run by corporate syndicates. A similar consolidation characterized the anthracite coal fields of Pennsylvania. Deep in the earth, men and boys from Wales, Poland, and Germany, as well as from Russia and Austria-Hungry, worked, often knee deep in water, at the era's most hazardous occupation. By 1917, 180,000 miners extracted millions of tons of "hard coal" from this region.

Before dawn, the whistle from the mine would blow, and the miner would head to the pit site, outfitted in overalls and rubber boots, a lamp attached to his cap, and a tin lunch pail in hand. Helpers were met and all would descend, via an elevator cage, down the mine's main shaft into the semidarkness of lamplight. The cage stopped at various levels of the shaft, where miners and helpers went off into tunnels or "gangways" to work their individual faces. The long, heavily timbered gangways contained narrow-gauge tracks along which mules hauled coal to elevator shafts where it was hoisted to the surface. The mining crew carried the tools needed for a day's work: picks, shovels, drills, blasting powder, fuses, and lumber. After testing the roof, the miner drilled holes for his explosives and began firing. After each detonation the crew separated large bits of slate from the coal. The miner continued blasting until he had "cut" his day's quota of coal. The laborers filled buggies and mules pulled the loads through the gangway to the surface elevator.

A skilled miner, although he toiled in the most dangerous of all industries, controlled the work pace of his underground domain. He contracted with the mine operator to work a face at a certain price per car or per ton; he supplied the tools and powder and paid his laborers. He served what amounted to a two-year apprenticeship before being eligible to take the required state examination that would certify him as a "skilled miner." Success meant the ability to respond, in English, to at least twelve questions regarding mining practices.

Young boys usually drove the mine's mules (figure 2.6). They worked for a barn boss who maintained an underground stable where the animals were fed, watered, and kept permanently. Using no reins to drive his charges, a boy would stand on the front bumper of a car and either shout commands or direct the mules with a whip. A typical driver took care of a dozen working chambers with one mule, moving six cars a day in and out at each face.

Colliery buildings, located near the mine shaft's mouth, housed other workers. Unlike the men who contracted to work underground, these men were company employees and received hourly wages. Many labored in the high coal-breaking building. This singular wooden structure towered over the coalfield landscape. Cars of coal traveled up an inclined plane to the breaker's top, where they were tipped and their contents emptied into revolving cylinders that separated the coal according to size. A series of chutes carried the coal down again, past "breaker boys," whose job it was to sort out the slate and other refuse material. Sometimes old men or injured miners who were no longer able to work underground would return to this first job they held in the mines, hence, the popular refrain: "Twice a boy and once a man is the poor miner's life." Frigid in winter, sweltering in summer, filled with coal dust and bleeding fingers in all seasons, the coal breaker, boy or man, labored in a vile environment.

Coal workers suffered and died in appallingly large numbers from both accidents and the everyday environment in which they worked. In the late nineteenth century, it has been estimated that three miners were killed every two days in the anthracite fields and tens of thousands were seriously injured or maimed. Accidents came from roof collapses, runaway coal buggies, flooding, and faulty explosives. Dangerous coal gases—the dreaded "fire-damp" (methane), "black damp" (carbonic acid), and "white-damp" (carbonic oxide)—brought death and disability. Highly volatile coal dust caused miner's lung (black lung) disease as well as frequent mine explosions and fires.

With injury so frequent and accidental death so commonplace, fatalism colored everyday mining life. An ominous blast of the mine whistle at an off hour, the baleful church bells, and the eternity of silent waiting by the wives and children, who would take up the vigil at a mine head, were all familiar. Everyone in a

typical coal patch had kin—a father, son, brother, or other relative—who had been brought from the shaft as a dirt-caked, man-
gled corpse. All knew the frequent rituals of the family wake and
the community burial (figure 8.10).[17]

The independence of skilled contract miners survived elsewhere in the American work force in the small, custom workshop.
Unlike lumber, mine, or oil sites, workshops were urban. They
clustered either near a city's commercial hub or in its manufacturing districts, adjacent to the larger mills and plants to which they
often sold specialty parts or for which they provided contract
services. In Philadelphia, for example, these workshops, employing between three to eight people, assumed two forms: the craft
shop and the sweatshop.

While craft production declined appreciably throughout the
nineteenth century, decorative ironwork, fine harnesses and sad-
dlery, and sign printing remained products of craftshop teams.
The Tacony Iron and Metal Company, best known for casting the
enormous statue of William Penn atop Philadelphia's city hall, for
example, made custom sculptures for parks, plazas, and public
buildings. Contract shop work offered workers identities of both
place (the work space was small, multifunctional, and personal)
and trade (a fraternity of craft techniques and traditions). Here
employers discussed wages, hours, and shop conditions face to face
with the employees.[18] Craft shops minimized specialization. In
Chicago, for instance, Jewish glove makers resisted the subdivision
of labor that was common to large factories even though it promised better wages. "You cling to the variety," said one worker who
preferred to craft the entire product rather one part of it, "the
mental luxury of first, finger-sides, and then, five separate leather
pieces, for relaxation, to play with! Here is a luxury worth fighting
for!"[19]

Sweatshops were concentrated in the clothing and needle
trades. Rather than conserving a traditional craft, the sweatshop
signaled its disintegration, since the skilled tailor was replaced by
women, children, and immigrants doing separate tasks—cutting,
basting, embroidering, trimming, and hemming. Sweatshops
could be classified into two categories: inside and outside work. In
the first group one might find coat makers working in a rented loft,

warehouse, or rowhouse. "Inside" these buildings they would manufacture products for a contractor. "Outwork," on the other hand, was done not at a contractor's shop but in the worker's home. Generally, it involved work on "finished" garments, the raw sections having been picked up at the contractor's, and the finished pieces returned for counting, inspection, and tallying for periodic payment. Outwork might also include the manufacture of artificial flowers, cigars, toys, and paper cartons. Although sweatshops employed both sexes, the contractor's and foreman's jobs were invariably held by men. Most bosses were recent immigrants, often from the same European regions as their workers. Men "sweaters" averaged six dollars per week in the 1890s and women, four dollars. As with miners (who went unemployed for months during the summer when people did not heat their houses), sweatshop workers endured erratic work schedules and slack times.

Workers in garment sweatshops, along with those who labored in the expanding ready-to-wear industry, produced the period's workclothes. Outdoor male day laborers and skilled tradesmen all worked in short jackets, trousers, occasionally an apron, and usually a hat. Men laboring indoors looked much the same. Working women wore smocks, dresses with aprons, and shirtwaists and long skirts.

LABOR'S DAY

Workers, in such attire, marched in America's first labor day parade in New York City. Placards proclaimed "LABOR CREATES ALL WEALTH," "THE TRUE REMEDY IS UNIONIZATION AND THE BALLOT," and "EIGHT HOURS OF WORK, EIGHT HOURS OF REST, EIGHT HOURS FOR WHAT WE WILL." Although federal-government workers won an eight-hour workday in the 1840s, it was still not the norm for the approximately five thousand jewelers, masons, machinists, carpenters, iron puddlers, bricklayers, and printers who paraded on September 5, 1882.

The parade, planned by the New York Central Labor Union, stepped off from City Hall to the tune "When I First Put This Uniform On" from *Patience,* the latest Gilbert and Sullivan operetta. By the time it reached Union Square (where Terrence Powderly, the General Master Workman of the Knights of Labor and other dignitaries stood on the reviewing stand), displays of craft regalia and regimen were everywhere. Bricklayers demonstrated construction techniques; piano makers had one of their members playing on and at his work. Tools were carried as symbols of the individuality of various crafts. Many artisans smoked cigars to demonstrate they were at their leisure. One spectator wrote that "the whole thing gave a faint suggestion of the gathering of the guilds in past centuries."[20]

The march, as it continued up Fifth Avenue, symbolized the nation's economic polarities. Several thousand workers tramped through America's most ostentatious corridor of wealth and power. They passed Delmonico's restaurant and the Astor and Belmont mansions—whose inhabitants were vacationing in Newport for the season. If the consciousness of capitalism was not penetrated, its precinct was, by a militant procession that included the Progressive Cigarmakers Union, wearing red ribbons, bearing red banners, and accompanied by the Socialist Singing Society under a red flag.

By 1915 Labor Day had become a part of everyday life, President Grover Cleveland having signed in 1894 a federal law establishing it as a national holiday (figure 2.1) honoring the contributions of working people to America. Its observance officially demarcated summer from autumn, becoming a pivotal date after which schools opened and amusement parks closed, vacations (for the middle class) ceased, and advertisements for fall fashions began. Labor Day was the only official holiday that most workers enjoyed between July Fourth and Christmas. (Thanksgiving, although proclaimed a national holiday by President Abraham Lincoln in 1863, was a workday for many laborers until the 1930s.) Unions and other labor associations used Labor Day, as they did May 1, to call strikes, issue manifestos, or demonstrate solidarity, which assumed many forms: picnics, excursions, athletic competitions, and dances. Pageants dramatized the laborer's plight. The 1,029-member-cast extravaganza, performed by the Paterson silk workers before a standing-room-only crowd of over fifteen thousand in New York's Madison Square Garden in 1913, was only the most famous of these frequent displays of class consciousness.

The identity of workers also assumed iconic forms. Ornate membership certificates hung in many a trade unionist's parlor. Union badges, brightly colored and decorated on one side, were worn to parades and meetings; members reversed these fabric badges (black on the opposite side) when attending co-workers' funerals. The Knights of Labor devised special oaths, passwords, handshakes, and regalia. Clothing—the leather apron, the folded paper box cap, the blue-denim overall—identified workers in class and caricature. So did the carrying of a metal dinner pail, an artifact successfully manipulated ("Four Years More of the Full Dinner Pail") by the Republican party to reelect President McKinley in 1900.

Uniforming also shaped workers' consciousness. At mid-century, the police in Boston and New York were identified by a leather badge or a "star-shaped copper shield." By 1876 both cities required uniforms that were based vaguely on regular army garb; urban firemen also acquired uniforms with a military flavor. Over the next sixty years, regulation wear came to other municipal employees (streetcar drivers, sanitation workers, subway operators), to postal workers, and to railway employees. Some utility companies uniformed their employees, as did service firms.

Workers protested their employers' unwillingness to raise wages or to improve factory conditions by urging boycotts of products and affixing union labels. Pioneered by the needle trades of the Amalgamated Clothing Workers and the International Ladies Garment Workers Union, this strategy also alerted the public to unsanitary sweatshop conditions and displayed an iconography that, like national-brand advertising, competed for the consumer's choice.

MILLS AND PLANTS

The massing of labor in large-scale mills or plants characterized two-thirds of American industrial work by 1900. Measured by the average size of their labor force, eleven of the nation's sixteen largest industries more than doubled in size by that date, a year when over 1,063 work complexes had payrolls of more than 500 workers and 443 had more than 1,000 wage earners.

Early American manufacturing centers, particularly grist, saw, and textile mills, followed watercourses to create rural industrial villages, such as Rockdale, Pennsylvania, or Cohoes, New York. By the mid-century, coal-fired steam engines led to a new generation of mills, now freed from their waterside locations and planted in cities. By 1900 electricity added a new option.

In the early 1820s, the cotton-textile industry in Lowell, Massachusetts, emerged as the archetype of many mill towns. Less dramatically, other industries—arms manufacture and iron rolling—moved swiftly toward factory dimensions. Company mill towns, communities dominated by a single firm or industry (often responsible for planning and running it), proliferated in places such as Manchester, New Hampshire (Amoskeag Company); Kannapolis, North Carolina (Cannon Mills); and Sparrows Point, Maryland (Pennsylvania Steel). In large urban areas like Troy, New York, or Cincinnati's Mill Creek Valley, distinct mill districts emerged. These environments had their own banks, breweries, churches, ethnic clubs, saloons, and newspapers.

Mills existed primarily to house machines and to produce goods. Inside their walls, several generations of craftsmen, laborers, farmers, and peasants underwent a massive transformation involving new work habits. In Herbert Gutman's terms, the mill changed "prefactory people" into "modern industrial workers" within the brief period of 1843 to 1919. Mill work made a truly *new* worker's world, one more specialized, disciplined, and mechanized. This industrial world of work often forbade singing, drinking, joking, smoking, or conversation on the job and it denied ethnic workers time to celebrate their national holidays and holy days (the Greek Orthodox Church had over eighty festivals) or to keep (as for Jews) the Saturday Sabbath. It also harbored death and bodily harm— one statistician estimating in 1913 that twenty-five thousand workers were killed each year in industrial accidents and another seven hundred thousand were maimed or disabled. This world of work became, in the words of Richard Edwards, a "contested terrain," in which workers and managers struggled for control of time and talent, energy and expertise.[21]

"The different branches of the trade are divided and subdivided so that one man may make just a particular part of a machine and may not know anything whatever about another part of the same machine," machinist John Morrison told a Senate committee in 1883. "There is no system of apprenticeship. You simply go in and learn whatever branch you are put at, and you stay at that unless you are changed to another."[22] By reducing work to a series of repetitive tasks done by an undifferentiated mass of laborers, mills limited a worker's control of production. Mill rules enforced this control of time and person. In place of the cycle of heavy work followed by leisurely breaks for conversation and pints of beer, which characterized the work patterns of independent artisans in their own shops, came the continual pace of work synchronized with machines.[23]

Unlike craftsmen, industrial workers did not own their own tools. The factory's means of production—its power looms, stamping presses, and forging hammers—were controlled by factory owners who, in the interests of productivity, continually sought technological innovations that would allow them to manufacture their product faster, cheaper, and with less human labor. Machinery determined the speed of human labor. "I made 80 pairs of shoes an hour," noted a female operator of the new (1862) McKay stitching machine in Lynn, Massachusetts, "because that's how fast the machine runs." To one member of the Knights of Labor, the extensive introduction of machinery into the workplace meant the degradation of labor: "The men are looked upon as nothing more than parts of the machinery they work. They are labeled and tagged, as parts of a machine would be, and are only taken into account as a part of machinery used for the profit of the manufacturer."[24]

Layoffs usually resulted when mills introduced new machinery. For example, when textile manufacturers in Fall River, Massachusetts, replaced spinning mules with ring spinning frames, this innovation left a thousand highly skilled spinners competing for eight hundred jobs. With the introduction of new pneumatic iron-molding techniques in the McCormick farm-implement plant, the managers dismissed the entire iron molders union and replaced them with unskilled recruits. More efficient machinery eradicated the jobs of heaters and rollers in steel mills, glassblowers in glassworks, and weavers in hosiery mills.

Women often replaced men in the increasingly mechanized

mill, so that by 1900 they constituted a fifth of the work force. By 1915 they also worked in linoleum factories, tanneries, and electronics industries. In textile mills, canneries, the garment industry, and food processing, they dominated the labor force.[25] "These operatives," reported a Department of Labor investigator of the New England shoe mills in 1906, "are very conscientious . . . and considered more reliable than men. They perform their tasks quietly and rarely give their employers any trouble. Men who are paid more for the same work are often less productive."[26]

The industrial plant, a work environment that was different in scale from the mill, emerged in early twentieth-century America. In 1915, Armour's Chicago slaughtering and packing plant employed over 6,000 workers; the United States Steel complex housed 9,000 workers at Homestead, Pennsylvania; and the Ford Plant at Highland Park, Michigan, employed 16,000 workers. Plants became minicities, complete with their own railroad terminals, water supplies, energy sources, telephone networks, fire departments, and security forces. Requiring vast amounts of space, new plants reoriented transportation patterns and housing markets. Although some, such as the Disston Saw and Stetson Hat works in Philadelphia, resulted from the steady expansion of nineteenth-century family mills, others like General Electric in Schnectady were massive sites that were newly built in outlying areas.

American industry had been moving toward mass production throughout the nineteenth century. Important developments in the manufacturing of firearms (the interchangeability of parts), in tool-and-die companies (precision jigs and gauges), in grain milling and iron foundrying (the handling of materials by conveyor belts), in can making (special or single-purpose machinery), in steel production (time-and-motion efficiency studies), in meat packing (slaughterhouse "disassembly" lines), and in bicycle manufacturing (sheet-metal stamping and electric-resistance welding) preceded the Ford Motor Company's introduction of a chain-driven assembly line in its Highland Park plant in 1913–14. The Ford engineers borrowed from past ideas and techniques. They applied them to more complex tasks (putting together five thousand parts to build a car) and carried them further than had been done to date.

Ford's production engineers, as David Hounshell documented, first experimented with a "line" in the subassembly of magnetos.[27] Under the old system of bench-building a magneto, a worker assembled the entire unit, from start to finish, in about twenty minutes. On April 1, 1913, the Ford engineers decided to try another way. They positioned twenty-nine workers beside a long, waist-high row of magneto flywheels that rested on a sliding surface. A foreman instructed the workers to attach one particular part of the assembly or perhaps start a few nuts or just tighten them and then shove the flywheel down the line to the next worker. The workers continually repeated their assigned routine. At the shift's end, the workers who, individually, usually assembled 35 magnetos per day at their benches had put together 1,188 on the line, or roughly one every thirteen minutes and ten seconds per worker. The workers complained of aching backs from stooping over the line, so the engineers raised the work level several inches. Some workers seemed to drag their heels, while others worked too fast. The engineers found that by moving the magnetos at a set rate with a chain, they could control the pace: speed up the slow ones and restrain the eager. Thus, within the year, by moving the magnetos with a continuous chain at a set speed and lowering the number of workers to fourteen, the line yielded an output of 1,335 magnetos in an eight-hour day, or one every five minutes, compared to the original twenty. The same technique reduced engine assembly from ten hours to six.

Ford's engineers next decided to put the most symbolic mass-production operation, the final or chassis assembly, on line (figure 2.7). Using their time-and-motion studies, they placed chassis parts and the men to work with them at different intervals along a 250-foot path. Over the next year, all the elements of this line—its length, divisions, manpower, and speed—were manipulated. The line was raised, lowered, speeded up, slowed down. Men were added and taken off. By April 1914, three such lines were in full operation, and the workers along them built 1,212 chassis assemblies in eight hours, or one every ninety-three man-minutes.

Adapting humans to serve as mechanical extensions of continually moving machinery exacted its toll, resulting in a high turnover of workers. To ensure that 15,000 laborers would be on the lines daily, Ford had to hire 53,000 people a year. To buy the stability of its work force and to thwart union organizing, the company cut the workday to eight hours in 1914 and instituted a wage-and-bonus system that raised laborers' earnings to five dollars per day, about twice the norm for industrial workers. The five-dollar day attracted much publicity and many job applicants. (The next year the company had to hire only 6,500 new employees.) The downside of high earnings surfaced within a month after Ford announced it. As an anonymous housewife wrote to Henry Ford in 1914: "The chain system you have is a slave driver! My God! Mr. Ford. My husband has come home and thrown himself down and won't eat his supper—so done out! Can't it be remedied? . . . That $5 a day is a blessing—a bigger one than you know but oh they earn it."

Workers resisted the increased mechanization, standardization, and automation of the workplace in many ways, the strike being the most visible and dramatic (figure 2.2). In addition to being direct responses to economic and working conditions, strikes became expressions of working-class identity, representing, in Alan Trachtenberg's words, "a defiance of the cardinal norm of everyday life: compliance with the authority of employers." The "readiness to strike," with "its attendant consequences of economic hardship, beating and arrest," according to Trachtenberg, resulted from wage cuts, new technology, and "a more fevered competition among businesses at a time of increasing consolidation and concentration of economic control."[28]

Turbulent labor-capital struggles bred fears of a second civil war or widespread urban anarchy; such confrontations also contributed to the growth of state power to impose social order. Following the bloody and destructive railroad strikes of 1877, a network of new armories were erected in large cities to house a standing "national guard." Public and private police forces, militia, and detective agencies all expanded in number and presence in Victorian America.[29]

Visible Hands

CONTRACTORS AND ENGINEERS

American business underwent a revolution in size, power, and organization in the generation after the Civil War. Several factors stimulated this phenomenon: an increasingly accessible, continually expanding home market; the country's enormous mineral wealth and fossil fuels; the pro-industry policies of both state and federal governments—including land grants, protective tariffs, favorable taxation, and the absence of direct intervention or regulation in most economic activities; and the widespread legal and economic use of incorporation.

The trend toward bigness, centralization, and incorporation in American business is an oft-told tale. Less well known is the influence and expansion of middle managers, many of whom had engineering backgrounds, who played crucial roles in changing the mass production and mass distribution of manufactured goods.

Middle managers, the middle-class professionals (figure 2.9) whom Alfred Chandler identified as the new "visible hands" of late nineteenth-century American business, first worked for the railroads. In that industry, an economy of scale developed, since a large railroad operation demanded the daily coordination of hundreds of workers—brakemen, conductors, engineers, station men, clerks, and work crews—across thousands of miles of track. A railroad's annual financial transactions, collecting charges from shippers and passengers, presented a staggering accounting task. Comparable more to maintaining a large army than to running a family business, railroads (several of whom had former Civil War generals as presidents) "called for a military-like organization to evaluate, coordinate, and enforce decisions. The result was the modern corporation, with its bureaucratic departments (finance, production, purchasing, and marketing) and hierarchical chains of command flowing downward and outward." Their size and administrative hierarchy moved the railroads beyond entrepreneurial capitalism and into the era of managerial capitalism. By the mid-1890s, this managerial revolution spread to food processing, steel making, and farm-implement manufacture and then to oil, chemicals, and rubber.[30] It was no accident that one of the first to introduce railroad-management techniques into manufacturing was steel maker Andrew Carnegie, a former division superintendent of the Pennsylvania Railroad.

Prior to the 1870s, manufacturers entrusted the day-to-day operations of their shops or mills to first-line supervisors and skilled workers. Many foremen ran their departments as independent baronies, often controlling the hiring, firing, and promotion of their work force. Some even looked the part, as at the Reed and Barton whitesmithing works in Massachusetts, where foremen "customarily reported for work in silk hats, cutaway coats, and attendant accessories."[31] In addition to his responsibility for the men or women working in his department or area, a typical early nineteenth-century foreman had a say in determining the manner and timing of production and in ascertaining the cost and quality of the work.

An internal contract system of manufacturing, operating at various times in factories of the Northeast, contributed to the foreman's authority and autonomy. Under this system, used in the manufacture of firearms, sewing machines, and locomotives, highly skilled workmen became managers as well as workers. A firm agreed to provide a contractor with floor space, machinery, light, power, heat, special tools, patterns, and the necessary raw and semifinished materials. The contractor both paid and hired his labor force. As Harold Williamson pointed out in his history of the Winchester Repeating Arms Company: "The management credited the accounts of the contractor so much for every hundred pieces of finished work which passed inspection, and debited his account for the wages paid to his men and the cost of oil, files, wastes, and so on, used in production. Anything left over was paid to the contractor as a profit."[32] The contractor received a foreman's wage. A variation on inside contracting was the "helper" system. Working under a general foreman, mule spinners, for example, often "employed" their sons as helpers, glassblowers similarly hired and supervised their furnace boys, and iron puddlers and rollers recruited their "green" hands.

A general foreman approved such arrangements and had the authority to change them if they interfered with his main task of "getting the work out." His job, while lacking the independence of the inside contractor, entailed similar responsibilities. The foreman made many decisions about how the job was done and who did it. Usually, he recruited the men and women who worked under him through a labor agent, an immigrant go-between, a "boarding boss," or by his personal choice from the unemployed crowds that gathered around a factory's gates. The degree to which owners interfered in the foreman's empire depended upon the industry and the production process. In general, the foreman enjoyed the greatest autonomy in industries that used unit and small-batch techniques and had fewer prerogatives in factories that came closer to mass production.

Most foremen espoused the "driving" method of supervision to motivate their men. A combination of authoritarian rule and shop profanity, driving meant keeping workers at their assigned tasks to complete the day's assigned production quota. Contractors working with shop craftsmen used it, as did foremen supervising unskilled plant workers.

Whether he bossed a locomotive-repair gang or an assembly-line crew, the foreman had invariably worked his way up to his position. His skills, however, were not beyond the reach of co-workers; they, too, could "make foreman" one day. Formal education meant little; mechanical ability, training in a craft, and experience were all-important. As Daniel Nelson pointed out, "the convergence of skill and power made foremen conservative men, often uncompromising defenders of the status quo. Because of their success they looked askance at anyone or anything that threatened to change the 'shop culture' that had rewarded their ability and diligence. Understandably they were seldom receptive to union organizers or management 'reformers' who sought to strip them of their powers."[33]

MANAGERS AND ENGINEERS

By 1915 a foreman in a large plant labored in a work world that was considerably altered from that of 1876. His authority and responsibility had been subdivided and dispersed to other supervisors. As his power and prestige declined, those of the plant manager and his staff rose.

FIGURE 2.3. Tobacco curing, Nash County, North Carolina (ca. 1910). Photograph courtesy of the North Carolina State Archives.

FIGURE 2.4. Bonanza wheat farming, Oregon (ca. 1890). Photograph courtesy of the Washington State Historical Society.

FIGURE 2.5. Women office workers trimming currency (1907), from records of U.S. Public Building Service. Photograph courtesy of the National Archives Trust.

FIGURE 2.6. Lewis Hine, *Mule Drivers and Nipper Boys* (1909). Photograph courtesy of the Library of Congress, Division of Prints and Photographs.

FIGURE 2.7. Assembly-line workers installing pistons in Ford Model T engines, Highland Park, Michigan (ca. 1914). Photograph courtesy of the Henry Ford Museum and Greenfield Village.

FIGURE 2.8. Sample employee time card and time clock recorders, from the International Business Machines Company trade catalog (ca. 1920s). Courtesy of the Warshaw Collection of Business Americana, National Museum of American History.

This Body of Engineers
Build a *New* "33"—Self-Starting

FIGURE 2.9. The engineer as white-collar manager and expert advertisement (1912). Drawing courtesy of the Hudson Motor Car Company, *Colliers* magazine.

FIGURE 2.10. Parody of the Irish domestic servant (undated). Drawing courtesy of the Newberry Library.

ETIQUETTE.

MR. HOLWORTHY.—"Is Miss Roseleaf at home?"

RECENTLY ACQUIRED TREASURE, (who has been carefully instructed in regard to callers.)—"Yis; but I can't let ye up stairs till ye've put ye'r name in the dish."

New industrial managers brought about this change. They phased out the inside contract system, proposed incentive plans, and introduced white-collar workers to perform tasks that were formerly done by the foreman. Accountants filled out and tabulated "cost sheets" that detailed statistics about every aspect of production. Timekeepers monitored the workers' time on their jobs. Industrial-welfare secretaries kept track of the workers' lives away from the plant. Time-study engineers calculated the most efficient "system" for doing a particular job. Quality-control inspectors reviewed the finished work. Personnel departments, like the one instituted at the National Cash Register Company in 1902, did hiring and firing.

While their names—Charles Sorensen at Ford or Frederick Winslow Taylor at Midvale Steel—are often neglected even in general histories of American business, these new middle managers and their staffs changed how many Americans did everyday factory and office work. Trained as engineers, they introduced important technical innovations into mass production via their experiments with new materials, sources of power, designs of plants, and machinery. Equally significant was their social engineering of managerial procedures that were required to synchronize the workplace and to supervise the work force.[34]

"Systematic" or "scientific" management, as pioneered by Frederick Winslow Taylor and Frank Gilbreth and as described later, sought to decipher the intricacies of the work process in order to separate the thinking and doing of a job. Using cards or tickets, managers conveyed instructions to foremen and workers, detailing the scheduling and inventorying of work. Factory accounting, done by an enlarged clerical staff, meant additional management control. As James Bridge, a supervisor in the Carnegie steelworks noted: "The minutest details of cost of materials and labor in every department appeared from day to day and week to week in the accounts; and soon every man about the place was made to realize it. The men felt and often remarked that the eyes of the company were always on them through the books."[35]

No artifact summarizes the progress of the managerial revolution more graphically than did a corporation's organization chart. Here, in a streamlined flow chart, much admired by the efficiency expert, was a white-collar empire of general managers, managers, superintendents, and supervisors. Here, in sanitized precision, could be found new features of American big business: parallel product operations, foreign market expansion, research and development laboratories. Here, in an administrative hierarchy in which everyone knew his place but hoped to move to the one above, managers and supervisors were hired to control work in which they did not participate.

While the new corporate ladder had many administrative rungs, it had only one form of proper dress by 1915: the business suit. The suit, "the trusty blue serge" introduced in the 1890s, descended from several nineteenth-century forms of male dress, including the frock; the ditto suit (coat, vest, and trousers cut from the same cloth); and, most important, the sack coat. Suits, advertisements claimed, symbolized modern masculinity—the American male as thinker, expert, and manager. Whereas the "Perfect Gentleman" outfitted in a Prince Albert long coat personified the male sartorial ideal of the 1870s, the "Coming Man," dressed in a business suit, tie, and Arrow white collar-shirt, embodied the corporate ideal of the 1910s.

Between 1910 and 1920, the number of white-collar supervisory employees in manufacturing, mining, and transportation increased by 66.3 percent compared to a 27.7 percent growth in wage earners. This managerial concentration had two important ramifications. Many skilled craft workers ceased to be production workers. Instead, they now performed ancillary functions of planning, toolmaking, and setup. Mechanized production work came to be done by specialized operatives whose routines, output, and status were controlled by supervisory technicians. As David Montgomery pointed out, the number of these unskilled laborers also increased significantly. In the automotive industry alone, for example, the number of operatives grew from 21,091 in 1910 to 121,164 in 1920.[36]

This "new" industrial labor force did not develop, however, without resistance from workers. Traditional work habits of the shop artisan and rural peasant, as Herbert Gutman and Daniel Rodgers documented, continually opposed the imperatives of the mechanized factory system. Workers sought self-protection in cooperative, fraternal, mutual-benefit, and ethnic societies; they sought self-assertion through wildcat strikes, deliberate absentee-ism for personal reasons (a typical Polish wedding lasted three to five days), the observance of Blue Monday (absenteeism following a weekend), product boycotts, sympathy strikes, group control of piecework rates, and the "stint" (a day's production regulated by the workers), plus street parades, funeral processions, and solidar-ity rallies.[37]

TIME IS MONEY

Industrial capitalism's quest for regularity and standardization in the workplace, an environment that timed both men and ma-chines, had a long American history, dating at least to Benjamin Franklin's belief in his *Advice to a Young Tradesman* (1748) that "Time Is Money."

The Self-Winding Clock Company, a shadow corporation of Western Union, provided electric synchronized clock systems and daily time signals to factories, schools, and offices. An exhibitor at Chicago's 1893 exposition, the firm demonstrated its product's accuracy by regulating over two hundred clocks from its central pavilion. A "master clock," such as the firm's best model (The Autocrat), linked numerous "slave" or "controlled" clocks; it could be programmed to ring bells or trigger machines on or off.

Before the 1890s, many factories stationed at their gates a man or woman who logged a handwritten record of employees' names as they came and went; other companies assigned each worker a numbered brass check to present to the timekeeper, who re-corded each name and number in a ledger. In large firms, either method meant long waiting lines and daily arguments about who—the timekeeper or the worker—had the "right" time. Prom-ising promptness, order, and discipline, time clocks became stan-dard fixtures of many large plants and offices (figure 2.8). By 1907 many leading manufacturers in the time-clock industry had been bought up by the International Time Recording Company, later known as International Business Machines, or IBM.

"Time studies of work," claimed Frederick Winslow Taylor in *Principles of Scientific Management* (1911), "forms the basis of modern management." Taylor, a pattern maker, machinist, and industrial consultant, sought to standardize factory production with his stopwatch. At Pennsylvania's Midvale Steel, he first conducted time and motion studies in 1884 of the most efficient way for men to load pig iron. He and his followers went on to time and test needless motions and unproductive distractions in bricklaying, arms manufacture, and metal and steel making.

Taylorism, or scientific management as it was also called, struck many Victorians as a rational way to eliminate many economic and social evils. To a generation that was fascinated with timesaving in transportation (express subways or limited rail trains) and communication (the telegraph and telephone), it followed logically that to extract the maximum yield from a given effort with the least amount of time and money spent was an appropriate goal. Taylorism operated on four essential concepts: (1) the stopwatch analysis of each distinct work operation in order to fix its time "rates"; (2) the centralized planning and routing of a task's successive phases, regulated by synchronized factory time clocks; (3) detailed instruction, supervision, and monitoring (requiring workers to complete time cards for each job) of each worker's performance of his or her discrete task; and (4) wage payments based on each worker following those instructions and promptly "punching" the office time clock throughout the pay period.[38] Taylor's time imposed a machine logic on the workday of mills and plants. It choreographed the human motions of hands, arms, backs, and legs to perform with clocklike regularity.

Workers responded to the demands of the era's "new" time in different ways. Molders at the Massachusetts Watertown Arsenal and metal polishers in auto plants at Saginaw, Michigan, decided to strike rather than "go under the watch." Others accepted the machine time of the workplace, but demonstrated, lobbied, protested, and organized to shorten its day (the eight-hour-day movement) and its duration (a forty-hour week). The quest to lessen the American laborer's average work time was a major issue in many labor-capital confrontations, notably the Haymarket Massacre of 1886.

Office Work and Service Jobs

WOMEN TYPISTS AND MEN MONITORS

The industrial and managerial revolutions of late nineteenth-century America created the need for enlarged office bureaucracies that were capable of administering massive flows of men, materials, and money. As simple partnerships gave way to national corporations, "downtown" offices expanded. Beginning in 1886 with Chicago's Home Insurance Building, the country's first skyscraper, cities of capitalist towers—providing businesses with expanded office space and corporate symbols—arose to dwarf the other activities of urban life. Alfred Stieglitz's famous 1910 photograph, "Old and New York" captured this momentous change in a single image.

Prior to the 1870s, the typical business office was a small affair, totally staffed by men. Senior clerks, involved in most stages of a business transaction, controlled the rate at which the staffs worked. Most began their careers as office boys, eventually becoming copyists or bookkeepers, hoping ultimately to run a company of their own. The office staff generally enjoyed high status through regular contact with their employers, by the responsibilities entrusted to them, and because their wages equaled those of most skilled craftsmen.

Fifty years later, office staffs had changed dramatically. Clerks became clerical workers. By 1900, women made up more than a third of the clerical workers and by 1920, more than half. Because there were few job opportunities for women in the professions, except for nursing and teaching, literate women turned to office work.

These working "girls" tended to be native-born, white, young (eighteen to twenty-four years old), single women, an increasing number of whom tended to live away from home. Some learned their tasks directly on the job, but many took courses in the rapidly growing business schools, at the YWCA, or in commercial courses in the new high schools. In these courses, they pounded out the 1872 Republican rallying slogan for Ulysses S. Grant ("Now is the time for all good men to come to the aid of their party") and practiced William McKinley's famous speech at the 1901 Pan-American Exposition (a standard shorthand dictation exercise). Clerical jobs paid better than did many other jobs that were open to women. A high school graduate of the classical course who taught in an urban public school earned $450 per year. Her counterpart from the commercial course who worked in an office received $660, whereas most mill women made $260 per year. Hence, many women worked in offices for the money, as in Booth Tarkington's 1921 novel, *Alice Adams,* where a middle-class daughter goes into clerical work because of the failure of the family business. To many daughters of working-class parents, like Rachel Toomis in Dorothy Richardson's *The Long Day: The Story of a New York Working Girl* (1905), office work offered economic and social mobility and paid better than did factory work, domestic service, or clerking in stores.[39]

Whatever their motivations for working, few female office workers became office executives. A talented woman might be promoted to a lower-level managerial post, such as a supervisor of a typing pool or a head of a bookkeeping department, but she could never expect to become a junior executive or a full partner. Viewed by male monitors to have no ambitions, and hence unlikely to be dissatisfied if their jobs offered no prospect of advancement, women office workers became the equivalent of semiskilled workers in mills or plants.

The gender hierarchy of pay and power that characterized the office by 1915 also occurred, in part, because of specialization and technology. The clerical worker, instead of being an autonomous male clerk charged with the whole of a business transaction, acted primarily as a process worker in specialized departments (accounting, purchasing, auditing, credit, personnel, marketing, filing), each carrying out part of the work process. Perhaps the most potent sign of the clerical worker's parallel with the plant worker was the time clock's appearance in business offices by 1910.[40]

Ironically, the typewriter—the invention of a man, Christopher L. Sholes, who first exhibited it at the 1876 Centennial Exposition—both eased the entry of women into the formerly masculine office and enslaved them to subservient status once they entered it. When first marketed, it had no historical ties to either sex, which meant that female typists did not have to counter (as women did in factories) the argument that they were operating a "man's machine." By the 1880s, advertisers and office managers, however, changed this situation, claiming that the most efficient typing required the supposedly greater nimbleness of women's fingers. Hence, when Mark Twain, its staunch publicist, bought his first machine, the salesman had a "type girl" on hand to demonstrate it to him. In 1870, 4.5 percent of the stenographers and typists were female; by 1930, that figure was 91.8 percent.

Although some early typewriters resembled sewing machines (Remington) or had a semicircular keyboard (Hammond), by 1900, most office models were black, with white lettering on black keys, and had a sturdy metal carriage—all suggesting an efficient and reliable industrial design. What about the machine's operators, who quickly became known as "typewriters"? How were they designed?

Shirtwaists and skirts dominated women clerical workers' everyday dress (figure 2.5). Costing from fifty cents to seven dollars, shirtwaists fulfilled the expectations of everyone, ranging from the affluent matron to the girls who made them. When artist Charles Dana Gibson sought to capture "the typical American girl" of his time, he depicted her "a new woman, a steel-engraved lady," in the standard costume of shirtwaist and skirt.

Many office women emulated "the Gibson look" because it was fashionable and practical. Technical training manuals urged dressing for success and advised a middle ground in clothing, one neither too feminine (avoid "fluffy, frilly furbelows") or too masculine (shun "tweeds and cheviots"). What was most appropriate to the everyday business environment? A black skirt and a white shirtwaist, resembling in color and effect, the sober, organized, clean look and lines of the secretary's typewriter.

ENVIRONMENT AND EQUIPMENT

Typewriters were only one office innovation. Desks and furniture were redesigned and new machines installed to manage the work and workers more efficiently and profitably. Desks, as Adrian Forty traced, changed first. The standard nineteenth-century senior clerk's desk, such as the famous Wooton Rotary Desk, had a high back with pigeonholes and drawers in it, and sometimes a roll top. A clerk seated at such a desk could see his work in front of him, but no one else could see what he was doing without coming to look over his shoulder. Such a desk "represented a small personal domain, the roll top closed to secure its privacy." The Modern Efficiency Desk, designed for the Equitable Assurance Company in 1915, suggests a totally different view of everyday office work. Gone was any sense of a worker's private enclave. The new flat-top desk was only a table containing shallow drawers. Managers periodically inspected desk drawers to check a clerk's volume of "in" and "out" work.

The standardization of desks, arranged in a uniform order on the office floor, extended even to providing identical rulers, paper clips, erasers, and pens. Office managers argued that instead of "a large supply of different pens to suit handwriting idiosyncrasies, one nib style would be more economical" and give a firm's paperwork more uniformity. Thus, "even in handwriting, the most individual and personal characteristic left to the clerk," nonconformity meant inefficiency.[41]

Scientific management, promoted by manuals like Walter D. Scott's *Increasing Human Efficiency in Business* (1915), should have been applied with equal force to everyone in an office. Managers, it turned out, enjoyed different environments than did workers, although their basic activities in terms of time-and-motion studies—sitting, reading, or writing at a desk—were the same. While clerks had standardized dip pens, managers wrote with fountain pens (perfected by Lewis Edson Waterman in 1884). The redesign of the clerk's desk failed to apply to an executive's desk. Although centralized filing had eliminated the need for storage and efficiency required no more space than necessary for writing, executive desks, usually situated in glass enclosures or separate rooms, continued as obvious status symbols. Their size and style immediately established who was boss.

With the exception of the dictaphone—the one new (1885) business machine personally used by the executive and hence disguised in a wooden cabinet to make it more appropriate furniture for the manager's suite—other new office technology (such as the mimeograph and addressing and adding machines) was overtly

mechanical and industrial in appearance. Painted black and supported on tubular metal frames, these new mechanisms, run by
the female staff, either speeded up or further segregated office
tasks.

Even everyday filing took on a new format. Take, for example,
the traditional nineteenth-century record-management procedures of a federal government office handling a letter sent to the
Treasury Department from one of its routine correspondents.[42]
First, a clerk registered it according to the writer's name, date of
the letter and date of its receipt, subject, and the division to which
the letter was given for reply in a central file. These files were
ordered alphabetically by the writer's name or office and then
chronologically. Eventually, these incoming letters were bundled
with red or white woven-cloth string (hence the expression,
"bureaucratic red tape") and eventually bound into sets of
volumes by year. The answer to that letter retraced the same
route. Government files were, therefore, multiple, permanent,
and unwieldy. Though no private firm approached the amount of
a government department's paperwork, the traditional file of
chronological press books slowly gave way to other systems. With
the use at the century's end of the humble manila folder—portable, resortable, and expandable—and its four-drawer, vertical file
cabinet, the chronological tyranny of the press-book archive was
broken.[43] All the information on an account, a transaction, or an
employee was enveloped in one thin, easily accessible, file.

SERVICE: DOMESTIC, SALES, CIVIL

While the proportion of women in industry and office work increased substantially in the late nineteenth century, domestic service remained the era's dominant form of "women's work." In
1870 the first census carefully recorded working women: one-half
of all female wage earners worked as domestic servants; roughly
one million women servants made up one-twelfth of the total labor
force. By 1920, however, only a sixth of American women worked
in "private or public housekeeping," creating what many middle-
class women bemoaned the age's "servant problem." In New York
City, for example, while there had been 188 servants for every

1,000 families in 1880, the ratio dropped to 141 in 1900, and to 66 in 1920.

Household service changed in other ways. By the 1890s, "domestics" replaced "help" or "hired girls" in name and fact, reflecting transformations that recast work roles and family life. The hired girl, much like the hired man, worked in a society of small producers. In addition to household chores, she often helped out with the home production of homespun textiles or cheese, eggs, and milk. Families commonly hired temporary help in times of special demands—birth, death, or illness. Rural people hired women to help with the extra work (in fields and kitchens) of harvest seasons. City folks needed girls for spring and fall house-cleaning. The hired girl, sitting and eating at the family's table, shared their food and their family circle. Usually, she had been recruited through a network of kin, neighbors, or friends. She worked by the day, by the task, or by the season. When she lived with her employer, both anticipated only a temporary stay.

By contrast, employers of "domestic servants," or "domestics," recruited their household workers in institutional contexts. Some employers published want-ads in newspapers. Others contacted church groups and welfare organizations. Some used the "intelligence office," an employment agency specializing in supplying servants. In exchange for a fee (ranging from fifty cents to a dollar), often required of both parties, the proprietors of these agencies (usually women) brought together two sets of women: the servers and those to be served. Sidney Fisher, whose wife, Bet, patronized "Mrs. Bourke's intelligence" in Philadelphia in 1870, fumed at the ordeal. "It is a most disgusting business, this of running to intelligence offices, and unfit for a lady. Bet always meets ladies elegantly dressed in one room waiting to choose, and a crowd of hideous Irish monsters in another waiting to be chosen. Out of the lot it is rare to be able to select one fit to enter a decent house."[44]

The Irish "Bridget" or "Biddy" became the ethnic stereotype of the American domestic by the 1850s (figure 2.10). Biddy jokes celebrated her inadequacies. Biddy answered the door by yelling through the keyhole; Biddy, accustomed to descending by a ladder, walked down stairs backwards. Irish women—who, more than any other immigrant group, came to America unaccompanied by families—dominated the domestic job market.

Live-in domestics were expected to be at work or on call before the family arose from bed and after it went to sleep. They were allowed little time off, the standard being one evening or afternoon a week and one day (usually Sunday) every two weeks. The lack of genuine free time frustrated domestic workers, especially since they could not regularly participate in the era's expanding night life of cultural, educational, and entertainment activities. "My first employer was a smart, energetic woman," a former servant reported. "I had a good room and everything nice, and she gave me a great many things, but I'd have spared them all if only I could have had a little time to myself."[45]

Domestics received pay "in kind" (room and board, sometimes used clothing) and in wages. Servants resided in segregated and sparsely furnished areas of the house, generally above or beside the kitchen or in the attic. Most domestics could not entertain visitors or suitors in their quarters, look forward to enjoying regular seasonal holidays on their own, or treat themselves to the family larder without permission. Unlike the hired girl, the domestic ate alone, in the kitchen, usually the leftovers of the meals she had cooked and served that day. Her mistress often dictated her diet. If, for example, she worked for employers who were influenced by food reformers, she might be forbidden to drink coffee, tea, wine, or beer.

Although strikes by domestics, who were organized in the Household Union in Holyoke, Massachusetts, or the Servant Girls Union in Toledo, Ohio, took place, many domestics simply looked forward to the day when they could find other jobs. In Cohoes, New York, in 1881, the local newspaper declared that obtaining competent servants was "next to impossible" because of the nearby cotton mills. In 1897 Lucy Salmon—Vassar College's first history professor—wrote *Domestic Service,* which reported that former domestics rated waitressing, fruit picking, cannery work, and labor in shoe, textile, and clothing factories above household service. Most immigrants also left domestic service as soon as they reasonably could. In 1900, 60.5 percent of the Irish-born wage-earning women in the United States were servants, but only 18.9

percent of the children of Irish-born parents were.[46]

Although the working conditions of domestics had changed little by 1915, the age, marital status, and race of its workers did. As part of the general migration of blacks from southern farms to northern cities, many black women moved specifically to become domestics, recruited by employment agents who traveled the South offering them transportation and jobs. Such women accepted low wages for part-time, nonresident day labor. Black women, about a fourth of the servant population in 1900, constituted nearly half by 1930. "Unlike working-class white women," wrote Susan Strasser, "who throughout the nineteenth-century usually worked outside the home only before marriage or worked part-time to supplement their husbands' earnings, black women, as slaves and as freed women, had always worked outside their own households. In 1920, 33 percent of married black women worked, as opposed to only 6 percent of married native and 7 percent of married immigrant white women." Once a predominantly white and single labor force, American domestic service became increasingly black and married. Bridget, the full-time, live-in domestic of the late nineteenth century left the scene, replaced by Beulah, the part-time black maid of the twentieth.[47]

Retail selling jobs, largely unavailable to black women, expanded for native-born and, eventually, for white immigrant women. Although sales work paralleled clerical work in many ways, the latter generally required more training. Selling, when compared to factory work, however, commanded more status. As one early twentieth-century editor put it, "Maggie" in the mill became "Miss" in the store. In 1870, "saleswomen" were too few to be counted separately in the census records. By 1900, they numbered over 142,000. The figure doubled in 1920 owing to the proliferation of department and franchise stores.

Sales work, like domestic service, provided a context for the spread of middle-class tastes and expectations. This indoctrination began in the trainee programs for clerks, where personnel managers sought to erase telltale signs of working-class dress and demeanor while trying to acquaint employees with middle-class lifestyles so they might better sell the appropriate goods. It continued with manager's directives, regulation booklets, and the interaction with customers.

Clerks naturally resented elaborate store rules. In 1898, for example, the Hess Brothers of Allentown, Pennsylvania, distributed a manual listing no fewer than sixty-two "Store Don'ts," including "Never sit down," "Don't huddle with other employees," and "Don't dress dowdily, gaudily, or dudishly." Some clerks bypassed edicts they found unreasonable. For example, Massie, one of the three thousand clerks in O. Henry's "Biggest Store," chewed tutti-frutti "when the floorwalker was not looking" and "smiled wistfully" when he did.

Saleswomen, as Susan Benson has shown, found various ways to control their work. Apparel saleswomen, for example, learned to estimate, at a glance, a customer's clothing sizes and the cost of her outfit. A clerk who called "Oh, Henrietta," while waiting on a customer alerted her co-workers to the fact that the customer was "a hen," a difficult type. New saleswomen quickly learned how to maintain a "good book"—the amount of sales that constituted a solid day's work or "stint." "A saleswoman deviated from the stint at her peril: sales too far below it brought management down on her head, sales too far above alienated her peers. Within a given day, saleswomen tapered off their selling efforts as they approached the informal quota, sometimes calling other clerks with lower 'books' to take customers" while they did stockwork. A saleswoman's worst sin was to be a "grabber": to ignore the stint and to hog customers.[48]

Government employment also opened for more men and women in Victorian America. First hired by the Treasury Department in 1862, female clerks penetrated federal offices (previously an exclusive male enclave), setting a precedent for the influx of women clerical workers who entered business and government offices in the following decades (figure 2.5). By 1900, women constituted a third of all federal employees.

Two types of evidence—statistics and structures—demonstrate the dramatic growth of the federal bureaucracy and the increasing governmental presence in everyday life between the Civil War and World War I. In 1881 there was one federal employee per 502 people of the total population, compared with one per 237 people in 1911. Similar figures record the parallel expansion of government workers in state capitols and city halls. As civil servants and bureaucrats "made more of the fundamental decisions affecting people's lives," wrote Warren Susman, a new administrative state, "equal to any kind in Europe," emerged.[49]

Washington's burgeoning bureaucracy—new departments, such as Labor (1888) and Agriculture (1889), and new commissions like Civil Service (1883) and Interstate Commerce (1887)—aided the city's growth. Elsewhere government employment multiplied via local "federal presents" repeatedly pork barreled out of Congress: new customs houses, mints, immigration stations, federal penitentiaries, and combination courthouse–post offices everywhere. States rebuilt or expanded their capitols. The "county courthouse wars" of the 1880s and the City Beautiful movement in the 1910s were other manifestations of a nationwide government-edifice complex.

Progressive reformers like architect Daniel Burnham saw the new government offices as civic environments that would eliminate political graft and corruption. Who would dare pilfer from the public coffers in a building such as he proposed as Chicago's City Hall in 1909? Its noble classicism, Burnham believed, would condition a public servant's conduct. Similar objectives motivated those who passed the 1883 Pendleton Act, legislation limiting a political party's manipulation of federal-government jobs for patronage purposes. Before the 1880s, "To the victor belonged the spoils." Patronage followed party. Government workers could expect dismissal with changing election results. The Pendleton Act, modeled after a similar British law, established the Civil Service Commission, which introduced the merit system into everyday public employment through competitive examinations. At first only 10 percent of the 131,000 government workers came under the new regulations, but, by 1920, almost half of all federal jobs were so "classified."

Monitoring Money

WAGES, SALARIES, BUDGETS

Whether one "took home wages" or "was on salary" was a crucial distinction in worker's pay and status. Often, as in the textile, canning, and metal-working trades, wages were determined by some form of piecework. Wage workers were usually paid by the day or the week. They could not expect regular daily or weekly work, since their jobs fluctuated with seasonal conditions, the foreman's whims, and economic downturns. An 1887 study by Wisconsin's Department of Labor, Census, and Statistics reported an average yearly figure of sixty-one days of unemployment per man in all trades.[50]

The wage earner's daily experience with irregular employment differed markedly from that of the man who earned a salary. Clerks, for example, usually received a salary, not a wage, indicating that they could anticipate working without fear of a sudden layoff. They were paid weekly, bimonthly, or monthly. Salaried workers enjoyed other fringe benefits: leave time, sometimes with pay; more free holidays and regular vacation time; and sickness benefits.

Working "on commission," the way appliance salesmen and car dealers earned their pay, expanded with the growth of company franchising. As early as 1856, the Singer Sewing Machine Company sold its machines through salaried agents who worked on commission. Federal revenue agents received a percentage of what they collected. Insurance companies and business-machine firms also used the commission system.

In various company towns, wage earners were sometimes paid off in tokens, private coinage, or scrip redeemable only at the company's store or establishments favored by the dominant local industry. Most company stores extended credit to workers' families against the workers' scrip wage, but such indebtedness gave managers additional leverage against the workers in disputes over wages or working conditions.

Beginning with Carroll D. Wright's Massachusetts Bureau of Statistics on Labor in 1875, social scientists began to investigate

American workers' incomes, budgets, and expenditures. For example, studies, such as that of Louise Bolard More (table 2.1), revealed that the cash wages of working people varied significantly. However, as Clarence Long and John Modell charted, the real wages of many workers rose, at least statistically: The cost of food, clothing, and housing dropped.[51]

But such statistics can be misleading because the earnings of the skilled "aristocracy" of labor—locomotive engineers, machinists, master carpenters, printers, and other highly trained craftsmen—improved much more than did those of the unskilled workers at the bottom of the pyramid. The average annual wage for manufacturing workers in 1900 was only $435, or $8.37 a week. Unskilled workers were paid ten cents an hour on the average, about $5.50 a week. A girl of twelve or thirteen, tending a loom in a textile factory, might take home as little as $2 a week.[52]

Inflation and new patterns of consumption, plus changes in class relationships and family life, prompted researchers to monitor the salaries and budgets of the middle classes. Martha and Robert Bruère, for example, produced an intriguing study, *Increasing Home Efficiency* (1912), that analyzed systematically, for the first time, a significant amount of material on the differing lifestyles of the middle classes. Three of their case studies (table 2.2) demonstrate the earnings and expenditures of a Boston businessman (the Wells family), a Middle West farmer (the Parnells), and a California teacher (the Allison family).[53]

In 1914 a few middle-class Americans participated in a new ritual that eventually would become as perennial for most citizens as the spring equinox. On or before March 1 that year, 357,598 Americans confronted, completed, and filed a four-page government tax *Return of Annual Net Income of Individuals* that the Internal Revenue Service had enumerated, for no particular reason, as Form 1040. After a half century of congressional debate, heated public argument, and several Supreme Court tests, an annual personal income tax became law by means of the Sixteenth Amendment when it was ratified by Wyoming on February 3, 1913.

Throughout the 1890s, western Democrats, Socialists, Populists (who included it as a major plank in their 1892 platform), and various reformers pressed for a national income tax as a means of mitigating the country's growing inequities in wealth and income. For example, during a 1894 Senate debate, William V. Alley (Nebraska) argued, using federal census statistics, that 91 percent of the 12 million families in the United States owned only 29 percent of the national wealth and 9 percent controlled the other 71 percent.

Minor by current standards, the 1913 income tax rate was 1 percent on taxable income above $3,000 or $4,000 for married couples. Besides this tax, an additional surtax with progressive rates was levied on the amount of an individual's net income exceeding $20,000. The maximum rate anyone paid was 7 percent of earnings. The law allowed deductions, such as interest on loans, other taxes, and depreciation. No taxes were withheld in advance.[54]

A new occupation, the certified public accountant, expanded because of the income-tax laws. Accountants and auditors, important functionaries in steering corporations through proliferating state and federal legislation, had a significant role in drafting the 1913 tax law and to them fell the task of preparing the corporate tax returns that it required. The Federal Board of Tax Appeals permitted only certified public accountants (and attorneys) to argue taxpayers' claims before it. Corporate tax work led to the handling of complicated returns for middle-class individuals. By 1915, such professionals and small businessmen now said, "See my accountant," as well as "See my lawyer."

NICKEL EMPIRE—WHAT FIVE CENTS WOULD BUY

As the dime ("Brother Can You Spare One?") reigned as the coin of the depressed realm in the 1930s, the nickel symbolized many of the buying habits of the 1890s. What cost a nickel then demonstrates much about America's changing everyday food and transportation patterns, recreational interests, and consumer preferences. "A nickel's worth" also accounts for shifts in retailing, charitable giving, and the American language.

Nickel did not mean a five-cent coin until the 1880s. The first U.S. coin to be called a nickel was the copper-and-nickel one-cent piece of 1857, and the next was a three-cent nickel of 1865—used

TABLE 2.1. WORKING-CLASS YEARLY FAMILY BUDGET

Seamstress

Income

Mrs. M., sewing, 14 weeks, averaged $5.00 a week	$ 70.00
"　　　"　　　"　38　"　　　　"　　3.00　　"	114.00
Girl, 13, earned in summer	14.00
Mother, extra work	20.50
St. Vincent de Paul Society, grocery tickets	26.00
"　　　"　　　"　　　"　　　"　shoes	4.00
Charity Organization Society, for rent	11.50
Total	$260.00

Expenditures

Food	$130.00
Rent	92.75
Clothing	18.00
Fuel	13.00
Medicine	1.00
Moving expenses	3.00
Sundries	2.25
	$260.00

Factory Laborer

Income, January 1, 1904, to January 1, 1905, $489.

Expenditures

Food (about $4.00 a week)	$205.00
Rent, $9.00 a month	108.00
Gas and coal	26.00
Clothing	24.00
Clothing for baby	8.00
Furniture	45.00
Books and papers	7.80
Charity	3.00
Recreation in summer	7.00
Gifts	6.00
Loan	27.00
Kitchen needs	8.00
Miscellaneous (stamps, paper, thread, pins, etc.)	14.20
	$489.00

Glassworker

Income

Man, 51½ weeks at $14.00 (3 holidays deducted)	$ 721.00
Woman, for janitor's services, rent-free	132.00
Boy (15), 22 weeks at $3.50, 25 weeks at $4.00	177.00
	$1030.00
Gift from landlord at Christmas	10.00
Total	$1040.00

Expenditures

Food, $10.00 a week, including lunch-money	$ 520.00
Rent	132.00
Clothing	85.00
Light and fuel	48.50
Insurance, .60 a week	31.20
Papers, .11 a week	5.72
Union dues	6.00
Drink for man, $3.00 a week	156.00
Medical attendance	27.00
Church	13.00
Recreation for father and oldest boy	10.00
Sundries	5.58
Total	$1040.00

Source: The budgets for the seamstress, factory laborer, and glassworker are reproduced from Louise Bolard More, *Wage-Earner's Budgets: A Study of Standards and Cost of Living in New York City* (New York: Henry Holt & Co., 1907), 133–34, 146.

frequently to pay the then three-cent postage rate. By 1883, the Treasury Department issued a five-cent nickel (actually made of one part nickel and three parts copper) that became extremely popular. The new "five-cent piece," or "five-center," sported a Goddess of Liberty bordered with stars. This "Liberty Head" coin was a favorite of confidence men, who, sometimes with gold or silver plating on it, passed it off as a five-dollar piece, the Roman numeral V on the original not being followed by the word "cents." In 1913 the Treasury Department asked James Earl Frazer to design a new five-cent coin. Frazer incorporated two vanishing American symbols: the profile of an American Indian (a composite

TABLE 2.2. MIDDLE-CLASS YEARLY FAMILY BUDGETS*

Budget of the Wells Family, 1911

Item	Amount in Dollars	Percentage of Budget
Food	504.00	21.00
Shelter (mortgage, repairs, taxes)	396.00	16.50
Clothes	192.00	8.00
Operating costs		
Help	120.00	
Heat and light	96.00	
Carfare	72.00	
Refurnishing	54.00	
Subtotal	342.00	14.25
Advancement		
Doctor, dentist, medicine	132.00	
Church, charity	168.00	
Vacations, travel, books, amusement	39.00	
Incidentals	89.40	
Insurance (fire and life)	117.60	
Savings	420.00	
Subtotal	966.00	40.25

Budget of the Parnell Family, 1911

Item	Amount in Dollars	Percentage of Budget
Food	600	15.000
Shelter (taxes, repairs, improvements, etc.)	475	11.875
Clothes	450	11.250
Operating	625	15.625
Advancement		
College (son and daughter)	1000	
Insurance (fire and life)	148	
Vacation trips	200	
Gifts, charity, church	60	
Books, etc.	50	
Miscellaneous	182	
Savings	200	
Subtotal	1850	46.250

Budget of the Allison Family, 1911

Item	Amount in Dollars	Percentage of Budget
Food	216.00	12.0
Mortgage on home	360.00	20.0
Clothes	225.00	12.5
Operating costs		
Help	59.40	
Gas and electricity	41.40	
Telephone	23.40	
Carfare	70.20	
Laundry	14.40	
Subtotal	208.80	11.6
Advancement		
Insurance	91.80	
Church	10.80	
Books, etc.	64.80	
Amusements	50.40	
Incidentals	50.40	
Savings	522.00	
Subtotal	790.20	43.9

Note: Advancement expenditures for the Parnell family do not add up to $1850.

Source: The budgets of the Wells family and the Parnell family are from Martha B. Bruère, "What Is the Home For?" *Outlook* 99 (16 December 1911), 911. The budget of the Allison family is from Martha B. Bruère, "Experiments in Spending: The Budgets of a California School-Teacher and a Massachusetts Clergyman," *Woman's Home Companion* 38 (November 1911), 14.

*These tables can be found in Daniel Horowitz, *The Morality of Spending: Attitudes Toward the Consumer Society in America, 1875–1940* (Baltimore: Johns Hopkins University Press, 1985), 90–92. For the sake of clarity, Daniel Horowitz has adapted the figures and modified the form for this table and subsequent tables.

of three native models) and a silhouette of an American bison on the reverse side. The "buffalo" or "Indian head" nickel was minted until 1938.

Nickels bought anything and everything. One could open an account with them at the Worcester (Massachusetts) Five Cents Saving Bank. A stroke of the mechanical cheese cutter on a country store's counter yielded a diagonal cut that tallied "around a nickel's worth." Clerk's dipped into the store's proverbial bulk cracker barrel on the basis of "one handful, one nickel." Americans drank nickel beer and nickel coffee (a refill being free). Coca-Cola and Nathan's Franks cost five cents. Bob's Quick Lunch in 1904 offered several options for the worker's nickel: a large bowl of coffee and hotcakes, three rolls or three donuts, or a quarter of a pie, while other meals cost a double nickel. New candies (Cracker Jack, 1893; Tootsie Roll, 1896; Mary Jane's, 1912) and confections (flavored chewing gum, 1884; ice cream cones, 1904) came in five-cent packs. So did P. T. Barnum's circus peanuts.

A nickel took you most places in most cities. It was the standard fare on the Brooklyn Elevated, a Boston streetcar, a New York subway, and the Staten Island Ferry. In 1901, a nickel bought a taxicab's hire or an amusement park's ride.

Nickelodeons were only one form of cheap entertainment. Five cents got you onto the midway of a county fair, where any number of "nickel nickers" were anxious to take your coins at games of chance. In saloons you could play various mechanical games, such as box-ball, five minutes for five cents, or buy five-cent snacks from the Automatic Lunch Counter food dispensers. For a nickel you could use a public telephone or buy a dozen roses to impress a date. One nickel of Chinese firecrackers made for the holiday amusement of rural children celebrating Christmas. Most postcards and folded greeting cards also cost five cents.

So did life's little luxuries for men. Full plugs of chewing tobacco (like R. J. Reynolds' rural favorite, Brown Mule) came creased in nickel squares. (Recall, however, U.S. Vice President Thomas R. Marshall's famous 1912 campaign lament: "What this country needs is a good five-cent cigar!"). Cigarettes sold best in nickel packs. A shave and a haircut, a small bet on the ponies, and new shirt collar, all cost the same in 1896. A poor worker, as the title ("5 ¢ a Spot") of a famous photograph by Jacob Riis suggests, could spend a night in a flophouse for the same price as a cheap shot of whiskey. Women, too, had their five-cent worlds. In 1876 it cost a southern woman thirty-five cents to smell like Cape Jassamine, White Magnolia, or a Black Forest spring, but in 1912, sharecroppers' wives enjoyed the social advantage for a nickel if they bought, and thousands did, tiny bottles of "Hoyt's Five-Center" perfume. For a 1908 nickel, a city lady could buy a change purse, a Japanese folding fan, or a linen handkerchief. Hat pins, artificial flowers, a spool of thread, and hair combs cost the same.

Nowhere was the nickel empire more evident than in the five-and-ten cent stores of Woolworth and his imitators. (Sears, Roebuck mail-order catalogs regularly ran advertisements, "Look what 5¢ will buy!") Cash-line merchandising proliferated in vending machines that sold nickel candy, playing cards, crackers, cookies, toys, and chewing gum. By 1912, the New York City transit system sported over four thousand machines of all types along its lines. Nickel-in-the slot eateries also fascinated Americans as Horn and Hardart quickly discovered when it installed the country's first automat at 818 Chestnut Street in Philadelphia in 1902. The company's famous move to Manhattan's Times Square (Broadway and 46th Street opened in 1912) took in 8,693 nickels its first day. Office clerks, blue-collar workers, rooming-house residents, and after-theater crowds continuously put the announced number of nickels into slots, twisted a knob to open glass doors displaying their culinary wish, and took out one of Horn and Hardart's specialties: soup, pie, coffee, macaroni and cheese, roast beef. Automat food meant convenience, cleanliness, and cheapness—mechanized, in motion, all for a change purse of nickels.

Everyday reading habits changed with the introduction of the nickel. Dime novels sold for half the price by 1896. Multisection Sunday newspapers remained pegged at a nickel until after World War I. Some of the new magazines, for example, the *Saturday Evening Post*, sold for five cents in 1897. So did the Salvation Army's *War Cry*. American speech was influenced. "A nickel nurser" was such a tightwad that "he would try and rub the buffalo off a nickel." The Americanisms, "Not worth a plugged nickel" and "Don't take any wooden nickels" date from 1908 and 1915. Perhaps the surest indicator of the nickel's ubiquity as the country's common coin was John D. Rockefeller's self-conscious attempt to demonstrate both his wealth and his generosity. The world's first billionaire customarily gave out dimes (over one hundred thousand) to little children when he took his Sunday walks in Cleveland.

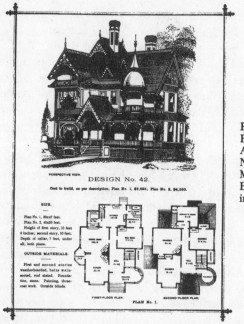

FIGURE 3.1. George F. Barber and Company, Architects, "Design Number 42, Eclectic Manse" (1892). From a Barber company housing trade catalog.

FIGURE 3.2. Sears, Roebuck and Company, "Modern Home Number 151, Progressive Bungalow" from the mail order home catalog (1914). Courtesy of the Sears, Roebuck Archives, Chicago, Illinois.

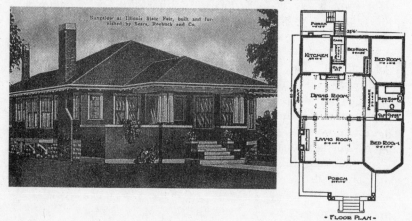

I N THE second half of the nineteenth century, Americans witnessed their country's greatest building boom to date. From Queen Anne mansions along avenues of affluence, such as Summit Avenue in St. Paul, to claim shanties in the Oklahoma Territory, from triple-decker apartment houses in Boston to bungalow courts in Fresno, a range of new architectural styles, building types, construction methods and materials appeared. Residential buildings accounted for 60 percent of total construction.

Three new house types appeared: the apartment, the sod house, and the bungalow. Several settlement patterns—the streetcar suburb, the ethnic neighborhood, and the Indian reservation—either developed or assumed new forms. Building and loan associations, mail-order financing, and real estate agencies offered new ways of buying and selling houses. Suburban home ownership became a possibility for an increasing number of blue- and white-collar families.

Whether they lived individually in boarding and lodging houses or as families in tenements and apartment houses, a growing number of urban dwellers lived in multiple-unit residences. With the development of commuter railroads and electric streetcars, American towns and cities grew more segregated. The sizes of houses and lots became conscious and visible symbols of social achievement or aspiration. The wealthy positioned themselves along exclusive thoroughfares, such as Euclid Avenue in Cleveland, or departed for elite suburbs like Shaker Heights outside the city.

Distinct working-class neighborhoods also assumed identifiable configurations.

Finally, the American house, whatever its size or location and no matter what the wealth or work of its inhabitants, underwent internal transformation. Several traditional spaces—the hall, the kitchen, and the parlor—changed several times in the era. The bathroom, of course, was totally novel. The expanse of the porch, lawn, and garden brought new routines to both home maintenance and domestic recreation.

Home Sites

RURAL HOMESTEADS, CITY HOUSES

Farmhouses, with one exception, took no special form or style in the late nineteenth century. Many that were located in long-settled areas had an additive look—the result of several successive stages or generations of expanding and remodeling.

Two folk-house forms of British colonial America, the I-house (figure 3.5) and the cross house, were common until 1900. The I-house, a residential form so named because of its popularity throughout Indiana, Illinois, and Iowa, consisted of a gabled structure, one room deep, two rooms wide, and two stories high. I-houses, also called "two-over-two houses," spread from the mid-Atlantic region to the upland South and as far west as Utah, where Mormon emigrants built what came to be "Nauvoo-houses," named after Nauvoo, Illinois, the town from which the Mormons fled in the 1840s. Cross houses contained six to eight rooms, organized by a cruciform plan. Such houses took to the Victorian fetish of adding porches with a special architectural passion. First a country house, by 1900 the cross plan populated many small American communities, where townspeople recalled its rural origins by calling it "a homestead house" (figure 3.5).

The breakup of southern plantations into semi-independent rental units (33,000 plantations of 1860 were subdivided into 93,000 smaller tracts by 1880) did not mean a drastic change (other than symbolically) in the residences of postbellum blacks. Many freedmen built their own isolated cabins, but some merely hitched a team of mules to their former quarters in the slave compound and dragged them off to the land they intended to rent or crop. Those who built, erected simple homes fashioned in various vernacular forms called dogtrots, tidewaters, saddle backs, or shotguns (figure 3.5). Constructed of pine and devoid of detail, these ubiquitous Southern rural farmhouses contained two to three rooms with lean-to kitchens out back and lean-on porches in front.

Shotgun or straight-through houses served as typical tenant farmers' homes along the Mississippi River and as company housing in the oil-boom towns of Texas and Oklahoma. Containing three or four single-story rooms aligned on a single axis, the shotgun also suited narrow urban lots. The building's origin, however, was rural West Africa, where it was called a *caille*. Black carpenters introduced it in New Orleans from where it migrated northward as far as Louisville and westward as far as Colorado. Since all rooms were arranged one behind another, usually with parallel interior doorways, one could supposedly fire a shotgun through the house without hitting any walls.[1]

Homesteading the vast open prairies, from southern Minnesota to Texas, produced a novel American farmhouse, a dwelling made of earth sods (figure 3.3). By 1890, over a million "soddies" dotted the region, with the largest concentration in Kansas and Nebraska. Most contained one room, one small window, one wooden door, and a dirt floor. Prairie sod (known as "Nebraska marble") made up the walls and roof. Although sometimes compared to the earth dwellings of American Indians—the Navajo hogans, the earth lodges of the Mandan, the adobes of the Pueblo—the origins of the soddie are European. Russian, German, and East European settlers who came directly to the High Plains knew Old World sod-building techniques; other migrants moving from the eastern states imitated their examples.

Before building a freestanding soddie, newcomers often resided temporarily in a dugout—a simple, square cave dug into the side of a ravine or south-facing hill. Dugouts invariably leaked during rains. In attempts to waterproof, disinfect, and beautify them, housewives whitewashed the interiors. They also suspended sheets from the ceiling, partitioning space into "rooms." They cooked outdoors whenever possible, putting a stove pipe through the earth roof in winter. Cave-ins often occurred; travelers unknowingly drove over dugout roofs at night, and stray livestock occasionally plummeted through them. Despite their discomforts, homesteaders built dugouts because they were quick and cheap. In 1872, the Elder Oscar Babcock, a Seventh-Day Adventist minister in North Loup, Nebraska, itemized the cost of his fourteen-foot-square dugout as follows:[2]

One window	1.25
18 ft. of lumber for front door	.54
Latch and hanging (no lock)	.50
Length of pipe to go through roof	.30
3 lbs of nails to make door, etc.	.19½
	2.78½

Once a family constructed a full sod house, the dugout was converted to a stable, pig pen, root cellar, or a storage shed. Homesteaders constructed soddies with available farming tools. A plow could cut a continuous row of sod four inches deep. A spade reduced the furrow strip to "sod bricks" about three feet long. Door and window frames were set in the wall, and the sod was packed around them. A frame, tin, or sod roof completed the building. The whole thing, as one pioneer said, was "made without mortar, square, plumb, or greenbacks."

A soddie in the Dakota Territory seemed to be a world away from a typical "city cottage" on Chicago's West Side (figure 3.4). To be sure, urban and rural housing had many differences: the density of neighborhoods, the building materials used, and the availability of utilities. Both, however, expanded home ownership for workers. Although the construction of tenements and apartments increased in American cities, at no time did multiresidentiality become the residential norm for the majority of middle-class or working-class people. The dominant goal, for both groups, remained the single-family detached home. Between 1890 and 1930, single-family residences accounted for anywhere from 56 percent to 80 percent of the nation's annual urban housing starts. It was a rare city in which dwellings sheltering three or more families (the legal definition of a tenement) made up over 20 percent of the total housing stock.[3] In seventeen of the twenty-eight largest American cities in 1890, the figure was under 5 percent. Lawrence Veiller, the era's foremost housing reformer, wrote in 1910 that "the normal method of housing the working population in our cities is in small houses, each house occupied by a separate family, often with a small bit of land, with privacy for all, and with a secure sense of individuality and opportunity for real domestic life."[4]

The term *laborer's cottage* served as a universal description of all types of unpretentious frame (sometimes brick) houses built between 1870 and 1910 with modest touches of the Italianate, Eastlake, or Queen Anne styles. Chicago's *Real Estate and Building Journal* listed a one-story, frame cottage with a parlor, kitchen, and two bedrooms for $600 in 1886–87. For slightly more than double this price, a worker might buy a two-story cottage, including an indoor bath, fireplace, and three bedrooms. A Queen Anne–style dwelling of seven rooms (including a sitting room, a parlor, and a tub bath) complete with a tower, cost $1,900.

Workers' cottages also appeared for sale in architectural pattern books, volumes of house plans, and mail-order catalogs. Pattern books offered advice on style and aesthetics at five dollars or more. House-plan books, on the other hand, sold for fifty cents or a dollar. George Palliser, an architect operating out of Bridgeport, Connecticut, built an enormous practice selling books of house plans, such as his *American Cottage Homes* (1878), which included "50 designs of Modern Low Priced Cottages and Workingmen's Homes." Robert W. Shoppell of New York, who published *Artistic Modern Homes of Low Cost* in 1881, expanded the house-plan trade, quickly establishing it as a major mail-order industry.[5] Shoppell clearly advertised the cost of plans and the total price for building the house. He expanded his business by offering home financing and by providing wholesale prices for developers of subdivisions.

Many companies offered to supply "original" designs if the published plans failed the needs of a prospective owner. Frank Lloyd

Wright recalled the standard practice of providing such "custom" house plans during his early days in a Chicago firm: "All [the architect] had to do was call: 'Boy, take down No. 37, and put a bay window on it for the lady.'"

Providing house plans encouraged some entrepreneurs to sell entire houses by catalog. George F. Barber, a provisioner of house plans in Knoxville, Tennessee issued a catalog in 1888 with illustrated plans of complete dwellings that could be built for five hundred to ten thousand dollars (figure 3.1). It remained for giant corporations, like Sears, Roebuck and Montgomery Ward, and large firms, such as the Radford Company in Chicago and Aladin Homes in Bay City, Michigan, to make a major impact on the American housing market.

Early in this century, over a hundred thousand families turned to Sears, Roebuck to purchase their homes. They made their choices from house catalogs (44 pages when first issued in 1908, peaking at 146 pages in 1918) that contained customers' testimonials ("All I did was order and wait for the boxcars to arrive"), photographs of erected houses and owners' names (to inspire customers' confidence), plus illustrations of the interiors (figure 3.8). Designs ranged from two-room cottages to twelve-room residences in various architectural styles. While the designs of cheaper houses carried only order numbers, the designs of more fashionable residences, in imitation of the aristocratic practice of naming the family manse, were called The Windmere, The Magnolia, or The Chateau.

After ordering, a buyer received packets of information by mail and shipments of materials by rail. Construction manuals came first, followed by blueprints and a certificate of guarantee. Numbers on the blueprints corresponded to numbers on the precut lumber and millwork. All the builder needed to do was match the pieces—averaging about thirty thousand not including nails or screws. In an era that was fascinated with speed but whose local carpenters had few power tools, the construction of mail-order houses was trumpeted as the "Instant Home." Sears, for example, estimated that its small prefabricated houses could be built in 352 carpenter hours, compared to 583 hours for a conventional one.[6] Cottages could be constructed in an eight-hour day. The mail-order house, like the sod house, meant that every man could be his own home builder.

The bungalow (figure 3.2), a house type new to the era, dominated the nation's mail-order market by 1915. Whether in Dalton, Georgia, where the "Farrar-Made" Home catalog offered the California Bungalow in eleven different house kits (one called "The Sacramento"), or in Waukesha, Wisconsin, where the R. L. Kenyon Company advertised its "Take Down House," a portable bungalow that could be assembled and disassembled at vacation retreats, the nation indulged in a bungalow craze that would last through the 1920s. Just as *cottage* is an appropriate label for so many of the late nineteenth century's vernacular houses, so too, the term *bungalow* adequately characterizes much of the American popular housing constructed during the first quarter of the twentieth century.

Promoted by its own trade journal (the monthly *Bungalow Magazine*), adopted by small contractors and subdivision developers, supported by home economists and feminists, and even sanctioned by architects (Greene and Greene of California established its reputations with it), the bungalow appealed to both middle-class and working-class home owners. Usually only one story or a story-and-a-half in height, the bungalow had a number of features, the most conspicuous of which was its wide, low-pitched roof extended to form a spacious porch. Construction materials varied according to the region: stucco and redwood on the Pacific coast, adobe in the Southwest, red brick in Midwest cities, board-and-batten in the South, and cobblestone and clapboard in the Northeast. A typical bungalow had an informal, multipurpose floor plan, with a combination living-dining area replacing the earlier parlor and hall.

While there are conflicting claims about the bungalow's first appearance, no one debates that Californians eagerly embraced and popularized it, so that the term *California bungalow* became interchangeable with the general style. In Los Angeles county, for example, the population tripled in size between 1904 and 1913, and approximately five hundred new subdivisions were opened with bungalows as the main housing stock.

The bungalow's diffusion west to east (an important reversal of the traditional transfer of cultural innovations in America) took place rapidly and widely. What began in southern California as a local response to a massive housing shortage accelerated elsewhere as a fashionable trend. For example, Boise, Idaho, built its first bungalow in 1904. Seven years later, the local newspaper observed that "bungalows far outnumber any other sort of home being erected. Citizens now refer to themselves as residents of "a bungalow city." Much the same could be said of large parts of Salt Lake City or Denver.[7] Chicago built brick bungalows. Westwood, a Chicago subdivision claiming to be "The World's Largest Bungalow Development," housed over a thousand families.

Why were so many Americans so taken with the bungalow? Promoters offered various answers: its southern California connotation of youthful, informal, healthy living; the flexibility of its design and easy maintenance; and its adaptability to various styles—it could be made to look Colonial, Moorish, Mission, English, Swiss, or even Oriental. The small-house design also had particular appeal to newlyweds. Its simpler construction and plainer decoration meant that a bungalow was easier to furnish. Many newly married couples of 1915 thought of the domestic residence differently from the way their parents saw it. Whereas the family manse built in the 1880s was viewed as a place in which to "settle down" for life, the younger generation often thought of a bungalow as only a first home in their quest for social and economic mobility. Many bought bungalows because they were inexpensive. Sears's prices began at $475, with many choices up to $1,500. The *Ladies' Home Journal* published a series of monthly articles in 1908, showing a variety of bungalow models priced at $1,000, $2,000, and $3,000 "for the bride who does her own work."

STREETCAR SUBURBS, PLANNED COMMUNITIES

Most urban dwellers walked to and from their homes, shops, and workplaces in American cities before the 1830s. New patterns served by new transport technologies, however, altered this compact urban environment of the pedestrian and changed American residential history forever.

While certain wealthy residents of New York City became suburbanites by working in Manhattan and commuting, by ferry, to Brooklyn Heights or Staten Island, the steam railroad extended suburbanization to cities that lacked water transport. A wealthy elite moved to places like Llewellyn Park, New Jersey (1853) or Lake Forest, Illinois (1861). Railroad suburbs developed outside every large American city by the 1880s. But the high cost of both outlying housing and train fares (together with extra commuting time) meant that only the affluent lived in these areas.[8]

The Eclectic Manse, a characteristic residence of the railroad suburb, symbolized its era. The massive, asymmetrical collage of a house (figure 3.1) exuded breadth, depth, and expanse. A large edifice with a substantial lot (more achievable in the suburbs), the manse, given its manorial origins, implied affluence and achievement through its elaborate, monumental facade. This residential ideal championed an idea of "artistic" beauty and individualistic design, hence the extravagant interest in all forms of ornamentation. The values of the middle-class Americans who populated the post–Civil War suburbs might be the same, but their residential exteriors and interiors were not. Finally, those who built Eclectic Manses saw their houses as symbolic statements of the owners' outlook and priorities. A following generation viewed the American home quite differently. Rather than a monument to personal success or an icon of a family dynasty, they saw the home more as a place of recreation and relaxation.

A small cluster of workers, unlike their affluent neighbors, lived *and* worked in the suburbs. These service people, employed as maids, governesses, laundresses, or gardeners, usually inhabited rental flats above stores or simple dwellings that surrounded the suburban railroad stations. In Brookline, Massachusetts, for example, the Irish servant population lived in small, inexpensive houses near the town center and station. Thus, the physical configuration of the railroad suburb tended to duplicate the developing class-segregated spatial patterns of cities—the poorest inhabitants living closest to the central business district, more wealthy inhabitants residing in commodious homes on the perimeter.

Streetcars, which played the largest role in creating workers' suburbs, did so in two typical ways. Car lines might be laid out to existing hamlets like Idlewild in Memphis or Weequahic in Newark, anticipating the transformation of such areas into suburbs, or car tracks might run through undeveloped land (often owned by railway executives) to create new residential communities like Cleveland Park, District of Columbia, Blue Island, Illinois, or Shadyside, Pennsylvania.[9]

Typical streetcar suburbs were nestled in the interstices between railroad suburbs and the city neighborhoods. They included modest single-family cottages and bungalows and, sometimes close along the trolley tracks, larger duplexes and quadplexes. Houses built directly along the streetcar lines often evolved into shops with apartments above them. A unique multifamily structure, the "triple-decker," developed in New England suburbs. Most triple-deckers were long, rectangular buildings with their narrow side toward the street, housing one family on each of their three floors. Often adorned with simple cottage detailing (although they had outgrown the cottage's scale), "deckers" featured front and back porches on each story. Triple-deckers, though rarely elegant and usually clad in clapboard or shingles, provided adequate space for a single family within a multifamily context.

Southern California suburbs developed the bungalow court—a residential environment, part minisuburb and part horizontal apartment house. The court consisted of ten to thirty bungalows geometrically arranged, often around a garden. Courts sometimes included a community recreational center, where residents, often bachelors and working women, could entertain. Two other residential types—the foursquare and the homestead house (figure 3.5)—appeared in American suburbs and small towns. Two stories high, the foursquare was set on a raised basement with the first floor approached by steps and a porch usually running the full width of its first story. With its pyramidal roof and an interior plan of four nearly equal-size rooms, it was also known as the American box, or the Midwest cube. Homestead houses were popular because their basic shape (a rectangle), like that of the foursquare (a cube), lent itself to unlimited (and economical) modifications, additions, and stylings. All of these houses types were examples of what architectural historian Alan Gowans called "The Comfortable House," a residence that was a reaction to and a replacement for the Eclectic Manse.[10]

Workers sometimes established their own residential enclaves, such as Mount Vernon, New York, developed by the Mechanics Mutual Protection Society in 1851. To avoid the "ruinous rents" and the "rapacity of landlords" in New York City, these artisans formed the Industrial Home Association No. 1, purchased 369 acres from Mount Vernon farmers, subdivided the land into a grid, and began building their own houses.[11] More common were company towns created by large industries, which built houses for workers to rent or purchase, such as Homestead, Vandergrift, and George Westinghouse's Wilmerding, all near Pittsburgh. To work its Berry Coal Mine, Standard Oil of Indiana placed a $1 million mail order with Sears for the immediate purchase of 152 frame dwellings in the "Standard Addition" of Carlinville, Illinois (Sears's subsequent catalogs included "The Carlin" as a model house for workers). Most company communities—Kohler, Wisconsin, Gary, Indiana, and Pullman, Illinois—were built using some form of prefabricated housing.

Pullman's architect, S. S. Beman, designed the industrial suburb's row-house residences with mass-produced millwork and bricks made on site. No dwelling was more than two rooms deep in order to ensure cross-ventilation and sunlight. The top floors featured skylights. Each home came equipped with an indoor water supply, gas fixtures for light and cooking, and an indoor water closet. Rents for such amenities, however, often amounted to almost half a skilled worker's monthly salary.

George Pullman owned everything in his town: He rented its church, library, shopping arcade, market, and other public facilities. He permitted no saloons and sanctioned his town manager's visits to workers' homes to enforce his forty-two-page manual of tenants' regulations. Residents resented this surveillance, as well as the company's refusal to sell the residences to those who wished to become home owners. Other tenant-landlord tensions continued to mount until the depression of 1894, when the Pullman company cut wages but not rents. These tensions, as well as other issues, sparked the Pullman Strike that year, which was one of the most bitter confrontations in American labor history.

Indian reservations (figure 1.2) constituted another "model" (and paternal) environment that was vigorously promoted by Victorian Americans. Although the United States used the reservation system as early as 1786, the postbellum period witnessed a wholesale attempt to impose the concept among tribes within the nation's borders. The Bureau of Indian Affairs created what were, in effect, government company towns throughout the American West. Power and influence centered on the government agent's house, where, for example, weekly government food rations, clothing, and farm equipment were issued and annuity payments were made. The federal schoolhouse (all instruction in English) ranked as the major instrument of acculturation; here children were taught to feel shame and contempt for their "blanket-Indian" parents and their tribal customs, kinship system, shamanistic religion, and communal (versus private) concept of land property. Clustered around the public school might be a church-related or mission school, particularly if the agency had been established in the Grant administration. On larger reservations there would also be a government physician's house, a constabulary headquarters for the Indian police (such deputies could have only one wife and had to wear white men's clothes, short hair, and unpainted faces), and general stores of the various government-licensed traders. Depending upon the tribe and the reservation, the Indians might live in traditional house types such as lodges or pueblos, or be pressed into government-built houses, gender-segregated dormitories, boarding schools, or multifamily shelters.

Even after the Dawes Severalty Act (1887) seemingly gave reservation Indians a chance at individual home ownership (by demanding that they adopt "the habits of civilized life" for which they would be allotted 160 acres of land to be held in trust by the federal government for twenty-five years), Indians continued to live in two residential worlds. While no longer clustered around the agency, they were still instructed by civil servants (white men working as agency superintendents; white women employed as field matrons) as to their hygienic practices, financial affairs, and even the furnishing and maintenance of their households.[12]

Home Builders and Financiers

CONSTRUCTION CONTRACTORS, SUBDIVISION DEVELOPERS

Balloon framing, a nineteenth-century construction innovation, contributed to the rise of the housing contractor and developer. Developed in the 1830s, the technique transformed American house-framing technology, replacing the traditional folk method of cumbersome girts and posts. In balloon framing, mass-produced nails joined standardized studs, joists, and rafters. Naysayers gave the method its derisive name because it seemed so ridiculously light that it would surely blow away. However, George E. Woodward, author of a popular plan book, *Woodward's Country Homes*, calculated in 1865 that the new frame cost 40 percent less than did the mortise and tenon one. The labor and materials that were saved through balloon framing contributed enormously to the boom in urban and suburban housing following the Civil War.

Contracting represented a new system of residential construction by the early 1870s. A contractor, usually a carpenter by trade, estimated a job and submitted a bid to an individual desiring a private home or to an investor underwriting a number of houses. If his competitive bid succeeded, he then set in motion a half-dozen or so subcontractors: masons, plasters, bricklayers, and painters.

Contractors usually handled the balloon framing and sometimes the excavating. The installation of hot-water and hot-air heating systems (beginning in the 1880s), and electric lighting (by 1900) required new expertise. House building became, by 1915, a process in which clients, investors, contractors, subcontractors, building and loan associations, unions, public health inspectors, and zoning enforcers participated. A contractor-builder did have help. He could consult published pattern and plan books. He reduced labor costs and expedited work by buying prefabricated house parts.

The daily routine of carpenter-contractors changed how wood was worked. First by steam and then by electric machinery, timber could be transformed rapidly into rough framing pieces or intricate embellishments. This mechanized woodworking increasingly occurred at the lumber mill, rather than at the construction site, shifting the house-building process from primarily one of the craftsmanship of artisans to that of the parts-assembly of laborers.[13] A writer in the 1887 *American Builder* regretted that the ancient folk adage "A workman is known by his chips" no longer applied. Instead, he reported: "We don't have any shavings in the houses now; they are all made at the mill."

Most nineteenth-century house contractors erected three or four houses or perhaps even a block of residences as their capital and inventories permitted. However, entrepreneurs, such as S. E. Gross in Chicago, Aaron Kaplan in Brooklyn, and Fernando Nelson in San Francisco, planned whole subdivisions, building and selling thousands of new homes a year. In an age that savored statistics, Gross listed his on the back of his advertisements (figure 3.6) that by 1892 claimed he had sold over 40,000 lots, built and sold over 7,000 houses, and launched over 16 towns and 150 subdivisions. He produced both simple $800 four-room workers' cottages and $5,000 nine-room dwellings for middle-class buyers. Advertisements for Gross's subdivision properties emphasized individualized houses, but most originated with his "builder's basic model," a design he manipulated to appeal to all buyers and budgets. His "easy payment" plan, with its remarkably liberal financing (as little as $100 down and $10 a month) made him a fortune and earned him the mayoralty nomination from Chicago's Workingman's party in 1889. His later years, however, illustrate the vicissitudes of the real estate market. The recession of 1907 wiped out his multimillion-dollar housing empire and left him bankrupt.[14]

Although new rental residences (such as the apartment) appeared in Victorian America, owning a detached, single-family home remained the national dream. In practically all American urban areas, the rates of home ownership increased, sometimes doubling, as in Baltimore, Omaha, Cincinnati, and Philadelphia. The 1890 census, first to count who owned a home, revealed this trend was not just a WASP, middle-class, or suburban phenomenon. Except for blacks, Hispanics, and Asians (who encountered housing discrimination unknown by other minorities), most ethnic groups actively aspired to owning their own residences. In 1870 it is estimated that approximately one in five Americans families lived in a place of their own; by 1920 that figure rose to one in four.[15]

Cheap land, inexpensive construction methods, favorable taxing policies, and the expansion of public utilities partially explain the thrust for home ownership. The sacrifices that working-class people were willing to endure to pay for a home, however, was probably the key factor. In Detroit and Pittsburgh, for instance, immigrants managed to purchase homes at rates equal to or above those of native-born Americans. Poles in Milwaukee's Fourteenth Ward rented first floors or basements to tenants and did without leisure and material comforts to buy modest bungalows. In Buffalo, Italians sent mothers (and sometimes children) to work, took in boarders, converted homes into workshops, and sacrificed a proper diet to save and buy houses.[16]

Some Americans obtained a home loan from a relative, an immediate family member, or a good (and prospering) friend who was leery of the stock and bond markets but willing to venture some money in neighborhood capitalism. Most families counted on renewing their mortgages three or four times before paying off the principal. Land companies also financed home buying. Free horse-car or trolley rides out to a promised construction site, a free lunch, refreshments, and entertainment often prefaced auction sales of land. Under the banners, GET A SLICE OF THE EARTH and OWN YOUR OWN DREAM HOME, lots were sold and terms arranged. The Blue Island Land and Building Company, south of Chicago, offered lots and houses in 1873 at 10 percent down; 20 percent in thirty days; and the balance in one, two, and three years with 7 percent interest per year. If you built on the lot within four months, the interest charge was waived.[17] Ground rents in Philadelphia and land contracts in Michigan assisted the purchase of homes by permitting buyers to lease a home lot for a nominal sum over a fairly long period. In the Midwest, Sears, Roebuck financed its mail-order houses as early as 1911, granting mortgages without meeting the borrowers or inspecting their collateral property. Loans typically ran for five years at 6 percent interest, payable in regular monthly installments. Before 1916, national legislation prevented most commercial banks from providing long-term, amortized mortgages; therefore, most banks that granted loans demanded a sizable (40 to 50 percent) down payment and required that the loans be paid back only in one lump sum, often at the end of three years.

BUILDING AND LOAN ASSOCIATIONS

Building and loan associations (B & Ls), first begun in Frankford, Pennsylvania, in 1831, financed many new houses built in Victorian America. These organizations offered average-income families the opportunity, as members of a corporation, to borrow mortgage money at a minimum interest rate (usually lower than a commercial bank). Individuals made monthly payments to buy shares in the association and, after proper scrutiny of their house plans and lot sites by the association's directors, had their funds, in turn, lent out as mortgages on houses costing between $2,000 and $7,000 dollars. Investors were paid 10 to 12 percent on their savings. Many associations supplied building plans to prospective buyers. While they tended to prefer suburban sites, the B & Ls also financed mortgages for urban row houses and bungalows.

In the twenty years after the Civil War, the B & L association became a national institution, spreading from large eastern cities to small western towns where credit was always in demand. When the Department of Labor conducted a survey in 1893, it found that only 9 of the 5,838 B & L organizations then in operation had existed before 1863. In 1901 new B & L mortgages were granted for 50,000 homes; in 1910, for 87,000; and in 1915, for 114,000.[18]

People with irregular earnings (day laborers), part-time employees (waiters), or agricultural families with seasonal incomes usually did not use the B & Ls. The primary clientele of the B & Ls were skilled workers with steady employment who met other bills (utilities, phone service, insurance) that people now paid monthly. Even with the advantages of the support of a B & L, the purchase of a house could strap a worker's family resources. Historian Clifford Clark cited an example of a coachman in Roxbury, Massachusetts, in 1879, who was earning $35 a month and began saving his money for a house. "Six years later, he put $200 down on an eleven-room house that cost $1,900. Monthly payments, at first $23.80, were afterward reduced to $18.80. Still, they ate up half of his monthly income. The same was true of a tailor in St. Paul, Minnesota. He joined a savings and loan association in 1876 and invested $10 a month until 1883 when he bought two lots for $700. Two years later he put up a two-story, eight-room house for $1,860. His monthly payments of $26 continued for eight years."[19]

Home ownership had a special utility for nineteenth-century workers whose wages declined as they aged. Since few pensions existed, old age could be a terrible experience (see Chapter 8), survived only by private charity or in the public poorhouse. If the mortgage was paid, however, a man and a woman at least would have a place to live rent free.

Paying the last mortgage assessment often prompted a celebration, sometimes burning the mortgage papers or hosting a block party. Foreclosures on lapsed mortgages were equally common. Between 1890 and 1894, more than eleven thousand foreclosures took place in Kansas alone. "It has been said," wrote Carl Vrooman in *U.S. Department of Agriculture Yearbook* (1916), "and I think with good reason—that more midland farmers' wives died of mortgage during those trying years than of tuberculosis and cancer together, and that more farmers' wives were sent to the madhouse by mortgage than by all other causes."

Housing with Others

BOARDING AND LODGING HOUSES

Boarding—paying money to live and eat with someone else—had become widespread in America by the 1830s. Economic pressures in these years were such that many workers' houses, originally designed for one-family occupancy, were subdivided and shared with boarders. The phenomenon extended to other classes. Newly married middle-class couples often chose, for a few years, to forsake establishing their own households. The Tremont House in Boston and the Franklin House in New York were early "fashionable" boardinghouses. The period saw the development of the Lowell boardinghouses, erected for young women who worked in the Massachusetts textile factories. Fannie Farmer, author of *The Boston Cooking School Cookbook* (1896) and the "mother of level measurement," received her culinary apprenticeship in her mother's well-known boarding establishment. Thomas Edison's research and development staff ("The Menlo Park Gang") lived at Sarah Jordan's Boarding House in New Jersey.

For the middle class, boarders contributed income and often filled excess rooms in spacious Eclectic Manses—bedrooms or whole floors not yet needed or now vacated by grown children. Widowers or widows might take in boarders or become boarders themselves. Boardinghouses run by the middle class for that class usually had pretensions to gentility. Most required references or letters of introduction. Many stipulated the bounds of the boarder's space (usually one's room, the parlors, and the dining room); some prohibited the use of alcohol, and a few had evening curfews. Although entire families did board (young married couples or widows with children), the more typical boarders were young single men and women who were just beginning their careers. Some boardinghouses developed a local reputation as homes for newspaper, legal, or theatrical people, while others were known because of the proprietress's conversation or cuisine. Outstanding food encouraged a "boardinghouse reach."

To supplement their income—particularly to have a regular sum for monthly rent or mortgage payments—many workers' families rented rooms and provided meals. In 1890, 44,000 families reported that they shared their quarters with one or more boarders; by 1900 the figure had almost doubled; and by 1910, it had reached 164,000 when as many as one-third to one-half of all urban Americans were either boarders at some time (usually in their early adulthood) or lived in a home where boarders also resided.[20] Women usually took charge of the boarders. While taking in boarders added to a woman's housework (more people eating more food, dirtying more dishes, soiling more bed linen), having boarders offered women employment, particularly those who did not wish to work outside the home or were denied such job opportunities because of gender prejudice, or who, of necessity, needed to stay at home with their children.

In middle-class boardinghouses, a single, multicourse meal was served, family style, at an appointed evening hour. Providing meals for laborers, many of whom worked a swing shift (a twelve-hour day and a twelve-hour night) in mines and mills was more complicated. Women who kept boarders with separate meal accounts often cooked separately for each person in the house; sometimes, as Margaret Byington reported in her study *Homestead,* "they fried different kinds of meat in one pan, each with a tag of some sort labeling the order." These women, in other words, ran home restaurants.

Boarder and landlady became archetypes for vaudeville humor. Popular songs recalled boardinghouse characters and courtships. Immigrant novels featured the boarder as a fact of life. For instance, in Anzia Yezierska's 1900 novel *The Bread Givers,* a Russian Jewish family debates whether the father can continue to use a bedroom for studying the Torah or whether, in economic desperation, the family must rent it to a boarder.

Social reformers decried "the lodger evil," a type of residence where single men or women could rent a room for the night, week, or month, but could not obtain meals. Called different names in various cities—"furnished-room houses" (Philadelphia), "rooming houses" (Chicago), and "lodging houses" (San Francisco)—the typical lodging house rented a room for from one dollar to seven dollars a week (or its multiple by the month).[21] As described in Albert B. Wolfe's *The Lodging House Problem in Boston* (1906), the average rooming-house structure was about twenty-five to forty years old, first built as a downtown residence for an upper-class family who had subsequently moved away. Women usually kept these lodging houses, often maintaining several simultaneously, while living in the basement of one. Originally single-family dwellings, many rooming houses had only one toilet facility to serve the needs of their dozen or so residents. Often hot water was available only on certain days, forcing tenants to use the public baths.

Things were worse, however, for those who lodged in the "cages" or "cribs" of flophouses (figure 7.2). Renting from 40 cents for a single night room in a converted commercial loft building, to a 25-cent cubicle in a five-by-seven-foot cage in a warehouse, to a 10-cent or 5-cent flop space where one slept wherever one found room, was the lot of more than 10 percent of Boston's population in 1906. In the rented crib or cage, there was just enough space (with a bed and perhaps a chair) to allow the occupant to pull off his or her clothes. Only slightly better was the typical lodging house in a Chicago working-class neighborhood described by Edith Abbott: "The beds were not clean, and very often were occupied by relays of men, the day shift and the night shift. The bedding scarcely becoming cold after one occupant had left it."[22]

Many flophouses operated primarily during the winter. They had no permanent installations and often no heat. Some furnished old mattresses, rags, or blankets as bedding; others had long rows of canvas hammocks or slings; most simply offered patrons (men and women) a dry place on the floor where they could sleep on newspapers or on the bedrolls they carried. Many flophouses were as temporary and transient as the clientele they housed. Nonetheless, they could be profitable to their owners. Housing reformer Jacob Riis knew a wealthy New Yorker who operated three such lodging places and made $8,000 a year clear profit.[23]

For urban young men and women who did not live with a family and wanted to avoid boarding or lodging, philanthropists, social reformers, and religious groups built various institutional residences. While the residential wings of the YMCA and the YWCA became the most famous, each major city devised its own version of the home-away-from-home for such single people. By 1915, there were fifty-four nonprofit hotels, clubs, and apartments for women in New York and twenty-four in Chicago. In Manhattan there was a Junior League Hotel for Women and the Tuskegee and Hampton Hotels for black women. Jane Addams organized Chicago's Jane Clubs, whose members rented houses, elected a resident steward, and paid three dollars weekly board. The boarders did the lighter housework, but hired servants cooked the meals.

TENEMENTS: SPECULATIVE AND MODEL

Warehouses, factories, breweries, and residences were adapted as multifamily dwellings in post–Civil War America. New tenements were erected on sites where previous buildings had been razed or where earlier frame structures had been moved to the rear of the lot as alley houses. Defining these nineteenth-century multiple-household structures is as complicated now as it was then. *Tene-*

ments and *apartments,* terms often used synonymously, referred
to dwellings designed to accommodate three or more separate sets
of tenants, living independently of one another, under a single
roof and doing their cooking on the premises; both connoted, in
the eyes of their critics, dense urban living, although tenements
and apartments also appeared in suburbs and small towns. One
frequent, but not constant, difference between an apartment and
a tenement was that the former usually had (after the 1890s)
private sanitary facilities, while the latter often had only communal plumbing.

Tenements came in many shapes and sizes. Real estate speculators created one type by buying up large family homes (vacated
by upwardly mobile families) in central city neighborhoods in the
hopes that the houses could be torn down eventually to make
room for commercial development or for manufacturing or warehousing purposes. Edith Abbott, a lifelong housing investigator,
who wrote *The Tenements of Chicago* (1936), saw these ad-hoc
tenements still expanding in 1910. She noted that on the city's
near southside, such housing units came both furnished and unfur-
nished. "Light Housekeeping Rooms" described a furnished unit.
Such residences, usually one or two rooms, served as cheap efficiency apartments for poor workers who wished to do their own
cooking. Their hallmark by 1915 was the ubiquitous gas plate on
a zinc-covered shelf in a bedroom corner. As with boarding and
lodging houses, widows or single working women usually
managed such units, residing in one of them.

In eastern cities before the Civil War and elsewhere thereafter,
investors built specifically designed "tenant houses," normally
three stories high, with a family on each floor and in the basement.
Some contained only one room per floor, with an enclosed stair-
way leading from one floor to another. In Philadelphia, locals
called them "bandboxes" or "father-son-holy-ghost houses." Many
laborers and newly arrived immigrants and their boarders called
these cramped quarters home. The alley tenement developed in
Washington, D.C., as a two-story box, twelve feet wide by thirty
feet deep. The living room and kitchen constituted the first floor,
with the second devoted to sleeping quarters. Initially homes for
white workers' families before the Civil War, Washington's alley

houses became the residences for blacks who later migrated to the city.[24]

A larger multifamily structure, popularly known as the "railroad tenement," housed four families per floor. This ninety-foot-long rectangular block occupied almost all its narrow lot save a ten-foot rear yard. Of the twelve to sixteen rooms per floor, only those facing the street or alley received direct light and air. There were no indoor toilet facilities or hallways.

In 1879, the *New York Plumber and Sanitary Engineer* sponsored an architectural competition for the design of a model tenement that would be ideal for both a landlord and tenants. The former required at least a 7 percent return on his investment; the latter was to be guaranteed sufficient light, fire protection, ventilation, and sanitation. Of the 190 designs submitted, the winning entry by New York architect James E. Ware, Jr., was quickly labeled the "dumbbell" because its plan had two narrow air shafts within an otherwise solid (one hundred by twenty-five-foot) rectangular (four- to six-story) block. Since most tenements abutted each other, these air shafts proved totally inadequate for providing light and air to the inside rooms. Instead, they became garbage dumps and fire hazards. Most dumbbells contained four housing units per floor: two four-room flats in the front and two three-room flats in the rear. Seven-by-eight-foot bedroom alcoves stood between the kitchen and a parlor bedroom. The public hallway contained communal toilets. Although criticized as unhealthy and inhumane, the dumbbell form proved economically profitable to New York City speculators. After a state tenement law adopted Ware's air-shaft dimensions as an approved minimum standard later that year, the dumbbell became the prevailing model for the city's new tenements until it was outlawed by state legislation in 1901.[25]

To counter such conditions, a number of individual philanthropists and housing reformers sponsored experiments that they hoped would raise the building standards of the average contractor, lower the greed of the typical investor, and improve the living conditions of the renters. With no thought of urging municipal, state, or federal governments to build or subsidize housing, these reformers believed that a merger of capitalism and altruism would benefit the worker-housing market. They erected various model housing projects—for example, Alfred T. White's Home and Tower Buildings (1877–78) in Brooklyn, New York, or Edward Waller's Francisco Terrace (1895), designed by Frank Lloyd Wright in Chicago—to demonstrate how philanthropy could be combined with profit.

Two final comments should be made about tenement housing—model or otherwise. First, the stereotype of a tenement owner as an absentee landlord living in the suburbs but controlling numerous properties throughout the city is false. Tenement owners often came from the same ethnic or racial group who occupied a tenement district. The owner frequently lived in the district or close by. Such individuals, for example, Italians and Jews in late nineteenth-century Philadelphia, used tenement real estate and landlordship as an avenue to upward economic mobility.[26]

Second, neither the model nor the dumbbell tenement typified multiple-family living conditions in most American cities. Although they attracted the attention of social reformers in their time (and of historians since), tenements never constituted more than a fraction of the housing that was built. New York's Lower East Side, the case study most frequently cited because of its extensive slum housing, did, indeed, contain densely crowded tenement districts and vile living conditions. A similar density of tenements, however, appeared in few other cities. Instead, all sorts of multiunit dwellings, made of masonry, brick, or wood and rarely more than three stories high, characterized multifamily housing for the urban working class.[27]

THE APARTMENT HOUSE

America's earliest apartment buildings, the Hotel Pelham built in Boston in 1855 and the Stuyvesant "French" Flats of New York in 1869, appealed to well-to-do families and bachelors. Sometimes called apartment-hotels, they contained a luxury hotel's amenities (public dining rooms, room service, steam laundries, and maids and other servants), and their permanent guests lived in room suites of various sizes.

The apartment-hotel captured the nation's fancy with its mechanization and centralization of domestic tasks. It featured hot-water heating, bathrooms, kitchens (for those who wished them), telephone service, and, by the late 1880s, electric lighting and appliances. Elevators were the technical marvel and mainstay of the apartment-hotel and its less sumptuous progeny, the studio and the efficiency apartment. First hydraulic, later electric elevators transported residents and their guests to and from their quarters, while a separate service elevator ferried servants and deliveries. "We were talking about your apartment, Mrs. Roberts. It's charming," remarks a guest in the W. D. Howells' play, *The Elevator.* "It *is* nice," her hostess replies. "It's the ideal way of living. All on one floor. No stairs. Nothing. All these apartment hotels have them."

The first apartment-hotels sought to look like large, rambling family mansions in order to allay suspicions that they were not proper for middle-class life. By the turn of the century, this restraint was abandoned as grandiose and opulent towers rose to twenty stories and spread over entire city blocks. The Ansonia in New York City and the Ponce de Leon in Los Angeles made no concessions to the appearance of conventional residences. They were examples of the age's fascination with giantism, as well as the apartment's increasing influence in American life.[28]

Middle- and working-class Americans inhabited less exclusive but more extensive apartment houses. These servantless and serviceless living units ranged in size from an entire floor of a building to a single, multipurpose room that included kitchen and sanitation facilities. Family flats or apartments were usually three- or four-room ensembles. Built by real estate firms, insurance companies, and private investors, they spread out along the streetcar corridors of most American cities. In its mail-order catalogs of houses issued after 1911, Sears, Roebuck sold such apartment houses, complete with living room fireplaces.

Between 1900 and 1915, one final type of apartment, the efficiency, became common in West Coast cities. This one-room-and-bath apartment appears to have first developed in the San Francisco Bay area and, like the bungalow, spread eastward. The efficiency featured disappearing or folding beds and portable, collapsible furniture, such as disappearing tables for dining nooks. As one journalist described these hideaway gadgets, "everything is collapsible, sliding, folding, built-in, grooved, or hung on pivots." By 1911, tiny cooking areas called "buffet kitchens" were common enough in San Francisco apartments to be considered in proposed new housing codes. By the end of the decade, these tiny (six-by-eight-foot) spaces were popularly called "kitchenettes." They epitomized a new trend toward simplified cooking and a reliance on packaged foods.

Household Utilities

WATER AND WASTE

By 1915 the middle-class house became increasingly connected to a growing maze of pipes, wires, ducts, cables, conduits, and mains. While the new forms of utilities—heat, light, power, and sewerage—altered home life, the pace and place of the changes were uneven. The wealthy got such services before the poor, city residents before farm families, and, to an extent, easterners before southerners and westerners.

In the 1870s, the task of lugging fresh water into the home and carrying dirty water and liquid refuse out of it marked the daily routines of most American women and children. By 1915 many rural families and city dwellers still had no running water inside their living quarters. Late nineteenth-century rural householders got water by multiple means: buckets filled at water courses, cisterns, and rain barrels; kitchen pitcher pumps located over farmhouse wells or connected to tanks maintained by windmills. Urbanites obtained water from barrels filled by water-hauling tank wagons, from street hydrants in tenement courtyards or water taps in tenement hallways, or through a house plumbing system connected to public water mains.

Municipal waterworks owed their existence more to public health crises than to consumers' demands for water. The widespread yellow fever epidemics of the 1790s forced Philadelphia to pioneer the country's first major public water-supply system. Other cities followed Philadelphia's lead, so that by 1876 most cities with populations of more than ten thousand had some kind of municipal water supply to some of their neighborhoods. By

1915, similar services reached communities of five thousand.[29]

Rural towns constructed hilltop reservoirs to dispatch water, via gravity, through wood, iron, and steel pipes. The water tower, usually the community's tallest public structure and frequently emblazoned with the community's name and population, loomed as one of small-town America's most visible icons. Homer Croy, writing of a Missouri town in *West of the Water Tower* (1923), noted: "The tower was a town character; the city revolved around it almost as much as the court house, or around the square. Picnic parties were held at its base; boys climbed up the little iron ladder, which seemed to reach to infinity, as high as courage lasted and scratched a chalk mark on the red brick; then the next boy tried to raise it."

Municipal concern for a water supply did not necessarily mean responsibility for its disposal. Sewerage collection lagged behind water supply. Before the 1850s, no city had adequate sewers to remove human waste from houses. In the 1880s, however, urban areas began constructing sewerage systems, although most were largely for the collection of storm water. City ordinances usually forbade people to dump wastes in them. Some home owners contracted with scavengers (night-soil men) or farmers to collect wastes from privy vaults; others dumped waste in backyards, the front street, storm sewers, or vacant lots. Adoption of the water closet, first installed in urban dwellings, further exacerbated the problem.[30]

HEAT AND LIGHT

Throughout the nineteenth century, Americans experimented with different ways to heat their homes and cook their meals. Patents for cast-iron parlor stoves and kitchen ranges proliferated beginning in the 1840s. Made in small foundries, such as the Dowagiac Round Oak Stove Company in Michigan, house stoves came in all shapes, styles, and sizes. At the 1915 Panama-Pacific Exposition, one could still see displays of box, cannon, globe, or "pot-bellied" stoves, with all manner of flues, dampers, and grates.

In frontier communities almost anything combustible was burned to keep warm. Homesteaders on the southwest Plains in the 1880s used mesquite, corn cobs, and cow chips. Euphemistically called "surface coal" and "grassoline," dried cow manure provided a cheap, abundant, fairly efficient, if somewhat odorous, fuel. Even after railroads brought coal to this region, settlers continued to maintain a chip shed. Urban dwellers fueled their stoves and later their furnaces mostly with coal. So did American industry. Coal tonnage increased from 15.2 million in 1870 to 127.8 million in 1920, making the mining of both hard and soft coal vital to the national economy.[31]

Despite their many stoves (over seven thousand models patented by 1910), most Americans who lived through winters north of the Ohio or Missouri rivers endured cold from mid-November to mid-April. Families resigned themselves to awakening to chilly mornings after nights spent sleeping in unheated attics and second-floor bed chambers. As Alice LaCasse, a New Hampshire textile worker recalled: "We had a big stove in the kitchen and three grills in the ceiling, so that in the winter a little bit of heat went up to the second floor, but hardly any at all reached the third and fourth floors."[32] To counteract the cold, some heated iron ingots, ceramic "bed bricks," and soapstones to serve as bedwarmers.

Central heating, largely a middle-class comfort enjoyed by some working-class families only after World War I, transformed the American home by both cluttering it and enlarging it. Cast-iron radiators, developed in the 1890s, and brass floor registers complicated interior decoration on the first and, later, the upper stories. The cellar expanded into a basement. Typically an ill-ventilated hole in the ground with stone walls and an earthen floor, the cellar was used only for storing items that were not affected by dampness. Basements, on the other hand, were larger, drier, cleaner spaces, often walled in Portland cement rather than in stone.

The home laundry entered the basement only in a piecemeal fashion. Before the early twentieth century, the Monday chore that Nevada diarist Rachel Haskell called "the Herculean task which women all dread," took place in many places: backyard, wash house, back porch, or kitchen. A piped-in water supply and a water-carried sewerage system, along with new washing machines, gradually centralized the work of soaking, rinsing, soaking, sudsing, scrubbing, scalding, bluing, starching, and drying clothes in the basement.[33]

Artificial lighting drastically altered everyday life in the postbellum American house. Slowly, by means of new fuels (gas and petroleum), power sources (electricity), and a myriad of lighting devices, the daily natural cycle of light and darkness no longer conditioned human activities. Rural families lit their homes with traditional methods, such as tallow candles, floating tapers (in assorted greases), and oil lamps that burned lard, whale, cottonseed, and castor oils, turpentine, or camphor. Kerosene, a petroleum derivative, came into wide use after the discovery of oil in Titusville, Pennsylvania, in 1859. "Kero" reigned as the country's most important oil refinery product, with gasoline viewed as only a petroleum by-product until the advent of the internal combustion engine.

The care and feeding of kerosene lamps meant their daily filling, wiping, and wick trimming; weekly washing of the chimneys and shades; and periodic rewicking. Despite their operational demands, fire hazards, odor, and soot, kerosene lamps (like coal stoves) fostered living in a space defined by a specific light or a heat source. Immigrant memoirs and rural autobiographies of the period often reflect on the family closeness generated by the central stove or a room's center lamp.[34] Central heating and electrical lighting tended to disperse such family circles. Centrifugal privacy replaced centripetal intimacy.

Gaslight offered an alternative to the dirt and demands of kerosene illumination—if the homeowner could afford its installation and if his home was located close to its supply. While manufactured gas (rather than natural gas) lit Rembrandt Peale's Baltimore Museum as early as 1816, its use in homes of the wealthy came in Victorian America, giving the period one of its romantic (but unrepresentative) sobriquets: The Gaslight Era. The mansions of a city's elite (who often capitalized the private or municipal gasworks) sported elaborate multilight chandeliers, ornamented with porcelain and glass shades.

Most Americans, however, initially experienced gaslights in public rather than in private places. Main streets (figure 1.8) and sometimes suburban streets (Cincinnati's Clifton area streets have been gaslit since 1853) first received gas illumination. So, too, did fashionable bars, department stores, and government buildings.

FIGURE 3.3. Solomon D. Butcher, *Peter M. Barnes Dugout and Sod House Near Clear Creek, Custer County, Nebraska* (1887). Photograph courtesy of the Solomon D. Butcher Collection, Nebraska State Historical Society.

FIGURE 3.4. Typical Chicago cottage, 54 West Chicago Avenue, Chicago, Illinois (ca. 1880–85). Photograph courtesy of the Chicago Historical Society.

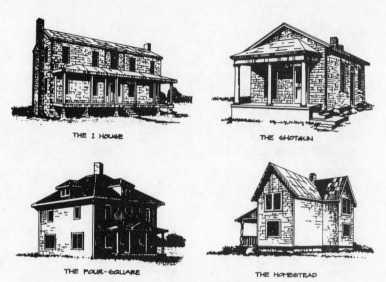

THE I HOUSE   THE SHOTGUN

THE FOUR-SQUARE   THE HOMESTEAD

FIGURE 3.5. Vernacular house types, 1870–1920. Courtesy of Allen Noble, M. Margaret Geib, and Yu Wang.

FIGURE 3.6. S. E. Gross, *Scenes Illustrating S. E. Gross's Enterprises,* from a promotional brochure (1892). Courtesy of the Chicago Historical Society.

FIGURE 3.7.   Solomon D. Butcher, *Interior of Mr. and Mrs. R. A. Acheson and Daughter, Watertown, Nebraska* (1903). Photograph courtesy of the Solomon D. Butcher Collection, Nebraska State Historical Society.

FIGURE 3.8.   Open plan combined living–dining room and furnishings, Sears, Roebuck and Company model bungalow, Illinois State Fair (1912). Photograph courtesy of the Sears, Roebuck Archives.

FIGURE 3.9. Advertisement for Hoosier kitchen cabinets, Hoosier Kitchens, Indianapolis, Indiana, *Saturday Evening Post* (1915).

FIGURE 3.10. Advertisement for Standard guaranteed plumbing fixtures, Standard Manufacturing Company, Pittsburgh, Pennsylvania, from *McClure's Magazine* (May 1914).

Gaslighting could also be found in some schools, hospitals, and factories.

Thomas Edison's development of an incandescent light bulb in 1879 and his marketing of a delivery system (generators, fixtures, lamp sockets, wiring, meters) opened the "energy wars" of the late nineteenth century. In the competition for the residential lighting market, gas lost to electricity. Gas, however, entered the home to fuel machines that did other work of everyday life. By the turn of the twentieth century, gas stoves, ranges, water heaters, and furnaces appeared, frequently sold through the gas companies themselves or manufactured by their subsidiaries. In 1899 roughly 75 percent of the gas being produced nationwide was used for illumination; by 1919, the percentage dropped to 21, while domestic consumption for heating climbed to 54 percent. Two years after Edison opened the world's first central generating station (significantly near New York's Wall Street) in 1882, five hundred New York homes and several thousand businesses used his electric lamps, wire, switches, and sockets. In 1907, 8 percent of the country's residences were wired for electricity, a figure that grew to 34.7 percent by 1920.[35]

New lighting and heating options oriented the home differently to the surrounding community. One bought kerosene or other fuel oils at a store or lumberyard or had it delivered periodically. Gas and electricity, however, involved no contact with a merchant or delivery man. One need not converse with the meter reader (a new occupation in Victorian America), only pay the bill by mail. Lighting devices fueled by the competing energies affected interior decor. Oil lamps and electric lamps (once a house had ample outlets) were portable; gas fixtures were not, a restriction to which furniture had to be adapted.

Electrical light appeared to have other advantages: a more regular light, no soot, and no need to ventilate. Not all home owners were convinced. Many feared its unknown consequences. For example, in the 1880s, one architect claimed that its use for residential lighting caused freckles. Other critics blamed it for fires, explosions, or electrocution. Families who put in electricity usually had their residences first wired only for lights. In a home being converted from gas, the same fixtures and conduits were often recycled. Portable lamps to be plugged into outlets were available as early as the 1880s, but were not in wide use until house wiring became less expensive.[36]

The new utilities altered everyday life in several ways. They changed a home's relationship to its surrounding neighborhood and altered the physical landscape above and below its surface. A household no longer depended upon itself for many of life's common needs. Forces beyond its domestic circle now dictated the quantity and quality, cost and availability of several of its vital life-support systems. To create this new network of telephone lines, water mains, sewers, and power cables required political and economic decisions by governmental and corporate enterprises, both of which assumed greater control over the home residence's shape, structure, and placement via zoning ordinances, fire regulations, and building codes.

The new utilities accustomed Americans to think of "systems" as a metaphor for modern life. Introduced to the idea by the railroad companies (the Pennsylvania System) and their related corporations (the Pullman System), they hooked up to or plugged into the Edison or Bell System.

A final, and perhaps the most important, ramification of the introduction of the new utilities for daily life was their gradual but increasingly widespread homogenization of the domestic environment. Pioneered first in American hotels and skyscraper office buildings, the new systems of heating, cooling, lighting, and waste removal blurred outside-inside differences in nature's temperature and climate; they also eradicated nature's time, replacing the natural rhythms of day and night with mechanical impulses of the electric light and electric clock.

House Spaces

PUBLIC AND FORMAL: HALLS AND PARLORS

The period 1876 to 1915 saw a major shift in housing standards and family ideals (compare figures 3.1 and 3.2). The first standard, the Eclectic Manse, with its ornate decor, numerous rooms, and domestic clutter, came under attack. In its place, architects, builders, and feminists argued for a more modern, progressive, Comfortable House. Reformers who advocated building California bungalows instead of Queen Anne villas similarly pressed for household equipment that would be simple, easy to clean, labor saving, and efficient.

Upon entering a typical Eclectic Manse, a visitor encountered a front hall, usually six to eight feet wide and twelve to twenty feet long, or considerably longer if it ran the length of the house. Its decor indicated the character of both the dwelling and its inhabitants. Decorating books recommended bright colors, a dado and a rail, and hand stenciling or wallpaper. Most front halls before 1900 included a staircase to the second story.

Large homes also had back halls and backstairs. As Kenneth Ames noted, Victorian architects often divided the front hall from the back with a real or symbolic barrier—"a door, lower ceiling, narrower passage, or change in wall or floor coverings"—thus separating the formal from the functional.[37] These two passageways segregated daily traffic: rowdy children and servants to the back and adults and visitors to the front; ordinary chores, such as carrying dirty laundry or slop buckets were confined to the rear, whereas dramatic descents to meet family members and guests demanded the front stairs.

A fully furnished front hall contained a hall stand, hall chairs, and a card receiver. A family's articles of personal costume (hats, coats, parasols, or umbrellas) bedecked their hall stand. Here clutter was class. Hall stands often had seats, where messengers, solicitors, and unexpected visitors rested while awaiting instructions. If the hall stand had no seat, other furniture, such as leather upholstered settees or a single straight side chair, might be provided.

Service people might temporarily occupy a hall chair, but they would never use the card receiver, the third artifact necessary for any properly furnished hall. Like the hall stand, the card receiver is now obsolete; so is the elaborate ritual of calling and card leaving. During its American vogue, 1870 to 1910, card leaving became an avenue for entering society, of designating changes in status or address, of issuing invitations and responding to them, of presenting sentiments of happiness or condolence, and, in general, of carrying on all the communication associated with middle-class social life.

Done almost exclusively by women in the afternoon, calling and card leaving entailed complicated social arithmetic. Since husbands did not normally accompany their wives, the wife left her husband's card where she visited. If the lady of the house was "at home," the visitor left two of her husband's cards on the card receiver, one for the lady of the house and one for the lady's husband. She did not leave her card, since she had seen the lady. If, however, the visitor called but the lady of the house was "not at home," she left three cards on the receiver, one of her own (etiquette books prescribed that a lady should leave only *one* card for a lady) and two of her husband's. The contents of a family's card receiver were sorted and evaluated. Decisions then had to be made as to how to respond—to pay an actual visit or only a surrogate one by way of a card (a call for a call or only a card for a card). Mark Twain, writing in *The Gilded Age,* lampooned the intricacy of these social rituals by commenting: "The annual visits are made and returned with peaceful regularity and bland satisfaction, although it is not necessary that the two ladies shall actually see each other oftener than once every few years. Their cards preserve the intimacy and keep the acquaintanceship intact."

Opposite the hall, behind closed doors and closed shades, lay the showplace of the Eclectic Manse: the parlor (figure 3.7), sometimes called "the first parlor," "the sitting room," "the front parlor," or "the front room." Affluent colonial and early Federal homes in the city or country usually contained parlors. One early New England house plan is commonly referred to as a hall-and-parlor, with the parlor located in the front of the house and often serving as the master bedroom. By the early nineteenth century, householders more commonly segregated sleeping quarters from social ones, using their parlor as a ceremonial and social space.

Etiquette manuals, domestic advisers, and furniture manufacturers nurtured the parlor culture; so did various public spaces. In addition to room displays at world's fairs and department stores, Americans experienced the aesthetic and cultural conventions of "public parlors," such as those found in the lobbies of hotels and businesses, photographer's studios, railroad cars, and steamboats.

Parlors or some type of "best room" transcended social class, economic status, or geographic location. Immigrant workers' wives sought to set aside a room or a part of a room for family culture. Rural farmhouses in Kansas and Georgia contained parlors, as did urban and suburban dwellings in St. Paul, Minnesota, or Rochelle Park, New York. Parlors, while differing in size, location, and furnishings, functioned similarly no matter what their inhabitants' status. They served as a stage for special domestic events (marriages, wakes, clergymen's calls, holy day and holiday celebrations), as the repository of a family's treasured possessions, and as the exhibit space in which the lady of the house demonstrated her (and, by association, her family's) artistic and cultural refinement.[38]

Families displayed their histories (framed photographs, marriage certificates, and the like) and their taste as consumers (lithograph prints, Rodgers's sculpture groups) in parlors that doubled as family museums. Designers created a special furniture form, the étagère, to house the numerous figurines, plants, artwork, heirlooms, and bric-a-brac that were commonly displayed on pedestals and mantels. Decorative artifacts and natural objects (sea shells or dried flowers), placed in the étagère, typified the nineteenth-century family's urge to collect and classify the exotic and the novel.

Women curated these collections, as well as other parlor artifacts and activities. In addition to overseeing (and periodically overhauling) the parlor's decor, the Victorian woman controlled its use, either by other family members (for example, as a courting area for her daughters) or by herself (as a place for gatherings of her ladies' society). In the parlor the Victorian woman had a semblance of a room of her own.[39]

Furnishings in a parlor changed over a family's history. The home interior of an immigrant who had recently arrived in America looked different from that a long-resident neighbor. Newlyweds in a worker's cottage could but anticipate how their rooms might look in the future. In an economy of expanding consumer choice, home furnishings came and went as never before, thus necessitating attics and basements.

When Margaret Byington surveyed the lives of Pittsburgh steelworkers in 1910, she noted that once families got a bit of extra space, they would allocate it not for more bedrooms but for a social room. "The first evidence of the growth of the social instinct in any family," she reported, "is the desire to have a parlor." Many families in *Homestead* attempted "to the inconvenience of other activities, to have the semblance of a room devoted to sociability."[40] Frequently that room was called the "front room," a phrase with a significance quite beyond its suggestion of locality. Furnishings might include a mixture of dowry wedding gifts, family heirlooms, mass-produced chairs, and a table. In the 1880s, factories in Chicago and Grand Rapids, Michigan, turned out ornate lines of inexpensive but "fancy" furniture for a working-class market. Manufacturers encouraged furniture stores in workers' neighborhoods to extend credit, particularly to customers who were willing to purchase furniture by the suite. The front room of a working-class home commonly contained an overstuffed parlor set (a lady's and a gentleman's chair and perhaps side chairs), a draped center table, and wall-to-wall carpeting. The description of a three-room home of Slavic immigrants in Jersey City, New Jersey, by a housing reformer verifies the attention to decorative details common to working-class parlor settings: "The walls are hung with gorgeous prints of many hued saints, their gilt frames often hanging edge to edge so that they form a continuous frieze around the walls. This mantel is covered with lace paper and decorated with bright colored plates and cups, and gorgeous bouquets of homemade paper flowers are massed wherever bureaus or shelves give space for vases."[41]

In addition to furniture, whatnot shelves, and bulky chiffoniers, the immigrant family's front room might also contain a bed, since workers' parlors often doubled as sleeping rooms. Such sleeping facilities might be folding beds stored elsewhere during the day or a stationary wood bedframe, piled high with feather comforters. An observer in Lawrence, Massachusetts, in 1912 described the interior of an Italian mill worker's home as boasting "pleasant vistas of spotless beds rising high to enormous heights and crowned with crochet-edged pillows."

Frontier and farm families also emulated the parlor ideal. In *The Northern Tier* (1880), Evan J. Jenkling, a federal land-office surveyor, described a Kansas setting that could have been found in many parlors across the nation. "In one of those dug-outs which I visited on a certain rainy day, a [parlor] organ stood near the window and the settler's wife was playing 'Home, Sweet Home!' " In addition to upholstered furniture, bird cages, and a tea set, there was also "a neatly polished shelf, supported by pins driven into the wall, containing the holiday gift books, album, and the indispensable household treasure, the family Bible."[42] Although well outfitted, country parlors saw limited use. The farm family lived mostly in its back kitchen. In the 1850s, the progressive agricultural press began a long campaign to transform the seldom-used parlor into a cheery family sitting room. "Anna Hope," a regular contributor to the *American Agriculturist*, recommended in 1857 that farm families "use and enjoy what we have and permit our children to use it," rather than "shut up a part of the house for weddings, parties, and funerals."

In proposing that a farm family's social space be called a "sitting room," rather than a parlor, rural writers recognized that rural Americans were simultaneously attracted to the city's consumer ways and threatened by them. Farm folks desired the forms of the urban parlor (a stylish center table and art objects) but wished them to nurture country life. Rural domestic reformers, therefore, argued that an informal, family- and youth-centered sitting room would help prevent young people from deserting the farm to seek work in the city. As one architectural historian demonstrated, the percentage of parlorless plans for farmhouses after 1880 substantially increased, particularly when the Grange movement endorsed the campaign for informal sitting rooms. Women, always admitted to the Grange with full equality, assumed a large role in promoting the sitting-room concept.[43]

To describe the urban parlor in detail would require the resources of several decorator's guides and furnishings catalogs. Fortunately, the parlor was the most photographed of all nineteenth-century American interior spaces. Hence, ample visual evidence survives of the densely draped, ornamented, and furnished space that symbolized the Victorian compulsion to purchase, accumulate, and display possessions. All the accoutrements found in the farmer's sitting room and the immigrant's front room (except the beds) appeared in the urban parlor. In addition, there might be a wider array of specialized furniture: davenport sofas, parlor cabinets, and library bookcases.

The furniture, manufactured by steam-powered woodworking technology in complex and ornate shapes, was invariably covered by all sorts of hand-sewn (by the mistress of the house and young girls), embroidered, or crocheted textiles. Lambrequins or horizontal borders of fabric draped the tops of windows, doors, shelves, and mantels. Needlework also disguised chairs, cushions, and pianos. Doilies and antimacassars or tidies were everywhere, attached to the backs of chairs or sofas to protect fabrics from the greasy pomades used by men.

Men and women knew where to sit, since parlor furniture was gender distinctive. Gentlemen's chairs were thronelike, higher than lady's chairs and with arms. Ladies chairs lacked arms (in part to accommodate their full skirts) and were designed to reinforce the era's postural requirements for women—to sit upright, away from the chair back, with one's hands folded in one's lap. Children sat similarly in side chairs and were, as a favorite parental injunction, enjoined, "to be seen and not heard." By the 1890s, the urban parlor featured various artifacts not usually found in workers' or farmers' homes. These artifacts included easels (to display prints or photographs), pillows (piled everywhere), and open-hearth fireplaces.

A middle-class cult of the fireplace emerged concurrently with and, in part, because of, the practicality of central heating. Well publicized in fashionable magazines, the colonial fireplace returned to the middle-class parlor, replete with romantic inglenooks or brightly tiled hearths. Elaborately carved mantels, a few in marble but most in painted and incised wood, provided urban and suburban parlors with a ritual center. Home owners did not seem to mind if hearths came with artificial logs, were often gas fired, or hid a furnace register. Carved and galleried overmantels became a place to display small sculpture, vases, or chinoiserie.

A large manse often included a room that was variously called the second parlor, the drawing room, music room, sitting room, or living room. This space might have a plain ceiling, walls finished either in plaster or in less ornate paper, and a cheaper, sturdier carpet. Another circular or oval table centered the family's activities. Unlike the formal parlor, the second parlor was more child oriented. In fact, the room sometimes doubled as a nursery because of its proximity to the kitchen. By the turn of the century it was sometimes called the children's playroom or the family room. Here the family entertained itself by reading, playing board games, or singing around a reed organ or an upright piano.

House plants frequently graced formal and family parlors. Manufacturers stimulated indoor gardening by producing decorative flower pots, hanging baskets, and miniature greenhouses, known as "Ward cages." Catharine Beecher, author of *The American Women's Home* (1869), strongly recommended growing house plants to help humidify a home's usually dry air in winter. Amidst the family parlor's plant life often stood a machine in the garden: a cast-iron sewing machine—probably the era's most significant domestic labor-saving device.

The formal and the family parlor came under attack from many quarters in the late 1890s. Architects, journalists, interior decorators, social reformers, and agricultural editors denounced the closed and cluttered rooms of the Eclectic Manse. Clarence Cook, author of *The House Beautiful* (1878), and Edward Bok, editor of the *Ladies' Home Journal,* called for the parlor's abolition. They objected to the custom of reserving the best for strangers, to the room's stuffy formality, and to its ostentatious display. In its place, they endorsed new floor plans, such as found in the Comfortable House types (the bungalow, the colonial revival), and advocated a new furnishing aesthetic (sanitary, efficient, and simple). In place of front and family parlors came a multipurpose space—the living room (figure 3.8)—designed for a more open, flexible domestic life.

Natural woods, exposed structural elements, and simpler furniture challenged the elaborate, upholstered and multilayered look so characteristic of the 1880s' parlor. White oak replaced horsehair. In the new decor, less became more. Open passage was created between the front parlor and the dining room behind it by leaving out either the door or the entire wall between the two rooms. The formal parlor slowly evolved into the intimate living room. In the former, public behavior prevailed; in the latter, family informality predominated. Parlors conditioned propriety; living rooms suggested coziness. Furnishing guides documented this major change in residential life. In 1897 Edith Wharton already acknowledged the decline of the parlor in her *The Interior Decoration of Houses.* By 1913, E. DeWald, author of the *House of Good Taste,* embraced the living room as the "true heart of the house," just as the parlor had been its "face." To cultural historians who maintain that middle-class Americans underwent a basic reorientation in the 1870 to 1920 era—from the culture of character to a cult of personality—the transformation of the parlor into the living room suggests a residential context for such a shift in the collective psyche.[44]

Complex and multiple reasons account for this gradual transformation: a changing attitude by the middle class toward industrialism, the impact of the home economics movement, a renewed search for authentic American design, and a "scientific" concern for a more efficient, ordered, and germ-free residential space. Such were the motivations of those whom architectural and family historians have called "progressive householders." By 1915 these remakers of the American house, primarily middle-class urban dwellers and suburbanites, had extended their influence to effect the domestic ideals of wealthy farmers but had had limited impact on immigrant and working-class families.[45]

A dining room, another formal space prior to the residential reformers' reorganization, was both a private place for family meals and a public room in which the family enacted mannered rituals of dining with guests. The room's sideboard and the main table competed for attention and space. Each was designed to carry the most ample culinary largess, as well as to exhibit the family table linen, carving set, china, stemware, and silver. Less affluent families could ape a wealthy table service when electroplating and other technologies brought "silverware" within the budgets of more households.

Middle-class Americans ate amply at their dining room tables. While all meats were considered staples, beef gained preference over pork, while lamb was rarely served. A wide variety of fruits and vegetables became available year round owing to food processing and refrigerated shipping. Salad, a meal course inspired by

French cuisine, gained wider acceptance as lettuce became less perishable. Head lettuce from California became commercially available in 1903 when a strain we now call iceberg was developed for long-distance travel.[46]

Working-class homes sometimes included dining rooms, but their inhabitants often used them only on holidays or special occasions. For example, Margaret Byington noted that even when a native-born American worker in *Homestead* had a dining room, "it did not live up to its name." In "five-room houses we find an area known as the 'dining room,' " she reported. "Though a full set of dining room furniture, sideboard, table and dining chairs, are usually in evidence, they are rarely used at meals. The family sewing is usually done there, the machine standing in the front of the window; and sometimes, too, the ironing, to escape the heat of the kitchen; but rarely is the room used for breakfast, dinner, or supper. The kitchen is the important room of the house."[47]

SEMI-PRIVATE: KITCHENS

Kitchens (figure 3.9), while increasingly more compact, more technological, and more efficient, nonetheless were the site of laborious daily housework. Plans for American single-family houses typically located kitchens in the back, although basement or "summer" kitchens could also be found. In the 1870s and 1880s, a short-lived trend developed among some American farm families to move the kitchen to the front of the house to give it a southern exposure and to site it toward the public highway.

Rural families usually took their meals in their kitchens. Some enjoyed abundant diets: dairy products, beef and bread, winter (root crops) and summer (stalk crops) supplies, fresh or dried fruit (particularly apples) punctuated and enlivened by daily doses of pickled condiments. Others, like many southern sharecroppers, endured a subsistence table, composed mainly of "white food," that is, fat pork, corn bread or corn pone, and molasses made from corn or sorghum.

Tenement kitchens took their orientation from their building's plumbing system when one existed. In addition to cooking and eating, family bathing, washing, and socializing occupied this cramped space. A board might be folded over the washtub and a cloth pinned over its rim to create a separate table. Folding bed transformed the kitchen into a boarder's bedroom at night. Kitchens could mean comfort. Mary Antin fondly recalled frequent visits to her married sister's kitchen in East Boston: "After the dinner dishes were washed, Frieda took out her sewing, and I took a book; and the lamp was between us, shining on the table, on the large brown roses on the wall, on the green and brown diamonds of the oil cloth on the floor . . . on the shining stove in the corner. It was such a pleasant kitchen—such a cozy, friendly room—that when Frieda and I were left alone I was perfectly happy just to sit there. Frieda had a beautiful parlor, with plush chairs and a velvet carpet and gilt picture frames; but we preferred the homely, homelike kitchen."[48]

Working-class kitchens often harbored various cottage industries: cigar rolling, garment assembly, laundering, sewing, ironing, and baking for hire. Entire families, each according to his or her skill, labored in the kitchen workshop after school, at night, or on weekends.

Coal and wood stoves and ranges dominated kitchen environments until smaller, lighter, steel versions began taking their place by the 1910s. Sometimes they were accompanied by tall, cylindrical hot-water heaters. Cast-iron ranges, the behemoths of the kitchen, were brooding hulks. Home economist Nellie Kedzie Jones, who wrote a women's column in *The Country Gentleman* from 1912 to 1916, described them well: "The best kitchen range," she said, "is none too good. You had better economize anywhere else than on that. Good cookery is impossible on a poor stove." A farm kitchen needed a large six-hole stove, with a firebox large enough to hold "quite big wood," a damper in the stovepipe ("a wonderful fuel saver"), and a large water reservoir ("you can't have too much hot water"). Jones celebrated the "indispensable" warming oven (also used for drying fruit), baking ovens with glass doors, "and, of course, a thermometer. Without it your baking is guesswork."[49]

A well-equipped kitchen of the 1880s would also contain a patented icebox or ice chest, frequently located on an outside wall so the ice-delivery man could regularly deposit fresh ice in the box from the back porch and need not enter the home. Families also kept their iceboxes in the pantry, the basement, or a carriage house. Root cellars, well pits, and spring houses also served as coolants in winter.

Refrigerators (a term coined by a Maryland farmer, Thomas Moore, in 1803 for his invention of a double-walled box for storing perishables with ice) became available only in the late 1910s. General Motors marketed its first Frigidaire in 1918 and it eventually became so popular that many people erroneously used this trade name as the generic term, calling all electric or gas refrigerators "frigidaires."

PRIVATE: BATHROOMS AND BEDROOMS

Not until World War I did the bathroom evolve into a special area (figure 3.10) containing a tub, sink, and toilet. In the Centennial year, only wealthy homes had bathrooms, that is, prescribed places for bathing. If they also had an indoor toilet, it would have been located in a closet or other storage area. The sink, stool, and tub migrated to the bathroom from elsewhere inside or outside the home. The sink originated as a wash bowl and pitcher set in individual bed chambers, the stool replaced the outdoor privy or the indoor chamberpot, and the tub derived from the portable tin-plated or wood tubs of the kitchen. The bathroom itself traveled about the house, being located in the basement, kitchen, utility room, and sometimes in the smallest bedchamber. Since it required a constant water supply, house remodelers and designers of new homes kept it close to the building's plumbing system.

Nineteenth-century Americans attended to their daily necessities in outdoor privies. The more fastidious called the privy "a house of office," or a "necessary house"; most folks knew it as the outhouse. Behaviors and beliefs surrounding privies made them favorite subjects of everyday humor. Stories of falling through the outhouse hole and being attacked from below by spiders, snakes, and bees were legion. Stealing, moving, or tipping over outhouses became Halloween rituals. When the Rockefeller Sanitary Commission (1909) and the U.S. Public Health Service (1912) attempted to impose a "sanitary privy" or to have indoor plumbing installed in farm homes, such groups often encountered resistance from rural men who saw no need for "one of them new-fangled white crock-flushers."[50]

Women found using the outhouse especially distasteful. Understandably, one of the early advocates of indoor plumbing was Catharine Beecher, who, in her household manuals, offered detailed advice about the two major sanitation systems advocated by those who sought to bring the outhouse into the main house. Beecher first endorsed the earth closet in 1849, a system of human waste disposal advocated by sanitary reformer George Waring. The earth system operated on the principle of dropping dry earth on human waste to induce rapid fermentation without the generation of noxious gases. The simplest form of earth closet was a wooden commode equipped with a back hopper filled with earth. Waring's model, movable to any room, required no water supply and no expensive jangle of pipes and fittings, as did the rival water-closet systems. Waring (and his imitators) argued that treated wastes could be recycled as fertilizer for gardens and farms. Impressed by this aspect of the Waring system, Horace Greeley claimed: "I think that America will be worth 25 percent more a hundred years hence than it would have been without it."[51]

Waring's approach, however, proved unfeasible in big cities, since the large quantities of treated waste had to be hauled away. Also the opportunity to get rid of wastes instantly, as in the water closet, had enormous appeal. Thus, despite concern over which bowls, traps, or vents to buy or what precautions to take to prevent the dreaded sewer gas, the water closet, a technology that flushed wastes immediately out of sight through a network of invisible pipes either to a municipal sewer or to an underground cesspool, proved the most attractive option for most middle-class Americans in dealing with one of life's daily necessities.[52]

Sears, Roebuck, which had offered few plumbing furnishings a decade earlier, by 1910 sold separately or as a suite bath tubs (with claw feet), "toilet closets," and "lavatories." The white trio of tub, toilet, and sink (freestanding or wall hanging), each aligned along a wall and compressed into an average of forty-eight square feet, became a distinct architectural form. Unlike their migratory predecessors, these fixtures were each permanently attached to networks of water and waste. The fixtures came in standard sizes, with standard fittings, many made by a plumbing manufacturer appropriately named American Standard. Edward and Clarence Scott improved (1899) upon commercially prepared toilet paper (which sold in bulky packages of five sheets) by selling toilet "tissue" that came in small perforated rolls, its whiteness matching the other standardized bathroom fixtures.

Tenement dwellers rarely enjoyed the amenities of the private bathroom. While they might have a toilet and a basin in their flat, communal bathing facilities might be in the building's basement or not exist. Or the reverse could be true. They might take baths in portable tubs somewhere in their quarters and attend to their sanitary needs in a collective toilet down the hallway or out in the alley.

Personal hygiene, for many nineteenth-century Americans, began in the bedchamber. A washstand with a decorated washbowl and pitcher, a sponge, a towel, and a strip of oilcloth for the floor's protection constituted the essentials of daily cleansing. A middle-class bedroom might also contain a chair or two, a bureau or dresser, and, of course, a bed. Since Victorians considered bedchambers their inner sanctums, not shown to anyone outside the immediate family, the decor of these rooms was often sparse. Home economics manuals recommended that bedroom walls be painted, but many people disregarded such advice, preferring colorful (and cheaply priced) patterned wallpaper.

Proper bedsteads mirrored class preferences. By 1915, middle-class decorators claimed brass and iron to be more sanitary than ornate wooden furniture. High-posted bedsteads (necessary when ceilings were high and floors were cold) were replaced by lower ones of simplified headboards and footboards. Traditional furniture forms, however, continued to fill the bedchambers of immigrant and farm families. The one artifact that nineteenth-century immigrants carried with them more frequently than any other— either when coming to America or moving across it—was feather bedding. Jews, Italians, Slavs, and many other nationality groups viewed the bed (often unveiled at marriage) as an icon of the family's future happiness. The bed frequently dominated American ethnic bedchambers as it had European peasant homes. For example, Italian marriage customs prescribed that the bride's trousseau provide hand-sewn, heavily embroidered bed linens. Beds, as ornate and high as possible, sometimes required a stool to climb into them. Margaret Byington found a "high puffy bed with one feather tick to sleep on and another to cover" typical of the workers' homes in *Homestead*. [53] The bed also played a part in the rituals of death. Italian families often laid out their dead ceremoniously at home. Thus, the embellished bed served as a symbol of three crucial events of everyday life: birth, marriage, and death.

In the second half of the nineteenth century, nurseries and children's bedrooms, new to middle-class homes, housed various new devices. In this child-centered environment, furnishings included special wallpapers and pictures; child-scaled chairs, rockers, and tables; and, of course, toys. There no longer was a cradle, the bedstead of colonial American children; it had been replaced by the metal or wooden crib. So completely had the crib eclipsed the cradle that a 1890 volume of *The Upholsterer*, under the unequivocal heading, "The Cradle Is No More," asserted that "a cradle is a thing unknown nowadays. Go to the furniture store, and ask for cradles, and they will show you cribs, perambulators, hammocks, and bassinets."[54]

DAILY CHORES AND SEASONAL TASKS

Since antiquity, the word "attic" referred to the story above a classical cornice and the space under the roof. Victorian attics had many uses: as places to dry fruit, flowers, and laundry; as bedrooms for adolescents, unexpected visitors, or a housemaid; and as playrooms for children. A storehouse of discarded, outgrown, but not-quite-useless items, the attic attested to the vagaries of a consumer culture. Here householders stored furnishings they deemed still functional, if not fashionable. Basements, by design and default, served as storage and servicing areas for home life. Fuels as well as foodstuffs filled their confines. Basements, like attics, also doubled as children's playrooms and occasional sleeping quarters.

Much everyday housework involved daily, weekly, and seasonal home maintenance. For example, a six-day experiment, conducted in 1899 by Boston's School of Housekeeping, concluded that operating a "modern" coal stove required at least twenty minutes spent in sifting ashes, twenty-four minutes in laying fires, one hour and forty-eight minutes in tending fires, thirty minutes in emptying ashes, fifteen minutes in carrying coal, and two hours and nine minutes on blacking the stove to keep it from rusting. It was heavy work: in the six days 292 pounds of new coal and 14 pounds of kindling were put in, and 27 pounds of the ashes sifted out.[55] Waste removal also demanded daily attention. Someone—a servant, a child, or a housewife—also had the daily task of carrying garbage, rubbish, and liquid waste (dirty dishwater, cooking slops, and, of course, the contents of chamber pots—"the most disagreeable task of domestic labor" according to Catherine Beecher) outside to the manure pile, garden plot, privy vault, or street.

Cleaning house also took enormous time and effort. In 1908, Ellen Richards, in a study typical of the era's fascination with statistics, calculated how long it took to clean an average house. To remove dust and tracked-in dirt, an eight-room house required eighteen hours a week. If the house had a furnace as well as open fireplaces, it needed four special cleanings of twenty hours each during the course of the year. More time was required if oil lighting fixtures, with their omnipresent lamp soot, were used. Washing the windows took ten hours a month. All told, concluded the author of *The Cost of Cleanness* (1908), these tasks took about fourteen hundred hours a year, or twenty-seven hours per week.[56]

Victorians customarily swept rooms and stairwells twice a week—on Friday or Saturday, in preparation for the Sabbath, and, if laundry was hired out, on Monday. The carpet sweeper, one of the late nineteenth century's most efficient and inexpensive innovations in home technology, somewhat lightened the cleaning chores. Immediately popular and affordable, hand-pushed carpet sweepers (such as those manufactured by the Bissell Company) literally swept the nation beginning in the 1880s. Numerous inventors attempted to improve on the hand sweeper by designing vacuum cleaners, but only when it was electrified (as was the first Hoover in 1908) did the vacuum sweeper begin to become a labor-saving device.

Housekeeping intensified at week's end, baking and cooking being done to avoid servile work on Saturday or Sunday. Many women also baked on Tuesdays or Thursdays. Even those women who had a domestic servant usually did their own baking, since most considered this culinary art a special demonstration of their domestic skill. In 1850 commercial bakeries produced less than 10 percent of the bread consumed in the United States. By 1900 the figure had risen only to 25 percent.

Fuel procurement, a continual task for most people, expanded in the late summer and early fall, when rural families cut and stockpiled wood supplies for winter use. By the 1880s, most urban dwellers placed their autumn orders with coal dealers. In 1869 Catharine Beecher advised that an average urban family needed three tons of anthracite in the Middle States and four in the Northern, for heat during the winter.

Coal dust and ash, along with other outside filth (mud and manure) and inside dirt (oil and gas soot) made spring and fall housecleaning a semiannual ordeal. Few housekeepers liked this "general house wrecking process," as one home economist described the usual week-long cleaning onslaught: "It breaks women's backs and causes men to break the Ten Commandments." "House's being cleaned," wrote the poet Emily Dickinson one spring. "I prefer pestilence."

Spring cleaning, as Susan Strasser documented, entailed more domestic disruption and manual labor than its autumnal counterpart.[57] Beginning usually in April or May, it generally involved removing carpets and heavy draperies for cleaning; washing all windows, mirrors, and floors; moth proofing and packing winter clothes; polishing furniture; removing winter stoves; scouring painted walls; and cleaning pantries, bins, and the furnace (if there was one). Fall housecleaning entailed removing screens, reinstalling stoves, and sweeping chimneys. Bedding received special attention: blankets, comforters, and ticks were washed, mattresses were cleaned, and pillow feathers were rejuvenated.

While houses might be repainted prior to winter's coming, such maintenance normally took place in spring or summer. Porches often received an annual painting, and some house features were given a yearly whitewash: the front facades of southern rural cabins, the interiors of soddies on the Plains, and many (as Tom Sawyer knew well) a picket fence. Done only approximately every four to six years, painting the entire house was labor intensive, particularly as the palette of available colors expanded and the woodwork of the Eclectic Manse became more elaborate. By the 1870s, the American paint industry perfected machinery to grind pigment fine enough to remain suspended in oil. Also developed were tight-sealing metal cans in which this "ready-mixed" product could be shipped safely over long distances. (Heretofore, home-owners depended on local painters who mixed a white lead base, linseed oil, turpentine, and color pigments for each job.) Two decades later, national firms, such as Lucas, Seeley Brothers, and Sherwin-Williams, began promoting their standardized paint products via colorful sample chip cards, brochures, and architec-tural pattern books.

By then, a middle-class house built in Central City, Colorado, or in Biloxi, Mississippi, could be painted in the identical color tones of greens, olives, grays, yellows, and browns—colors much darker and richer than those advocated by pre–Civil War architects. Two color schemes dominated house painting in postbellum America. The "brown decades," aptly chronicled by Lewis Mumford, fea-tured russets, ochres, and maroons during the period 1870–90. A neoclassical vogue, prompted by colonial revival architecture and the "white cities" created at the Chicago (1893) and St. Louis (1904) world's fairs, made white and pastels stylish by 1900–20. Many owners of homes built in the 1870s gave their residences a completely new look after the turn of the century. A case in point is the seaside resort of Cape May, New Jersey. The clapboard cottages, hotels, and churches that were once a riot of polychromy had almost universally been repainted white by World War I.

House Exteriors

PORCHES: FRONT AND OTHER

The American sitting porch, the most prominent feature of all Victorian house fronts, first appeared on southern houses in the eighteenth century. House types elsewhere featured only stoops or small entranceways that were often not roofed. As an early cultural and environmental response to its region's hospitality and subtropical summer, the southern porch underwent a national diffusion beginning in the 1850s. By World War I, the front porch reigned as a national icon of respectable domesticity. It became such a symbol that after several national political conventions, astute campaign managers of presidential hopefuls, such as William McKinley, would arrange for the country's press corps to take photographs of candidates on their front porches in rocking chairs being folksy and friendly. In the estimate of one party boss, "a rambling porch was worth 300,000 votes." Dissenters also took to the porches. In the seven-month Paterson Silk-Workers strike in 1913, crowds of twenty thousand gathered around Pietro Botto's front porch (in the streetcar suburb of Haledon, New Jersey) to hear radical labor leaders like William Haywood and Elizabeth Flynn advocate the eight-hour day, minimum-wage standards, and the solidarity of workers during the strike.

Porch culture thrived on its public-private nature. Like the hall, the porch acted as a transitional zone between familial and communal life. To be sure, it had its utilitarian function as a workplace for household chores, particularly in the southern vernacular dogtrot house, but its cultural importance was even greater. For the children, it became a place to play in rainy weather; for young couples, it served as a courting place—its swing, the site of countless marriage proposals; for the old, it offered a hospitable place for watching the world go by.

Not only the Eclectic Manse featured porches, but so did the modern Prairie, Craftsman, and Mission designs of the Comfortable House ideals. California bungalows and Midwest foursquares made the porch an architectural prerequisite. Moreover, the porch proliferated elsewhere about the house in specialized progeny: breakfast, sleeping, and sun porches—each a particular size and geographic orientation. Informal native and oriental wicker and willow furniture furnished such porches. So did potted plants, birdcages, rockers, hammocks, and grass rugs.

Back porches generated their own customs. In the Jim Crow era, black people usually approached a white household only by its rear access. For both black and white, country and city folk, back porches were multifunctional spaces, places to air bedding in summer and to store perishable food in winter.

LAWN AND GARDEN

Only country estates and city mansions had large, manicured lawns before the 1870s. Grass had to be cut either by grazing stock or by wielding a scythe. Since most average house owners had neither the space to accommodate the former nor the time and inclination to do the latter, the typical home grounds were left as rough meadows cut down, at best, once or twice a growing season.

The lawnmower, an English invention of the 1830s put into large-scale production by several American firms by the 1870s, contributed to the trend to make the lawn a necessary element of the suburban house. In that decade, for example, the Chadborn and Coldwell Manufacturing Company of Newburgh, New York, launched the production of its "Excelsior" mower, a hand-propelled device that contained spiral rotary blades positioned in front of a lawn roller. By 1874, annual production reached fifteen thousand, and design was offered in various sizes and prices.

Achieving a verdant, weed-free front lawn became an obsession for many Americans by 1915. Contests were held for the greenest, largest, most original, and most improved lawn. For example, before the Democratic National Convention of 1900 in Kansas City, Missouri, a local newspaper offered a prize for the best-kept lawn. Citizens expanded this idea and raised $1,200 in prize money for twenty-six additional awards for the best lawn, floral and garden displays, and the neatest vacant lot.[58] Ironically, as Americans quested for the perfect lawn, their perennial bête noire, *Digitaria valorum* (a form of millet), arrived in America via immigrants from Eastern Europe. This transported cultivar, commonly known as crabgrass, proliferated throughout the nineteenth century as an everyday bane in any serious lawnowner's existence.

Lawns fostered lawn games. Imported from England in the late 1860s, croquet became an immensely popular American pastime by the 1880s. Illustrations of farmsteads showing rural families playing the game appear in Midwest county atlases of the period. Lawnless families traveled miles to play on a friend's lawn; towns organized teams. But croquet was more than just another fad: It was a popular outdoor game designed for equal participation by both sexes and by all ages.

Americans ornamented as well as played on their lawns. Exaggerated plant forms took center stage. Ornamental grasses and boldly colored foliage plants were popular, weeping beeches were often grown as single specimens, and tall castor beans might be surrounded by an exotic combination of cannas. Artifice, in the form of manufactured ornaments, also adorned the expanse. Classical urns and vases vied with cast-iron and stone dogs, stags, and lions.

As with indoor furnishings, lawn furniture reflected the specialization that was becoming increasingly common in everyday material life. Of course, many people simply moved chairs and tables out of the house, but others purchased furniture, such as lawn swings, hammocks, or lounges, that were specifically marketed for outdoor use. To make the lawn an outdoor parlor, cast-iron chairs and settees (fabricated in naturalistic patterns) appealed to middle-class budgets, while gardeners with more modest incomes had to settle for similar forms in wicker or reinforced steel wire.

Victorian Americans devoted much attention to amateur gardening. A new leisure activity, it involved middle-class suburbanites, such as the novelist George Washington Cable, who wrote books and articles on the vogue, as well as on the family members of silk worker Pietro Botto, who filled their modest yard with cold frames, arbors, and flower beds. National and local garden clubs began, as did the garden section of the weekend newspaper. New serials, such as *House and Garden* and *Better Homes and Gardens,* appeared. Herbert Hemenway's *How to Make School Gardens* (1903) introduced the subject into urban grammar-school curricula. Census records reveal that seedsmen and nurserymen increased 275 percent between 1870 and 1930.[59]

Ornamental gardening blossomed with unprecedented diversity, color, and content in an age that exuded the flowery in many facets of everyday life. Carpet bedding—geometric floral designs made with different colored plants of graded heights—flourished. Home owners drew their models for this gardening arrangement from public parks, where designs of flower baskets or floral clocks (an emblem popular at suburban railroad stations) were planted against a slope to show off the display. Carpet bedding was a floral analog to the Eclectic Manse's exterior facade and interior decor.

Another planting innovation, actually an importation, was the herbaceous border, a seemingly natural planting of hardy perennials and wild flowers. Sometimes described as the Arts-and-Crafts garden and largely the inspiration of Britisher Gertrude Jekyll, this garden format had its impact on American middle-class gardens through such periodicals as *Country Life in America* and Gustav Stickey's *The Craftsman*. Like the Progressive bungalow it surrounded, the new garden design was touted as more natural, less structured, and more informal than were the plantings that accompanied the Eclectic Manse. This "natural garden" was thought to be more apropos of the smaller, simpler 1910 Comfortable Home and the landscape antithesis of ostentatious carpet bedding.

Prior to the Civil War, noted Patricia Tice, "a new plant variety was matter-of-factly named after its place of origin (Concord grape), the originator (Wilson strawberry), or a growing characteristic (Early York Cabbage)." By 1900 seedsmen attempted to capture consumers' attention with more evocative names: for instance, "new tomato strains were called the Conqueror, the Acme, and the Paragon." Such a large number of strawberry plants were marketed that amateur gardener Charles Dudley Warner exclaimed in exasperation: "There are more berries now than churches; and no one knows what to believe."[60]

While this home gardening craze mostly affected the growing middle class and its aspirants, it would be a mistake to assume that new immigrants, factory workers, or rural people did not share in it. Although fountains or elaborate carpet beds typically did not highlight their lawns, simple beds of geraniums on either side of a front walk and the ubiquitous flower urn (store bought or handmade) did. Working-class back gardens tended to be functional: fruit trees were chosen over ornamental species and vegetable plots over expansive lawns. Economic downturns accentuated these emphases. For example, during the depression of 1893, Detroit mayor Hazen Pingree implemented a plan to enable workers on relief to grow their own food. Pingree wanted to show critics of the relief program that those without jobs were willing to work. He found several thousand acres of vacant land in Detroit and appealed to the owners of these sites to let unemployed people plant them. In the first year the value of the crops exceeded the money spent in establishing the program. "Pingree's Potato Patches" attracted national attention, and in the following three years, garden-allotment programs were established in many major American cities.[61]

Lawns received less concern and tree planting more attention in rural areas. In addition to planting windbreaks, home owners also set out trees, individually or in groups, to commemorate a marriage, a sequence of childbirths, or other special events in the family or even the national history. Wedding and children conifers often graced nineteenth-century Midwestern farmsteads. Tree groves marked the 1876 Centennial and the twentieth century's beginning in 1900. Arbor Day, a significant enthusiasm of the Great Plains in the 1890s, continued a tree-planting tradition begun by New England village improvement societies in the 1870s.

Home gardening, like much else in Victorian America, spawned competition. Initiated by new associations, such as the Rotary Club (1904), the Boy Scouts and the Girl Scouts (1912), and established organizations like county fairs and the Women's Christian Temperance Union, gardening contests multiplied from 1890 to 1915. During periods of labor unrest, strikes, and lockouts, large factories, including the National Cash Register Company of Dayton, sponsored them to pacify workers. John C. Olmsted, son of America's most famous landscape architect, and Liberty Hyde Bailey, an eminent American plantsman, oversaw model gardens for the NCR's 2,500 workers.[62] The best-kept premises, the most beautiful effects, and the most decorative window boxes received prizes.

Home gardening, at first thought, might appear to be only a surface phenomenon, a growing aspect of everyday life but nevertheless a peripheral one. Yet, in its simple way, it demonstrated several ironies of Victorian America. The expansion of gardening and related concerns for urban and national parks coincided with the era's unprecedented exploitation of the country's natural resources. Loggers and miners uprooted as others planted. In another context, home gardening became a leisure pursuit for many middle-class Americans only after industrialization changed the country from an agrarian republic to a manufacturing nation. Finally, on the home grounds of domestic life, gardening further reinforced Victorian gender roles. With the advent of the manicured lawn (assumed to be a masculine responsibility), the ornamental flower garden (like the domestic residential interior) became a largely feminine preserve.

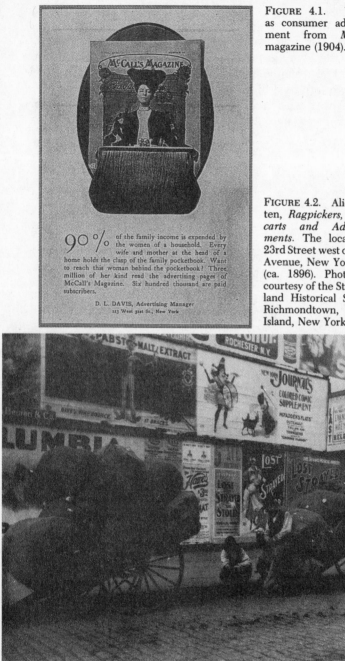

FIGURE 4.1. Woman as consumer advertisement from *McCall's* magazine (1904).

90 % of the family income is expended by the women of a household. Every wife and mother at the head of a home holds the clasp of the family pocketbook. Want to reach this woman behind the pocketbook? Three million of her kind read the advertising pages of McCall's Magazine. Six hundred thousand are paid subscribers.

D. L. DAVIS, Advertising Manager
113 West 31st St., New York

FIGURE 4.2. Alice Austen, *Ragpickers, Handcarts and Advertisements*. The location is 23rd Street west of Third Avenue, New York City (ca. 1896). Photograph courtesy of the Staten Island Historical Society, Richmondtown, Staten Island, New York.

4

꧁ _____

B<small>Y</small> 1915, according to marketing trade journals, American
women (figure 4.1) spent more time shopping than did American
men. They accounted for close to 90 percent of all consumer
spending in the United States. "Give the lady what she wants"
insisted Chicago department store entrepreneur Marshall Field.
New chain and franchise stores, the rise of women's magazines,
such as *Ladies' Home Journal,* and the proliferation of gender
advertising sought to do exactly that as the nation gradually
shifted from a society of producers to one of consumers. The "good
life" came to mean the "goods life."

Why did American consumer habits gain such momentum from
1876 to 1915? Briefly put, more people (middle class and working
class) had more money and more time to purchase more goods,
mass-produced more cheaply and advertised more widely. Annual
earnings per working person rose in the period and the work week
declined—for factory workers, from approximately sixty-six hours
in 1850 to sixty by 1890, and then to fifty-five in 1914.[1] Simultaneously, the sheer variety and amount of goods increased. Department stores and mail-order catalogs turned local markets into
national ones. New institutions of commercial leisure—amusement parks, vaudeville, and spectator sports—suggested that fun
could be bought like anything else. New products and new materials appeared. Plastics like Celluloid (1872), Bakelite (1907), and
cellophane (1912)—all synthetic creations unavailable in nature—
initiated whole new lines of everyday products.

The emerging consumer culture received scrutiny from various observers of American life, among them Edward Bellamy, Ignatius Donnelly, and Thorstein Veblen. A lesser-known theorist, Simon N. Patten, suggested that increasing levels of consumption meant, as the title of his influential book indicated, nothing short of a *New Basis of Civilization* (1907). Until the mid-nineteenth century, argued Patten, every society (including America) had to cope with an economy of scarcity. But industrialization had, for the first time, made a surplus possible. Society's task was, therefore, no longer how to make do with less, as it always had been, but instead how to live with much more.

Traditional Buying and Selling

DAILY SHOPPING

People bartered and peddled goods and services before and during the rise of an everyday consumer culture in Victorian America. Trading surplus foodstuffs for tools, clothing, medicine, and liquor remained a common practice among many farm families well into the twentieth century. In addition to selling summer produce, farm women and their daughters put up applesauce and sauerkraut for fall markets; they also offered household products for sale—feathers for pillows and homemade brooms, soap, baskets, and potted plants.[2]

Itinerant peddlers—whether "damn Yankees" working southern homesteads, Alsatian Jews selling consignment goods across the Midwest, or Italian street vendors hawking wares in an urban neighborhood—sold everything from special goods to personal services, including dentistry and portraiture. Peddlers brought commodities that general stores might not always have on hand; thus, they introduced cosmetics (Avon, 1886) and household aids (such as Fuller Brush, 1905) into America's homes.

Urban peddlers usually worked circuits a day's travel from their homes. Many were, or became, daily delivery men, vending commodities, such as dairy or baked goods, meats, or produce. Others hawked the "off-the-peg" clothing that tailors made during seasonal slack periods. City peddlers also sold (or bartered) ice, coal, and firewood while buying rags, scrap metal, and recyclable trash (figure 4.2). Such peddlers often worked out of a city's public market like Boston's Faneuil, New York's Fulton, or San Antonio's Military Plaza. In addition to foodstuffs, customers at San Antonio's market could purchase consumer goods, such as jewelry, notions, and home furnishings.

Groceries, like most necessary goods, were sold in markets and stores on a credit system. Prior to the 1880s, customers presented their orders to clerks who filled them. Accounts (figure 4.3) were periodically tallied (weekly, monthly, or yearly) and bills were paid. Cash-and-carry transactions were atypical for most people. Low-income people bought in small quantities and invariably on credit. For many, daily shopping also meant an adversarial context. Before department and chain stores adopted a fixed-price policy for merchandising, sellers bargained individually with buyers, asking a price determined by a particular buyer's social position, need, and desire for a particular item. The price finally paid for an item varied with the customer's haggling skills and the merchandiser's selling abilities.

COUNTRY STORES

In rural stores, customers could see, feel, and even taste a merchant's goods. In addition to the customary spatial arrangements in which counters and shelves along the store's right side were devoted to dry goods; those on the left side to groceries, tobacco, sundries, and patent medicines; and the rear to kerosene, whiskey, and meat barrels, country storekeepers by the 1890s used many techniques to showcase luxury merchandise, such as cuckoo clocks, chromolithographs, and stereoscopes.

Some bought glass display cases shaped with ogee curves, filling them with cutlery and glassware. Dye companies, candy firms, cosmetics dealers, and chewing-gum manufacturers provided the stores with colorful product dispensers. For example, one store promotion of "Merrick's Six Cord Soft Finish Spool Cotton" was shaped like a great cylinder and whirled around showing all thread gauges and colors. Seed companies, such as those of the Shakers and W. A. Burpee, contributed chromolithographed exhibits to enhance seasonal displays.

The commercialization of Christmas took place in countryside emporiums just as in urban department stores. In southern stores, for instance, special displays in various geometric shapes were made of coconuts, apples, oranges, and nutmegs. Children's toys and Christmas ornaments were suspended from the ceiling, while special promotions of suitable gift ideas (Martha Washington's Perfume Waters selling for $1.05 or a Harrington & Richardson pistol for $2.98) were stocked near the main counter's credit book. Also prominently arranged everywhere were firecrackers, black powder, and Roman candles—material culture that even the poorest rural Southerner deemed essential to a festive Christmas celebration.[3]

By the 1890s many country store merchants had installed a "five-and-ten-cent counter." Imitating the merchandising concept that F. W. Woolworth pioneered in 1879, country storekeepers began displaying a tempting assortment of items—crochet hooks, wash basins, baby bibs, watch keys, and harmonicas—that one could buy for the smallest units of change. Butler Brothers in Boston, wholesale jobbers to the country trade, specialized in providing the country merchant with cartons of mixed goods of price-focused quality.

Country merchants often sold by example. In rural communities, for instance, they were the first to install a telephone, to buy a regulator wall clock, or to use a box camera. Their informal endorsement of these and other new products (samples of which they frequently received from jobbers) added credibility to a product's quality in an era that thrived on testimonial advertising.

Despite his initial monopoly of a rural community's trade and the credit liens he held on many customers, the storekeeper widely advertised his wares. For example, he placed large ads for special sales and seasonal promotions in local weeklies. By 1900, he was also touting his goods through the picture postcard, bulk mailings of handbills, free calendars, and even his own business cards.

In mounting these promotional campaigns, national advertisers and traveling salesmen assisted local storekeepers. Patent medicines, the first national brands that country store owners stocked, became popular "Called For" goods by customers who had read about them in the agricultural, religious, or regional press. Drake's Plantation Bitters or Radway's Ready Relief were also promoted by the extensive publishing network of free "medical" almanacs sent to country merchants every November to stimulate holiday sales, as well as to mark the coming New Year.

The national-brand advertising that appeared in almanacs and other rural publications soon forced country storekeepers to join the "packaging push." Innovative store owners recognized that the artifact in which a product was boxed or bottled could be more appealing than the article itself. The trend away from displaying generic goods in barrels, jars, bins, and sacks to preparing individual consumer units of wrappers, packets, cartons, and containers was a gradual but continual shift in American store marketing. As early as the 1870s, a local merchant could purchase, in various shapes, sizes, and colors, "Pasteboard Caddies" on which his business name could be printed and in which he could apportion tea, sugar, coffee, and other bulk staples according to the preferences of his customers. More frequently, however, the local merchant let national manufacturers do his promotional packaging. Commodities, such as Mail Pouch chewing tobacco in individual bags instead of forty-pound loaves of plug or Quaker Oats in a sixteen-ounce cylinder instead of an eight-pound sack, increasingly stocked the shelves of country stores after 1900.[4]

Eventually even the cracker barrel, one of the country store's revered icons, succumbed to the new consumer culture. With the formation of the National Biscuit Company in 1898, the firm began marketing Uneeda Biscuits—a five-cent package of soda crackers in an airtight, patented, moisture-proof package. National Biscuit initiated such a lavish, nationwide advertising campaign to sell the new item that economic historian Alfred Chandler identified it as a prototype for modern mass distribution.[5] Traveling salesmen from National Biscuit worked crossroads stores with a particular intensity, distributing posters for barns, livery stables, and railroad depots. These drummers also used promotions and premiums to "drum up" interest in their new product, providing Uneeda watch fobs, cuff links, and stick pins for storekeepers and their favorite clientele. The campaign succeeded. Uneeda biscuits quickly registered monthly sales of over

10 million packages. Promoted with a trademark (a profile of a boy in a yellow storm slicker) and a slogan ("Lest you forget, we say it yet, Uneeda Biscuit"), the product inaugurated the first million-dollar advertising campaign in the United States, as well as some less successful imitators, such as Uwanta beer, Isagood soup, and *Ureada Magazine*.

Drummers played a vital role in rural consumerism. They kept rural merchants abreast of what they had learned from their trade journals, their professional association (Society of Commercial Travellers), and other clients visited on their circuits. Drummers served as informal financial consultants, economic forecasters, and market analysts to local storekeepers. The subjects of innumerable off-color "Farmer's Daughter" jokes and yet the founders of the Gideon Bible Society, the turn-of-the-century drummers were the perfect liaisons between the commercial worlds of country and city. With the latest-style haberdashery, knowledge of urban sports, arts, and entertainment, and sample cases of the most up-to-date city goods, the drummer's rotational visits to the country became something of a community event.

Innovative Retailing

THE DEPARTMENT STORE

Victorian America inaugurated a new era of city shopping. When John Wanamaker opened a new Philadelphia store in 1876, only a few dozen U.S. department stores existed. Five decades later, over a thousand stores were visited by a hundred thousand shoppers daily. Department stores, like railroad stations and skyscrapers, became symbols of urbanity and artifacts of community identity. Major urban centers had several: R. H. Macy's and Gimbel's in New York, Marshall Field's and Meyer and Schlesinger in Chicago, and Jordan Marsh and Filene's in Boston. Smaller cities likewise had their impressive consumer palaces—Rich's in Columbus, Kaufmann's in Pittsburgh, and The Emporium in San Francisco.

A. T. Stewart's "Cast-Iron" Palace opened in New York in 1862 and, following the example of Aristide Boucicaut's famous Bon

Marché in Paris, introduced practically all the retailing practices found in the American department store: special attention to women consumers (his famous "Ladies Parlor"), a fixed-price policy, departmentalized stock (including everything from baby carriages to funeral "black goods"), centralized management, an impressive store building, shopping amenities (continuous organ music to entertain customers), and bargain sales. Macy, Field, and Wanamaker all acknowledged their merchandising debts to the pioneer merchant they called "Stewart the Great" and "King Stewart."

Wanamaker's of Philadelphia (figure 4.6) typifies the department store's role in consumer culture before World War I. At the 1876 opening of his "New Kind of Store," over seventy thousand people entered the three-acre bazaar, the "largest space in the world devoted to retail selling on a single floor." The store contained 129 counters, some two-thirds of a mile in length, with 1,100 stools in front of them for the shoppers' convenience. It was lit by day with stained-glass skylights and at night by great gas chandeliers. Wanamaker's later features became commonplace to department stores everywhere: a restaurant, electric displays, white sales (adapted from France), and U.S. parcel post delivery. At one time or another Wanamaker's sold about every kind of merchandise, including automobiles and airplanes.[6]

Department stores developed as a new building type. Towering over a parade of pedestrians and a web of streetcar lines, they usually featured a great court, a grand staircase, or an immense rotunda topped with a classical dome. They rivaled the monumentality of the metropolitan art museums that were being founded simultaneously in large American cities. Murals, such as those of Boardman Robinson depicting the history of commerce for Kaufman's in Pittsburgh, filled their interiors. So did public sculpture: Wanamaker's immense *American Eagle* (first exhibited at the 1904 World's Fair in St. Louis) and Siegel-Cooper's smaller replica of Daniel Chester French's *The Republic* (executed for the 1893 World's Fair in Chicago) made the department store a free art gallery. Several department stores—Wanamaker's, Field's, and Filene's—were designed by Daniel Burnham of Chicago, the era's most prolific architect of mammoth structures.[7] Their openings became national events, such as when President William Howard Taft dedicated a new Wanamaker's in 1911.

As meccas of consumerism and materialism, department stores pioneered the modern arts of commercial display to promote what one interior designer called "the intensification of desire." Like world's fairs, with which they had many parallels, department stores used changing interior arrangements, fashion shows, and holiday pageants, as well as outdoor parades, street fairs, and carnivals to sell merchandise. In their unprecedented use of color, store managers transformed the drab interior of the dry-goods house into a sumptuous theatrical set. Customers first saw in the department store, as in no other institution, the visual explosion of new colors manufactured from new chemical dyes. "Fast colors," in all combinations and tints, invaded all realms of retail display, packaging, advertising, and goods.[8]

With the cheaper manufacture of plate glass by the mid-1890s, larger, stronger, clearer display windows dominated the design of department stores. Such windows, magical stages created by designers like L. Frank Baum (also author of *The Wonderful Wizard of Oz*, 1896), presented commodities to pedestrians who shopped without even entering a store. At Christmas they often became tableaux of animated figures relating ancient holy-day legends as they subtly encouraged contemporary holiday spending.[9] Window shopping democratized consuming, making it an urban ritual open to all classes at all times. For example, most Saturday nights in 1898, Mary Antin, a young Jewish immigrant, and her girlfriends would "march up Broadway, and [take] possession of all we saw . . . or desired," staying out "till all hours." In a "dazzlingly beautiful palace called a 'department store,' " she and her sister, in a memorable rite of passage, "exchanged our hateful home-made European costumes . . . for real American machine-made garments, and issued forth glorified in each other's eyes."[10]

Department stores developed new customer services for shoppers who spent several hours (sometimes the entire day) in their emporiums. Rest rooms and women's lounges led the way to restaurants (often called tea rooms) and reading rooms. Nurseries for customers' children, complaint and credit bureaus, post offices, and ticket agencies became store features. The stores borrowed from other public institutions. By 1920 the department store was a miniature zoo (Bloomingdale's in New York had an enormous pet store), a botanical garden (floral shops, miniature conservatories, and roof gardens), and a library. As early as the 1890s, when merchants started to build their own auditoriums, department stores became theaters, putting on plays, musicals, and concerts. In 1904 Richard Strauss conducted the world premier performance of his *Symphonia Domestica* in Wanamaker's New York store.

Customer amenities were available to the shawl as well as to the carriage trade. They helped convert feminine shopping—always something of a social undertaking—into even more of a social art. Marshall Field had a particular genius for satisfying both society matrons and shop girls in his theater of shopping and spending. He insisted that his clerks call all women "Ladies," making everyone actresses in their consumer indulgence in the era's "pecuniary canons of taste," Thorstein Veblen's term for a new ethic that considered all people equal if they had the money to acquire certain goods. "The principal cause of the stores' success," one shopper wrote in 1892, "is the fact that their founders have understood the necessity of offering a new democracy, whose needs and habits" are satisfied "in the cheapest possible way," providing "a taste for elegance and comfort unknown to previous generations."[11]

Although department stores sold practically everything, items of fashion became a mainstay. Christmas and Easter, claimed the department stores, required new clothes, as did the summer vacation and school's fall opening. Victorian dress styles could be chronicled in the changing fashions of department stores. Beginning with the rounded, full-skirted, bustled costumes of the 1870s, through the elongated mode of the skirt and interchangeable shirtwaist in the 1890s, to the practical one-piece dress for home ("crackerjack lines") and street wear ("lingerie" dresses) of the 1910s, American women shopped women's departments for their apparel.

Department stores, mail-order firms, and other retailers contributed to the standardization of American dress. In 1861, the need to mass-produce Civil War uniforms resulted in guidelines for common sizes based on the examination of recruits. With some notion of what most men of a particular height should weigh and what their average measurements were, a new statistical science, anthropometry ("the measurement of body's sizes"), developed along with a factory-made, ready-to-wear clothing industry first for men and then eventually also for women. By the 1880s, garment retailers steadily expanded their range of "regular" sizes until they reached from size 32 to over 50—"every size clothes for every sized man." By 1915 American men also had a wide choice of ready-made clothing designed for business, sports, and specialized occupations. By that time, it was possible to walk into a clothing store, indicate that one was a "44" and put on a suit or jacket that, with little or no alteration, would satisfy a critical eye.[12] The standardization of women's and misses' clothing took place more slowly, but by 1910 Sears, Roebuck featured women's suits in even and odd sizes, from 32 to 44, each size in three different body proportions.

Massive store sales—white, clearance, and anniversary sales— quickened the tempo of the changes in style and encouraged buying sprees. So did the bargain basement, a store department in which unsold goods were featured at reduced prices to generate high turnover and to clear other floors of distressed, discontinued, or surplus merchandise. Although Wanamaker's "Bargain Room" first promoted the concept among big stores in 1888, it was Edward Filene's Automatic Bargain Basement that perfected the form. Established in 1909, and several years later the scene of a silent movie called *One Flight Down* (one of many films made in or about department stores), Filene's differed in several respects from most bargain floors. It automatically reduced its merchandise 25 percent after twelve selling days, slashed the price again by 25 percent on items remaining after eighteen days, and reduced it by a further 25 percent after twenty-four days. Theoretically, all items went to Boston charities at this point, but little merchandise survived shoppers by that time.

As has been shown (in chapter 2) department stores expanded the American labor force, creating new jobs and redefining old ones in the retail business. Male floorwalkers evoked the owner's masculine presence by their omnipresence. Dressed in either a black frock or a cutaway coat and high collar, they patrolled the aisles as Charlie Chaplin parodied the type in his film *The Floor-walker*. They kept their staff "up to the standard of dress, deportment, and activity," also serving as a buffer between salespeople and irate customers.

Middle-class women found jobs as merchandising managers, buyers, advertising agents, and sales representatives, a job so new that it inspired Edna Ferber to fictionalize it in *Emma McChesney and Co.* (1915). By 1900, women became the dominant sex behind the sales counters. Managers and customers welcomed them as better salespeople. "Women have more tact and accuracy than men," claimed Wanamaker. "There is far more reciprocity in fine manners between women and women."[13] Others argued that female clerks understood the department store's women clientele because they themselves wished similar possessions. Many female customers supposedly found it easier to share their desires with them than with men. Fitting new garments was also simplified.

CHAINS AND FRANCHISES

The expression *chain stores,* in usage by 1915, described a group of similar stores under common ownership. Cash-and-Carry served as the motto of these stores. In contrast to department stores, which succeeded by offering some of the personal services traditionally associated with neighborhood merchants, the new chain stores made a virtue of their economies of scale. Whereas the department stores operated on systems of credit and installment buying, chain stores featured price-focused goods. In 1859 George Gilman and George Hartford opened a small tea store on New York's Vesey Street that they pretentiously called The Great American Tea Company. Showmanship, as Daniel Boorstin documented, enticed consumers to their doors: gift premiums, pagoda-shaped cashier cages, and a great green parrot prominently in evidence on the main floor. Gilman and Hartford expanded the name of their store to The Great Atlantic and Pacific Tea Company in 1869 (figure 1.4), the year the country's coasts were connected by the nation's first transcontinental railroad. Having gradually added other prepacked groceries (spices, coffee, condensed milk, and baking powder) to their line, the A&P boasted a chain of sixty-seven stores by 1876. In the years between 1912 and 1915, the A&P Co. reputedly opened a new store every three days.[14]

Other chains, Grand Union (1870s), Kroger (1880s), and Jewel Tea (1890s), changed the way many Americans did their grocery shopping. Food chains, for example, doubled during the period 1900–20, with the number of stores increasing eightfold. With lower overhead and larger per-unit profits than independent grocers, chains offered lower prices through large-scale purchasing. Lower markups attracted consumers from lower-income groups, while wealthier shoppers tended to stay with traditional grocers.

Many neighborhood merchants and the National Association of Retail Grocers claimed that the chains threatened the American way of local life. Congressional representatives from small towns delivered jeremiads against chain-store consumerism, insisting that it dissolved a neighborhood's identity and contributed nothing to the cohesion of a community. However, the anti-chain-store movement, like the opposition to mail-order catalogs, mounted, at best, a rearguard action in its complaints.

Grocery chain stores eventually evolved into supermarkets. Clarence Saunders, a Memphis, Tennessee, merchant, opened the novel Piggly Wiggly chain of stores in 1916 that were set up so that customers passed through turnstiles and followed a predetermined course, which forced them to view all the merchandise displayed on the store's shelves. In this scheme of "self-service," the captive buyer confronted commodities he or she had not necessarily come to purchase. The seller had entrapped the buyer by a new architecture and technology of distribution designed to promote "impulse buying."[15]

A similar psychology influenced variety chain-store entrepreneurs, such as F. W. Woolworth, who, beginning in the 1870s, helped give consumer goods the attraction of price, rather than function or quality. Woolworth's rationale was simple. If an attractive item, say a Christmas decoration or a cosmetic kit, was offered at a reasonable price, "the customer would buy it if he needed it—but if the price was low enough, and in convenient coin, perhaps the consumer would purchase it on the spur of the moment" because "it was only a nickel."[16]

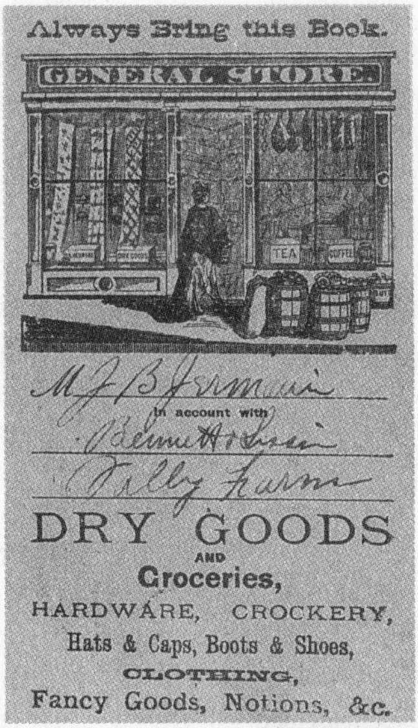

FIGURE 4.3. Cover of general store credit book (ca. 1890). Courtesy of the Warshaw Collection of Business Americana, National Museum of American History.

FIGURE 4.4. Harry Grant Dart, "Picturesque America" (1910). Cartoon courtesy of the Library of Congress, Division of Prints and Photographs.

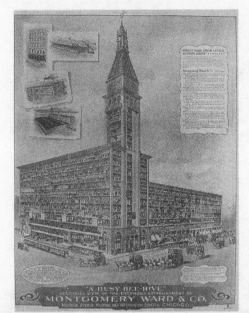

FIGURE 4.5. Montgomery Ward & Company, "A Busy Bee-Hive" (1896). Chromolithograph courtesy of the Chicago Historical Society.

FIGURE 4.6. Interior of the Grand Depot, John Wanamaker Department Store, Philadelphia (1876). Lithograph from Herbert A. Gibbons, *John Wanamaker.*

FIGURE 4.7. Racial stereotyping in advertising. "The Chinese Must Go" (ca. 1880s). Chromolithograph courtesy of the Library of Congress, Division of Prints and Photographs.

FIGURE 4.8. Use of children in advertising. Promotional handout, Genesee Pure Food Company, Leroy, New York (ca. 1910). Courtesy of the Warshaw Collection of Business Americana, National Museum of American History.

FIGURE 4.9. Electricity in the home. Magazine cover, *Electric City Magazine* (May 1912).

FIGURE 4.10. Rise in dental hygiene magazine advertising, Florence Manufacturing Company, Florence, Massachusetts (1904). Courtesy of the Warshaw Collection of Business Americana, National Museum of American History.

Before Woolworth merged his company with five others in 1911, his nickel or dime price (unchanged until 1932 when twenty-cent items appeared) and his "browsers wanted" policy boasted 319 five-and-dime stores throughout the world. The 1911 merger almost doubled the chain's total number of stores to 596, doing sales of more than a million dollars a week.[17] The corporation, also the world's largest restaurant chain, served thousands of meals over its lunch counters, at which many department store salesclerks (who could not daily afford their employers' tea-room prices) took their midday meal.

The Woolworth idea paralleled the concept of franchising, another retailing technique pioneered by I. M. Singer & Co. in the 1850s in its efforts to market sewing machines. Independent businessmen agreed to pay Singer a fee of $60 for each sewing machine sold within a geographic area defined as their exclusive territory. They, in turn, agreed to sell these machines at a price of $125 apiece. Other industries moved into this same pattern of franchising the right to sell a particular product, often in a particular locale. For example, as early as 1899, Coca-Cola licensed operators with the rights to bottle its patented syrup; in 1902 Louis Liggett, along with forty druggists, established the Rexall company, franchising its name, logo, and products to independent drug stores. In the early twentieth century, General Motors, lacking the capital needed to open retail outlets, began selling its vehicles through a system of car dealerships. The first franchises included owners of bicycle shops and hardware stores who sold cars as a sideline. Aggressive local dealers obtained a site, built a showroom and sales lot, and sold the cars that the companies sent them annually. Other auto-related goods and services—gas, oil, and tires—as well as motels and fast-food restaurants—eventually joined in the franchising of the American roadside.[18]

THE MAIL-ORDER CATALOG

"There's a Haynes-Cooper catalog in every farmer's kitchen," remarks a Wisconsin woman in *Fanny Herself,* Edna Ferber's 1917 novel depicting the Chicago mail-order industry. "The Bible's in the parlor, but they keep the H.C. book in the room where they live." Often called "Farmer's Bibles," the mail-order catalogs of the Chicago giants—Montgomery Ward and Sears, Roebuck—expressed a secular hope for salvation from want. There was, for example, the oft-quoted folk tale of the little boy from rural Idaho who, upon being asked by his Sunday School teacher where the Ten Commandments came from, unhesitantly replied, "From Sears, Roebuck, where else?"[19]

In 1872 Montgomery Ward staked out rural-consumption communities through a loose affiliation with the Grange movement and made his Chicago firm the farmer organization's official supply house. His chief competitor, Richard Sears, a former Minnesota railway agent who got into the mail-order business in his spare time selling watches, launched his company in 1886. Two decades later, Sears claimed his was "The Largest Retail Supply House in the World," selling ten thousand other items in addition to a watch every minute. The key medium for displaying his merchandise was the semiannual consumers' guide, as his mail-order catalog began to be labeled with its 1894 edition. Mail-order catalogs compressed a city's shopping district into a five-hundred-page volume. Not only did each new edition add more lines of merchandise, it enlarged the range of consumer selection. By 1910, an estimated 10 million Americans annually shopped by mail.

Catalogs affected every aspect of American daily life, from love and birth to loneliness and dying. For example, a Kansas farmer wrote Sears in 1899: "Find enclosed one check; please send one wife Model #1242 on page 112 as soon as possible." A Minnesota consumer, anxious for embalming fluid for a near-death husband, wrote Montgomery Ward at the turn of the century: "When you send the stuff please send instructions with it. Must I pour it down his throat just before he dies, or must I rub it on after he is dead? Please rush."[20]

Unlike the country store or the department store, where customers could inspect products, mail-order merchandising required constant attention to its credibility. Country store merchants continually warned their customers that mail-order purchases invited disappointment, poor-quality goods, and downright fraud. To counter such charges, Sears and Ward jammed their catalogs with beguiling illustrations and folksy descriptions. Ward's provided instructions for ordering products in ten languages. Sears introduced early catalogs by a personal letter. "Don't be afraid that you will make a mistake," he assured potential customers. "We receive hundreds of orders every day from young and old who never sent away for goods. . . . Tell us what you want, in your own way, written in any language, no matter whether good or poor writing, and your goods will be sent promptly to you."[21]

Both Sears and Ward guaranteed their customers satisfaction or an immediate cash refund. Both used their catalog covers to depict their Chicago stores (figure 4.5) as industrious beehives of diligent clerks filling thousands of orders daily from a seemingly inexhaustible cornucopia of products. So that skeptical customers could get a look at company operations, Sears sold cheap sets of stereopticon slides depicting his offices, plants, and warehouses.

In 1905 Sears developed a plan, sometimes called his "Iowaization" scheme because it was first implemented in Iowa, to secure additional consumers. The company sent two dozen catalogs to each of its current Iowa customers asking them to give these catalogs to friends or neighbors who did not already have one. The customers were also asked to send to the company the names of the people to whom they had given catalogs. Sears monitored who ordered what, giving premiums to those who got new orders from their friends and relatives. When Iowa sales outstripped all other states', the company applied the concept elsewhere. Rural patterns of kinship and friendship that had developed, in part, by weekly and seasonal visits to country stores, local merchants, and county fairs, thus became capitalistic networks for new ways of buying and selling. Consumers themselves became private distributors and promoters of goods. With the spread of mail-order merchandising, many rural people who had lived, to a large extent, on a barter or extended credit system, now became immersed in a money economy.[22]

Several actions of the U.S. Post Office—bulk mail rates, postal money orders, rural free delivery (RFD), and parcel post—had an enormous impact on the success of mail-order consumerism. Perhaps of most significance was the beginning, in 1896, of a nationwide RFD system of direct-to-the-home mail delivery. Endorsed by Postmaster General John A. Wanamaker and championed by the Grange, other farmers' organizations, and the mail-order houses, it was fought bitterly by the express companies, local storekeepers, and the National Association of Grocers. Similar combatants waged a similar battle with similar results over parcel post.

Rural delivery made mail-ordering simple and direct. "If you live on a rural route," advised the catalogs, "just give the letter and money to the mail carrier and he will get the money order at the post office and mail it in the letter for you." By 1920, a fifty-pound package could be sent by the new (1913) parcel post from Chicago anywhere in the country and a seventy-pound package could be sent anywhere in its first three postal zones. For example, in that year, of the 787 Wisconsin farm families who were sampled about their consumer habits, 38 percent bought an annual average of $58.91 worth of mail-order goods. Another survey along a Midwest rural route showed that every family received an average of seventeen mail-order parcels a year.[23]

Catalogs prompted heated consumer conflicts. Country storekeepers and small-town editors waged a prolonged and vitriolic anticatalog campaign. Local merchants, such as R. E. Ledbetter in George Milburn's novel, *Catalogue* (1936), urged townspeople and farmers to bring in their catalogs to a "Home Town Industry Jubilee and Bonfire," where country store owners paid a bounty of a dollar in trade for every new catalog turned in to fuel a huge bonfire they staged in the town's public square. Prizes of up to fifty dollars were offered to those folks who collected the largest number of "Wish Books" for public immolation.

Small-town merchants won some of the antimail-order battles, but they eventually lost the mail-order merchandising wars. Many country storekeepers capitulated and acted as agents for Sears or Ward, placing the wishbook next to their counterbooks. Democrat Gene Talmadge, later governor of Georgia, knew his constituents well when, during his many successful campaigns, he told them: "Your only friends are Jesus Christ, Sears, Roebuck, and Gene Talmadge." Proof that other rural Americans shared his faith is the town of Seroco, North Dakota, an acronym that honored the Sears, Roebuck Company because the company's catalog was the first piece of mail to reach the village post office.

Catalogs influenced other aspects of everyday rural life. Install-

ment buying came to the countryside through mail-order merchandising. The "Farmer's Bible" doubled as an encyclopedia in
many rural schoolhouses. Children practiced arithmetic by adding
up orders, did geography from its postal zone maps, and tried
figure drawing by tracing the catalog's models. The "Big Books"
(1,064 pages in 1921) served as home almanacs, since they usually
contained inspirational readings, poetry, and farming and household tips.

Channeling Wishes

MIRROR MAKERS: MEDIUMS AND METHODS

Advertising underwent a major transformation in personnel and
purpose in postbellum America. By 1900, American advertisers
spent $95 million a year, which marked a tenfold increase over the
amount spent in 1865. By 1919, the figure exceeded a half billion
dollars.[24] Early advertising agents, first called brokers, acted as
middle men, selling space in newspapers to individual advertisers.
The space they sold was limited to advertising columns of small
agate type. Led by N. W. Ayer and Son of Philadelphia in the
1880s, however, agencies like those of J. Walter Thompson and
Lord & Thomas broke out of the classified tradition with new
formats. Such agencies prepared display advertisements for department stores and, by the decade's end, for manufacturers such
as Proctor and Gamble. Based in New York and Chicago, mostly
staffed by young men from small-town, Protestant America, the
advertising firms employed art directors, account executives,
copywriters, and marketing experts.

As another new addition to the middle-class labor force, the
admen discovered the new social science of psychology, claiming
its applicability to "demand creation" for consumer goods.[25] Aca-
demicians, such as Walter Dill Scott, a professor of psychology (and
later president) at Northwestern University, lectured advertising
executives on the application of psychological theory to advertising practice.

Scott borrowed ideas from the experimental psychology of Wil-
helm Wundt (under whom he studied at Leipzig) and the develop-

mental psychology of William James (whose *Principles of Psychology* he recommended as required reading for all advertisers). He conducted behavioral experiments to test the reactions of people to visual stimuli, such as colors, typefaces, and graphic images. He mailed millions of questionnaires to discover attitudes toward certain kinds of products and reactions to different sorts of advertising. In *The Theory and Practice of Advertising* (1903), Scott discussed such concepts as mental suggestion and association, arguing how such factors could create an advertisement's mass appeal. Armed with this rationale, many advertisers not only claimed the potential of stimulating consumers to greater spending but exhibited a new confidence in their ability to do so. For example, Paul Cherington declared that the purpose of advertising was to increase consumerism by undermining the "savings instinct." "The strength of this instinct is only relative," he asserted in *Advertising as a Business Force* (1913), "and here the consumer is vulnerable."[26]

As will be noted again in chapter 5, American everyday life was a highly visual culture by 1915. Print predominated, but pictures proliferated. In popular culture, for example, the visual crowded the verbal for attention (figure 4.4). Advertisers both made and minded this ever-expanding iconographic inventory to stimulate consumption, manipulating images to sell everything from breakfast foods to beauty aids. Indicative of the growing competition of the visual with the verbal is the name change the industry's early trade journal underwent by the 1920s. *Printer's Ink*, begun in 1895, evolved into *Advertising Age* by 1916.

Advertisers, as Stephen Fox argued, led the American consumer through four overlapping cycles of advertising "styles" in the brief compass of two generations.[27] These shifts occurred in older promotional methods like outdoor advertising, as well as in newer concepts like national-brand marketing.

In the 1890s, American consumers got their advertising in two contending styles. The first, pioneered by John E. Powers while working for Wanamaker's, stressed plain talk, direct and factual copy, and the importance of content in selling. A second, sometimes called the "jingles and trade character" style—widely used by the Calkins and Holden firm for clients as diverse as the Lackawanna Railroad and Cream of Wheat cereal—attempted to pique curiosity, beguile the commuter's short attention span, and gently but persistently remind the public of its product. The vernacular severity of the "commonplace" style had its opposite in the peppy musical characters of the "jingles" approach. Representing the former were ads such as those for the National Cash Register Company; suggesting the latter were Force cereal's "Sunny Jim" series.

By the turn-of-the-century, other ad approaches appeared. Instead of general claims, folksy personae, or catchy slogans, advertising executive Albert Lasker insisted that an ad should offer a concrete "reason why" the product was worth buying. Consumers would respond to advertisements that were clear, rational forms of salesmanship on paper. Soon "impressionistic copy" or "atmosphere advertising," however, challenged the reason-why format. Its leading advocate, Theodore F. Macmanus, a star copywriter for several auto manufacturers, argued for advertisements that pitched their products obliquely, by suggestion or association. Often drawing theoretical support from the new claims of psychology, atmosphere advertising featured opulent art and striking layouts. While each of these advertising approaches claimed to be "totally new," they were obviously indebted, in concept if not in form, to the earlier contrasting types: the cognitive plain-talk versus the affective jingle paralleled the intellectual reason why versus the emotional atmospheric layout. In addition to these basic ad formats, some merchandisers resorted to blatant racism and ethnic bigotry to sell their goods (figure 4.7).

In addition to traditional formats (handbills, circulars, and posters), advertisers took special advantage of the rapid growth of the metropolitan press (see chapter 5). Department stores like Wanamaker's took full-page advertisements in the metropolitan dailies and featured specialized merchandise (particularly clothing) in Sunday supplements. Wanamaker also advertised his wares through paid newspaper advice columns that instructed consumers about the latest trends in style, etiquette, and fashion appearing as merchandise on his counters.

Before the 1870s, few American magazines carried advertising. Polite editors considered it crass. Two leading women's magazines, *Godey's* and *Peterson's,* did surrender their back covers to the Great American Tea Company, but inside they restricted advertising to less than a page per issue. The genteel literary monthlies—*Atlantic, Harper's, Scribner's*—were underwritten by publishing houses that filled back pages with ads for their own books. *Harper's,* for example, turned down adman George Rowell's offer of eighteen thousand dollars for a back cover promoting the Howe Sewing Machine.

J. Walter Thompson, however, pressed magazine advertising from the agency side of the business, and Cyrus H. N. Curtis promoted magazine publishing through advertising. Thompson worked to make serious magazines more commercial; Curtis made popular journals more serious. Together they helped transform the American magazine, formerly a cultural arbiter of the elite, into a vehicle for middle-class identity and consumerism. Thompson sold advertising for Pabst beer, Mennen talcum powder, Kodak film, Prudential insurance, and Durkee's salad dressing in the "best" magazines—*Atlantic, Harper's,* and *Century*—as well as in the "newest"—*Munsey's, McClure's,* and *Everybody's*—that were designed for middle-class clientele. Curtis created the *Ladies' Home Journal* in 1883, achieving a circulation of several hundred thousand a decade later. In 1897 he bought the struggling *Saturday Evening Post,* reduced its price to a nickel, and by 1904 claimed seven hundred thousand subscribers.

Magazines flooded homes and newsstands (figure 5.1). Whereas in 1885 there were only four monthly magazines with circulations of one hundred thousand, each costing at least thirty-five cents a copy, by 1905 there were twenty such magazines, most selling at ten or fifteen cents, with a combined circulation of 5.5 million.

Critics pondered advertising's transformation of periodical and newspaper publishing. "The advertiser, rather than the subscriber, is now the newspaper bogie," wrote E. L. Godkin, editor of the *Nation* in 1900: "He is the person before whom the publisher cowers and whom he tries to please. . . . There are not many newspapers which can afford to defy a large advertiser." On the other hand, the fictional Mr. Dooley, author Finley Peter Dunne's sage of Chicago's South Side, complained indignantly that he had bought his favorite magazine and found over a quarter of its pages devoted to literature. "Why, he had started reading an ad only to find it was really an article!" If this dangerous trend continued, he warned, people would stop reading magazines: "A man don't want to dodge around through almost impenetrable pomes an' reform articles to find a pair iv suspinders or a shavin' soap."[28]

Advertisers promoted everyday consumption with extraordinary spectacles. Wanamaker, for example, orchestrated parades through the streets of Philadelphia and gave a suit to everyone who returned one of his hot-air advertising balloons. To promote buying, department stores resurrected older holidays and dreamed up new ones, such as Ladies' Day and the Fete d'Autumne, particularly directed at women consumers. Women, in turn, appropriated such advertising strategies to promote women's rights. As William Leach documented, suffragists conducted marches and pageants echoing those arranged by department stores. A purple, violet, and gold color scheme unified the Washington suffrage parade of 1913. "Yellow rallies" were held in New York, with marchers wearing yellow capes and carrying "yellow balls of light in the shape of lanterns." In May 1914 twelve little girls dressed as butterflies, symbolizing the suffragette states to date, led decorated floats and bedecked automobiles in a parade through Louisville, Kentucky.[29]

Outdoor advertising (figure 4.4) assumed a new scale. Promoters of patent medicines set the pace. For example, anyone riding a train between New York and Philadelphia in the 1870s could not miss learning the virtues of Dr. Drake's Plantation Bitters as proclaimed by the passing signs on barns, houses, billboards, and rock outcroppings. Sides of wagons, taxis, and delivery vans carried advertising. Inside streetcars and subways, weekly promotions competed for the commuter's pocketbook. In cities mammoth electric signs were found aside and atop buildings. Six stories high and topped by a forty-foot-long green pickle, the Heinz Company's sign, "57 Good Things for the Table," in New York advertised with the aid of 1,200 light bulbs.

Heinz's slogans, trademarks registered with the U.S. Department of Commerce, typified another advertising innovation. New federal legislation, passed in 1881 (and frequently amended), became the basis for a boom in trademarks: There were 121 registered trademarks in the United States in 1870 compared to over 10,000 filed in 1906 alone.[30]

In the mid-1870s a New York soap-making firm, Enoch Morgan's Sons, produced a small gray cake of scouring soap. The Morgans went to their family physician and asked for an impressively Latin-sounding name for the new product. "Sapolio," said the doctor. At first Sapolio was only a seasonal product, selling most heavily for spring and fall house cleaning. In 1884 the firm hired an advertising agent, Artemas Ward, who over the next two decades, by numerous inventive devices, made Sapolio the most generally recognized trade name of the day. Other advertisers promoted similar national identities for everyday products, such as tobacco, house paint, chewing gum, toiletries, soft drinks, breakfast cereals, and innumerable packaged foods.[31]

The "Battles of the Brands" changed patterns of consumption. For example, in less than half a century, corporate giants like Gold Medal and Pillsbury flour virtually eliminated small-town flour mills. National-brand advertising altered country-store merchandising, promoting greater price competition (if not quality). Along with other new innovations in corporate advertising, it inverted traditional methods of selling goods. Instead of going first to a wholesaler who then conveyed his goods to the retailer, many manufacturers of national brands now increasingly appealed directly to consumers, relying upon advertising to create a demand for their products. Besieged by would-be buyers of Kodak cameras or Arrow collars, the modern retailer placed his order directly with the manufacturer.

National-brand advertising nurtured "consumption communities"—groups of people drawn together, not by political persuasion, nor by racial or ethnic identity, but rather by buying and using the same products, whether they lived in Grinnell, Iowa, or Grosse Pointe, Michigan. As Daniel Boorstin noted, the new consumption communities consisted of "people with a feeling of shared well-being, shared risks, common interests, and common concerns." This feeling came from consuming the same kinds of objects: from "those willing to 'Walk a Mile for a Camel,' to those who wanted 'The Skin You Love to Touch,' or those who 'put their faith in General Motors.'" The national-brand advertisers "constantly told their constituents that by buying their products they could join a special group, and millions of Americans eagerly joined."[32]

CONVENIENCE, COMFORT, CLEANLINESS

Three areas of merchandising—family diet, domestic comfort, and personal hygiene—aptly demonstrate how consumerism pervaded the routine lives of middle-class and working-class Americans.

Food and beverages became highly advertised products only in the 1880s. The concept of the convenient, sanitary, novel, "package"—tin can, glass bottle, sealed cardboard box—transformed marketing strategies by proving that raw goods could be profitably turned into standardized products with national brand names. Canned or packaged foods had a threefold impact: They introduced hitherto unknown foods (or foods eaten only by the wealthy) to a wide American market; they provided easier access to diverse food in isolated regions; and they enabled middle- and working-class women to escape some of the time-consuming work of daily food preparation.[33] Advertisers trumpeted the purity of canned foodstuffs. No human hand touched "Stacey's Workdipt Chocolates," Schlitz cooled its beer in "filtered air," and Boston housewives could buy "Huckins' Hermetically Sealed Soups."

Advertisers also touted processed foods as sophisticated and up to date; being condensed, evaporated, and concentrated, such food and drink claimed to provide more for less. By the turn of the century, canned goods were promoted as scientific and efficient for a generation that prized such values in factory and office, bathroom and kitchen.

As shall be shown in chapter 6, the new cereals changed the traditional meat-and-carbohydrate breakfast. Processed foods likewise transformed the nineteenth-century formal midday dinner, its evening "tea," and supper meal. By 1915, many family eating occasions became shorter and more fragmented. Canned soup, as Campbell's repeatedly told consumers, could be a meal in itself for lunch. So, too, could prepared spaghetti, meat stews, and casseroles. Cooking such foods required only heating them. Convenience foods also invaded evening meals as packaged cake mixes, puddings, and fruit cocktail. The Genessee Pure Food Company of LeRoy, New York, touted Jell-O (figure 4.8) almost from its invention in the 1890s as America's "most quick and easy" dessert. Frank Woodward, an expert in mass marketing, sent salesmen touring the country in special Jell-O trucks to demonstrate the simple preparation of his product at church socials, country fairs, and lodge picnics. Using captivating pictures of young Elizabeth King, "The Jell-O girl," in advertisements beginning in 1904, Woodward also distributed recipe booklets, dessert dishes, and souvenir spoons to make Jell-O a household word by 1915.

The nineteenth-century humorist Josh Billings once observed that "the history of man's necessities is the history of his inventions." While the Victorian era did not invent electricity, it did harness it so that numerous domestic "necessities" seemed mandated to use its power. For example, in the 1910s, Samuel Insull and his Commonwealth Edison staff in Chicago built a sales organization that sold electricity and electrical appliances as mass merchandise through daily newspaper appeals and a free publication called *Electric City Magazine* (figure 4.9). The company also created a chain of fancy appliance stores. Door-to-door salesmen canvassed the city's neighborhoods giving housewives the free use of electric irons for six months. Liberal installment plans stretched the cost of house wiring and appliances over a two-year period. To include the working-class consumers, Insull contracted with subdivision developers to wire new homes for $12, with an additional fee of $2.50 for each outlet. This "entering wedge incentive" as one solicitor called it, usually worked, "so that almost before the householder realized it, he is relying on electricity for his light and various other needs and wondering how he could have gone without it for so long."[34] By 1915, the electric home symbolized the middle-class home. Many electrical devices (the hot plate, coffee pot, immersion heater, chafing dish, and toaster) assisted in the preparation of food, particularly fast, one-step meals. Others, such as electric shaving mugs and curling irons, aided personal grooming.

Diverse promoters sold electric devices that supposedly cured acne, excessive facial hair, cold sores, pimples, dandruff, and, of course, baldness. No bodily process was neglected. Part of the attention such advertisers gave to health products merely continued the patent-medicine hyperboles of early decades. Another part, however, operated on the premise that an industrial society demands uniformity and standardization in ready-made clothing, canned foods, civil servants, and assembly-line workers. "As statistical norms (pulse, temperature, height, weight) became increasingly used to establish national criteria for well-being," argued Robert Atwan and his colleagues, "public tolerance for physical and psychological deviation declined. Advertisers learned that they could manipulate people into thinking themselves either too fat or too skinny, too tall or too short, too restless or too lethargic, too constipated or too diarrhetic."

To profit from such anxieties, advertisers publicized two ideals of the human body: the machine and the model. "The human 'machine,' with its familiar assortment of gears, pipes, tubes, and levers (nervous system wires came with electricity), offered the public a convenient image of internal efficiency and precision— 'runs like a machine' became synonymous with good health. The photogenic model, on the other hand, with her flawless complexion, sparkling teeth, and shapely limbs, represented the external standards of human presentability—the eternal 'after' of countless advertisements."[35]

An enormous amount of pharmaceutical and toiletry advertising (figure 4.10) hinged on standards of efficiency and presentability. In the apt summation of Atwan and his colleagues: "Keep fit and fit in, work like a machine and look like a model." King Gillette's patented (1895) safety razor and disposable blades not only contributed to the full beard's decline and spared men frequent trips to the barber shop but claimed to provide "the modern man" with an opportunity each day to be the "master" of his own time and appearance. Its successful promotion established greater male uniformity in personal grooming. During the Civil War, men grew all manner of beards, mustaches, and other forms of facial hair—goatees, Billy Whiskers, and sideburns (named for Union General A. E. Burnsides) out of necessity and for style. Soldiers in World War I were provided with 3.5 million Gillette razors and 32 million blades to keep the armed forces looking clean shaven, trim, athletic, energetic, and youthful.[36]

To do their daily work better (and also look healthier), American men by 1920 were also urged to eat Force breakfast food, use Pebeco tooth paste, wear an Ingersoll watch, and smoke Tuxedo pipe tobacco (Ty Cobb did) or Lucky Strike cigarettes (Douglas Fairbanks's favorite), after which one chewed Pep-O-Mint Life Savers.

Two ideals of feminine beauty developed over the period 1870–1920. The earlier model was voluptuous and plump, with a full, almost round face; her hair style was termed *à la Madonna* (when pulled back and often braided on each side of her head) or *chignon* (when braided and coiled into a large roll at the back of the head) to balance the backward thrust of her full skirt's bustle. The actress Lillian Russell, first lady Lucy Hayes, and, of course, Queen Victoria herself helped spread this ideal. After 1900, notions about beauty changed as the Gibson Girl offered another model—tall and commanding, slender and athletic. This "new" woman wore her hair *à la pompadour* (a full but not ornate style that emphasized the front rather than the back of the head); or as a *Marcel* (created by French hairdresser Marcel Grateau, who arranged hair in symmetrical waves over the head with a curling iron); or as an American creation: the *bob* (a close-cropped, straight style fashionable after 1910). English actress Jane Harding, dancer Irene Castle, and numerous magazine illustrators popularized these models.

Not without coincidence, given Victorian consumer trends and advertising's cult of physical allure, did a national cosmetics industry emerge in American cities by the 1890s. By the first decade of the twentieth century, the beauty parlor achieved its modern form. Beauty salons, along with commercial entrepreneurs such as Elizabeth Arden and Helena Rubinstein, and department stores promoted national brands of rouge, lipstick, and mascara. Rouge first became popular. As historian Lois Banner has traced, from rouge sticks to lip glosses and finally to eye shadow the movement was speedy. In 1910 beauty writer Elizabeth Reid wrote that "the mania for make-up has spread from the theatrical profession up and down the line, from the aristocratic lady in her private car to the saleswoman and the factory girl." Every restaurant, hotel, and store of any importance, she asserted, kept a supply of cosmetics in their women's rest rooms. Exclusive beauty shops concocted and sold their own preparations, while cosmetics manufacturers spent sizable sums on advertising in the new women's magazines. Most handbags, noted Reid, were sold outfitted with sample cosmetic accessories.[37]

With all sorts of new, mass-produced goods appearing almost daily, advertisers hoped to entice everyone. While much of the new retailing first sought out a middle-class market, advertisers also endeavored to raise workers' expectations for higher standards of material living. For example, after the mother in the novel *Bread Givers* begins to take in boarders and her daughters get full-time jobs, they begin refurnishing their house, buying a table "so solid it didn't spill the soup all over the place," "regular towels" to use instead of old rags, a new soup pot, and plates and utensils "so we could all sit down at the table at the same time and eat like people." As they got used to having new things, they began to want more: "We no sooner got used to regular towels than we began to want toothbrushes. . . . We got the toothbrushes and we began wanting toothpowder to brush our teeth with, instead of ashes. And more and more we wanted more things, and really needed more things, the more we got them."[38]

FIGURE I.1. The World's Columbian Exposition as the White City, the Electricity Building, Chicago (1893). Photograph courtesy of the Chicago Historical Society.

FIGURE I.2. Racial prejudice in Chicago's White City. "Darkies' Day at the Fair," *Puck* magazine (1893). Courtesy of the Library of Congress, Division of Prints and Photographs.

᪐

CHICAGO launched its first world's fair with rituals similar to those opening the Centennial Exhibition. Following a Columbian hymn, ode, and march, President Grover Cleveland, the first Democrat elected to the White House since 1856, read the required presidential address. Shortly afterward, he pressed a button that sent electricity pulsating through the fair site. A shroud fell from Daniel Chester French's giant *Statue of the Republic* and, since the United States had no official national anthem, an orchestra played "America, The Beautiful."

Whereas the Philadelphia fairgrounds could be compared to a pleasure park, the Chicago setting evoked a planned, albeit idealized, urban environment. Its scale, density of buildings, and municipal services all suggested a model metropolis. As the first "City Beautiful," it influenced the next two decades of American urban design.

The Columbian site came dressed in the architecture of Beaux Arts classicism. Around a formal court with its central Administration Building clustered buildings housing what Americans, in the 1890s, deemed basic to their economy: Railroads, Machinery, Manufactures, Agriculture. Two buildings, Mining and Electricity, signaled the expansion of the extractive industries and the growing utilization of a new source of power. Encircling a miniature park called The Wooded Island, one found Louis Sullivan's Transportation Building, the Women's Building and its adjoining Children's Building, plus two massive structures of state: the Illinois Building and the United States Building. Finally, to the west stretched the Midway Plaisance, a mile-long recreational corridor.

Although the White City contained few residences, many exhibits displayed trends in domestic life. For example, the growing competition between gas and electricity as home utilities could be seen by visiting three different model kitchens. In the Manufacturers and Liberal Arts Building, period-room settings of furniture, display cases of tableware, and showrooms of textiles went on for miles.

While many states contributed extensive housekeeping exhibits, New York constructed an actual residence. Katherine Davis, a Rochester social reformer, coordinated the designing and furnishing of the Workingman's Model Home. She imagined a young engaged couple—a laboring man earning $500 a year and a woman, a domestic servant, making $156 a year plus board—as its prospective buyers. Their house, a two-story, wood-frame dwelling, built at a cost not to exceed $1,000, contained a front parlor, a kitchen, and a bath with a tub and water closet. The upstairs had a front bedroom and two smaller children's bedrooms. A range and room stoves heated the house. In the two-year engagement Davis conjectured for her hypothetical couple, she calculated that the two could amass $400, of which $100 would be kept as savings, leaving $300 for furnishing their mortgaged dwelling. Lists of what such household items cost were posted next to the objects throughout the home exhibit. Similarly, Davis priced and displayed all the clothing that her hypothetical family (to which she added an eight-year-old boy, a five-year-old girl, and an infant) would need over a year. Finally, she researched feeding this "average" family. Calculating both the cost of foods in Chicago markets and the nutritional content of her purchases, Davis prepared daily meals during a month of the fair and served them to a policeman and an Irish widow with three children.[1]

In the Electricity Building (figure I.1), another model home suggested the domestic future: electric stoves, hot plates, washing machines, and carpet sweepers, plus electric doorbells, fire alarms, and innumerable lighting fixtures. The Westinghouse Company's mammoth dynamos symbolized to Henry Adams a new energy force whose application to common life seemed unlimited. As the telegraph and telephone dramatized electricity's potential at Philadelphia, now phonographs and Kinetoscopes suggested still newer types of communication at Chicago.

Electricity illuminated miles of consumer goods displayed throughout the forty-four acre Manufacturers and Liberal Arts Building, the largest department store the world had ever seen. Many of the wares that were exhibited were for sale and carried price tags so visitors could do comparison shopping. Among the most popular items were Morris chairs, the "Clasp Locker or Unlocker for Shoes" (an early slide fastener or zipper), garden furniture, bathroom fixtures, baby carriages, and rural telephones. As Burton Benedict has pointed out in *The Anthropology of World's Fairs* (1983), such products could be used as fences or bridges: In world's fairs, exhibitors were mostly building bridges, expanding their markets, but they, as well as their customers, recognized the importance of goods as fences to mark off one status group from another.[2] The enormous range of goods at the Chicago fair provided a cornucopia of material culture that not only catered to middle-class taste but helped to form that taste.

"One of the manias dearest to Americans consists in meeting in groups and founding societies apropos of everything and apropos of nothing," wrote French composer Jacques Offenbach in 1877. "Any pretext is good, and associations abound in the United States." World's fairs provided a special forum for the middle-class's penchant for the associative life. The Philadelphia fair hosted national gatherings of Odd Fellows, Knights Templars, the American Banking Association, and the Socialist party. The Chicago fair established a separate World's Congress Auxiliary of 14,000 members, who organized 139 national conferences attracting more than 700,000 participants. Most popular were those on education (at which G. Stanley Hall and John Dewey spoke), labor (with addresses by Samuel Gompers and Henry George) and women (at which Julia Ward Howe and Frances Willard were featured speakers). The World's Parliament of Religions, lasting seventeen days, reflected both American pluralism and the country's anxiety over the future of belief in an age of increasing materialism.[3]

Chicago's Midway Plaisance in the course of a summer became known simply as "the midway," a new term subsequently applied to commercial entertainment zones common to county fairs, tent chautauquas, or trolley parks. Unlike Philadelphia's "Centennial City"—an Elm Avenue strip of restaurants, ice-cream parlors, dioramas, and beer gardens located just outside the 1876 fair's main entrance—Chicago's midway achieved a degree of official status, since the fair's organizers classified it under a Department of Ethnology. The polyglot midway presented a diverse counterculture to the moral earnestness of the White City. Here the Court of Honor and the *Statue of the Republic* gave way to the Streets of Cairo and George Ferris's Wheel. Fair goers, on foot or in hired chairs, made their way through a riot of attractions: Turkish bazaars, Hawaiian volcanoes, Hagenbeck's circus animals. Flesh was flaunted—by world heavyweight champion Jim Corbett, by hootchy-kootchy dancer Little Egypt, and by bodybuilder Bernarr MacFadden.

Visitors could ride several types of railroads, make a 1,500-foot ascent in a captive balloon, or, for fifty cents, purchase two revolutions on the Ferris Wheel, the unofficial icon of the dynamic, heterogeneous midway. Chicago's answer to Paris's 1889 Eiffel Tower, Ferris's 264-foot bicycle wheel in the sky dominated the landscape. With thirty-six cars, each larger than a Pullman coach and capable of holding 60 people, the wheel, when fully loaded, rotated 2,160 people in the air.

The Columbian exposition featured living ethnological displays of nonwhite cultures. These exhibits of people, rather than goods, appeared on the midway, juxtaposed with wild-animal acts, joyrides, and other side shows. The village displays frequently reinforced American racial prejudices and ethnic stereotypes. Often depicting people as curiosities (the Javanese) or trophies (the Sioux), the exhibits were staged along what one contemporary called "a sliding scale of humanity." Nearest to the White City were the Teutonic and Celtic races, represented by the two German and two Irish enclaves. The midway's middle contained the Muhammadan and Asian worlds. Then, continued the observer, "we descend to the savage races, the African of Dahomey and the North American Indian, each of which has its place" at the remotest end of the midway (figure I.2). Blacks repeatedly petitioned Congress for Afro-American exhibits in both the fair's main structures and in the state pavilions, but the only official display mounted presented the Hampton Institute's educational program.[4] While Chicago had a growing black population, discrimination barred them from the fair's construction crews and clerical staffs.

Other tensions at the fair revealed additional paradoxes that were emblematic of American culture at large. For example, Daniel Burnham's Beaux Arts prescription at the fair for the model American metropolis seemed at odds with his architectural firm's downtown (in Chicago and elsewhere) modern skyscrapers—awesome vertical towers that radically altered urban life. The displays in the Women's Building contrasted with activities in the World Congress of Beauty ("40 Girls from 40 Countries"). Buffalo Bill's Wild West shows drew sell-out audiences, while a thirty-two-year-old Wisconsin professor named Frederick Jackson Turner told his colleagues at a meeting of the American Historical Association at the fair that frontier America was over.

A greater paradox was yet to come. In 1893 Americans honored the duke of Veragera and the Spanish Infanta as the diplomatic representatives of the country that, four hundred years earlier, had dispatched Columbus on his epic voyage; five years later, many of those same Americans cheered the military humiliation of Spain in what Secretary of State John Hay would call "that splendid little war."

Daniel Burnham, in typical Chicago bravado, claimed the

Columbian Exposition to be the third greatest event in American history, the other two occurring in 1776 and 1861. Unlike those at the Centennial, Americans in 1893 reveled in their historical identity. At this fair the Colonial Revival style characterized many state pavilions, the first commemorative postage stamps and coins were issued, and a new holiday and new ceremony were added to everyday life. Francis J. Bellamy, an editor of *Youth's Companion*, proposed a plan for the fair's dedication (Columbus Day, October 12, 1892) whereby children across the country could participate in concurrent celebrations in their schools. Bellamy drafted the Pledge of Allegiance to the flag of the United States, which the federal Bureau of Education circulated to teachers nationwide. As a hundred thousand people in Chicago witnessed the fair's dedication and the pledge's recitation, millions of children around the country also promised their national allegiance, thus beginning a ritual that has since been repeated daily in the schools.[5]

Chicago in 1893 also introduced Americans to Cream of Wheat cereal, Aunt Jemima pancake mix, Postum, Juicy Fruit gum, Shredded Wheat, and Pabst Blue Ribbon (the fair's award-winning beer). That year, rural telephone companies proliferated as the 1876 Bell patents expired; *McClure's* magazine was first issued at 15 cents a copy; Sears, Roebuck sent out its first 500-page catalog; and the "Sooners" and thousands of other would-be Oklahomans staked out the Cherokee Strip. The murder trial of Lizzie Borden, a thirty-two-year-old spinster from Fall River, Massachusetts, monopolized the gossip of fair goers, as did a children's street chant: "Lizzie Borden took an axe / And gave her mother forty whacks. / And when she saw what she had done / She gave her father forty-one."

In Washington, D.C., Coxey's Army (figure 1.9) chanted, 1,500 strong, to demand relief for the unemployed as the country's worst economic depression to date deepened owing to the era's continuing boom-bust business cycles. Wall Street stocks plunged on May 5, with the market all but collapsing on June 27. Six hundred banks closed their doors, thousands of business firms failed, and seventy-four railroads (including the Philadelphia and Reading, the North Pacific, Erie, and the Santa Fe) went into receivership.[6] As the World's Columbian Exposition closed on October 29, 1893, its flags were lowered to half staff to mourn the brutal death of Chicago's five-term mayor, Carter Harrison, by an assassin's revolver at his home the night before. Four more years of widespread unemployment, labor protest, farm foreclosures, business bankruptcies, and economic turmoil were only beginning.

FIGURE 5.1. Detroit Photo Company, *A Characteristic Sidewalk, Newsstand, New York City* (ca. 1900). Photograph courtesy of the Library of Congress, Division of Prints and Photographs.

FIGURE 5.2. Comet Theatre, Third Avenue between 12th and 13th Streets, New York City (ca. 1910). Photograph courtesy of the Quigley Photographic Archive, Georgetown University Library.

5   COMMUNICATING

Victorian Americans witnessed an unprecedented diffusion
and a diversification of communication techniques. The circulation of daily newspapers, for instance, increased sevenfold, the
number of post offices tripled, the sale of postage stamps increased
eight times, the volume of telegraph messages grew by a factor of
seven, and the publication of new books tripled.

Various innovations, some as simple as the penny postcard (introduced in 1873), others as complex as Ottmar Mergenthaler's
linotype machine (1884), stimulated what many historians regard
as a "communications revolution." Its implications were wide
reaching. "Consciousness itself was altered," claimed Warren Susman. "The very perception of time and space was radically
changed."[1] By 1915, Americans kept in touch not only through
traditional personal contact and correspondence but also via new
mechanisms, such as the telephone. The phonograph, snapshot,
and motion picture suddenly made experience repeatable. These
new means of communications transmitted some messages that
were recorded and relatively permanent and others that were
transitory and erasable; many emphasized visual and aural experience over purely verbal expression.

Pictures proliferated, making the era a highly visual civilization.
Newspapers by 1915 included halftone photography, comic strips,
and rotogravure sections. Chromolithographs, stereoscopes, and
snapshot albums filled middle-class homes. New Yorkers saw the
nation's first "moving pictures" in 1896.

Extending Verbal Discourse

LETTER WRITING AND MAIL SYSTEMS

The written and printed word provided news, ideas, and companionship for those who were unable, because of isolation or distance, to communicate with others in person. While almanacs, newspapers, and trade catalogs disseminated public information and amusement, the letter sustained individual relations. Americans who were concerned about the safe arrival of an immigrant relative, the health of a friend homesteading in the Nevada Territory, or the fate of their business awaited the mails. To order goods, take an extension course at a state university, pay bills, send money home, join the Chautauqua movement's book-of-the-month club, express their views in a newspaper, or pledge their love, Americans wrote letters.

Several developments encouraged Americans to write more. The eighteenth-century's common "lead" pencil, a slender wooden cylinder at the tip of which a point of lead is exposed for writing, went into mass production a century later, selling at two for a penny by 1900. Lewis E. Waterman manufactured the first practical "hydraulic" or "fountain pen" with an ink reservoir in 1884. Writing paper, now machine made with wood pulp replacing rags as its primary raw ingredient, became available to virtually any pocketbook; its varieties, grades, colors, and finishes multiplied.

Although illiteracy rates dropped significantly (see chapter 7), not everyone wrote his or her own letters. Country merchants (whose stores frequently housed local post offices) often served as amanuenses for patrons. Rural-free-delivery (RFD) mailmen did the same along their routes. Settlement house workers performed similar services, often helping immigrants complete money orders to send back home. One historian estimated that in 1907, U.S. postal money orders, valued at nearly $100 million, were mailed to Italy alone.

Manuals of epistolary etiquette proliferated as social conduct, at least for the middle class, became more complicated. Mourning, for example, received special attention. Manuals advised the bereaved person to begin his or her first year of mourning for a spouse by using mourning stationery: black-edged paper, envelopes with a black border and sealed with black wax, and calling cards with quarter-inch black borders. The thickness of the black borders decreased as mourners neared their second year of formal grief.

Postal rates continually dropped in the late nineteenth century. The first adhesive postage stamps—a five-cent Franklin and a ten-cent Washington—humorously called "lick and stick" when issued in 1847—prompted the children's game, Post Office, by 1854. In 1863 first-class postage dropped to three cents, irrespective of distance, and twenty years later it decreased again to two cents per half ounce. Proliferating postage stamps (the first U.S. commemorative series was issued for the 1893 Columbian Exposition) also prompted a new hobby, philately.

Before 1863, everyone picked up and deposited his or her own mail at the post office or paid a letter carrier an additional two cents service fee per letter. Free home delivery began during the Civil War in the larger Northern cities, and the service was extended in 1873 to other urban areas populations of 20,000, and then to towns of 10,000 by 1887. RFD started in 1896 on an experimental basis.

Residential mail delivery produced two common sights of everyday life: the mail box on the landscape and the postman on his route. At first, home mail boxes, left to the discretion of the resident, appeared in sundry shapes, sizes, and colors. On rural routes, individuality reigned. In North Yakima, Washington, an observer reported in 1897: "one man has a lard pail hung out on a fence post; three or four have nailed up empty coal oil cans, and a few have utilized syrup cans. . . . Old apple boxes, soap boxes, cigar boxes, and in one instance a wagon box, adorn the entrance to farms all over the valley."[2] By 1902, the federal post office set standards for the size and construction of all personal boxes, requiring that they bear the marking "Approved By the Postmaster General."

City mail carriers often delivered in both the morning and the afternoon. After 1871, they might work out of a branch post office; in addition to sorting, delivering, and collecting mail, they sold stamps, postcards, and money orders. At one time, they administered oaths to Civil War veterans when completing pay vouchers for the delivery of pension checks. They provided their own shoes and uniforms.

Rural carriers, beginning in 1896, had similar responsibilities but purchased additional equipment. Almost every rural mailman before World War I had to have at least one horse, a harness, and a buggy. Many maintained two horses, and those with long routes kept additional teams. By 1914, a carrier made an average yearly salary of $1,200, part of which, of necessity, went for horse stabling, feed, and the maintenance of equipment.

Many rural carriers delivered more than mail. In the early years of the service, they brought weather reports from the telegraph or newspaper office. They monitored a community's vital statistics—deaths, births, engagements, and marriages. They kept patrons posted on each other's health, the price of goods in town, who was planting, and who was harvesting. Enterprising businessmen advertised in the *R.F.D. News* ways for rural carriers to make extra money by taking orders for household goods, distributing free samples of products, or selling insurance. "They sell," said the *New York Sun* in 1904, "provisions, dry goods, furniture, horseshoes, farming implements, fertilizer, chocolate caramels, and tar roofing; take subscriptions for newspapers, magazines, and turf investment bureaus; insure lives and houses, erect lightning rods, and put down driven wells. One Iowa mail carrier's delivery business grew so large he towed three large wagons of merchandise as he delivered the mail."[3]

Congress curtailed such practices in 1904, but with the introduction of a domestic parcel post system in 1911, the government entered the package business on a new scale. COD ("Cash-on-Delivery" or "Collect-on-Delivery") was only one of several postal innovations. Others included special delivery service (1886), postal savings banks (1911), and the beginning of air mail service (1917). The number of post offices expanded (figure 5.3), reaching their peak (76,945) in American history in 1901. More than 70,000 of these centers of local life were fourth-class stations, and, after two decades of consolidation, their number dropped to 41,102 by 1920.

POSTCARDS AND GREETING CARDS

First introduced in 1873 as a promotional mailing device for businesses, hotels, and resorts, the postcard turned out to be one of the era's crazes. After 1906, when Congress authorized messages on one-half of the address side, the cards served as short letters. In that year, 770.5 million cards were mailed in the United States. By 1909, this number had risen to 968 million; the Illustrated Postcard Company alone produced 3 million cards a day.

Collecting postcards proved immediately popular. Many publishers produced them in a numbered series to encourage the habit. They also marketed postcard albums. To display cards effectively in stores, E. I. Dail, a drummer from Lansing, Michigan, invented a special revolving steel rack in 1908. The device enabled customers to wait on themselves. The concept—an early form of self-service merchandising—led to display racks for books, magazines, comics, greeting cards, and sheet music.

A break with the traditional epistolary style in favor of a clipped new form of communication, postcard messages suited an age of speed and convenience, with people using them to acknowledge that "they had received your letter and will write soon." Travelers posted cards to relate their progress (especially when changing trains); they also purchased them as mementos of vacations and excursions.

Actual photocards (photographs developed and imprinted as postcards) were made by national companies, such as the Detroit Publishing Company (which alone produced some sixteen thousand different views) and by small-town druggists who sent photographs or negatives to Germany (where many U.S. cards were printed before 1906). Every aspect of everyday life survives in this visual archive of three-by-five-inch images: holiday celebrations, fairs, circuses, beauty contests, and baby pageants. Postcards promoted bigotry as well as cosmopolitanism; many that featured black, Indian, or Oriental subjects fostered racist and ethnic stereotypes.

Postcards served as the poor man's greeting card. Mother's Day (1911) and Father's Day (1913), two new American holidays, could be remembered with a postcard or with a more elaborate greeting card enclosed in an envelope. The printed Christmas card first appeared in the United States in 1874, brought out by Bavarian-born Boston lithographer Louis Prang. Like other Christmas innovations of Victorian America—Thomas Nast's Santa Claus (1881), the Christmas bonus (1899), the electric Christmas tree (1902), and the Christmas club (1910)—Christmas cards contributed to making a folk holy day (quietly celebrated in antebellum America) into a nationwide festival of consumption.[4]

METROPOLITAN NEWSPAPERS AND NATIONAL MAGAZINES

Although the transformation of the content, format, and readership of the metropolitan press is the main story of American journalism between 1876 and 1915, it should be noted that the weeklies and semiweeklies that were published chiefly in rural towns also grew and had their influence. For example, the two states carved out of the Dakota territory contained 25 dailies and 315 weeklies at the turn of the century. By that date, 18 million Americans subscribed to publications, such as the *Algona Pioneer Press* (Iowa), the *Lacon Home Journal* (Illinois), or the *Greencastle Banner* (Indiana), compared to 15 million who bought an urban paper everyday. As Edgar Howe and William Allen White would point out, these eight-to-ten-page papers, often the work of a single editor-printer, detailed local news; their format was predictable, their style vernacular.[5] Many subscribers received their papers through the mails, since, as early as 1851, weeklies could be mailed postage free within the county where they were published.

By contrast, the metropolitan daily was graphic, multiple (nine to ten editions a day), and big (twenty-four to thirty-six pages). While the period's competing editors—Joseph Pulitzer, Edward Wyllis Scripps, and William Randolph Hearst—made the headlines, an army of reporters, copy editors, artists, photographers, columnists, admen, printers, and newsboys made the newspaper. These metropolitan papers, using new technologies such as high-speed ("lightning") presses and news services coordinated by telegraph and telephone, both chronicled and changed everyday life. Their number doubled (from 971 to 2,226) between 1870 and 1900.

How do we explain this growth? What made the metropolitan press so popular? To begin with, evening dailies gradually outnumbered morning editions three to one. Although evening papers dated from the eighteenth century, they expanded with the nineteenth-century development of kerosene, gas, and finally electric lighting as publishers sought to catch people heading home from work and shopping. Sunday newspapers grew as publishers promoted reading the Sunday paper as a diversion and ritual for people who were tied to offices or factories six days a week. They expanded it to include special Sunday supplements on travel, sports, and entertainment, as well as features like Sunday comics, horoscopes, crossword puzzles, and a Sunday magazine.

Dividing the Sunday edition into separate sections paralleled changes in the daily's format where a reader, with the help of graphics, columns, and indexes, increasingly sought out the special departments particular to his or her interests. Segregating news reports, editorials, features, and advertisements, argued Gunther Barth, imposed "a verbal order on chaotic urban life." "The ancient practice of throwing all news items together into the columns of a paper without reference to either character or locality, is gradually but surely dying out," the *Journalist* stressed in 1887: "It is comparatively rare now-a-days to find a wedding following a murder, and a church dedication after a raid on a disorderly house."

Women, who had been largely ignored by antebellum journalism, were courted as readers of the metropolitan press. For example, in 1883, the *New York World* provided fashion news and beauty tips. *The Philadelphia Inquirer,* in the late 1880s, featured "women topics" ranging from child care to serialized novels in its Sunday Section. About the same time, a "Woman's Page" (furnished by the Bok Syndicate) came with the Sunday edition of the *St. Louis Republican;* here one found a "Room and Boarders Directory," biographies of well-known women, club and society news, plus household and fashion hints.[6]

Sports pages appeared in American papers by the 1880s. Joseph Pulitzer, expanding the sports reporting pioneered by weeklies, such as the *Spirit of the Times* and the *National Police Gazette,* staffed his *World* with several experts to write on baseball, horse racing, bicycling, and boxing. A sports page served as a surrogate for men and boys who could not watch, much less play, the games of summer. Baseball news dominated and seemed especially suited to being retold via the newspapers. Sports pages everywhere celebrated the statistic. In charts, tables, and box scores, fans could search out "firsts," compare averages, and note exceptions.

Three new features—the advice column, the human-interest story, and the local color column—widened the appeal and the urban imperialism of the metropolitan press. Although the *New York World* ran a series of "advice letters" briefly in 1883, "Dorothy Dix" (Mrs. Elizabeth M. Gilmer) seems to have launched the first true advice column in 1896 in the *New Orleans Picayune*. Two years later, "Beatrice Fairfax" (originally Marie Manning) introduced the feature into the *New York Journal,* where, by 1915, it spawned a popular song "Beatrice Fairfax—Tell Me What To Do." Syndication quickly spread the views of newspaper counselors to millions. Though they specialized on suggestions to the lovelorn, these counselors also advised on many other aspects of everyday conduct.

Human-interest stories also helped personalize the anonymity of city life for urban readers. As Gunther Barth suggested, such "stories related the complexities of urban actions from the perspective of village life. Their intimate scale made it possible to identify people 'lost' in the daily shuffle, bypassed in the pursuit of riches, their misery ignored by neighbors as well as officialdom." Short human-interest features singling out "seemingly anonymous people fostered the recognition of divergent urban life-styles."[7] These reports paralleled the short stories of O. Henry, collected in *The Four Million* and *The Voice of the City* (some having first appeared in the *New York World*)—stories that focused on the local and the typical. Chicago local colorists like George Ade or Peter Finley Dunne created a literature of everyday life within a thousand-word limit story. Their daily columns, featuring such characters as "Mr. Dooley," "Doc Horn," and "Pink Marsh," interpreted the nineteenth century's greatest news story—the rise of the city—to Victorian Americans. Dunne's fictional vignettes emanating from Dooley's working-class saloon on "Archey Road"

(Archer Avenue) in Chicago achieved national prominence through syndication. Ade's work remained best known to Midwestern newspaper readers via his column, "Stories of the Streets and Town."[8]

The typographical boredom of the pre–Civil War newspaper layout gave way to new graphic displays. *Frank Leslie's Illustrated Newspaper* (1855) pioneered the wider visual documentation; by the 1880s, dailies like Pulitzer's *World* made woodcut and steel-engraved illustrations essential to news reporting and cartoons. A decade later, cartoons led to comics. Richard F. Outcault drew a single-panel cartoon, "Down Hogan's Alley," for the *World* Sunday editions of 1893. Its hero, an odd-looking youngster (figure 5.7) who wore a long night shirt, monitored the everyday antics of residents in a New York slum. The paper's printers, who had been experimenting with techniques to introduce color, suggested that the boy's shirt should be yellow to attract the readers' attention. The "Yellow Kid" appeared on February 16, 1896, beginning the tradition of Sunday color comics. Outcault lettered his flippant, slang-laden comments right onto the "Kid's" nightshirt; soon the Yellow Kid's likeness adorned everything from lapel buttons to cigarette packs. To some, the color comics and the papers in which they first appeared symbolized all that was ugly about the aggressive, garish, new journalism; they therefore labeled it "yellow journalism." When William Randolph Hearst lured Outcault and his creation to the *New York Journal,* the *World* promptly hired another artist, George B. Luks, to continue the series. Hence, for a time, two of the era's most famous yellow journalists, Hearst and Pulitzer, competed for circulation supremacy with two "Yellow Kids."

Thousands of kids—the era's newsboys and -girls—distributed the metropolitan papers. These urchins of the streets, exemplars of "pluck and luck" in many Horatio Alger novels and examples of the exploitation of child labor in many Lewis Hine photographs, cajoled their customers into buying newspapers whether they wanted to or not. Their aggressive salesmanship dated back to the 1830s. At that time, Benjamin H. Day bypassed the customary list of subscribers for his new penny paper and sold, cash in advance, one hundred copies of the New York *Sun* for sixty-seven cents to boys who pocketed thirty-three cents after they had cornered a hundred buyers.

Youngsters also hawked magazines on city streets and, working door to door, sold subscriptions. Aided by improved methods of manufacturing paper, printing, and photoengraving, plus the cheaper mailing rates established by Congress in 1879, these new magazines (figure 5.1) sought a mass national audience. The British critic William Archer remarked: "There is nothing quite like them in the literature of the world—no periodicals which combine such width of popular appeal with such seriousness of aim and thoroughness of workmanship."[9] They were all family magazines, and if some of them became mediums for the muckrakers of the next decade, they published nothing radical. Without sensationalism, they presented readers with a livelier style than the established journals and a lavish use of illustrations. A brief review of the *Ladies' Home Journal* and the *Saturday Evening Post* suggests their appeal.[10]

Edward Bok's *Journal,* a feminine but not feminist publication, preached a conservatism that reassured homemakers of the properness of their traditional roles. Bok introduced fiction by the best new writers, inexpensive house plans by Frank Lloyd Wright, and special departments like "Ruth Ashmore's Side Talks With Girls," which received an average of ten thousand readers' letters a year. He used the *Journal* to elevate American taste, lecturing his readers on the virtues of rugged Mission-style furniture and on the immorality of Queen Anne interiors.

What Bok did for the *Ladies' Home Journal,* George H. Lorimer paralleled in the *Saturday Evening Post.* By 1913, the *Post* claimed a weekly circulation of over two million, making it the most widely distributed magazine in the world. In its pages were the stories of Booth Tarkington and Stephen Crane, the political philosophies of Senator Albert J. Beveridge and William Jennings Bryan, the arts commentaries of Oscar Hammerstein I and John T. McCutcheon, sports coverage by Alonzo Stagg and Jack Dempsey, and the illustrations of P. C. Leyendecker and Norman Rockwell. With its histories of business and industry, biographies and autobiographies of self-made entrepreneurs, and political commentary favorable to the Republican Party, the *Post* exuded middle-class stability and taste.

New weekly and monthly popular magazines promoted the short story as a genre in American letters and the feature article as a stock item in American journalism. Moreover, there was hardly an important novel of the period that was not serialized or excerpted in their pages. The *Saturday Evening Post*, for example, published Frank Norris, Owen Wister, Ellen Glasgow, Edith Wharton, Theodore Dreiser, Willa Cather, and Sinclair Lewis. Investigative reporting, made famous by Ida M. Tarbell and Lincoln Steffens, the personal interview, and eventually the photo essay were all pioneered in the American magazine. The front covers and interior graphics (Charles Dana Gibson first drew the Gibson Girl for *Colliers*) of these magazines formed new artistic sensibilities as the back covers and advertising displays stimulated new desires in consumers.

Electronic Media

TELEGRAPHS AND TELEPHONES

Samuel F. B. Morse first intended to use his 1838 invention of the telegraph solely for government communications. Quickly, however, others saw additional markets. Soon newspapers began publishing "Telegraphic News," causing the *Philadelphia Public Ledger* (May 22, 1844) to claim: "This is indeed the annihilation of space." By 1858, the transatlantic cable successfully transmitted European news to the front page of American papers. To economize on the costs of telegraph news, editors formed press associations. The telegraph shifted the definition of news. An editor no longer awaited information; he dispatched reporters who went out to look for news to keep the telegraph clicking and the presses running.

In his patent application, Alexander Graham Bell first called his invention "an improvement of the telegraph." Bell recognized, as did many others, that while the telegraph system provided an expandable, high-speed, communication network, it still did not offer the advantages of actual human dialogue, the intimacy of a personal voice, or the dual exchange of conversation. Although it condensed space, the telegraph remained an elite, almost mysterious artifact, accessible only through an operator who was trained to transmit its messages in code. Numerous intermediaries stood between the originator of a telegram and its recipient. Not so with the telephone; it ultimately permitted instant, person-to-person communication.

Bell, a teacher of the deaf and a student of electromagnetic induction, searched for a mechanical analogue of the human ear's membrane to act as a transmitter and a receiver of the human voice. By 1876, his efforts to enlarge the capacity of an experimental telegraph led him to a theory of how it might be done: "If I could make a current of electricity vary in intensity, precisely as the air varies in density during the production of a sound, I should be able to transmit speech telegraphically." He and his assistant, Thomas Watson, accomplished this feat for the first time on March 10, 1876. As they began an experiment on a new transmitter, Bell accidentally spilled some battery acid on his clothes and called in dismay, "Watson, come here! I want you." Watson, in another room, heard the message clearly from the diaphragm of his receiver, rushed down the hall to Bell's room—and the two men knew that at last they could send human speech over an electric wire.[11]

The first central telephone exchange, serving twenty-one subscribers, opened in New Haven, Connecticut, in 1878. From this office came the first telephone directory, one that listed only names and addresses, since phone numbers were not yet used to identify patrons. As phone networks grew, larger switchboards were needed. So were more operators. Young men were first employed, but their unreliability, rowdiness in the exchange, and tendency to talk back to callers prompted their replacement by women.

Women soon monopolized this new service industry (figure 5.4) supposedly because of their more pleasing voices and nimbler fingers and their willingness to work for ten dollars a week. Often called "hello girls" in the 1880s, by the early 1890s they were known, as was the local telephone exchange, as "Central." At first, new operators started work with little more than a few friendly hints from the next woman on the board, but eventually Bell training programs and floor supervisors standardized the etiquette of operators. Operators first asked: "What number?" By 1904, a Bell-company regulation insisted on the query "Number Please?" spoken pleasantly with a rising inflection. In 1912 the New York Telephone Company summarized the qualities of a good operator with the mixed metaphor: "The Voice With a Smile."

Several hundred operators worked around the clock in urban phone exchanges. In rural areas and small towns, "Central" was often a single individual at a small switchboard in a home or store. According to a 1905 magazine article, among typical requests of the local operator were the following: "Oh, Central! Ring me up in fifteen minutes, so I won't forget to take the bread out of the oven." "Say, Central, I have put the receiver of the phone in the baby's cradle, and if she wakes up and cries, call me up." "Central, ring me up half an hour before the 2:17 train in the morning. See if it's late before you call, please."[12]

Many of these rural operators worked for telephone companies that competed with American Telephone & Telegraph (AT&T) when its first telephone patents expired. By 1900, more than a thousand independent local exchanges had been established in Iowa alone. That year Bell had 800,000 telephones in service, compared to some 600,000 for the independents, and assets of over $120 million, in contrast to the independents' $55 million. Thousands of do-it-yourself telephone systems existed in remote areas served neither by Bell nor the independents. Farmers would pool resources, cut their own poles, buy the necessary wire, insulators, phones, and a switchboard, and install their own system for a few dozen rural families. In 1907, the U.S. Bureau of the Census counted 17,702 separate, private, rural circuits with 565,000 telephones and 486,000 miles of wire in service.[13]

Many towns had two telephone companies and two phone books. Some communities in Iowa had three. Businesses, in particular, had to maintain and advertise "Both phones" or be unavailable by telephone to one set of subscribers or the other. Competition lowered rates but caused inconvenience. Competing systems sometimes mirrored class differences. In Minneapolis, for example, the Bell system catered to the socially elite, while the competing Tri-State Telephone Company served just about every-body else. Beginning in 1908, T. H. Vail, the head of the Bell empire, launched a policy of buying up the independents under the slogan, "One Policy, One System, Universal Service."[14] By 1913, when the Justice Department invoked the Sherman Anti-Trust Act and pressed AT&T to stop such purchases unless approved by the Interstate Commerce Commission, the Bell system had already eliminated its major competitors and was on its way to becoming the largest U.S. corporation.

Over its first forty years, the telephone developed from a rectangular black box (1876) to a large microphone (1880), to an upright desk set (1892) with a mouthpiece-transmitter on a vertical stalk and a butter stamp for the earpiece-receiver. Wall sets were also available. In 1891, a Kansas City mortician, Almon B. Strowger, patented the first automatic direct-dial system. Strowger—at least according to legend—had been having trouble with local operators who, he was convinced, deliberately gave busy signals or wrong numbers when potential customers called him. Accordingly, he set out to invent a switchboard system that would eliminate the operator. He succeeded in creating one that would accommodate ninety-nine phones. Direct dialing, however, did not come into widespread use until the 1920s.

Telephone usage expanded quickly. Americans owned 1.3 million phones in 1900, a figure that grew to 13.3 million in 1920. Within a year of its debut at the Centennial Exhibition, the telephone had been used in news reporting, for advertising, and for long-distance communication. By the end of the 1880s, it sped up the time it took to get the doctor, reduced the time required for shopping, and expanded the time for conducting love affairs. Anytime telephone talk gradually replaced afternoon card calling; instead of requesting a name and address, you asked for a phone number. Finally, it also marked, as one biographer of Bell put it, the final "conquest of solitude."[15]

Telephones raised new questions of etiquette for users, as well as for operators: What should appropriate telephone manners be? How does one answer the telephone properly? Thomas Edison suggested that the caller be greeted not with "Hello" but with "Ahoy, ahoy!" Proper conduct on a party line also required definition. A new temptation had been introduced into farm life, reported *The World's Work* in April 1905. A farm wife, who had telephone service for just a few months, was asked how her family liked it. Her reply: "Well, we liked it a lot at first, and do yet, only spring work is coming on so heavy that we don't hardly have time to listen now."[16]

Telephones slowly changed the way Americans talked. Language became less formal, phone conversations being less mannered than letter writing. New expressions—"Give me a ring" or "I'll give you a buzz"—entered American speech. Quickly the telephone captured popular fancy and became a subject for greeting cards, vaudeville skits, and popular songs: "Drop a Nickel, Please," "Hello Central, Give Me Heaven," "Call Me Up Some Rainy Afternoon," and the favorite, "All Alone by the Telephone."

PHONOGRAPH AND AUDIO CULTURE

The telephone's development influenced the phonograph's invention. In 1877, after Thomas Edison had perfected a better transmitter for Bell's phone, he worried that the high cost of telephones might limit their use. Thus, Edison sought a device on which a person could record a spoken message and then take the record to a central station where it could be transmitted to an addressee over a telephone. The instrument that Edison designed consisted of a rotating, grooved metal cylinder around which a piece of tin foil was wrapped to record and play back the sounds. In December 1877 Edison tried out his model, shouting the verses of "Mary Had a Little Lamb" into the machine's brass tube. The machine played back Edison's voice to him and his assistants. "I was never so taken aback in all my life," he later recalled. "Everybody was astonished. I was always afraid of things that worked for the first time."[17]

Edison quickly patented the device and formed the Edison Speaking Phonograph Company to manufacture and exhibit the instruments around the country. James Redpath, founder of a thriving lyceum bureau in Boston, took charge of training traveling promoters, providing each with an instrument and a quantity of tin-foil "blanks." As a show property, the phonograph won immediate success. A single "exhibition" phonograph earned as much as $1,800 per week, talking in any language, imitating the sounds of animals, and reproducing music. Skeptics would be invited on stage to test the phonograph for themselves; they came and subjected the apparatus to all the different sounds of which the human voice is capable. Each sound was captured, recorded, and repeated.

Despite his awareness of its potential, Edison neglected the further development of the phonograph in favor of the incandescent lamp. By the mid-1880s, however, others moved into the business with new patents (using wax cylinders and an improved stylus) and new names (gramophone). They developed phonographs for public nickel-in-the-slot operations that played musical selections. The nickels with which people commanded renditions of marches performed by John Philip Sousa's U.S. Marine Band and Stephen Foster's nostalgic ballads mounted at a lucrative rate. Even an Edison-company subsidiary took to installing these prototype jukeboxes in neighborhood soda fountains and saloons. One coin-operated phonograph in a New Orleans drugstore averaged $500 a month in receipts in 1891, while the average player earned about $60 a week.[18]

Edison's cylinder machines had to compete with the gramophone machines developed by Emile Berliner, a German immigrant who simplified both the recording and reproducing processes. Instead of a cylinder, Berliner developed a flat master disc from which thousands of duplicates (first called "plates," but by 1896 known as "records") could be made from a single original recording.

To entice home owners to purchase phonographs, companies sold the machines on the installment plan: five dollars down and three dollars per month for seven months. The Victor Talking Machine Company also entered the competition, promoting one of the lasting images in American commercial iconography—a small black-and-white dog, Nipper by name, listening to "His Master's Voice"—to advertise its products.

Victor also transformed the phonograph (figure 5.9) into a piece of furniture. In its early forms, the whirling turntable, the metal tone arm, and huge flared horn made the phonograph an ugly, mechanical contrivance. To overcome the objections of many women who refused to have such a contraption in their homes, engineers designed a phonograph that would be accepted, like the piano, as a piece of stylish furniture. First developed in 1906, the new instrument was a four-foot-high console, made of "piano-finished" mahogany, with the horn pointed downward and enclosed in the cabinet. A lid kept the turntable and tone arm out of sight. The Victrola became the generic name for any American floor-model phonograph and set the design standards for a decade.[19]

By 1914, Americans had bought more than 500,000 phonographs annually, and seven years later yearly production exceeded 100 million. One reason for this expanding audio culture was that the country had gone dance crazy around 1910. Taxi dance halls, school proms, and lodge cotillions became the rage. Columbia Records took special ads in the *Saturday Evening Post* to promote their "authentic dance tempo" records. Victor replied by engaging Vernon and Irene Castle, the nation's ultimate arbiters of ballroom dancing, to supervise the making of all Victor's dance recordings. Whereas Americans in the 1890s might sing around the parlor organ or piano, by 1915 they now often danced around the victrola.

Widening Visual Experience

THE CHROMO CIVILIZATION

In 1884 Charles Congdon, writing in the *North American Review,* called his age one of "over-illustration," so filled was it with visual stimuli. And these illustrations, more often than not, relied on color to carry their messages. Color and its symbolism fascinated the era. The war of conflicting economic theories was fought by "Silverites" and "Greenbackers" over a "gold" standard. Yellow signified an unsavory brand of journalism, as well as a threat posed by Asian immigration. Cultural critics saw the era as brown (Lewis Mumford), mauve (Thomas Beer), or pretentiously gilded (Mark Twain). Emma Lazarus's 1883 poem, "The New Colossus," spoke of America as a "Golden Door," and Louis Sullivan designed just such a golden portal in his Transportation Building for the 1893

Columbian Exposition. The White City was a presentation of America's architectural fantasies, the White Fleet its imperial longings, and the Great White Way its road to entertainment.[20]

In his 1889 novel *A Connecticut Yankee in King Arthur's Court,* Mark Twain's hero finds himself in a dark, cold medieval tower, longing for his favorite "little conveniences." The Yankee described his lodgings: "There was no soap, no matches, no looking-glass—except a metal one, about as powerful as a pail of water. And not a chromo." Describing his East Hartford home, the Yankee recalled: "you couldn't go into a room but you would find an insurance-chromo, or at least a three-color God-Bless-Our-Home over the door—and in the parlor we had nine."

A chromo, as Twain's description suggests, was a type of pictorial representation. Technically its proper name was chromolithograph, meaning any lithograph printed in colors using two or more lithograph printing stones. In America, however, the term also took on a more focused definition, one shaped by purpose as much as by process. As art historian Peter Marzio noted, by the 1860s chromolithography also meant "the color lithographed reproduction of an oil painting or watercolor, or at least the full-color picture of some religious, heroic, or landscape subject."[21]

The mass-produced chromolithograph led E. L. Godkin to label the United States "a chromo civilization." In Godkin's estimate, the chromolithograph symbolized the debasement of high art and culture. To others like Louis Prang, however, it was the true democratic art, a technique and a format by which fine art might be reproduced, packaged, and distributed to the masses. Many of America's nineteenth-century painters (John James Audubon, Rembrant Peale, Winslow Homer, Edward Moran, Asher Brown Durand, and Albert Bierstadt, among others) had their work chromolithographed, their names made household words through the medium. Eastman Johnson's evocations of daily life were especially popular.

Americans brought chromos (ranging in price from a half-cent to twenty dollars, with an average cost of about two to three dollars) at lithograph offices, such as Currier and Ives's famous shop ("Grand Depot for Cheap and Popular Prints") in New York. They were also available for purchase from art galleries, museums,

FIGURE 5.3. Rural post office, Searsburg, Vermont (ca. 1910). Photograph courtesy of the Library of Congress, Division of Prints and Photographs.

FIGURE 5.4. Advertisements for orders by telephone. From the *Complete Directory of Chicago and Vicinity* telephone book (January 1904). Courtesy of the Chicago Historical Society.

Shopping by Telephone is a Most Convenient Way

"Private Exchange-One"

There is a growing satisfaction in shopping by telephone with us. Every effort is being made to make it so. Every order, inquiry, or request will be quickly and intelligently cared for. Every section of this store is at your service.

Call for "Private Exchange-One" and then ask the operator for the section you wish to speak with. If in doubt, explain briefly to the operator, who will give proper connection. For directory of sections, see page 90.

Marshall Field & Company
State, Washington, Randolph and Wabash Ave.

FIGURE 5.5. Underwood and Underwood, *The Stereograph as an Educator* (1901). Stereograph courtesy of the Library of Congress, Division of Prints and Photographs.

FIGURE 5.6. Elizabeth S. Green, "Children's Kodak," advertisement, *Colliers* magazine (1906).

FIGURE 5.7. "Hogan's Alley on European Tour," cartoon, *New York World* (1897).

WHAT THEY DID TO THE DOG-CATCHER IN HOGAN'S ALLEY.

FIGURE 5.8. Cassily Adams, *Custer's Last Fight* (1896). Chromolithograph advertisement courtesy of the Amon Carter Museum, Fort Worth, Texas.

CUSTER'S LAST FIGHT.

The Original Painting has been Presented to the Seventh Regiment U.S. Cavalry

BY ANHEUSER BUSCH BREWING ASSOCIATION.

ST. LOUIS. MO. U.S.A.

FIGURE 5.9. Advertisement for the Victor Talking Machine Company, *Saturday Evening Post* (1915).

FIGURE 5.10. Joseph Byron, *The Automatic One-Cent Vaudeville* (1904). The location is 48 East 14th Street, New York City. Photograph courtesy of the Byron Collection, Museum of the City of New York.

and traveling salesmen. Fraternal organizations gave them to their members. Children received them as school prizes. Commission agents, insurance salesmen, and merchants offered them as promotional giveaways. Chromos were displayed in offices, saloons, and residences. In her influential guide, *The American Woman's Home* (1869), Catharine Beecher specifically recommended certain chromolithographs for the impact they would have on domestic "correctness of taste and refinement of thought." Her choices for the parlor: Johnson's *Barefoot Boy,* Robert L. Newman's *Blue-Fringed Gentians,* and Bierstadt's *Sunset in the Yosemite Valley.* Prints were also available on temperance, history, transportation, and sports. In the 1880s Currier and Ives, catering to the growing racist sentiment, published a "Darktown" humor series of seventy-three prints parodying blacks as hapless imbeciles.

The chromo also served as an advertising medium. The earliest chromo ads combined fine-art images with commercial messages, but by the 1880s advertising forms appeared that contemporaries called "commercial art." Railroad, circus, and vaudeville companies generated an impressive chromo legacy; so did patent-medicine, fire-insurance, and farm-equipment companies. Some firms, like Anheuser-Busch of St. Louis, commissioned images that would appeal to their customers and hang where their product was sold. The Anheuser-Busch brewery had Cassilly Adam's *Custer's Last Fight* (figure 5.8) chromolithographed in 1896 and distributed by the thousands to the nation's saloons, making it, in the estimate of art historian Robert Taft, the most popular picture in America.[22] Chromolithographers changed the greeting card industry, brightened the stationery of innumerable businesses, and gave a new dimension (with buttons and memorabilia) to presidential campaigning by 1896.

THE STEREOGRAPHING OF AMERICA

At the turn of the century nearly every American parlor contained a viewer called a stereoscope (figure 5.5) and a basket of stereographs, or stereo views, cards with two almost identical photographs glued on a three-by-six-inch mounting. A caption identified the image and a text on the card's opposite side further explained the picture. When the card was viewed through the stereoscope, its two images fused, creating the seemingly magical illusion of a three-dimensional picture.

Produced by the millions in America from the 1850s through the 1930s, the craze for stereographs reached its height before World War I. For example, the Underwood and Underwood Company of New York produced 25,000 stereo views per day and sold 300,000 stereoscopes in 1901. One could purchase views from photography studios, through opticians and art shops, and by mail. Sears, Roebuck used its catalog network to offer the lowest prices possible, selling a stereoscope for 28 cents and 100 views for 20 cents in 1908. Other big producers relied upon large forces of door-to-door salesmen who were recruited each summer from colleges and universities.

Stereographs, like chromos and postcards, depicted every possible subject. The earliest (1854) "American Stereoscopic Views" by Frederick and William Langenheim portrayed scenery from Philadelphia to Niagara Falls. The American wilderness, particularly the Great West, held the interest of devotees of stereographs throughout the century. In 1898, Underwood and Underwood developed what it called "The Underwood Travel System," which consisted of a boxed set of stereo views of a particular country or region with a guidebook and maps describing the places pictured. The captions on stereographs were printed in six languages.[23] Exotic peoples fascinated middle-class Americans, who bought thousands of stereographs on American Indians, natives of the South Pacific, and the peoples of the Far East. Part of this intrigue paralleled the U.S. imperial expansion in the 1890s. As a medium, stereography allowed ordinary citizens to participate vicariously in the visible effects of the country's political and economic conquests. Thus, they collected stereo views of the anthropology exhibits of the World's Fairs, the Great White Fleet at sea, and the building of the Panama Canal.

Celebrities, such as presidents, actresses, baseball stars, boxers, and opera singers, all turned up in stereograph collections. News events—the Alaska Gold Rush, the Siege of Port Arthur, the Wright Brothers' early flights—had their stereographs. Disasters, local or national, invariably brought forth views. By 1908, you could also relive, via stereo views, the Johnstown Flood of 1886, Charleston's 1893 Hurricane, or the San Francisco Earthquake of 1906.

"Conduct Stereos" dramatized how to behave by depicting people, often rural bumpkins, blacks, or immigrants who did not know how to mind their manners. Temperance groups distributed visual variations on "The Drinker's Progress." Grammar schools bought stereoscopes for classes in geography, natural science, and art. Public libraries filed views in special cabinets, allowing patrons to check out images as they did books.

Viewing and exchanging stereo cards was one of the things that a family, a courting couple, or friends did for amusement at home. Stereographs also symbolized conspicuous consumption, both in their possession (particularly if you could show off the most recent issues) and in the claim to "refinement" and "culture" that their use implied. Underwood and Underwood, for instance, promoted its "travel system" by citing the schools and universities that used the system as a teaching device and quoting endorsements by prominent educators.

Finally, viewing and collecting stereo cards was another of Victorian America's new hobbies. Oliver Wendell Holmes, for instance, once boasted that he had seen more than one hundred thousand stereo views. Accumulation fascinated middle-class men and women. To gather a complete set of the views of a topic or activity intrigued individuals whose peers collected postage stamps, sheet music, chromos, or picture postcards.

SNAPSHOTS: EVERY PERSON A PHOTOGRAPHER

America's most popular hobby, amateur photography, received a major boost with the perfection of the dry-plate developing process, roll film, and the manufacture of inexpensive, easy-to-use box cameras. Photography, part of American life since the work of the daguerreotypists of the 1840s, did not become an average person's skill until the 1880s. With the advent of George Eastman's hand-held Kodak camera came the possibility of photography for everyone.

Eastman, the son of a penmanship teacher who set up the first commercial college in Rochester, New York, took up amateur photography in 1877 while working as a bank clerk. He wearied, however, of having to lug about cumbersome paraphernalia: glass plates, a camera the size of a soap box, a heavy tripod, several lenses, and, since the pictures had to be developed on the spot, a darkroom tent of chemicals. The equipment even for a single day's outing commonly weighed more than a hundred pounds.

After several years experimenting with dry plates, Eastman first patented a way of coating paper strips with a photographic emulsion. Later he used the recently invented (1873) Celluloid instead of paper, thereby creating a film that could be rolled on a spool. By 1888, he started selling his first roll-film camera. Pricing it at twenty-five dollars, he called it the Kodak, a name he made up. Eastman hit upon Kodak as a trademark because it was short, distinctive, and pronounceable in any language. The camera's operations were simplicity itself: (1) pull the string, (2) turn the key, and (3) press the button. "You press the button—We do the rest."[24]

Included in the purchase price of a Kodak was a roll of film, together with the processing of its hundred pictures. When the owner had used up the roll, he or she sent the whole camera back to the Rochester factory. The factory returned the camera (loaded with a new roll of film) and mounted pictures of all the successful prints for ten dollars. To any American with twenty-five dollars, however ignorant of chemistry or photography, the Kodak system promised the power to become an artist.

In 1900, Frank Brownell, Eastman's chief camera designer, produced the cheapest and simplest Kodak yet, the Brownie (figure 5.6), costing one dollar and made especially for children. The Canadian writer and illustrator, Palmer Cox, had, in the 1880s, popularized the mythical creatures, Brownies, in his books and poems published in the popular American children's magazine, *St. Nicholas.* In early advertisements, particularly in the children's periodical press, the dwarf Brownies were always illustrated with the Kodak camera. Competitors, like Ansco and Sears, introduced cameras named Buster Brown and Kewpie.

To promote the snapshot camera as "a universal hobby to make mementos for the future," Eastman advertised not only in the photographic press, but especially in the mass-circulation magazines. He engaged the skills of American artists, such as Frederic

Remington and Edward Penfield. Many of the promotions featured young women, for example, the Brownie Girl, setting a type of gender advertising (figure 5.6) that was integral to the company's selling image. To maintain consumers' interest, Kodak sponsored camera clubs for both children and adults and staged amateur photography contests—one attracting over twenty-six thousand people to New York's National Academy of Design in 1897.

Cheap cameras and inexpensive film meant that, for the first time, ordinary people in considerable numbers had the means to make their own pictures. What did they photograph? How did their pictures differ from the images created by the professional photographers of period?

To answer the second question first, the snapshot made possible a new kind of informal portrait, one freed from the constraint imposed by the presence of a professional stranger, one for which the individuals being photographed relaxed and adopted a less inhibited pose. Snapshots revealed society's lighter moments, its off-duty rather than official face. Moreover, there was a strong tendency to "clown" for the camera when it was in the hands of friends or relatives. Here was a facet of everyday life, actually a remarkably human and common one, which had remained largely unrecorded visually until the snapshot camera provided the means to capture such humor.

Many family snapshot albums, assembled from the 1890s to 1920, share perennial themes. No two family albums are the same and yet all are alike.[25] Most snapshots fall into obvious categories, the first being family and friends. Although professional photographers might be engaged to document milestones in the family history—weddings, graduations, anniversaries—snapshots were usually also taken of these events. Given the sunlight requirements of the first Kodaks, most early images were made outdoors. However, unlike the professional photographer who usually placed his subjects in front of their house, snapshot-camera buffs often favored the backyard for their settings. By 1915, amateur photographers also increasingly used a new prop in their pictures. Whereas the traveling photographer of the 1870s often marshaled several artifacts—a sewing machine, an ancestral portrait, a carriage—to accompany his cabinet photograph of the family, the snapshot often clustered everybody around a single prized possession: the family car.

Children dominate the turn-of-the-century snapshot album, indicating not only the greater ease by which they could be photographed at home (rather than at a photographer's studio), but the new adult view of them as a distinct life stage. The snapshot camera became a desirable, even indispensable, accessory to take along to a trolley party, a union picnic, a bicycling expedition, an auto-camping trip, or a sporting event. In time, the practice of keeping a traveler's diary or journal declined; people brought back pictures, rather than prose, from where they had been.

A final subject category found in most pre–World War I snapshot albums would be the documentation of extraordinary events. Soldiers and sailors carried cameras during the Spanish-American War to record their experiences; even more took Kodaks abroad to Europe in 1918. Local community events always received snapshot attention: the entry of the circus or the chautauqua into town, the region's first amusement park or air show, or an area train wreck or urban flood.

The Birth of a Film Nation

KINETOSCOPES AND NICKELODEONS

In his autobiography, *The Age of Confidence* (1934), Henry Seidel Canby, remembering his youth in Victorian America, identified one physical change in his hometown that aptly symbolized a larger shift in America's pattern of behavior: the opera house had been turned into a movie theater. With ten thousand movie theaters playing to a nationwide audience of over 10 million weekly in 1910, movie theaters were doing a greater volume of business than all the legitimate theaters, variety halls, dime museums, lecture bureaus, concert halls, circuses, and street carnivals combined. Only vaudeville outranked the movies at the time.[26]

In the past, popular amusements, such as those just named, had evolved from diversions that were originally the prerogative and pleasure of the wealthy. Thomas Edison thought this would also be the case with motion pictures and that they would primarily serve educational purposes. Instead, movies first appealed to the masses, not to the classes; a new cultural form, their popularity grew from the bottom up rather than being dispersed from the top down.

The primitive Kinetoscopes of the 1890s and the theater palaces of the late teens showed only silent movies, even though "talkies" were technologically possible before they were introduced in the 1920s. Filmmakers apparently wished it that way, realizing that the silents, through the universality of pictures, would continue to appeal to an audience of immigrants who spoke many different languages. As films came to be distributed nationwide, the movies gave everyday life a new simultaneity. Thousands could be watching the same movie anywhere in the land at the same time. Like the mail-order catalog and the mass-circulation magazine, movies made parts of American common culture truly common.

Throughout the nineteenth century, people sought to create the illusion of motion. Artists created panoramas, long strip paintings unrolled from giant upright scrolls in front of an audience, that fascinated Victorians who compared the visual experience to that of seeing an event from a moving train.

In the 1870s both Americans and Europeans explored ways of photographing rapidly moving objects. The most famous of these experiments took place in California at the Palo Alto stud farm of railroad magnate and university builder, Leland Stanford. To win a $25,000 bet that a galloping horse sometimes has all four hooves off the ground, Stanford asked landscape photographer, Eadweard Muybridge, to record the motions of a running horse. Muybridge, using a series of first twelve, later twenty-four cameras in a row, each shutter being tripped by a string as the horse ran past, proved that in a canter, all four hooves of a horse are periodically off the ground.

A decade after Muybridge's experiments, Thomas Edison, who knew the photographer's motion studies, began working "upon an instrument which does for the eye what the phonograph does for the ear, which is the recording and reproducing of things in motion, and in such a form as to be both cheap, practical, and convenient." Using Celluloid film, Edison fabricated a Kinetograph to take motion pictures, and a Kinetoscope to show them. The latter was an advanced peep-hole device with a fifty-foot strip of perforated (an Edison innovation) 35 mm, black-and-white film that moved between a light and a revolving shutter.[27]

Edison exhibited a number of Kinetoscopes at the Chicago World's Fair, and thereafter they were installed in Kinetoscope parlors (figure 5.10), billiard rooms, penny arcades, or storefronts. The Kinetoscope's subjects were a varied lot. You might see ninety seconds of a man sneezing, a girl dancing, or a child being given its bath. Vaudevillians juggled Indian clubs, threw custard pies, or built human pyramids. Their makers called these brief films "actualities"—short scenes of everyday people and events. The wonder of moving figures brought a steady flow of coins. Promoters quickly realized that if one could convert the Kinetoscope into a projecting machine the number of people who could watch a motion picture could be expanded enormously.

Although the first successful public attempt to project a moving picture was at the Cotton States Exposition in Atlanta in 1895, the first American commercial exhibition of "living pictures" took place a year later as an "added attraction" following the regular vaudeville show at Koster and Bial's Music Hall in New York. This showing included a scene from a prizefight (always popular with Kinetoscope fans), a brief dance number, and waves rolling in on the beach at Dover, England. The *New York Times*, in what was perhaps the first movie review, said the films were "wonderfully real and singularly exhilarating."[28] Motion pictures quickly became a fixture on vaudeville programs, often the concluding number. Although vaudeville promoters did not realize it at the time, the "added attraction" would, in the short course of two decades, become the main attraction as vaudeville houses were converted to movie theaters.

What might you see at the end of a vaudeville program if you stayed for the "moving pictures"? At first, a strange potpourri that might include scenes of William McKinley's inauguration, such celebrities as Buffalo Bill and Annie Oakley, moving trains and automobiles, Queen Victoria's funeral, Sandow the Strong Man, and Bertholdi the Contortionist. By the turn of the century, American films told simple narratives. One example was Edwin S. Porter's *The Great Train Robbery* (1903), an eleven-minute film often acclaimed as the first western—although it was shot in Dover, New Jersey. Telling the simple tale of a train robbery and the pursuit and capture of the robbers, Porter also pioneered several camera techniques, one being a close-up of a bandit firing directly at the camera, which caused people in the audience to duck, scream, or even faint.

Film historians dispute who opened the first nickelodeon theater. Storefront movie theaters existed as early as 1896 in New Orleans and New York, and all-movie "electric" theaters had begun in Los Angeles and Chicago by 1902. In 1905, however, the first use of the term *nickelodeon* to describe a movies-only, storefront theater seems to have been by either John Harris or Harry Davis who, in that year, named their small movie houses in Pittsburgh and McKeesport, Pennsylvania, The Nickelodeon. More important than who was first was the nickelodeon's audience and how it grew. Five thousand nickelodeons (figure 5.2) stretched across the United States in 1907 claimed *Scientific American,* twenty thousand operating by 1910 with a daily audience of a quarter million people.[29]

In *Our Times,* Mark Sullivan provided a concise description of a typical nickel theater: "In almost every case a long, narrow room, formerly used for other business purposes. . . . At the rear a stage is raised. Across it is swung a white curtain. Before the curtain is placed a piano, which does service for an orchestra. Packed into the room as closely as they can be placed are chairs for the spectators, who number from one hundred to four hundred and fifty. Directly above the entrance is placed the moving-picture machine, which flashes its lights and shadows upon the white curtain dropped in front of the stage. Many of the machines are operated by means of a tank filled with gasoline or some similarly inflammable material."[30]

The quality of projection left much to be desired. The intermittent feed mechanism on the early projectors made the screen image pulse or flash with an eye-straining flicker effect (hence the Americanism, *flicks*). Moreover, the pace of movement on the screen changed frequently because most hand-held cameras produced variations in the rate of frames per second. Projectionists,

however, distracted the audience from these problems by deliberately slowing down or speeding up the action to produce a comic
effect—a prizefighter falling back to the canvas with leisurely de-
liberation or a chase scene at breakneck speed. Everyone loved
seeing films run backward.

Programs lasted no more than fifteen or twenty minutes, short
enough for children to watch after school, a housewife to visit any
time during the day, and factory workers to see coming home
from work. Film historian Robert Sklar found that families were
apt to spend an evening or Saturday afternoon together engaged
in migrating between a number of theaters to view their offerings.[31] In the beginning, most nickelodeons were located in or
around working-class and immigrant neighborhoods. Promoters
also found that business was best where four or five storefront
theaters crowded together at the intersection of trolley lines or
along a principal shopping street in a workers' district.

The expanding film audience demanded a constant flow of new
pictures. Over half the four thousand films released annually were
imported from France, Germany, and Italy. Soon American studios sprang up in shacks, auditoriums, and lofts in New York City,
New Jersey, and Chicago. Their varied output included an adapta-
tion of Frank Norris's novel *The Pit,* and *The Perils of Pauline*
(1914), a weekly serial of melodrama romance. Everyday life
themes were depicted in such films as *The Song of the Shirt* (1910),
a story of work in a sweat shop; *The Typewriter* (1902), a presentation of office humor; and *The Kleptomaniac* (1905), a saga set in
a department store.

MOTION PICTURES AS MASS MEDIA

The number and notoriety of the nickelodeons brought movies to
the attention of the middle class by 1908. Many churches, reform
groups, and some settlement house workers initially condemned
the film houses as silly and time wasting, if not pernicious to morals. Censorship began erratically but escalated by 1907 in New
York City, then the center of motion-picture production, when
Mayor George B. McClellan revoked all the licenses of the city's
six hundred movie-theaters because of objections from the city's
clergy. Mayor McClellan announced that future permits would be

granted only if the theater owners agreed not to operate on Sundays and not to show pictures tending "to degrade the morals of the community." The movie producers got the message. Nine production firms had just organized the Motion Picture Patents Company, with the intention of creating a monopoly. Like several industries in the Progressive era, they created a self-regulating body (eventually known as the National Board of Review of Motion Pictures, or NBR) that, they hoped, would put a stop to local censorship.

The NBR, aligned with local municipal codes and licensing legislation, was one of several developments that brought middle-class Americans to the movies.[32] Other factors were an upgrading of films, both technically and thematically, as well as a new type of motion picture theater. The result was that between 1908 and 1915, films went from shorts to photoplays, and nickelodeons changed from a diversion of neighborhood storefronts to entertainment housed in sumptuous downtown edifices. Surviving nickelodeons often underwent a change of name and a face-lift, as when Marcus Loew refurbished his Brooklyn storefront theater, changing its name from the Cozy Corner to The Royal. As reformers successfully pressured movie exhibitors to clean up their theaters, to install paramilitary ushers to protect women and ensure order, and to remove objectionable films, middle-class patrons flocked to films with the same enthusiasm as did immigrants and workers.

The movies of the 1910s helped broaden this expanding audience. Within less than a decade, films evolved from the peephole quickies to longer playlets, historical dramas, and ultimately fullfledged vehicles for stars. D. W. Griffin's *The Birth of a Nation* (1915), a three-hour epic in which a southern family is saved from unruly blacks by the Ku Klux Klan, spoke to the racist anxieties of the day. Its cinematic techniques—dramatic fadeouts, switchbacks, and close-ups—also suggested that American movies could be an art form of interest to middle-class audiences.[33]

The middle class also took to Mack Sennett's 1914 comedy, *Tillie's Punctured Romance,* starring Marie Dressler and a newcomer—an odd little man with a postage-stamp mustache who wore baggy pants, carried a cane, and walked with a queer waddling gait. Within two years, Charlie Chaplin was a star with universal appeal and a salary of $670,000 for a year's work. Two other middle-class role models, Mary Pickford, "America's Sweetheart," and her frequent leading man, Douglas Fairbanks, showed Americans how to cope with and overcome the pressures and pitfalls of modern urban life.

By 1915, Americans were watching longer, better-made, more artistic movies in larger, more elaborate, and expensive moving-picture palaces. The new theaters first followed designs that were then fashionable for public buildings, hence, the classical facades of such theaters as The Empress in Owensburg, Kentucky, The Supera in Grand Rapids, Michigan, and The Elite in Carthage, Missouri. Like libraries, state houses, and museums, movie houses claimed to educate and ennoble as they entertained.

Inside the new temples of culture, massive pipe organs and accommodations for a full-scale orchestra replaced the jangling pianos of an earlier day. Although the new theaters moved uptown, their seating arrangements remained fairly democratic.[34] While the loges were slightly more expensive and the balconies were segregated for blacks, even the most expensive seats were usually no more than 45 cents. Most often there were two seat prices, ranging from 5 cents to 15 cents. In 1913, when it cost from 40 cents to $1.40 to see stage drama, movie admissions averaged 7 cents.

Astute theater managers recognized that attending a film could mean more than watching the screen. They realized that the movie house could be a dream palace, a place of escape and fantasy like the new amusement parks. To this end, the marquee became an electric-light extravaganza. Neoclassical designs gave way to more exotic architecture. Dreamlands—Babylon, Granada, Riviera—inspired the decor and names of new houses by the late 1910s. Inside, huge mirrors, statues, tapestries, and carpets gave the moviegoer the sense of being in a palatial estate. "With a little architectural hocus-pocus," wrote Lewis Mumford of these houses, "we transport ourselves to another age, another climate, another historical regime, and best of all to another system of aesthetics." Aping the palaces of the rich, these "atmospheric" theaters became playgrounds for everyone. As Mumford summarized: "They offered a gilded mansion for the weekly invasion of those who lived in stuffy apartments, or a gorgeous canopy to spread over a cramped and limited life, a firmament for cliff-dwellers, a place where even the most menial can stalk about with the vague feeling for the moment we have taken hold of romance."[35]

FIGURE 6.1. Whiting View Company, "Sunday School Picnic in Rural Districts" (ca. 1915). Photograph courtesy of the Library of Congress, Division of Prints and Photographs.

FIGURE 6.2. Reginald Marsh, *George C. Tilyou's Steeplechase Park* (1926), tempera. Courtesy of the Hirshhorn Museum and Sculpture Garden, Smithsonian Institution, Gift of Joseph H. Hirshhorn, 1966.

6

❧_____

THE TERM *Gay Nineties* persists as a common image of late nineteenth-century America. Like all stereotypes, it contains some truth. Although work dominated much of Victorian everyday life, the period also provided more leisure for more people.

While family picnics and community socials remained popular, Americans also flocked to public, commercial recreations. The new entertainments, although quickly exported to the countryside, originated in cities. Middle-class and working-class people, women as well as men, mingled freely at them. To some, the new recreations represented a new view of leisure, one that promoted sensuality and frivolity, thrill and impulse; to others, the innovations in entertainment challenged the genteel ideal of recreation that stressed the activities of the mind over the pleasures of the body.

Many middle-class Americans could play only if persuaded they were also improving themselves and not wasting time. Hence, their annual vacation often meant a stay at a chautauqua resort or a health spa. Most workers could not afford a week in the mountains or at the seashore. They took leisure when they could—an evening at a neighborhood saloon or *turnverein,* a Saturday afternoon at the nickelodeon or the vaudeville house, or a Sunday or national holiday at a city park or amusement park.

Family Fun

HOME GAMES—PARLOR, PORCH, AND PLACE

A town might have its "old whist crowd" and "young dancing crowd," William Allen White wrote of family entertainment in Kansas in the 1890s, its "lodge crowd," its "church social crowd," and its "surprise party crowd." Whatever the crowd, White noted that its enjoyment took place in the parlor, on the porch, or on the home grounds.[1] Weddings, reunions, and holidays (Christmas being the most elaborate) were familial celebrations. By 1915, two new holidays, Mother's Day and Father's Day, celebrated the family itself. Families also recreated at Grange picnics, county fairs, or Christian Endeavor suppers. White's reference to whist suggests card playing as one Victorian "past time." Other favorite card games included euchre, five hundred, bridge, seven-up, flinch, and Authors. Board games, such as Wall Street Brokers, Nellie Bly, Twenty Questions, Going to Jerusalem, and Caroms, remained popular into the twentieth century, as did checkers, dominoes, and chess.

Young girls, along with their mothers, spent leisure hours at needlecrafts. In shadow boxes and under glass domes, they arranged dried flowers, seeds, and shells to display their artistic talent, as well as to provide ornaments for the Victorian manse. Woodburning, or "pyrography," fascinated the whole family and yielded scores of blackly etched necktie holders, pipe racks, and jardiniere stands.

Reading filled the leisure hours of many Victorian women. Religious novels like Lew Wallace's *Ben Hur: A Tale of the Christ* (1880), westerns, such as Owen Wister's *The Virginian* (1902), and sentimental sagas like Kate Douglas Wiggin's *Rebecca of Sunnybrook Farm* (1903) found their way to many parlors and porches. Best-sellers in the 1890s included Arthur Conan Doyle's *Adventures of Sherlock Holmes*, James Barrie's *The Little Minister*, Charles M. Sheldon's *In His Steps*, Robert Louis Stevenson's *Dr. Jekyll and Mr. Hyde*, Stephen Crane's *The Red Badge of Courage*, Winston Churchill's *Richard Carvel*, and Frank Baum's *The Wizard of Oz*.[2]

By the 1880s, books written specifically for "American youth" had become a distinct literary genre. Horatio Alger's fiction sold widely. Alger wrote 135 novels (or one novel 135 times) preaching the virtues of frugality, industriousness, sobriety, and punctuality. Other popular books included the Frank Merriwell stories (200 volumes) created by William G. Patten and the Stratemeyer Literary Syndicate, which, beginning in 1906, churned out series after series, including *Tom Swift, The Bobbsey Twins, The Hardy Boys,* and *Nancy Drew.*

Families frequently gathered around parlor organs, pianos, pianolas (self-playing or mechanical pianos), and phonographs for "a sing." Common in rural and workers' homes by the 1890s, parlor organs seemed especially suitable for the hymns and sentimental ballads so loved by the Victorians. By the turn of the century, however, anyone with serious social and musical pretensions had a piano. Everyone knew that the great composers used it and that it served as the accompaniment for outstanding singers; moreover, almost all published sheet music was written for voice and piano.

Three lawn games—croquet, archery, and lawn tennis—influenced middle-class recreation at home. Both sexes played these gentle and genteel sports. Croquet spread westward, and many accounts relate its popularity throughout the small towns of the Midwest. During its greatest vogue, manufacturers sold playing sets with candle sockets on the wickets for night playing. Lawn tennis began simply as an exercise of hitting the ball back and forth over a net, but it quickly became more competitive. More active than croquet or archery, tennis appealed to young men and women.

PICNICS AND SOCIABLES

Family and group picnics (figure 6.1) at and away from home—at municipal parks, fair grounds, or along rural roads—took place throughout the summer. Decoration Day opened the picnic season, and Labor Day concluded it. The Fourth of July was its acme. An English traveler in 1870 notes that on that day, "picnics are going off in every direction—quiet little church picnics, Sunday school picnics, working people's picnics, Fenian picnics, picnics of a hundred societies and associations."[3] Picnics, as the photography of the period documents, were dress-up times; women might wear one of the stylish lingerie dresses, while men often sported a coat and tie.

Grangers often held their annual picnic on Independence Day. After a morning of political oratory, out came basket lunches of cold fried chicken, corn bread, potato salad, and beer and lemonade or Root Beer, "the National Temperance Drink" created by Charles E. Hires, a Philadelphia pharmacist. Band concerts or sports events took place during the afternoon: wrestling matches, races of all kinds, a baseball game, and, the most popular of all rural diversions, pitching horseshoes. "Nothing more picturesque, more delightful, more helpful," Hamlin Garland recalled, "has ever risen out of rural life. Each of these assemblies was a most grateful relief from the sordid loneliness of the farm."[4]

Urban workers also celebrated July Fourth outdoors. The 1885 picnic of the Worcester, Massachusetts, Ancient Order of Hibernians, for example, which attracted three thousand to four thousand participants, started quietly with dancing and a clambake. In the afternoon, track and field events, wrestling, and a tug-of-war took place. Contestants competed for cash prizes, and the spectators bet on the outcomes. The day's activities also included sparring matches. Boxing was illegal in Massachusetts, but sparring exhibitions provided a legal cover for this popular sport. After the official bouts, other private contests broke out among the picnickers. Heavy drinking appears to have nourished the brawling that went on into the night. Even the Irish-controlled *Worcester Daily Times* observed "young men in different parts of the grove who were on the muscle."[5]

Working-class Swedes in Worcester celebrated the 1885 Independence Day in a different fashion. Many went to church picnics, whose routine followed a predictable formula: services at church; a march to the picnic grounds; religious and patriotic remarks by the minister and the Sunday school superintendent; hymn singing, lunch, ice cream, and lemonade; and, finally, informal games and sports. Other Worcester Swedes observed July Fourth under the banners of the Svea Gille Club, the Viking Council of the Mystic

Brotherhood, or even the Scandinavian Socialist Club. These gatherings took on a livelier tone than did the church picnics.[6]

The Hibernians and the Svea Gille were part of a phenomenal increase in over five hundred new clubs, organizations, and associations throughout the United States. The nationwide enrollment in such groups grew to over 6 million by 1890, making up about 40 percent of the male population over the age of twenty-one. Many had ladies' auxiliaries (Daughters of Rebekah, Pythian Sisters) to organize chicken-pie suppers, corn roasts, picnics, cake sales, and dances.[7]

Everyone seemed to be joining some temple, clan, castle, conclave, hive, or lodge. Some participated for the sake of the sickness and death benefits many orders provided. Others took out membership to maintain business contacts. But such reasons only partially explain the stampede to become members of the Ancient Arabic Order of Nobles of the Mystic Shrine (figure 6.3), the United Order of Druids, the Tribes of Ben Hur, the Independent Order of Gophers, the Prudent Patricians of Pompeii, or the Concatenated Order of Hoo-Hoo. Towns had one or more lodges, their membership often embracing every element in its society. Lodge memberships in other communities marked the locale's social stratifications.

The elaborate ceremony and ritual of fortnightly meetings provided "such a striking contrast to workshop or factory, to the dull level of so much home life, that their appeal could hardly be withstood. . . . Any one might find himself a Most Illustrious Grand Potentate, Supreme Kahalijah, or Most Worthy and Illustrious Imperial Prince on lodge night."[8] In colorful regalia, men departed the everyday world of work and worry for a momentary pageant of mystery and make-believe. Perhaps a similar escapism explains the late nineteenth-century's delight in costume balls and Halloween parties, as well as dressing up for elaborate historical tableaux and pageants.

THE MIDDLE-CLASS VACATION

In 1910 a *New York Times* reporter put the question, "How long should a man's vacation be?" to several men of affairs. President

Taft recommended two to three months. New York Supreme Court Judge Henry Bishoff suggested two months for professional men, one month for businessmen, and two weeks for clerks. Other opinions ranged from two weeks to a month and a half. Even those who were reluctant to prescribe an exact time agreed that the pressures of modern life necessitated an annual vacation.

By the early twentieth century, summer holidays had become common for middle-class Americans. A New York Department of Labor study found that of the 1,500 factories investigated, 91 percent gave paid vacations to their office staffs, whereas few gave them to their hourly wage workers.

Where did these lawyers, merchants, and businessmen go for their holidays? In the two decades immediately before the outbreak of World War I, a significant number (an estimated two hundred thousand each year) traveled to Europe. Travel agencies made all the necessary arrangements for transatlantic crossings (on steamships like the *Lusitania*) and Continental tours (the cost varying from $400 to $600) with assurances that they provided "experienced escorts" and guaranteed "girls carefully chaperoned."

Many Americans took vacations for health reasons. Because the hydropathy cure enjoyed great popularity, older spas, such as White Sulphur Springs and Saratoga Springs, prospered. New watering places like French Lick in Indiana and Hot Springs in Arkansas also provided settings in which people could drink or bathe in curative mineral waters. Fresh mountain air attracted tuberculosis patients, hence the popularity of Colorado Springs and Ashville, North Carolina.[9]

Hotels like the Coronado in San Diego, Mohank Mountain House in New Paltz, New York, and the Chalfonte in Cape May, New Jersey, became major tourist attractions, affluent travelers journeying from one to another as on a pilgrimage for the ultimate in leisure. Victorian resort hotels featured grand verandas, places for viewing and being viewed. The veranda of the Grand Hotel on Mackinac Island, Michigan, for example, extended 880 feet, so that guests could see the sun rise on one Great Lake and set over another, giving them the feeling of being at sea. The veranda's expanse, enclosed but exposed, allowed guests to take in the outdoors without completely engaging in nature.[10] Here, one recuperated from forays onto the beach or into the mountains or sat with one's sketchbook, binoculars, or Kodak and recorded the view. Here, families replicated the rituals of the porch culture they knew back home: conversation, reading, and people watching.

Ocean Grove—a mile-long beachfront community bordered by two interior lakes on the New Jersey shore—was only one of almost a hundred scenic campgrounds, established by such denominations as the Methodists, that developed into resorts.[11] Gothic summer cottages and over a hundred tents (figure 6.5), rented from the Ocean Grove Camp Meeting Association, clustered around the main tabernacle, which grew from a large tent to an open-air building to a permanent auditorium by 1894. Lots in the community were sold by the association with ninety-nine-year leases to "people of good moral character" who lived on streets in the camp with names taken from well-known Methodists and the Bible. The faithful came in droves each summer, particularly during the August camp meeting, when daily religious services were held, sometimes at the water's edge.

Ocean Grove, like many vacation sites within reach of large American cities by railroad, also served as a one-day excursion holiday for workers. Special events like "Salt Water Day" enticed these tourists. A New Yorker, for example, could board a train from the city at 5:00 A.M. and arrive in Ocean Grove in time for breakfast. The round-trip excursion ticket cost $1.85, a hotel breakfast 50 cents, and if the visitor stayed on for dinner it cost 75 cents. For a modest fee one could go rowing on the lakes or go to the oceanfront, where bathhouses rented for 75 cents a day and bathing suits were rented by the hour, a card stamped with the time pinned to the suit.

Another excursionist's mecca, Atlantic City, New Jersey, was Ocean Grove's exact opposite. Harrison Rhodes, in his 1915 *Vacation America* guide, commented that the waves of "the Atlantic bow in amazed admiration before gigantic piers which bear aloft whirlwind vaudeville, and one-step dancing, and the wild music which pulsates in the soft warm night. Theaters and movies abound. Lion-tamers and snake charmers and curio-shops flourish. It was," he concluded, "a dreadful place, and yet oddly enough, it is . . . exactly what the majority of us really like."[12]

To many who were new to the middle class, a spin along the resort's famous Boardwalk on a "roller chair" (made famous by the 1905 song, "Why Don't You Try, or The Rolling Chair Song") was a chance to ape the wealthy. George A. Birmingham, a visitor to Atlantic City in 1913, speculated: "In towns and rural districts where men and women live their ordinary lives, work, love, and ultimately die, it is the rarest thing possible to see any grown person wheeled about in a perambulator or bathchair." To be photographed in such a chair was the "epitome of nouveau bourgeois."[13]

People who were new to minimal affluence, as well as to the rituals of pleasure travel, often clustered with their own kind and kin—hence, the rise of ethnic resorts, such as St. Petersburg in Florida, Connaught-on-Lake Erie, Tent City outside San Diego, and the Jewish Catskill resorts depicted in Abraham Cahan's 1917 novel *The Rise of David Levinsky.* Others rediscovered the country and farm, taking family vacations in the White Mountains, pictured by William Dean Howells in *The Landlord at Lion's Head* (1897). By 1915, Americans also vacationed in two newly opened tourist areas: the Florida shore and the national parks.

Florida's "boom" started with Henry Morrison Flagler, a former partner of John D. Rockefeller, who established a chain of resort hotels down the east coast of Florida from St. Augustine to the Keys in the early twentieth century. Flagler linked these hotels with a railroad that provided the impetus for much of the state's subsequent development. He named his St. Augustine hotel for the sixteenth-century Spanish explorer, Ponce de León, who had searched Florida for the fabled Fountain of Youth. Opened in 1888, Flagler promoted the hotel to Americans who were seeking similar rejuvenation. From St. Augustine (where Flagler also built churches, a hospital, a city hall, and schools, paved the streets, and installed municipal utilities), his railroad and its hotel chain went

on to Daytona and then to Palm Beach, where he built the Royal
Poinciana Hotel in 1894.

Unlike Flagler's polished yellow-and-white resorts, the new national parks projected an image of natural wilderness—a concept
with considerable appeal to a coalition of middle-class Americans
whom historians have identified as part of "a back-to-nature"
movement. Peter Schmitt, for example, called the movement "a
search for Arcadia"—an urban response that valued nature's spiritual impact above its utilitarian significance and one that involved
tourists, teachers, clergymen, bird-watchers, scout leaders, city
planners, and suburban commuters.[14] The Sierra Clubs (founded
in 1892 by John Muir), the beginning of the Boy Scouts and Girl
Scouts, and the appearance of new outdoor periodicals, such as
Forest and Stream, contributed to the national park movement.
The movement's official promoters, beginning with Yellowstone
in 1872, certainly saw American nature as wilderness, but they
also thought of the parks as tourist attractions. At Yellowstone, for
example, the Great Northern Railroad received the concession to
build a massive hotel two hundred yards from the Old Faithful
geyser, the wilderness area's most spectacular feature. As the
number of national parks increased—Yosemite, Grand Canyon,
Glacier, Mount Rainier, Yellowstone, Crater Lake by 1915—so did
their visitors. Roads and buildings multiplied. Most parks admitted
automobiles, more than fifty-five thousand visitors touring by car
in 1917. Fewer than ten years later, the number would be four
hundred thousand. By then, over half the visitors to Yellowstone
came by auto and half of them camped.[15]

Sporting Life

PHYSICAL FITNESS

Dioclesian Lewis's *New Gymnastics for Men, Women and Children* (1862) played a leading role in the late nineteenth-century
cult of physical culture. It went through ten editions, serving as a
standard text for calisthenic exercises in schools, gymnasiums, and
homes for twenty-five years. Lewis included women in his classes

and in his normal school program, where he trained physical education teachers. Using bean bags, hoops, and rings in what amounted to isometric exercises, Lewis also advocated working out with a four-foot-long "wand" or pole that was adaptable to sixty-eight different activities. He developed exercises for Indian clubs—turned wooden devices shaped like bowling pins. A diary account of Anne MacDonald in 1885 suggests the popularity of Indian clubs among young women in Rochester, New York: Anne and her friend Daisy went to a "Methodist social where they are to swing clubs"; over the next month, the two girls also performed at the Central Church, the Unitarian Church, and Lake Avenue Baptist church.[16]

Anne MacDonald also went regularly to a local gymnasium (figure 6.4) and a natatorium during the 1880s. Such facilities were becoming more available in large cities. But if one's locale lacked a gym, one could purchase a "parlor gymnasium." Included in such home equipment were rubber wands, rowing devices, and pulley weights. German immigrants contributed significantly to the fitness movement. Many followed Friedrich Jahn, whose teaching led to the development of gymnastic societies called *Turnvereins,* or Turners' Clubs, in centers of German immigration such as St. Louis, Milwaukee, and Cincinnati. Other national athletic clubs, including the Bohemian Sokols, Polish Falcons, and Caledonian Clubs, met with the Turnvereins in citywide gymnastic and sports competitions. The Turnverein philosophy influenced the American public school system. In Chicago, for example, school board president Luther Haven introduced the idea of having teachers incorporate several daily exercise periods as a permanent part of the city's grade and high school curricula.

Dudley Sargent, Harvard's first professor of physical training, helped make physical education part of the collegiate curriculum. He, and others who formed the American Association for the Advancement of Physical Education in 1885, saw fitness as best achieved by athletic contest, rather than by gymnastic performance. To many whom Sargent trained (Theodore Roosevelt and Henry Cabot Lodge were in his undergraduate classes), games became not only physical but ideological. Physical education instructors, coaches, and alumni, as Harvey Green documented, also envisioned the objective of such "games" to be winning as well as conditioning. Although Sargent attempted to curb the rise of highly competitive intercollegiate sports, by the time of his retirement in 1919, the philosophy of winning dominated.[17]

Luther Gulick, also a disciple of Sargent, took his mentor's philosophy in another direction as he transformed the Young Men's Christian Association into a sports-and-fitness organization. At the YMCA's Training School in Springfield, Massachusetts, he trained physical education directors to head new YMCA facilities. (James Naismith, a staff member at the training school, devised the game of basketball there in 1891.) Gulick turned out 50 new enthusiasts in 1885; that number grew to 244 annually by 1900. Gulick and his students promoted "muscular Christianity," believing a sound mind in a sound body would make for a saved soul.

Almost everyone who was caught up in the physical-fitness mania had ideas about proper diet. Some insisted the body had to be properly purged, either mechanically or dietarily, to be fit and clean. Cathartics, mineral waters, and laxatives became increasingly popular as some people worried about "autointoxication" and "internal cleanliness." Other health reformers developed theories about the proper way to eat. Horace Fletcher insisted that by chewing food thoroughly (thirty times or more), people would digest their food more easily and use their food more efficiently.

If not all Americans changed how they ate, many changed what they ate—especially for breakfast. In 1876, a typical middle-class breakfast demanded a heavy, cooked meal: beefsteak, bacon and eggs, fried potatoes, wheatcakes and sausage, porridge, donuts, and fruits. By 1915, many took breakfast out of a box of ready-to-eat, "cold," brand-name cereal (figure 6.7). Part of this change in the everyday diet of Americans came about because of the competition among health reformers, particularly John Harvey Kellogg and C. W. Post, who, in the 1890s, launched the breakfast-food industry in Battle Creek, Michigan.

Kellogg, a Seventh-Day Adventist, joined the city's Western Health Reform Institute as its nutritionist, later heading and renaming it the Battle Creek Sanatorium, which thousands of health seekers and food faddists affectionately called "the San." Besides prescribing large doses of bran, zwieback, Graham crackers, and caramel cereal coffee for everyone, Kellogg advocated his own health foods, such as Granola and "Granose," his variety of wheat flakes developed in response to Henry Perky, a Denver vegetarian restauranteur who created Shredded Wheat in 1892.

Earlier in the decade, C. W. Post had come to the "San" for treatment of heart trouble. He stayed nine months, but found no relief and so, in 1892, he established his own health home, La Vita Inn, where he banned tea, coffee, and physicians. By 1895, Post entered the health-food business, manufacturing a coffee substitute (made from bran, wheat, and molasses) called Postum Cereal Food Coffee, which became known to millions as Postum. He next introduced Grape-Nuts (1898). In 1906, he also began marketing corn flakes that he first called "Elijah's Manna," with a picture on the box showing a raven dropping food into the hands of the prophet Elijah. Complaints from the clergy and the religious press forced him to change the name to Post Toasties.[18]

William K. Kellogg, John Harvey's brother, countered Post with a corn-flake cereal that he named Kellogg's Toasted Corn Flakes, with the punning slogan, "the sweet heart of the corn." By 1915, American stores stocked numerous cereals that were unknown thirty years before, despite critics who called the new breakfast foods "shredded doormats," "Gripe nuts," and "Eata-heapa-hay."

ROLLERS, WHEELERS, MOTORISTS

Approximately every two decades, Victorian Americans popularized a new motion sport. In the 1870s roller skating appeared, followed by bicycling in the 1890s, and auto motoring in the 1910s. Each entailed personal movement, expanded the speed and range of one's mobility, and was first a participatory and then a spectator sport.

Roller skating, first fashionable among the New York City elite who vacationed at Newport, originated in the 1860s. A decade later, the sport spread across the country, with rinks of hard maple floors built in nearly every city and town. By paying an admission fee of twenty-five or fifty cents, men, women, and children could participate in races, fancy skating, and dances or just be content to go around in circles. Metal and wood roller skates could also be rented at the rinks, which commonly had a gallery above, where spectators could watch the show below. New York's Casino accommodated one thousand spectators and one thousand skaters.

While thousands circled the roller rink, out on streets and roads, others bicycled for pleasure and exercise. Different types of bicycles, such as velocipedes, had been in use before the introduction in the 1870s of the "high-wheeler," a vehicle with a large front wheel and a small back one. Riding the high-wheeler took skill and balance; few, if any, women rode it because female clothing, particularly the full skirt, made it almost impossible. Changes in the bicycle's form made it a sport for everyone when, in 1884, John Kemp Stanley designed a "safety" bicycle, a machine with two wheels of equal size joined by a tubular frame. By 1887, the Victor, a safety bicycle with a dropped frame and no crossbar, appeared for women. Pneumatic tires, enclosed gears, and coaster brakes completed the evolution of "the wheel." By 1888, fifty thousand men and women cycled in America, a number that doubled two years later when 312 U.S. firms were manufacturing 10 million bicycles.[19]

Although a new bicycle cost far less to purchase and maintain than did a horse, the initial investment was still not cheap. In the nineties, Chicago cyclists could buy a Columbia, made by the Pope Manufacturing Company, or an A. G. Spaulding bicycle for $90. Bargain hunters, the *Chicago Inter-Ocean* reported, could pick up a "good used" Monarch for $50 or a "shop-worn" model for $35.

After buying a wheel, many cyclists promptly joined one of their community's cycle clubs. By 1895, there were five hundred in Chicago, each with its own colors and uniform. In addition to participating in endurance rides and competitive events, members could enjoy reading rooms, group outings, and social events. The Hermes Club charged a five-dollar initiation fee and fifty cents for monthly dues. Most clubs were interested primarily in cycling and socializing, but the Viking Cycling Club's prospectus announced tersely that "this club and its associates control 1,800 political votes and will support those candidates favorable to wheelmen and wheeling." The fifteen thousand members of the League of American Wheelmen, founded in 1881, took a similar stand in lobbying for better roads and highways on a national level.[20] Their journal was aptly titled *Good Roads*.

The automobile, like the bicycle, prompted new leisure experiences for the middle class (figure 1.10). Those who initially engaged in "automobiling" had either a sense of adventure or a financial interest in the new automotive industry. In spite of frequent breakdowns and poorly marked roads, automobiling provided them with a freedom of action and direct contact with the landscape that was unknown to passengers of trains and ships.

Motoring first required instruction. Driving schools in large cities provided preliminary practice in shifting gears and steering behind dummy wheels before a pupil ventured on to the road. Whether out for a single Sunday afternoon drive or a longer auto-camping trip, early motorists prepared for the worst. One guidebook suggested that an auto camper carry "a standard tool kit along with extra spark plugs, tires, and tubes, socket wrenches, jacks, shovels, cables, a grease gun, and a sheet of cork from which to make emergency gaskets." A tire pump, an extra gasoline can, and several water bags for overheated brakes were also recommended.[21]

In 1914, the Lincoln Highway Association attempted to coalesce auto manufacturers, road builders, and the motoring public in a grand promotional scheme to mark and improve a transcontinental highway honoring Abraham Lincoln. Carl Fischer, founder of the Prest-O-Lite Company and the Indianapolis Speedway, initiated the project by proposing a "coast-to-coast rock highway." With the goal of linking Boston and San Francisco via the best and most direct route across the midsection of the country, the Lincoln Highway, for the greater portion of its 3,389-mile length, coincided with what would later be named U.S. Route 30. In the teens, however, red, white, and blue bands painted on telephone poles, trees, barns, and other objects identified the routes. Other national organizations mapped and marked scenic or historic routes, such as the Yellowstone, Pike's Peak, and Dixie highways. Consequently, along one 1,500-mile stretch of road in the West, telephone poles carried the markers of fifteen different highway associations.

FIGURE 6.3. Ancient Arabic Order of Nobles of the Mystic Shrine (ca. 1910). Photograph courtesy of the Library of Congress, Division of Prints and Photographs.

FIGURE 6.4. Girls' gym class, Seward Park, Chicago (ca. 1915). Photograph courtesy of the Chicago Historical Society.

FIGURE 6.5. Tent life in Ocean Grove, New Jersey (1873). Photograph courtesy of Jennifer Boyd and Timothy McMahon.

FIGURE 6.6. Neighborhood saloon, New York City, *Harper's Magazine* (ca. 1885).

FIGURE 6.7. Advertisement for Egg-O-See cold cereal, Egg-O-See Cereal Company, Chicago (ca. 1895). Courtesy of the Warshaw Collection of Business Americana, National Museum of American History.

"Take That Meat Away"

We will have no more meat or heavy, hard-to-digest foods on our breakfast table this Summer. We never felt so well in our lives as we did last Summer, when we made EGG-O-SEE the foundation of every meal."

If you do not use EGG-O-SEE for EVERY meal, you should at least make it the LAW OF YOUR BREAKFAST TABLE, and insure Summer Health and vigorous happiness for your entire household.

EGG-O-SEE is Nature's own food—the whole wheat in its most tempting, delicious and sustaining form.

More EGG-O-SEE is eaten each day than all other similar foods combined. This is the strongest endorsement ever accorded any food by the American people.

Costs no more than the ordinary kinds—large package 10c.

FREE—our "back to nature" book—tells how to get well and keep well by natural means. Sent free on application—write today.

EGG-O-SEE CEREAL COMPANY, Chicago

FIGURE 6.8. The National Summer Game, University of Notre Dame Baseball Team (1893). Photograph courtesy of the University of Notre Dame Archives.

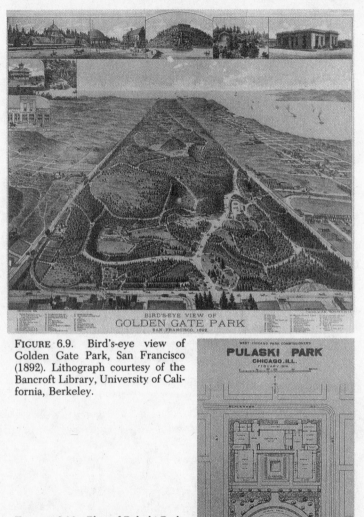

FIGURE 6.9. Bird's-eye view of Golden Gate Park, San Francisco (1892). Lithograph courtesy of the Bancroft Library, University of California, Berkeley.

FIGURE 6.10. Plan of Pulaski Park, Chicago, Illinois (ca. 1915). Drawing courtesy of the Chicago Historical Society.

SPECTATOR SPORTS

Sports in America assumed new forms in the second half of the nineteenth century. As Allen Guttmann summarized the new trend, athletic events like track and field and ball games, such as football and baseball, became professionalized to the point "where some men devoted nearly all their time to them." They were "nationally organized, thoroughly quantified, and marked by an unprecedented mania for the modern sports record" and the importance of winning.[22] This specialization put skilled players on the field and unpracticed spectators in the stands. A culture of spectatorship developed. While horse racing continued to have its influence and intercollegiate football gained popularity, boxing and baseball obsessed Victorian Americans. Both had evolved from traditional folk recreations, but by the end of the nineteenth century, each had become a money-making, commercial enterprise. Both were connected with the themes of strenuousness and competitiveness that were touted by politicians, journalists, and jingoists.

Paintings by George Bellows *(Both Members of the Club)* and Thomas Eakins *(Between Rounds)* suggest that prizefights were no place for a lady or, in theory, a middle-class gentleman. Bareknuckle prizefighting, illegal in most states, took place clandestinely in saloon halls, commercial gyms, and backwoods arenas. Club fights were part of the male culture, a milieu symbolized by and reported on in *The National Police Gazette*.

John L. Sullivan started out by traveling the country offering $50 and later $1000 to anyone who could last four rounds with him. Between 1882 and 1892, he bloodied one challenger after another. Although he endorsed the new Marquis of Queensberry rules, Sullivan also fought without them. In 1889, for instance, he battered Jake Kilrain for seventy-five rounds and over two hours in one hundred-degree heat before three thousand fans deep in the Mississippi woods. The spectacle also commanded the attention of followers of prizefighting elsewhere in the country who crowded into barber shops, hotel lobbies, and poolrooms awaiting messages from telegraph operators about the details of the endurance test. Still other fans followed the contest in the new sports pages of the daily newspapers.[23]

Race rivalry entered the boxing ring when Jack Johnson, a black fighter, won the heavyweight crown in 1908. Such a feat rankled many white Americans. Johnson aggravated the hatred of him by gleefully besting every "great white hope" who fought him. On July 4, 1910, he took on James Jeffries in Reno, Nevada. The clearly partisan band played the racist song "All Coons Look Alike to Me." Racial slurs greeted Johnson's entrance into the ring. As the telegraph sent word of Johnson's easy victory, violence erupted around the country. In Houston, Charles Williams openly celebrated Johnson's triumph, and a white man "slashed his throat from ear to ear"; in Little Rock, a group of whites killed two blacks after an argument about the fight in a streetcar; in Norfolk, Virginia, a gang of white sailors injured scores of blacks; in Wilmington, Delaware, blacks attacked a white, and whites retaliated with a "lynching bee."[24]

Baseball eclipsed boxing as the nation's leading spectator sport by 1915. Fans crowded the grandstands and packed the bleachers on summer afternoons to watch professional teams. "The fascination of the game," *Harper's Weekly* commented in 1886, "has seized upon the American people, irrespective of age, sex or other condition." Salesclerks and assembly-line workers, business managers and stenographers enjoyed the national game.

American baseball (figure 6.8) developed out of two children's games, rounders and town ball, brought to the United States by English immigrants. Contrary to popular myth that places the game's beginnings in bucolic Cooperstown, sports historians document its emergence in eastern cities, beginning in the 1840s. Two decades later, a dozen clubs existed in New York, four in Chicago, and nine in New Orleans, all with distinctly middle-class players and spectators. The Civil War accelerated the game's diffusion. A professional team, the Cincinnati Red Stockings, toured the country in 1869 taking on and defeating all comers. Seven years later, a professional National League was founded (the American League dates from 1901; the first World Series from 1903).

By the 1890s, baseball had assumed its modern form: a standardized diamond, formal rules, and a published schedule of games. It also attracted working-class people to its fields and stands. Irish-American and German-American owners and players were disproportionately prominent in the post–Civil War years, hence, the great heroes: John "Honus" Wagner, "Iron Man" Joe McGinty, "Pop" Anson, and Michael "Slide, Kelly, Slide." Black players, barred from major teams by the 1867 rules of the National Association of Base Ball Players, formed their own leagues.[25]

William Commeyer appears to have been the earliest baseball promoter to charge admission to watch a game. In Brooklyn in 1862, he built the first enclosed field in the country, graded the diamond, and erected a clubhouse. He left an even more enduring mark on the everyday routine of American spectator sports by having played at the game's beginning "The Star Spangled Banner," which, by a presidential order in 1916, became the official anthem of the United States.

Public Entertainments

THE NEIGHBORHOOD SALOON

"The saloon, in relation to the wage-earning classes in America," noted Walter Wyckoff, who had studied it in researching his book on *American Workers* (1900), "is an organ of high development, adapting itself with singular perfectness to its functions in catering in a hundred ways to the social and political needs of men." As Wyckoff suggested, saloons (figure 6.6) played several roles in late nineteenth-century worker culture. They provided the services of a neighborhood center; they offered a semipublic (largely male) preserve away from work and home; and, perhaps most important, they were the most popular leisure environment for male workers from the 1870s until the enactment of Prohibition in 1919.

By 1897, licensed liquor dealers in the United States numbered over 215,000, and unlicensed "blind pigs" and kitchen bars represented an estimated 50,000 additional drinking outlets. In Chicago, saloons outnumbered groceries, meat markets, and dry goods stores counted together at the turn of the century. In 1915, New York had over 10,000 licensed saloons, or one for every 515 persons; Chicago had one for every 335, San Francisco had one for every 218, and Houston had one for every 198.[26]

Urban saloons assumed many forms. In a city's business district, well-appointed ones catered to businessmen and professionals. At the other end of the spectrum, waterfront dives and barrelhouses served sailors, tramps, and the very poor. German-style beergardens proliferated in immigrant communities, as well as in suburban areas. These public drinking spots catered to families, allowing women and children to be part of the activities. Tables and chairs replaced the long bar, and the food served was as important as the beer in attracting trade. Music was essential, often involving brass bands, soloists, and vaudeville performers. The Summer Bazaar Garden, which occupied Boston's Mechanic's Hall Building in the late 1880s, had a military band, as well as a full orchestra. Its facilities included billiards, bowling, a rifle range, dancing, and skating. Faust's Roof-top Garden in St. Louis, Frank Lloyd Wright's Edelweiss (or Midway) Gardens in Chicago, and Pabst's Whitefish Resort outside Milwaukee were other typical beer gardens.

Workers' saloons came in three basic types. The occupational saloon drew its customers from a particular trade or from a nearby mill or plant. For example, prior to the formation of the International Longshoremen's Association, saloon keepers frequently hired men to work on a city's docks. In Buffalo, at the turn of the century, sixty-three of the city's sixty-nine union organizations met in saloon halls. Ethnic saloons, more an evening business, were centers of immigrants' communal celebrations like weddings and holidays and meeting places for fraternal orders and clubs. The neighborhood saloon might attract a local, multiethnic crowd and provide an institutional base for ward politicians. Many saloons in America simultaneously served all these constituencies. They did not, however, normally serve middle-class patrons, who preferred to drink at home, at private clubs or country clubs, or in hotels.

Although urban saloons varied greatly in appearance, atmosphere, and the character of both the barkeepers and the clientele, John Kingsdale argued that they shared several common characteristics: "Often located on a corner for maximum visibility, the typical workingman's saloon was readily recognizable by its swinging shuttered doors and front windows cluttered with potted ferns, posters, and advertising displays." Inside, a bar counter (often affectionately called "the long mahogany") ran the length of the room, paralleled by a brass footrail. "Across from the bar might be a few tables and chairs, a piano, pool table or rear stalls." Interior walls might sport advertisements and chromolithographs of John L. Sullivan, *Custer's Last Fight* (figure 5.8), or standard barroom nudes like *Andromache at the Bath.* Breweries increasingly furnished saloons with such popular art, as well as all their fixtures. In most saloons, draft beer sold for a nickel and whiskey for ten or fifteen cents. "Men drank their whiskey straight—to do otherwise would have been considered effeminate—followed by a chaser of water, milk, or buttermilk."[27]

The everyday work routine of a saloon began early, usually at 5:00 or 6:00 A.M., serving workers a morning bracer with the coffee they carried in their lunch pails. The morning also involved preparing the free meal for the lunch crowd. After the hectic midday press, the barkeep took care of teamsters, who dropped in throughout the afternoon. Later the saloon did a brisk trade at its side or back door when wives and children came to carry out beer in buckets, cans, or pitchers (called growlers) for the evening meal. Finally, in the evening hours, the saloon returned to being a workingman's domain.

Saloons furnished the only free toilets in many cities, provided teamsters with watering troughs for their animals, and supplied all patrons with free newspapers. Many times, saloon keepers also cashed checks and lent money to customers. Saloons doubled as convenience stores, selling cigars and cigarettes, headache powders, and bonbons—nicknamed "wife pacifiers." Often they acted as communications centers, places where workers picked up their mail, left messages, had access to a telephone, heard the local political gossip, or learned of work opportunities.

Saloons also functioned as restaurants. Shortly after the Great Fire of 1871, a Chicago barman named Joseph C. Mackin, after trying various attractions to entice patrons to his saloon, began serving a hot oyster free with every drink. Although the claim is impossible to verify and his competitors quickly copied and expanded his idea, historian Perry Duis considers Mackin to be a candidate for the inventor of the free lunch. In any event, the idea spread across the country; within a decade it was a institution. Usually set out about eleven o'clock each morning and left until three in the afternoon, the free lunch came with the purchase of a nickel beer. Salty and spicy to provoke thirst, lunch fare was usually ample: cold meats, sandwiches, hard-boiled eggs, bread, wursts, sliced tomatoes, onions, and radishes. Sometimes soup or stew was served. Some Chicago saloons contracted with caterers like the William Davidson Company, but most often, the proprietor's wife prepared the lunch (she also filled in as a bartender). A large saloon on Chicago's near northwest side reputedly spent $30 to $40 each day ·on "15–20 pounds of meat, 1½–2 bushel of potatoes, 50 loaves of bread, 35 pounds of beans, 45 dozens of eggs, 10 dozen ears of sweet corn, $1.60–$2 worth of vegetables."[28]

The saloon supported and reinforced an all-male culture that was separate from the world of women and the demands of family. As Jack London put it in *John Barleycorn* (1913): "In the saloon, life was different. Men talked with great voices, laughed great laughs, and there was an atmosphere of greatness." Drinking rituals reinforced male solidarity. The prevailing custom of "treating" serves as an example. In the estimate of observers as diverse as Upton Sinclair, Thorstein Veblen, and the Anti-Saloon League, it typified saloon life: Each man treated the group to a round of drinks and was expected to stay long enough to be treated, in turn, by others. Occasionally, the barkeeper treated patrons, but he also manipulated the rite of hospitality to his own benefit. One historian, who traced treating to the folk customs of rural Ireland, called it "a norm of equality and solidarity," implying "resistance to individualism as well as acquisitiveness." Indeed, he suggested, "the whole saloon going experience affirmed communal over individualistic and privatistic values."[29]

As is well known, the saloon played a significant role in big-city machine politics. As a working-class club, it provided a natural stage, particularly at the ward or precinct level, for politicians and an excellent base for organizing the vote. Saloon keepers frequently entered politics. Lincoln Steffens's story in *The Shame of the Cities* (1904) became a famous joke: The fastest way to empty any city council chambers was to stand at its rear and shout, "Your saloon's on fire!" Part of the barkeep-politician's success lay in his interest in everyday neighborhood issues: who needed a job, who was sick or in need of food, who had just died, and for whose family one should pass the hat down the bar. One fictional saloon keeper, Mr. Dooley, created by Finley Peter Dunne and based on Chicago bar owner Jim McGarry, became a nationally syndicated commentator on local and national politics.

THE SODA FOUNTAIN

When pressed to suggest a substitute for the saloon, temperance advocates often pointed to the soda fountain as an alternative institution. By the end of the nineteenth century, the soda counter had become a characteristic feature, if not the social center, of many local drug stores. Elegant soda parlors became separate businesses that did a brisk trade in concoctions of carbonated water, syrups, and ice cream.

Interest in the medicinal qualities of effervescent waters, both natural and artificial, first prompted drugstore owners to install counters to dispense "soda water" (a form of artificial carbonation using sodium bicarbonate or baking soda) to cure ills, such as constipation, indigestion, and obesity. Soda water combined with various syrups and extracts—lemon, ginger, sarsaparilla—proved extremely popular by the mid-nineteenth century. At this time, Baltimore milk dealer Jacob Fussell, using a mechanical ice cream freezer, transformed his leftover cream into bulk ice cream. Fussell's economy of scale enabled him to sell his product cheaply and widely from Boston to Washington. He also sold huge quantities to Union supply officers during the Civil War. As with condensed milk, American veterans returned home with a fondness for commercial ice cream.

Ice cream and soda water served as the soda fountain's main staples. In 1874 Robert M. Green, a soda-fountain manufacturer working a concession at Philadelphia's Franklin Institute, substituted vanilla ice cream for the sweet cream he usually mixed with syrup and carbonated water. Green's profits soared. His will dictated that "Originator of the Ice Cream Soda" be engraved as his epitaph.

The last quarter of the nineteenth century saw the intense competition among soda-fountain owners leading to innovations both in the aesthetics of their establishments and the novel drinks and desserts their operators dispensed. Out of this experimentation came several mainstays of the American soft-drink industry. A pharmacist in Atlanta, John S. Pemberton, developed a carbonated water and syrup mix as a headache cure in 1886. He and a partner named it Coca-Cola because its ingredients included extracts derived from Peruvian coca leaves and African cola nuts. Pepsi-Cola first competed with Coca-Cola in 1896, when Calab D. Bradham began marketing it from New Bern, North Carolina. Two American confections—the sundae and the ice cream cone—developed along with the soda fountain. The sundae originated in the 1890s and the ice cream cone first appeared at the 1904 St. Louis Exposition.

THE VAUDEVILLE HOUSE

"The vaudeville theatre," wrote actor Edwin Milton Royle in *Scribner's Magazine* (October 1899), "is an American invention. There is nothing like it anywhere else in the world." Vaudeville had roots in several American entertainment traditions. The most direct connection was the variety show, performed in saloon music halls and involving an assortment of singers, dancing acts, and comedy sketches. Usually considered male entertainment, the rowdy variety hall featured performer-audience interaction: Patrons hissed, stamped, jeered, and shouted their approval or displeasure.

A new generation of promoters decided to clean up variety and to sell it to a middle-class audience in the early 1880s. Tony Pastor's New Fourteenth Street Theatre (1881) in New York marked an early attempt to take variety out of the concert saloons and thus to avoid the stigma of serving liquor and catering only to a raucous male clientele. However, it was Benjamin Franklin Keith, a Boston showman who had worked in circuses, tent shows, and dime museums, who fashioned the vaudeville that appealed to a family audience.

Variety, minus its off-color jokes, its profanity, and its saloon context, became vaudeville with some additional appropriations from other forms of popular entertainment. The minstrel show contributed the classic vaudeville exchange among the interlocutor and his comedian end-men, as well as its tradition of blackface performers. From the circus and wild west shows, vaudeville borrowed animal and acrobat acts, gymnasts and strong men like Eugene Sandow, The Modern Hercules. Burlesque and melodrama furnished humorous plays shortened to twenty-minute sketches and farces reduced to pantomimes. It also contributed the dancers that evolved into the vaudeville's corps de ballet. The new family show occasionally also borrowed from the legitimate stage, as when it booked stars such as Sarah Bernhardt and Ethel Barrymore.

At first glance, a typical vaudeville bill appears to have been little more than a jumble of sentimental ballads, trained animals, comic songsters, brief skits, ethnic humor, and innumerable dancing acts. In fact, the bill was a meticulously planned and precisely executed performance arranged (and constantly rearranged) to amuse its audience. Promoters structured it toward an exciting climax, what vaudevillians called the "wow finish." A typical bill for big-time vaudeville might include a nine-act or seven-act show, depending on whether there was an intermission. A small-time show might feature only five acts. Big-time circuits also meant a matinee and an evening program, one or more headliners or stars on every bill, and higher admission fees (25 cents to $1.00) than for small-time "vaude." A small-time show usually meant a split week (two different shows a week), frequently included three to six performances every day, only occasional headliners, and lower admission fees (5 cents to 25 cents).

A good vaudeville show's pace, particularly its development of the "continuous show," paralleled the tempo of urban life. F. F. Proctor, following the Boston lead of B. F. Keith, who introduced the continuous performance idea in 1883, promoted his vaudeville program with a showman's injunction:

AFTER BREAKFAST GO TO PROCTOR'S
AFTER PROCTOR'S GO TO BED

Promoters sought to have an audience all the time. They also wanted as all-inclusive an audience as possible. As Royle summarized it in 1899, vaudeville "appeals to the businessman, tired and worn, who drops in for half an hour on his way home; to the person who has an hour or two before a train goes, or before a business appointment; to the woman who is wearied of shopping; to the children who love animals and acrobats; to the man with his sweetheart or sister, to the individual who wants to be diverted but doesn't want to think or feel; to the American of all grades and kinds who wants a great deal for his money. The vaudeville theatre belongs to the era of the department store and the short story."[30]

The vaudeville house, unlike the saloon, especially welcomed families, in front of the lights and behind them. Families formed several famous vaudeville troupes: The Four Cohans, The Seven Little Foys, and the Four Marx Brothers. Families frequented theaters on holidays and Saturdays, with some theaters offering group rates. Attending a matinee after shopping at a downtown department store became a customary outing.

Vaudeville—a moderate, moral, middle-class form of play—also dramatized many underlying aspirations of the American people. For example, the skits, the sketches, and the star system all urged the audience on to the pursuit of success. The cult of the celebrity, as on the film screen and on the sports field, gave Americans new models for emulation. Headliners like Will Rodgers or George M. Cohan became new American heroes. Fanny Brice, Nora Bayes, and other female stars inspired other women to imitate their clothes and coiffure, their makeup, their jewelry, and (for some) their independence.[31]

Ethnicity, its tensions and its triumphs, permeated the vaudeville experience. For some immigrants—Sophie Tucker (Abuza), Harry Houdini (Weiss), and Al Jolson (Asa Yoelson)—the vaudeville stage became a ladder to personal success. For many others in the audience, the theater became a setting for spoofing, stereotyping, and sympathizing with the Irish and Italians, Germans and Jews, as well as blacks and "rubes" fresh from the countryside. These comic and exaggerated exposures of many people's prejudices tended to temper ethnic hostilities, since the audience usually recognized a common humanity in other nationalities. Unlike the insular ethnic theater, vaudeville drew the residents of the polyglot city together and gave them a glimpse not only of themselves but of how others saw them.[32]

As with new movie theaters, the vaudeville house itself also came to be a show. B. F. Keith furnished "gentleman's smoking and reading rooms," as well as "suites of rooms for exclusive use of lady patrons, furnished with dressing cases and every toilet requisite—all free." Marble walls, large mirrors, brass appointments, plush carpeting, upholstered chairs, and thousands of electrical fixtures filled the palaces.

THE COUNTRY FAIR

Many rural Americans first saw demonstrations of electricity's new uses at a county or state fair. Such annual fairs marked the agricultural harvest and provided a seasonal gathering of country and town people. Most histories of American fairs stress their role in celebrating the rural economy and farm life. Early on, however, fairs assumed commercial and recreational roles, acting as showcases of national consumer products and as festivals of urban play activities.

The Great Granger's Annual Picnic Exhibition at Williams Grove, Pennsylvania, displayed all types of consumer products. Begun in 1873, this major regional fair grew from a one-day event attracting 10,000 people to a week-long program by 1885 when over 150,000 people from 29 states attended. Visitors to the fair often became temporary residents of Williams Grove as campers, renters of cottages, hotel patrons, and boarders in private homes. Firms displayed 1,329 lots of merchandise under the heading "Commercial Exhibits" in 1892. The goods ranged from bedroom furniture to kitchen stoves, from parlor suites to sewing machines. Frequently, a consumer could do comparative shopping within the fairground, since various models and brands of the same product were often demonstrated. In 1910, for instance, 37 different washing machines were exhibited. By the turn of the twentieth century, rural consumers could view and test-drive the latest automobile models, such as the Locomobile, that were on display. The Williams Grove fairs of 1912 through 1916 included auto shows. Newspaper comments in that decade noted the increasing number of those attending who now came by car as opposed to the hordes that formerly came by rail.[33]

State fairs and some county fairs looked like small towns by 1915. Flimsy wooden buildings, tents, and temporary sheds and pens gave way to massive structures of brick, steel, and concrete. Legislative appropriations, plus profits from the fairs, built machinery halls, children's and women's buildings, baseball parks, auditoriums, concessionaire stands, nickelodeons, post offices, and retail stores.

Just as Americans first introduced an amusement zone to world's fairs, so they also pioneered in expanding popular entertainment at the agricultural fairs. Horse racing remained a standard fixture. Minstrels, band pavilions, circuses, games of chance, vaudeville shows, amusement rides, and exotic food concessions were features of fairs by 1900. A fair's midway introduced country folk to the city amusement park's mechanical rides. Here one could purchase an ascent on a Ferris wheel, a hot-air balloon, or a barnstorming airplane. If more excitement was still required, one might take in a motion picture show or pay to see a disaster extravaganza, such as "San Francisco's 1906 Earthquake."

The bazaar of popular culture that came alive at a fair after dark was a nocturnal experience largely unknown to rural communities. First gas, then arc, and then electrical lighting set the stage. Amusement rides, dance halls, and side shows usually remained open until midnight. Nightlife—with its constant movement and colorful lighting, false-front architecture, and advertising hype— made the midway one of the spatial and cultural antecedents of the commercial strips that developed in American cities with the spread of the automobile.

Park Outings

PLEASURE GARDENS

New York's Central Park, built (1858–78) by Frederick Law Olmsted and Calvert Vaux, served as the prototype for a municipal-park movement that spread across the nation. Minneapolis owned no parkland in 1880 but had 1,400 acres a decade later.

Cleveland expanded its park system from 93 acres in 1890 to 1,500 by 1905. Los Angeles had 6 acres in 1880 and 3,700 in 1905. Similar park development took place in Boston, Chicago, and Kansas City. Olmsted, his firm, or his disciples designed many of these urban public parks. San Francisco's Golden Gate Park (figure 6.9) aptly represents these pleasure gardens that provided a vast landscape of trees, meadows, and quiet waterways. Here families could stroll, picnic, listen to concerts, and go boating. The grounds covered thousands of acres; the designers planned and planted the park to create the effect that one was removed from the city, away in a pastoral retreat.

To achieve this end, pleasure gardens initially permitted few buildings or sculpture. Translucent conservatories were allowed, since they displayed exotic plants. Pergolas, bandstands, and pavilions, often constructed of trees with the bark intact, maintained rusticity. Eventually, however, these picturesque structures gave way to neoclassical formalism when museums, art galleries, and zoos invaded many scenic city parks in the 1890s. Unlike the grid street pattern of the typical American city, carriage ways and footpaths in parks meandered. An Olmsted innovation, first introduced in Central Park, separated vehicular from pedestrian traffic.

Cities established parks for many reasons, among them to prevent cholera and other infectious diseases, to increase real estate development, to allow healthy recreation, to curtail alcoholism and promote temperance, to promote civic pride, and to control and civilize an unruly urban populace. Olmsted's own rationale remained constant throughout his long career. To him the park exemplified a three-dimensional landscape painting that acted "in a direct remedial way to enable men to better resist the harmful influences of ordinary town life and to recover what they lose from them."[34] The pleasure garden, designed as a quiet rural retreat, served as an antidote to metropolitan clutter, noise, and congestion. Although its naturalness might at first give the appearance of virgin landscape, much of it resulted from the deliberate hand of man. Nowhere is this more evident than in the several pleasure-garden parks—Fairmount in Philadelphia, Jackson in Chicago, Forest in St. Louis, and Harbor View in San Francisco—that evolved from carefully planned world's-fair sites.

To refresh the city dweller by providing rural scenery made sense to the middle- and upper-class gentry who supported pleasure parks and who sat on their governing commissions. To these individuals—who also favored other middle landscapes, such as suburbs, chautauquas, and college campuses—the pleasure park provided the appropriate environment for promenading and contemplating. Promoters of parks saw the pleasure garden as an environment for sedate family fun: croquet on the meadows, boating on the lagoons, carriage riding on the paths. The prohibitions were many: no gambling, no dancing, no soliciting, no raucous music, no alcohol, and no activities at night.

Disputes arose over the appropriate use of pleasure gardens. Two distinct and conflicting definitions of the park—the upper-class concept, with its emphasis on cultural enlightenment and the refinement of manners, versus a lower-class definition emphasizing fun and games—surfaced in cities such as New York, Worcester, and Chicago. An incident in Brooklyn's Prospect Park in 1908 points up these differing views. Over several successive summer Sundays, the park police arrested several dozen East Side immigrants who had taken the nickel ride to the park from Manhattan. The rules they were accused of breaking were satirized in the following excerpt, "The Prospect Park Commandments," from *The Brooklyn Daily Times:*

> Thou shalt not play with a ball.
> Thou shalt not walk on forbidden grass.
> Thou shalt not bring thy luncheon nor even bags of fruit.

By the turn of the twentieth century, another type of municipal park emerged in American cities. Users often referred to this model as the "play ground" as opposed to the "pleasure garden." Galen Cranz has called this recreational landscape the "reform park," since it grew out of two ideas of the Progressive reformers—their agitation for children's playgrounds and their belief that recreational needs were best served at the neighborhood level.[35] Pulaski Park (figure 6.10) in Chicago aptly demonstrates this change in the history of American parks.

Usually only a block or two in size, a typical neighborhood park and its fieldhouse resembled its surrounding commercial buildings, factories, and apartments. Fieldhouses, a new building type, usually included meeting rooms, a gymnasium (figure 6.4), and showers. Playing fields surrounded the building. Such parks also had outdoor play equipment, (particularly slides and swings) and sandboxes for toddlers. Swimming and wading pools became common. Large neighborhood parks might also include handball, tennis, and basketball courts. Almost all, by 1920, had electric lighting for night activities.

This change in the design of parks reflected a shift in middle-class attitudes toward more active recreation. It also expressed the perspective of reformers, who sought to counter the growing commercialization of leisure with the physical activities of sport. Pressure for "sports and games" instead of "repose and contemplation" in public parks came from individuals like Jane Addams, Jacob Riis, and Lillian Wald, who founded the Playground Association of America in 1906. Some city park administrations also changed their philosophy and, as in the case of the Worcester, Massachusetts, park board, also altered their names, becoming Parks and Recreation Commissions.[36]

Unlike the pleasure garden, which had no facilities for dancing, a fieldhouse gymnasium converted into a neighborhood ballroom. Grounds could be rented for community festivals, family reunions, and holiday parties. Fieldhouses often served as community centers, where fraternal orders met, bicycle clubs held meetings, and English-language and naturalization classes took place.

AMUSEMENT MIDWAYS

Whereas recreation at a neighborhood park could be a daily event in good weather, attending an amusement park usually involved a special excursion on a holiday or weekend. Admission meant passage into an illusionary world of fantasy, complete with bizarre architecture, exotic shows, and thrilling mechanical rides. Conceived and designed as a "total" play experience, the amusement parks had their antecedents in resort areas, such as Atlantic City, New Jersey, and Long Beach, California, which sought to extend their popularity and business by adding amusement rides. The midways at state and world's fairs likewise contributed to the amusement park's evolution. By 1915, nearly every American city had a major park, many featuring two or three. Boston's Revere Beach, Philadelphia's Willow Grove, Atlanta's Ponce de Leon Park, Cleveland's Euclid Beach, Denver's Manhattan Beach, and San Francisco's The Chutes were meccas for a fun-seeking public. Dominating them all in size, scope, and fame was Brooklyn's Coney Island.

Coney Island first became fashionable in the 1870s as an upper middle-class seaside resort on Brooklyn's southern shore. In 1893 and 1895 fires destroyed most of the entertainment sector in West Brighton, but in their wake several local entrepreneurs developed new attractions that they enclosed in separate amusement parks. First came Captain Paul Boyton's Sea Lion Park, with its dramatic waterslide, Shoot-the-Chutes; then in 1897, George Tilyou's Steeplechase Park, named for the mechanical race track that ringed its perimeters. By 1903 Sea Lion Park, under new ownership, became Luna Park. Finally, Dreamland opened across the street in 1904. Thus, the "New Coney Island" was not one, but several amusement parks. Together they comprised a form of leisure that, in the phrase of Luna Park manager Frederic Thompson, was "the business of amusing the million."

From May until September, Coney Island, unlike most pleasure gardens, stayed open until 10 P.M., sometimes later on holidays. Most individual attractions at the parks cost a nickel or a dime. Sometimes, however, there were special prices, as in 1905 when Steeplechase Park began offering a combination ticket of twenty-five rides for twenty-five cents. Many people who could afford only the nickel carfare traveled to Coney Island just to watch the crowds.

Those crowds included all social classes: salesmen, families, clerks, secretaries, professionals, shop girls, and laborers. Two surveys of working-class expenditures in Manhattan in 1907 and 1909 found that workers' families made one or two excursions a year to Coney Island.[37] In contrast to the pleasure garden, the neighborhood park, or their own residences, Coney Island presented its patrons with fantasy and illusion. Like the vaudeville house and the movie palace, parks such as Luna and Dreamland appealed to popular notions of magnificence. As stage sets, amusement parks provided romantic extravagance for those who walked along their promenades and midways. The Steeplechase's dramatic cyclorama, A Trip to the Moon, took visitors in a spaceship to a lunar landing site, where they met the Man in the Moon upon his throne and dancing moon maidens who, as part of the fantasy, pressed bits of green cheese upon them as souvenirs of their escape from Earth.[38]

Coney Island became an "Electric Eden" at night. Borrowing from the example of the Chicago 1893 Fair, Frederick Thompson illuminated his Luna Park with a quarter-million electric lights. To dwarf this extravaganza, the designers of Dreamland erected a 375-foot central tower that would anticipate the famous Tower of Jewels at San Francisco's World's Fair of 1915. To eclipse Luna's nighttime display, Dreamland installed a million electric lights, one hundred thousand for its tower alone. In his 1913 painting *Battle of the Lights, Mardi Gras, Coney Island,* Joseph Stella evoked the riotous spectacle of sound, sight, and sensation that the amusement park could create.

The amusement park gave visitors a chance to test themselves against the machines—railroads, elevated trains, and inclines—that dominated daily urban life. Inspiration for some Coney Island rides, for example, the Switchback Railroad or the Flip-Flop Railway, came from modes of transportation used in such industries as mining. Scenic railroads, also called roller coasters, exaggerated the twists and turns of urban elevated lines. Coney Island's Leap-Frog Railway gave riders a vicarious sense of being in a simulated head-on train wreck. Here riders experienced risk under relatively safe conditions and enjoyed a minor catharsis of the noise and speed that were becoming increasingly common in the industrial world.[39]

Roller coasters and Ferris wheels—fundamental artifacts for any park after 1900—simulated flight and speed. Given the age's fascination with motion and the monumental, they quickly became the criteria by which any amusement park was measured. Who had the tallest, fastest, most thrilling coaster or wheel? Less mammoth rides, for instance, the Human Toboggan, also enjoyed immense popularity. So did fun-house attractions: Steeplechase Park's Human Whirlpool (a large turning hardwood saucer that, as its speed increased, tossed riders to its rim); the Barrel of Fun (a huge, slowly revolving cylinder that frequently rolled patrons off their feet and brought strangers into sudden, intimate contact); or the Blowhole Theatre (where concealed compressed air jets sent hats and skirts flying). These rides and activities threw people off balance, dispelling, if momentarily, serious adult concerns in the sensations of the immediate moment.

An essential element of Coney Island's appeal and that of amusement parks elsewhere was, as John Kasson suggested, "the contrast it offered to conventional society, everyday routine, and dominant cultural authorities." Coney Island provided "an area in which visitors were temporarily freed from normative demands. As they disembarked from ferryboats with fanciful names like Pegasus, or walked toward the amusement parks along Surf Avenue, they felt themselves passing into a special realm of exciting possibility, a distinctive milieu that encouraged types of behavior and social interaction that in other contexts would have been regarded askance."[40]

The amusement park's celebration of visceral, sensory, participatory play (figure 6.2) temporarily suspended many social conventions. As one observer noted, "Coney Island has a code of conduct which is all her own." This looser, less Victorian code, manifested itself in numerous ways. Many mechanical rides threw men and women into each other's arms. Young couples could venture unchaperoned into the Laugh-in-the-Dark or the Tunnel-of-Love.[41] Period photographs and postcards all suggest the delight in informal, less decorous behavior. Release rather than restraint characterized the mood.

Like vaudeville, amusement parks featured varied entertainments, such as bathing facilities, band pavilions, dance halls, and circus attractions. Like vaudeville, amusement parks celebrated the city—its transport technology, its man-made physical environment, and its speed, anonymity, and heterogeneity.

Unlike pleasure gardens that nurtured communing with nature, amusement parks offered the mechanisms for mastering nature. Amusement parks made no pretensions to educate, uplift, or edify the masses who passed through their gates; they were strictly in the entertainment business. People who came to Coney Island, wrote Frederic Thompson in the 1907 *Independent*, "are not in a serious mood, and do not want to encounter seriousness. They have enough seriousness in their every-day lives, and the keynote of the thing they do demand is change. Coney Island represents a different world—a dream world . . . gayer and more different from the every-day world."

FIGURE 7.1. Graduation and Recognition Day (ca. 1890), Chautauqua Literary and Scientific Circle, Chautauqua, New York. Courtesy of the Chautauqua Assembly.

FIGURE 7.2. Charity Salvation Army lodging house (1897). Photograph courtesy of the Byron Collection, Museum of the City of New York.

7

❧

TRUSTING in the Lord Jesus Christ for strength," read the pledge of the Christian Endeavor Society, founded by Congregational minister Francis E. Clark in 1881, "I promise Him I will strive to do whatever He will have me do." In addition to attending weekly devotional meetings and monthly gatherings for special consecration to "promote an earnest Christian life," members of the society (3.5 million members in 1910) promoted a wide range of social and educational crusades. To many of them, church and school were common wellsprings and bastions of American Christianity and nationality. Religious fervor and educational earnestness were the warp and woof of a moral fabric that interwove everyday schooling and believing. To American Victorians, the active verb, to strive, and its synonyms of purposeful, didactic exertion—to contend, to struggle, to endeavor—aptly summarized this interconnection and interaction of worship and learning.

The interrelation was explicit in some aspects of the culture. French Catholics in New Orleans, German Lutherans in St. Paul, Minnesota, the Amish in Lancaster County, Pennsylvania, Mennonites in Shipshewana, Indiana, and Hasidic Jews in Brooklyn established and maintained religious schools that taught an additional "R" besides those of the traditional curriculum. Similar denominationalism characterized over a hundred church-related institutions of higher education founded between 1870 and 1920; several would be important contributors to the university movement of the 1890s.[1] Sunday schools (which sometimes met in public-school buildings) evangelized and educated children. Sunday school teachers began the enormously influential Chautauqua movement (figure 7.1), a school-church institution whose main aspiration Alan Trachtenberg characterized as "the sacralization of culture in America."[2] Crusades, often initiated at a local school board or church vestry to protest alcoholism (figure 7.9), juvenile delinquency, prostitution, gambling, drug abuse, and pornography, all combined interdenominational fervor, religious rhetoric, social science research, and political science methods to press for moral reformations.

Schooling Youth

COMMON SCHOOLS AND KINDERGARTENS

Victorian Americans expanded their primary educational system in scope, size, and substance. Whereas in 1870 elementary schools enrolled 57 percent of the nation's youngsters sometime between five and eighteen years of age, the figure passed 75 percent by 1918. More children also spent more time in the common schools, the average days attended rising from 45 a year in 1870 to over 90 in 1918.

In many rural, one-room elementary schools, a single teacher taught children from ages six through fourteen. Such schools usually had a rough tripartite division into beginning, intermediate, and advanced work, with reading, writing, spelling, and arithmetic stressed in the first phase; geography and nature study added in the intermediate phase; and history and grammar included in the advanced phase. During a school day that lasted from 8 A.M. to 4 P.M. in the winter months, the students learned the four Rs: reading, 'riting, 'rithmetic, and recitation. *McGuffey's Eclectic Readers* were commonly the texts to be memorized and recited. Between 1836 and 1922, approximately 122 million copies of these readers were sold, with the strongest sales being from 1870 to 1890.

As the titles of many McGuffey stories suggest—for example, "Respect for the Sabbath Rewarded," "The Bible the Best of Classics"—the readers included spiritual as well as reading lessons. McGuffey's didactic tales instilled other beliefs, such as "the primary purpose of government is the protection of private property; wealth was an outward sign of inner salvation; prolonged poverty was a sign of God's disapproval; and, to succeed in life, one needed to be sober, frugal, and energetic."[3] Although they were designed to be used in coeducational classes, the readers only occasionally featured girls as principal characters. In this neglect, the textbooks reflected the male sexism of the age and the common belief that the female (as opposed to the male) character possessed few moral defects.

School boards adhered to the symbol of woman as the paragon of moral virtue in their preferential recruitment of female teachers. An occupation that was originally a masculine preserve in the eighteenth century became a feminine one (86 percent) by the early twentieth century. However, as the curriculum and administration of common-school education underwent standardization, the careers of these schoolmarms usually went no further than their classrooms. Their role was defined as being moral and loving teachers, supervised and managed by male principals and superintendents.

During the decades following 1876, city schools took the lead in the development of the eight-year school system.[4] The bureaucratic organization of a typical urban system included (1) an administrative hierarchy with defined roles for a superintendent, principals, assistant principals, and teachers; (2) graded levels of instruction in which students moved progressively from one plateau to another; (3) a common course of study for all schools to assure uniformity of the curricular content in all grades; and (4) an emphasis on order, efficiency, and regular attendance and punctuality by the students.

Bureaucracy in metropolitan public schools characterizes only one major trend in American educational history. The *de jure* segregation of blacks in the South and of Native Americans in the

West, as well as the *de facto* segregation of blacks in the North,
Chicanos in the Southwest, and Asians in the Far West, meant that
a significant number of American children did not attend schools
that were truly "common," that is, without distinctions regarding
race, class, religion, or ethnic background. Other Americans,
Roman Catholics and Lutherans, choose to have their children
remain outside the public schools. At its Third Plenary Council in
Baltimore in 1884, the American Catholic hierarchy decreed that
a parochial school must be erected near each Catholic church and
that parents must send their children to Catholic schools unless
they were released from that obligation by the local bishop.

Catholic parochial schools assumed identifiable characteristics.
Religious communities, such as the Sisters of Mercy or School
Sisters of Notre Dame, staffed their classrooms. Catholic publishers, including the Sadlier Company and Benzinger Brothers, supplied the textbooks and other curricular materials. Catholic
prayers and devotional practices structured the school day. In
some parochial schools, particularly those of German communities, students learned the native language of the immigrant parish
as well as English.

A new organizational unit, the kindergarten (figure 7.3), appeared in both parochial and public schools. Introduced by disciples of the German pedagogue, Friedrich Froebel (1782–1852),
into the St. Louis school system in 1873 and demonstrated in the
Women's Building at the 1876 Centennial Exhibition, the innovation spread rapidly, so that by the turn of the century there were
225,394 kindergartens in the United States.

As a method of early childhood education that was to lead the
child from a world concentrated on self to a wider society of
other children, the kindergarten movement (and its variants)
combined German idealism and some early behavioral studies of
child development. Froebel advocated a model maternal teacher
whose pedagogy should be passive and protective, not directive
and interfering. His kindergartens employed set routines of creative play through organized stories, songs, and games and
through the manipulation of Froebel "gifts"—colored forms and

shapes through which children might express their individual selves and develop both cognitive reasoning and affective understanding.[5]

William T. Harris, school superintendent in St. Louis, decided in the 1870s that the only way to save slum children from vice and corruption was to get them into kindergartens. Harris insisted that such preschools were necessary because traditional socializing agencies like the family, church, and community had collapsed in the slums. Hence, in addition to Froebel's original philosophy of placing the learner at the center of the educational process, the kindergarten in America also became an agent for urban social reform. In it, children aged 4 to 6 were taught cleanliness, politeness, obedience, and self-control. Reformers also hoped that the moral habits learned in kindergarten would influence a child's parents, particularly the mother. For example, the Plymouth Cordage Company saw its kindergarten as a way of removing the children from the house for part of the day, so the mother could give her undivided attention to housework. Kindergarten teachers at Plymouth made periodic visits to children's homes to interest the mothers in the children's work and to survey their students' domestic environments.[6]

THE RISE OF HIGH SCHOOLS

The early nineteenth-century high school, usually defined as any school beyond the elementary level in which students were taught "all those branches which fit a young man for college," tended to be elitist, male, classical, and private. Its early twentieth-century form, however, strove to be populist, coeducational, vocational, and public. School-attendance figures demonstrate the growth of this "new" high school. In 1890, 202,963 students attended 2,526 public high schools; by 1920, the number rose to 1,851,965 students in 14,326 public institutions.[7]

Unlike their great-grandparents, Americans raising offspring in the early twentieth century fretted more about the behavior of their teenagers than of their youngest children. Their concern—bolstered by several decades of public discussion on the nation's "youth problem" by educators and social scientists, magazine writers, and muckrakers—centered on juvenile misbehavior and delinquency. In popular guidebooks and magazines, as well as from chautauqua lecturers and church pulpits, middle-class parents were warned about two separate, but interrelated problems: their own children's possible misconduct and the influence of those already "gone bad." Pilfering, vagrancy, roaming the streets, petty larceny, drinking, begging, and fighting characterized "bad boys."[8] Reformers sought to deal with such behavior with two strategies: to establish a special legal status for the young, as in the Illinois Juvenile Court Act of 1899, and to enact compulsory education statutes (in every state by 1918) at the high school level.

Comprehensive high schools offered a diverse curriculum. In 1889 entering students in Muncie, Indiana, chose between two four-year courses, the Latin and the English courses, the sole difference between them being whether one did or did not take "the language." By the early 1920s, secondary school students in Muncie had twelve options: general, college preparatory, music, art, shorthand, bookkeeping, applied electricity, mechanical drafting, printing, machine shop, manual arts, and home economics.

High school became an avenue of economic mobility for working-class teenagers, who used its diploma to gain white-collar work. For instance, so many women students entered public high schools to take the "commercial course" by 1915 that the enrollment in such courses outstripped that of private business colleges.[9] Male students increasingly found graduation from high school a necessity for entry-level jobs as bookkeepers, cashiers, salesmen, and managers.

Segregating students into separate courses of study according to vocational goals, aptitude tests (pioneered by Hugo Munsterberg in 1910), or the evaluations of "guidance counselors" meant that high schooling could be a fragmenting experience. To counter charges that the differentiated tracking of the high school had antidemocratic implications, education reformers fostered programs that were designed to promote a collective "school spirit." One tactic, directed at the immigrant, insisted on all instruction being given in English; another made civics a required course for all students; a third instituted the homeroom period as a time for group activity and guidance. A fourth sought school unity through an expanded program of extracurricular activities, such as student government, clubs, assemblies, publications, and athletics (figure 7.4). School officials also claimed that athletic contests, particularly team sports, promoted good health, taught cooperation, and generated élan among spectators.[10]

GOING TO COLLEGE

In establishing new colleges and universities, Victorian Americans had several objectives: to accommodate heretofore neglected clienteles, such as women or minorities; to develop special curricular emphases, such as engineering or business; to represent religious values; and to serve particular localities or regions. Several universities, for example, Duke, Stanford, and Vanderbilt, resulted from capitalist philanthropy. As early as 1870, there were more American colleges, medical schools, and law schools than in all of Europe. With the increase in institutions came a corresponding increase in the student population. While less than a percent were in college in the 1870s, 8 percent were by the early 1920s. The increase in the number and proportion of women in college was due, in part, to the founding of such women's colleges as Smith and Vassar and new coeducational universities (figure 7.5). Black young people also participated in greater numbers, but almost entirely through all-black institutions, such as Fisk or Howard. While Catholics might go to Fordham and Notre Dame and Jews to City College and New York University, the American collegiate experience before World War I remained primarily a WASP phenomenon. For example, a survey of undergraduate liberal arts institutions in the mid-twenties revealed that 88 percent of the undergraduates were native born.[11]

Graduate and professional faculties, largely nonexistent before the Civil War, grew in the half-century thereafter. German universities, with their emphasis on applying scientific methods of research to all knowledge, including economics, history, and theology, provided the model. New institutions, such as Johns Hopkins University, adopted the German strategy from their founding (1876); established schools, such as Columbia University, transformed their curricula and administration to conform to its philosophy. In such institutions, teaching methods changed. Earlier nineteenth-century methods involved the learning of traditional forms of knowledge, often by recitation or through the explication of texts. University education replaced this pedagogy with lectures based on the results of research. The research seminar and the laboratory served as the contexts for training students under the supervision of a professor. As on the factory assembly line and in the business office, learning, too, came to be seen as quantifiable and specialized. One now took a prescribed number of courses (sometimes called units), each worth a designated number of credit hours.

Specialized academic research led to a proliferation of scholarly fields and subfields. An 1876 student surveying the courses available to him in a University of Wisconsin catalog would find thirty-five; one examining a 1915 course book could choose from over a thousand. A comparison of the two catalogs would also point out the recent development and new influence of the social sciences—economics, anthropology, and sociology—in the college curriculum.

This representative Wisconsin student's choice of courses resulted from the elective system pioneered by President Charles Eliot at Harvard in the 1870s. When Eliot began his tenure, Harvard's prescribed curriculum emphasized Latin, Greek, and mathematics and included some work in philosophy, history, physics, chemistry, French, and German. The only electives available were in the sciences and modern languages. Eliot expanded his faculty and encouraged the faculty members to do research and to present that work in specialized course offerings. By the early twentieth-century, Harvard's only course requirement for graduation was freshman English composition.[12] In addition to his elective system, Eliot introduced another perennial ritual of higher education. His brainchild, the College Entrance Examination Board, gave its first tests in 1901 as a means of standardizing college admissions.

In her survey of campus life, Helen Lefkowitz Horowitz suggested that by 1920 there were at least three student subcultures in the American undergraduate experience: college men (and women), outsiders, and rebels. The first two had existed since the late eighteenth century; the third developed in Victorian America.[13]

Male students who espoused "college life" put a high value on camaraderie, on bonds that united them with each other against the faculty. They supported the fraternity movement of the 1880s and sought membership in elite clubs and other student organizations that emphasized polish and style. Rowdy and hedonistic, the typical college male took part in campus athletics, battled townies, and hazed new students. This adolescent peer culture included individuals like Henry Siedel Canby at Yale, Theodore Roosevelt at Harvard, and Lincoln Steffens at Berkeley.

At new coeducational institutions, such as Cornell and the University of Michigan, most women students found themselves to be outsiders. Male students excluded them from extracurricular activities. Studious, polite, and hardworking, these women had male counterparts; both sought the approval of their teachers, not of their peers. These outsiders welcomed the emergence of a university context and the elective system. "Heading for vocations and the professions, they focused on the curriculum and sought to do well." They saw the "classroom as their area of combat and sparred with each other and their professors."[14] Not without reason did some of these undergraduate outsiders later enter higher education's establishment.

While certain individuals had always dissented from college life, a new cadre of undergraduates saw themselves as rebels in the 1910s. They identified with the unconventional artists, writers, and thinkers whom historian Henry May argued brought about "the end to American innocence." College rebels were as "excited about ideas as any outsider; they could be as hedonistic as any college man; but unlike the first two student subcultures, they did not view their undergraduate years as instrumental to future success." Unlike both the fraternity types and the outsiders, they recognized that campus life was not everything; beyond the university existed a world of economics, politics, labor unrest, and the arts. But unlike the outsiders, they challenged the college types for control of the campus newspaper and other activities. With its "mix of iconoclasm, radicalism, bohemianism, and opposition to traditional college conduct," the college rebellion included many of the luminaries of early modern American intellectual history, for example, Walter Lippmann at Harvard, Max Eastman at Williams, and Randolph Bourne at Columbia.[15]

The emergence of the university in America provided a matrix for the development of what Burton J. Bledstein called the "culture of professionalism." Institutions of higher education helped restructure middle-class society according to a "distinct vertical vision—one of career." American universities played a significant role in widening the influence of the established professions (medicine, law, and teaching), as well as validating the status of new ones (engineering, nursing, social work, science, and business administration). Higher education "made possible a social faith in merit, competence, discipline, and control" that came to characterize professional achievement and success. "The most emphatically middle-class man," Bledstein noted, "was the professional, improving his worldly lot as he offered his services to society, expressing his expanding expectations at ascending stages of an occupation." In the four decades after 1870, the number of all professionals increased four times to total 1,150,000 by 1910. In the same period, those in finance, accounting, and management trebled, amounting to 276,000.[16]

In effect, the "Gilded Age was also a guilded age," a rapidly evolving "credentialed society" in which individuals and groups reinforced and codified their status through professional societies, journals, specialized training, national meetings, and accrediting associations.[17] Take, for example, the middle managers of the new industrial order: An accountant working for Price, Waterhouse and Company probably belonged to the American Institute of Accountants, read the monthly *Journal of Accountancy* (1906), and might have taken his baccalaureate degree at one of the 114 colleges and universities that offered accounting programs by

1916. Factory and production supervisors invariably joined the American Society of Mechanical Engineers, or later the Society of Industrial Engineers, and read journals, such as the *American Engineer,* subsequently renamed *Factory* and later *System,* or *Engineering News,* which, in 1916, became *Industrial Management.* Such managers might have been trained at any one of the new engineering schools founded in the late nineteenth century: MIT, Purdue, Cornell, or Case Institute.[18]

Adult Education

THE CHAUTAUQUA MOVEMENT

From 1876 to 1915, the rate of illiteracy in the United States fell from 20 percent to 6 percent. The American tradition of self-improvement, combined with the penchant for voluntary association, produced an impressive array of educational enterprises—fairs, libraries, museums, college extension courses, social settlements, women's clubs, night schools, unions (figure 7.6), and professional societies—in which adults pursued knowledge. in post–Civil War America.

The Chautauqua Literary and Scientific Circle, begun by John Vincent in 1878, became the most systematic, national, and popular of these programs. The aim of the CLSC, as Vincent created it, was "to promote habits of reading and study in nature, art, science, and in secular and sacred literature, in connection with the routine of daily life . . . so as to secure to them the college student's general outlook upon the world and life, and to develop the habit of close, connected, persistent thinking."[19] Vincent coordinated the CLSC from its headquarters on Lake Chautauqua in New York's scenic Allegheny Mountains. Working from a booklist that included such works as Richard T. Ely's *An Introduction to Political Economy,* James Bryce's *The American Commonwealth,* and *The Autobiography of Lincoln Steffens,* chautauquans read and discussed such books over a four-year period. They did so in hometown study circles and during eight-week summer sessions at the New York headquarters. Vincent augmented the work of the local reading circles with a monthly publication called *The Chautauquan,* a periodical designed to assist readers with the required readings, offer hints for more effective study and discussion, and provide news of other circles around the country. Those who completed the four-year program received a diploma at the ceremonies of CLSC's annual summer "Recognition Day" (figure 7.1).

During its first year, 8,000 men and women enrolled in the CLSC, with 1,718 taking diplomas four years later. Enrollments rose to almost 200,000 during the early 1890s and to 300,000 by 1918. One historian estimated that some 10,000 local circles sprang up during the CLSC's first two decades, a quarter in villages with populations of fewer than 500 and half with populations of 500 to 3,500.[20]

The CLSC grew out of the cultural ethos that I have identified as striving. It combined religious feeling and educational earnestness. In 1874 Vincent, a Methodist clergyman, and Lewis Miller, an Akron, Ohio, businessman, started a summer program at Lake Chautauqua to train Sunday school teachers. In addition to instruction, the Assembly offered recreation on the lake and lectures on topics other than religious themes. Chautauqua grew to be one of Victorian America's most popular middle-class resorts. Hotels, clubhouses, lecture halls, boardinghouses, parks, classrooms, auditoriums, and permanent summer homes were built on its lakeshore.

Chautauqua's landscape had several spatial forebears: the residential college campus, the outdoor religious camp meeting, and the communitarian settlement. Its ambience also paralleled the American suburb, pleasure park, and world's fair. Although touted as a place of rest and relaxation, the daily schedule at Chautauqua left relatively little time for either. It began at 6:00 A.M. with morning devotions, then breakfast and a full morning of classes and discussion groups. While afternoons usually included a quiet hour and some time for recreation, afternoon classes and concerts were also scheduled. During the day children were sent to special

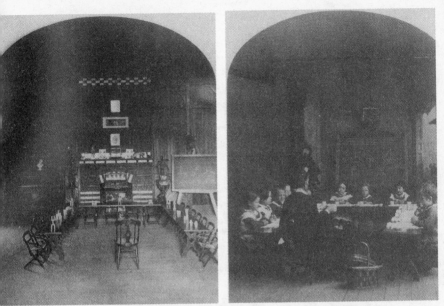

FIGURE 7.3. Kindergarten interiors, the Woman's Pavilion (1876), International Exhibition, Philadelphia, Pennsylvania. Stereograph courtesy of the Library of Congress, Division of Prints and Photographs.

FIGURE 7.4. Frances Johnson, *Track Meet, Central High School,* Washington, D.C. (ca. 1910). Photograph courtesy of the Library of Congress, Division of Prints and Photographs.

FIGURE 7.5. American history class, Professor Frederick Jackson Turner, University of Wisconsin–Madison (ca. 1894). Photograph courtesy of the State Historical Society of Wisconsin.

FIGURE 7.6. Arlington Branch, Number 500, International Workers of the World (ca. 1910). Photograph courtesy of the Archives of Labor and Urban Affairs, University Archives, Wayne State University.

FIGURE 7.7. Afro-American Baptism (ca. 1896). Photograph courtesy of the Cook Collection, Valentine Museum, Richmond, Virginia.

FIGURE 7.8. Evangelical street preacher tent wagon (ca. 1900), Chicago, Illinois. Photograph courtesy of the Chicago Historical Society.

FIGURE 7.9. "Inebriate's Express" (ca. 1900). Chromolithograph courtesy of the Library of Congress, Division of Prints and Photographs.

FIGURE 7.10. Frances Johnson, self-portrait with three symbols (beer, cigarette, and petticoat showing) of anti-Victorian female conduct (ca. 1896). Photograph courtesy of the Library of Congress, Division of Prints and Photographs.

kindergarten and youth-group programs. Vespers came after the dinner hour, followed by the day's major evening program (usually a speaker, such as Julia Lathrop or Jacob Riis) in the auditorium. A quiet bell closed the day at 10:00 or 11:00 P.M.

The success of the New York chautauqua spawned progeny elsewhere. Calling themselves "daughter" chautauquas or independent assemblies, these associations usually had their own grounds, preferably near a lake or wooded area with camping facilities. People came to attend lectures, scientific demonstrations (especially dealing with electricity), musical events, plays, and nondenominational religious exercises. Representative of the 292 independents founded by 1912 were those at Lakeside, Ohio, Winona Lake, Indiana, and Bay View, Michigan.

Keith Vawter, an energetic entrepreneur in the Redpath Lyceum Bureau in Chicago, put the chautauqua movement on the road in 1904. He furnished the talent, tents, advertising, and work crews for week-long assemblies that traveled, by rail, from small town to town. Much of a tent chautauqua's program consisted of music—involving orchestras, Swiss bell ringers, glee clubs, and string quartets. The lecturers, however, formed the backbone of the tent platform. The most popular included Senator Robert LaFollette, cartoonist John T. McCutcheon, humorist Opie Read, Eugene V. Debs, and Senator Warren Harding. William Jennings Bryan once gave fifty chautauqua lectures in twenty-eight days.

In 1920 there were 21 chautauqua tent companies operating 93 circuits in the United States and Canada. Programs were presented in 8,580 towns to 35,449,750 people. Chautauqua, whether in its mother, daughter, or itinerant forms, exercised an enormous influence throughout Protestant America. Theodore Roosevelt called it "the most American thing about America." Simultaneously it was a kind of moral vaudeville and an early institution of mass culture for the growing middle class. Its platforms served as forums for many of the paradoxes of Progressive thought, as well as for the anxieties of Evangelical conservatism.[21]

CITADELS OF SELF-CULTURE

Lorado Taft, a well-known Midwestern sculptor of civic art, gave chautauqua demonstrations of his techniques. He did so to encourage art appreciation, to inspire young sculptors, and especially to "awaken public interest in having community art galleries." In Taft's Chicago, new cultural institutions, including its Art Institute, multiplied in number and expanded in size within a generation. Wealthy philanthropists and genteel professionals like Taft created the Chicago Public, the John Crerar and the Newberry Libraries, as well as the city's Academy of Science and the Field Museum of Natural History. Similar scenarios of cultural expansion, underwritten by similar urban elites, took place in St. Louis, New York, Boston, Washington, and Philadelphia. These local Medici believed that by making available to the turbulent urban populace the best that had been thought and said in the world, they would stave off the anarchy that many feared might occur, given the growing ethnic, religious, class, and racial diversity of American cities.

Victorians especially valued libraries and museums as educational and civilizing agencies. Sometimes local libraries came into being through state legislation, as in Kansas and Wyoming. Often they originated as memorials to the local family or individual who endowed them, as with the Crane Public Library in Quincy, and the Ames Free Library in North Easton, both designed by H. H. Richardson in Massachusetts. Beginning in 1886, Andrew Carnegie took public libraries as his personal domain, and over the next three decades, he spent $39 million for 1,679 community library buildings across the country. In the era's tradition of business paternalism, he began first by making grants to towns and cities where Carnegie industries were located. Later he extended the opportunity to the rest of the country. In keeping with his belief in self-help, Carnegie required that the communities in which he built libraries agree to levy taxes to buy the books to fill them and allocate funds for their upkeep. Not everyone viewed the capitalist as the embodiment of altruism. Samuel Gompers, founder of the American Federation of Labor, believed that Carnegie made his millions at the expense of his workers. He advocated pragmatism, however, as a response to Carnegie's offered grants: "After all is said and done he might put his money to much worse acts. Yes, accept his library, organize the workers, and secure better conditions" he wrote a unionist, "and then the workers will have some chance and leisure in which to read books."[22]

SOCIAL SETTLEMENTS

In 1889 Jane Addams and Ellen Gates Starr, two graduates of the Rockford, Illinois, Female Seminary, founded America's first social settlement in the old Italianate Hull mansion on Chicago's near west side. As Addams later defined Hull House, a social settlement entailed "an experimental effort to aid in the solution of the social and industrial problems which are engendered by the modern conditions of life in a great city." Hull House resulted from three trends: "first, the desire to interpret democracy in social terms; secondly, the impulse beating at the very source of our lives, urging us to aid in the race progress; and, thirdly, the Christian movement toward humanitarianism."[23]

The social settlement idea originated in the British social Christianity of the early 1880s, when a number of university students took up residence in the poor Whitechapel district of London. The students named their house Toynbee Hall and used it as a base for living among the poor, developing cultural activities, educational programs, and social reforms in the neighborhood. In return, they hoped to receive a better understanding of the hard realities of urban life. Addams had visited Toynbee Hall in 1888, and the American settlement she established adopted several of its features.

Hull House residents, in Robert Bremmer's apt phrase, were dedicated to "social striving" as they sought to bring culture to their working-class neighborhood through art exhibitions, university extension classes, summer schools, Sunday concerts, and special lectures. Residents also engaged in lobbying activities on behalf of public libraries, parks, playgrounds, and improved schools. Hull House developed special-interest activities, such as a Paderewski Club of young pianists, a Jane Club for working women, and a Nineteenth Ward Club for young reformers. There were cooking and sewing classes, a free kindergarten and day nursery, a medical clinic and dispensary, and a Labor Museum designed to evoke in immigrant youths a sense of pride in the arts and crafts their parents had brought with them from Europe.

Progressives at Hull House also committed themselves to gathering statistical data about everyday life. As the first generation of college students who were exposed to the methods of the emerging social sciences, they erected their platform of social change on a foundation of numbers. Fact-finding was presumed to make possible a social scientific basis for rational social policy. Hull House residents collected figures on wage-earning children and the Cook County welfare system and gathered other vital and social statistics that they published in 1895 as the *Hull House Maps and Papers.* Elsewhere, residents of other settlement houses, individual reformers, and numerous governmental statisticians went about all forms of social fieldwork.[24] As a consequence, a great deal is known, at least in the aggregate, about mobility, birthrates, housing, fertility patterns, life expectancy, family size, mortality rates, and the causes of death of typical Americans during this period (see chapter 8).

A flood of specialized studies amassed statistics on the American poor. The "factual generation's" attempt to redefine poverty found an eloquent voice in Robert Hunter, who had served with the Chicago Board of Charities before working in the slums of New York City. Hunter's *Poverty* (1904), a book H. G. Wells called "compulsory reading for every prosperous adult in the United States," became a best-seller. In Hunter's definition, poverty meant the "lack of due food and lodging and clothing" that resulted—not from moral defects in personal character commonly attributed to the "unworthy poor"—but from "low wages, employment, ill-health, and accidents." Using statistics from unemployment rates, the files of charitable societies, industrial accidents, burial records of paupers, and wage rates, he concluded that one American in eight lived "in poverty."[25]

In addition to their "discovery" of poverty, social settlement workers "rediscovered" the asylum as they campaigned for additional institutions in which to incarcerate the growing number of individuals they considered to be deviant from their society's norms. As David J. Rothman has traced, they did so out of both "conscience and convenience."[26] Before the Civil War, the destitute, handicapped, orphaned, insane, and acutely ill were often housed together in municipal almshouses or county poor homes. Progressive reformers pressed for new agencies, usually supported by public taxes, that would "separate the delinquent, dependent, and defective" into specialized institutions, such as state orphanages, mental hospitals, and municipal workhouses. They also argued for the segregation of the criminally deviant into juvenile reformatories, state prisons, penal farms, contract or lease convict-labor programs, and federal penitentiaries. New York's Elmira Reformatory, opened in 1876, became a model for many new institutions that took first offenders aged 16 to 30; its emphasis on training for trades, educational programs, and parole prompted its imitation, in one form or another, by seventeen reformatories established by other states by 1913. Despite the "reformatory impulse" and its rationale of rehabilitation, the country's prison population continued to grow. That population almost tripled between 1870 (33,000) and 1920 (93,000), during which time thirty-one new state and federal penal institutions were constructed.[27]

Hull House became the best known of the early social settlements, thanks to Jane Addams' national reputation as a women's rights advocate, Progressive reformer, and peace-movement activist (she received the 1931 Nobel Prize for Peace). But every major American city had a settlement by 1900; a decade later, over four hundred existed, making the institution an established feature of urban life. Two common patterns characterized settlement workers. From 1889 to 1914, three-fifths were women and nine-tenths had been to college. Often outsiders or rebels when in college, many had made career choices to eschew marriage and pursue social action. Settlements frequently served as local forums for debating and disseminating political issues of special concern to women: temperance, child-labor reform, suffrage, workingmen's compensation, and equal rights legislation.[28] This coalition of interests, with the settlement as a campaign headquarters, became an informal third political party for women who were denied the franchise and major roles in the two traditional parties.

A final characteristic of settlement workers was their religious motivation. Addams and Starr were religious seekers. After a period of religious intensity, Addams was baptized in the Presbyterian church in 1888; Starr journeyed from the Unitarianism of her family to Episcopalianism in 1884 and ultimately embraced Roman Catholicism. Over two-thirds of the settlement workers came from ministerial families, and another third contemplated becoming clergy. In 1905 W. D. P. Bliss polled 339 settlement residents and found that 88 percent were active church members. Many came from youth organizations, such as the Christian Endeavor, the Epworth League, or the Student Volunteer Society.

Old Verities and New Practices

THE EVANGELICAL EMPIRE

Victorian Americans thought of themselves as a religious people. One of their presidents decided to annex the Philippines after several nights spent in prayer; another saw his campaign for reelection as a "Battle at Armageddon." Evangelical crusades for temperance, sabbath keeping, home missions, and Sunday schools involved thousands striving for a Christian America. Church membership and attendance increased steadily from 1870 to 1920. During the closing decades of the century, thousands of congregations of all faiths erected massive edifices in the greatest building boom in American church history.[29]

As church-going America expanded in statistical terms, belief assumed new forms. Ruptures caused by the Civil War over the slavery of blacks persisted as Methodists, Baptists, and Presbyterians failed to reunite during Reconstruction. Blacks, abandoned by southern churchmen, formed their own denominations, such as the Colored Methodist Episcopal Church (1870) and the National Baptist Convention (1895). In 1879, the Church of Christ (Scien-

tist) with headquarters in Boston received its charter of incorporation. By 1926, the institution had built over a thousand churches
across the country and numbered its membership at 202,098.
Christian Scientists traced their founding to Mary Baker Eddy,
who published the first edition of her best-known book, *Science
and Health According to the Scriptures,* in 1875. With many
parallels to New England Transcendentalism and the nineteenth-
century's continuing fascination with New Thought and spiritual-
ism, her teaching maintained that evil in general and physical
illness in particular could be overcome through prayer and a
deeper understanding of God.[30]

Popular religious ferment prompted George T. Bushnell, in a
1913 essay assessing "The Place of Religion in Modern Life," to list
a litany of recent trends: "organized philanthropy, social service,
laymen's missionary movements, Sunday school reform, spiritual-
ism, Christian Science, New Thought, theosophy, gifts of tongues,
psychical therapeutics—their number is without end."[31] Religious
statistician H. C. Carroll, author of *The Religious Forces of the
United States* (1912), could find no nation in the world to match
the variety of faiths present in fin de siècle America. Writing
amidst this growing religious heterogeneity, William James could
not have chosen a more apt title for his classic work, *The Varieties
of Religious Experience* (1902).

American Protestants, led by the Methodists, Baptists, Presbyterians, and the Disciples of Christ, acted as a semiofficial American
religious establishment—a fairly unified coalition within the context of friendly denominational rivalries. Together, they formed,
in the estimate of Martin Marty, a "righteous empire" of local
congregations and evangelical agencies. To summarize important
practices of American Protestantism from the Civil War to World
War I, it is useful to look briefly at three of its influential aspects:
its revitalized Sunday School movement, its most famous revivalist, and its most intense camp meeting.

Before the Civil War, Protestants developed a network of evangelical institutions to promote home and foreign missions, the
distribution of Bibles and religious tracts, and benevolence. The

Sunday school movement, which expanded enormously after the war, is a good example of how these voluntary societies organized religious impulses. Postbellum Sunday schools (figure 6.1) became the most important means for converting the unchurched. Families, it was argued, could best be saved through their children. Under the leadership of the Baptist B. F. Jacobs, "decision days" and "rally days" were held. Teachers were brought together in annual local and national conventions. "Each one win one" became the motto for many Baraca (for men) and Philathea (for women) classes, so that by 1913 these nationally organized groups involved several million members from thirty-two denominations. The Sunday school sometimes even overshadowed the local congregation, and the Sunday-school superintendent might be nearly as important a figure as the minister.[32]

William "Billy" Sunday, raised in an Ames, Iowa, orphan home, was a hard-drinking, woman-chasing, outfielder for the Chicago White Stockings from 1883 to 1890 before he joined the Presbyterian church, reformed, married, and became a YMCA worker. In Chicago, Sunday knew of Dwight Moody, a famous revivalist of the 1880s who preached what he called the "Old Fashion Gospel" and had founded the city's Moody Bible Institute in 1889. After serving a brief apprenticeship with another evangelist, Sunday set out on his own in 1896. He revamped revival meetings by introducing more zealous audience involvement with large choirs. Circus-style parades, led by big marching bands, were the processionals of his meetings, which took place, no longer in large tents, but in specially built, temporary, wooden churchlike arenas he called tabernacles. During his revivals, Sunday had up to twenty people in his on-stage troupe. Millions of Americans heard his rapid-fire, wisecracking, emotional sermons and tirades in which he mixed slang and baseball terms with his hatred of rum, prostitutes, card playing, and gambling.

Sunday, like many Protestant evangelists (figure 7.8) who toured the country at the turn of the century, supported the five fundamental beliefs affirmed that year at the Niagara Bible Conference: the divine accuracy of the Scriptures, the virgin birth, the deity and second coming of Jesus Christ, and His divine atonement for the sins of humankind. This orthodoxy received elaboration and promulgation in *The Fundamentals* (1910), the title of a popular twelve-pamphlet mini-encyclopedia, underwritten with a $250,000 bequest from laymen Lymann and Milton Stewart and published by the Los Angeles Bible Institute.

Methodists founded Ocean Grove in 1869 out of a deep concern for maintaining moral order in an urban-industrial society. Ocean Grove's founders and inhabitants, plus the thousands who vacationed there for a day, a week, or the whole summer (figure 6.5), believed deeply in what historian Robert Handy called "Christian America," that is, a faith in individual self-improvement (both material and spiritual), an intense nationalism, an obsession with private and public decorum, and a theology of Christian fundamentalism.[33] The Ocean Grove Camp Meeting Association prohibited dancing, card playing, theater going, and drinking in what was popularly known as "God's Square Mile." (Compare two of the Victorian era's reponses to the temperance issue in figures 7.9 and 7.10.) With its hotels, boardinghouses, and 9,600-seat auditorium, Ocean Grove in summer acted as the convention site for the Women's Christian Temperance Union, the Sunday School Union, and the Gideon Society, as well as annual meetings of state Baptist and Methodist associations.

Ocean Grove became most famous for its enforcement of "holiness Sundays." On Sunday, traffic was banished from the town's streets. No bathing, bicycle riding, recreation, or commercial enterprises of any kind were permitted on the Sabbath. Trains did not stop at the town depot. Residents went to church, often for both a morning and an evening service, and children attended Sunday school. In the afternoon, depending upon their age, the children might also attend a meeting of the Student Volunteer Movement or the Christian Endeavor Society.

Reading and home prayer were other ways of keeping the Sabbath in Ocean Grove and elsewhere in Protestant America. The Scriptures were the primary text, but religious novels, such as Elizabeth Phelps's *The Gates Ajar* (1868) were also appropriate.

Hymns were sung around the parlor organ, which often provided, in its Gothic casework, shelves and nooks for placing family mementos and religious objects (religious samplers, book markers, and home crosses) crafted by Victorian women. *Godey's* featured designs for building prie-dieux and Gothic wall brackets for holding Bibles, hymnals, and prayer books. Hair art entailed the weaving of strands of human hair (often of a dead relative) into shapes and designs, such as crosses or anchors, mounting them on a board, and then encasing them in glass. Also popular were chromolithographs on religious themes and temperance-pledge certificates.

BEYOND THE ANGLO-SAXON ZION

Unlike Protestants, who viewed their home as an appropriate environment for worship, Catholics saw the church as the primary space for religious activities. In 1880, Catholics already constituted the largest single religious group in the nation, with 6,259,000 communicants; by 1920, their number had risen to 19,828,000, largely because of the immigrants from eastern and southern Europe. Governed by a hierarchy of largely Irish and German extraction, American Catholicism divided into a multiplicity of national parishes—of Poles, Italians, Slovaks, and other nationalities.

In addition to providing religious services in familiar form and language, the Catholic national parish often developed into a neighborhood community center. For example, Chicago's St. Stanislaus Kostka parish built schools, an orphanage, a home for the elderly, a newspaper, and a cemetery. In other parishes, flourishing lay organizations, such as sodalities, altar societies, literary groups, and temperance societies (the Catholic Total Abstinence Union erected a fountain at the 1876 Centennial Exhibition) were part of everyday church life; so were popular devotions like Forty Hours, novenas, retreats, stations of the Cross, and parish missions. In a similar vein, there were harvest festivals, carnivals like the Italian *wiegiela,* and events venerating patron saints of the immigrants' home villages and ethnic heritage.

While American Catholicism emphasized communal expressions of belief, its adherents also expressed certain aspects of their faith in a domestic context. Popular devotions involved praying the Rosary and the daily Angelus, as announced by the chimes of mechanical "Angelus clocks." In a Catholic home, one might find religious calendars, often subsidized by parish merchants, listing Feast, Fast, and Ember days, and the Holy Days of Obligation; chromolithographs of the Sacred Heart of Jesus surrounded by flowers and candles (a frequent hallmark of Irish homes); crucifixes and saints' statues; family "charity boxes" for the poor; First Holy Communion certificates; and holy-water fonts near the doorways. Irish Catholic families continued the custom of weaving Palm Sunday fronds into St. Bridget's crosses as a means of protecting their homes.[34]

Like immigrant Catholics, black Christians were outsiders in Victorian America. Protestant antagonism toward each mounted during the 1890s. Jim Crow laws forced blacks to shop, eat, play, travel, and pray separately from whites. Blacks were also subject to personal violence; one estimate claimed that lynchings of blacks in the South took place on an average of three per week in the 1890s.[35]

In this segregated and hostile environment, black churches (figure 7.7) played vital roles. Institutionally, they became the most important agencies for providing structure and leadership to the beleaguered black communities in the aftermath of Emancipation. As the only local institutions that were completely controlled by black people, they grew rapidly, including about 43 percent of the black population by 1919. Their influence on the everyday life of black men and women, however, exceeded their membership statistics.

W. E. B. DuBois, in *The Souls of Black Folk* (1903), observed "that in the South, at least, practically every American Negro is a church member." DuBois went on to explain, "A proscribed people must have a social center . . . the Negro church of today is the social center of Negro life in the United States, and the most characteristic expression of African character." Booker T. Washington concurred: "The Negro Church represents the masses of the Negro people. It was the first institution to develop out of the life of the Negro masses and it still remains the strongest hold upon them."[36] Black worship, particularly its responsive and antiphonal character, usually involved a creative dialogue between the preacher and the congregation. Its spontaneous and musical spirit harkened back to a folk tradition forged in slavery as it also anticipated patterns found in modern jazz. The ministry, frequently in the Baptist or Methodist traditions, was virtually the only profession in which black men could assume leadership.

"Take a typical church in a small Virginia town," DuBois wrote, "it is 'First Baptist'—a roomy brick edifice seating five hundred or more persons, tastefully finished in Georgia pine, with a carpet, a small organ, and stained-glass windows. Underneath is a large assembly room with benches. This building is the central clubhouse of a community of a thousand or so Negroes." Various organizations meet there, noted Dubois, "the church proper, the Sunday school, two or three insurance societies, women's societies, secret societies, and mass meetings of various kinds. Entertainments, suppers, and lectures are held. . . . At the same time this social, intellectual, and economic center is a religious center of great power. Depravity, Sin, Redemption, Heaven, Hell, and Damnation are preached twice a Sunday with much fervor, and . . . few indeed of the community have the hardihood to withstand conversion."[37]

In 1880, some 250,000 Jews lived in scattered American cities. These immigrants came mostly from Germany, and they quickly acculturated to American ways. Their rabbis by then were beginning to be trained at the Hebrew Union College in Cincinnati, founded in 1875 by Isaac Wise; their synagogues had become temples, and their worship had been reformed in many places to the point where it resembled the era's liberal Protestantism, with organs, pews, hymn singing, sermons, and responsive readings in English. Jewish children attended public schools, and their parents aspired to, and largely achieved, middle-class status.

Over the next three decades, American Jewry expanded with the arrival of over 2 million poor, working-class, east European and Russian immigrants. In contrast to their German predecessors, these immigrants sought to maintain the everyday life of Orthodox Judaism that they had known in the European *shtetl* (small community). They organized synagogues and founded mutual-benefit societies to provide a range of services, from funerals to recreation; they established Jewish hospitals, young adult groups (YMHAs), orphanages, settlement houses (the Educational Alliance), and homes for the elderly. They began heder and Talmud schools that concentrated on instruction of the Hebrew language and the sacred texts. They established yeshivas or theological schools, where those who wished to be scholars or rabbis could receive advanced learning. Finally, they sustained a host of labor, Zionist, socialist, and other cultural institutions, including a Yiddish press and a lively Yiddish theater.

Their worship took place in *shuls* (synagogues), some of which were fairly imposing structures, others being improvised in tenement buildings. In Europe, the shul commanded daily attendance, but in America many Jews assumed it was necessary for only the more fervent among them to attend daily, provided there was a *minyan,* or group of any ten adult male worshipers. The majority used the facilities of the shul on the Sabbath—from sundown Friday to sundown Saturday, and on the High Holy Days—Rosh Hashonah and Yom Kippur. Worship involved readings from the Torah (Old Testament), an extended recitative prayer by a cantor, and private prayer.[38]

SOCIAL GOSPELS

A final religious movement, known in the 1870s as Social Christianity or Christian Socialism but more commonly called the Social Gospel by 1900, influenced American Protestantism. The Social Gospel grew out of tensions arising from rapid industrialization and urbanization. Bloody confrontations between labor and capital, inhumane conditions in factories, the squalor of the tenements, and the widespread use of child labor prompted various clergy and laity to call for a Christianization of the social order. The movement's standard bearers were varied. Washington Gladden, a hard-working pastor in several Congregational churches who helped organize the American Institute of Christian Sociology, was a founding member of the American Economics Association and wrote a score of books on the theme of his 1894 publication: *Applied Christianship: Moral Aspects of Social Questions.* Richard T. Ely, an economics professor at the University of Wisconsin, taught his classes with an interweaving of Christian ethics and social reform and tried to persuade his colleagues in the newly developing social sciences to infuse their research with Christian principles. The movement's major theologian, Walter Rauschenbusch, was a Baptist professor at Rochester Theological Seminary from 1897 to his death in 1919. He sought to make Christian ethics a staple of seminary education and published numerous books, among them *A Theology for the Social Gospel* in 1917. Others, like Charles Sheldon, a Topeka, Kansas, minister, applied the Social Gospel to fiction in works like his 1896 novel *In His Steps.* This sentimental tale sold over 6 million copies in twenty languages. It suggested that the ethical issues the average person encountered in everyday life could be governed by a single question: "What would Jesus do?"[39]

Paralleling the activities of the Social Gospel movement but not necessarily sharing its strategy of social reform or its liberal theology, was the Salvation Army. Like the settlement house, the Army (as it was called) originated in the East London slums, where evangelist William Booth began a ministry to the urban poor. In 1879 Booth dispatched his first "invasion force" to America, where, despite various schisms (one of which began the Volunteers of America), the Army grew rapidly. By 1904, when General Booth's daughter Evangeline assumed the U.S. command, there were 741 corps and outposts throughout the country. Urban Americans came to know the Salvationists' public performances. Open-air meetings and parades were standard fare, along with brass bands, drums, tambourines, singing, and hand clapping. Less known were the Army's lodging houses for the homeless (figure 7.2), evening schools for working children, rescue homes for prostitutes (where home economics was taught), and houses of industry for prisoners (where manual training was taught). Like settlement house workers, Salvationists tended to be young and female; they similarly protested social abuses, such as slum housing and child labor.

Settlement house workers and advocates of a social gospel, unlike most evangelistic reformers, tended to take an environmental approach to social change. Hence, they strove to reform society's structures—its municipal legislation, governmental policies, and social institutions—rather than to effect the conversion of individuals. In this objective they allied with other Victorian Americans—educators, prohibitionists, liberal theologians, and social scientists—who advocated reformist politics. Together, members of this coalition strove to effect and affect social change through education and moral strenuosity. Their religious stance in favor of a social gospel, in part, informed their political positions in favor of progressive politics. Indeed, the pervasive interweaving of Christian ethics and social reform at the turn of the century was nowhere better symbolized than in the Progressive party's 1912 campaign theme song: "Onward Christian Soldiers!"

FIGURE 8.1. James Baillie, *The Life & Age of Woman: Stages of Woman's Life from the Cradle to the Grave* (n.d.). Lithograph courtesy of the Library of Congress, Division of Prints and Photographs.

FIGURE 8.2. *Life and Age of Man: Stages of Man's Life from Cradle to Grave* (ca. 1850). Unattributed lithograph courtesy of the Library of Congress, Division of Prints and Photographs.

8

᷍᷍᷍_____

Historical demographers, such as Robert V. Wells, after looking closely at the census figures and vital statistics for 1770 to 1920, tell us that Americans underwent a significant transformation in how they experienced and thought about birth, marriage, children, and death (figures 8.1 and 8.2). In tracing the *Revolutions in Americans' Lives* (1982), Wells saw Victorian Americans playing an important role in and being influenced by several vital demographic trends. One was obvious: 25 million new immigrants, plus another several million individuals through natural increase, added significantly to the population. Yet there was a dramatic decline in childbearing. Beginning in the last quarter of the eighteenth century, American women began bearing fewer children, spacing children closer together, and ceasing childbearing at earlier ages. In 1900 American white women had half as many children as they had in 1800. A third fundamental demographic change was the gradual aging of the population. In 1880, only 3.4 percent of all Americans had reached the age of sixty-five. By 1920, the number of older Americans had risen to 4.7 percent. Finally, the second half of the nineteenth century saw a remarkable increase in the voluntary dissolution of marriages by divorce.

Birthing and Childhood

LYING-IN

In 1870 a typical American woman experienced childbirth as her counterparts had for millennia. As her pregnancy came to term, she alerted either her mother, her sisters, or neighboring women and usually a midwife. She then prepared to be "brought to bed" and to "lie-in" for the duration of her labor, delivery, and recovery. She retired to her bedroom or some suitable domestic space, with windows closed and shuttered. At her bedside, the midwife orchestrated the events of the next hours or days, while the attending corps of women comforted and shared advice. Husbands, brothers, or fathers gained only temporary access to this women's world, usually only after a successful birth or if the mother's life became endangered. This "social childbirth" experience united women and provided, as Carroll Smith-Rosenberg argued, one of the functional and social bonds that formed the basis of women's everyday domestic culture.[1]

Beginning in the mid-eighteenth century, male physicians entered the birthing room to supervise difficult births or to extract the fetus in the case of stillborns. By the early nineteenth century, upper- and some middle-class women enlisted both doctors and midwives to attend them because they believed the doctors had better training, improved technology (forceps of all types), and pain relievers (opium and laudanum). In 1846 Fanny Longfellow, spouse of the poet and first American woman to submit to anesthetized childbirth, hailed the new use of chloroform as "the greatest blessing of this age."

Others, including doctors, were not so sure. Protests surfaced on both medical and moral grounds. Some medical practitioners, believing that pain during labor was necessary to a healthy and safe birth, cited the Biblical injunction: "In pain thou shalt bear children." Others worried that mothers or their babies would be addicted to the narcotics or that women under aesthesia would behave illicitly or that doctors would take sexual advantage of them. Even Queen Victoria's eighth childbirth, under chloroform anesthesia in 1853, failed to quell all the critics.

As the use of anesthetics replaced natural childbirth, male doctors replaced female midwives. By the start of World War I, the number of white women using midwives had dropped sharply. Only 16 percent of white women in Mississippi and Wisconsin, for instance, had midwife deliveries by that time.[2]

Although physicians still delivered over half America's babies at the mother's residence in 1910, another shift had begun to transform this heretofore domestic event into an institutional procedure. In 1870 only the poorest urban women, pregnant mothers with few financial or social options, turned to public institutions, such as the Lying-In Charity Hospital in Philadelphia. By 1915, suburban, wealthy and middle-class women now increasingly gave birth in local hospitals (figure 8.9). They did so for two reasons. Hospitals and doctors promoted their obstetric care as safe and scientific, and women sought new anesthetics, such as scopolamine, or "twilight sleep," a cerebral depressant popularized by Marguerite Tracy's *Painless Childbirth* (1915). Normally only hospitals administered such drugs. With more hospital deliveries came a marked increase in cesarean sections—the surgical delivery of babies through the abdomen—when complications threatened either the mother or the child.

Maternity, the bringing forth of new life, carried with it the ever-present possibility of death. Even with new developments in pain relief, Victorian women continued to die as a result of pregnancy and childbirth. They feared the event as the most physically trying of their lives. Statistics for calculating maternal death rates—that is, the number of maternal deaths per number of live births, are difficult to come by for the entire period, 1870–1920. A New York study claims that one mother died for every 154 babies born alive in 1910; another report in 1917 put the total at 15,000 women dying each year. Only with the generation of women born in 1920 did the majority (57 percent) survive to see all their children grown. Death and debility resulted from many causes: hemorrhaging; the misuse of the forceps ("the hands of iron"), which caused lacerations to the mother and the child; and postpartum infections, especially "childbirth fever" (puerperal sepsis). Infant mortality affected a high proportion of families. Ten out of every hundred infants—and one out of every five black newborns—died by the age of one. Death came not only from birthing complications but from diseases and infections.[3]

Some women terminated unwanted pregnancies through home remedies or assistance from doctors. Harvey Green noted that "abortions were inexpensive and common in the late nineteenth-century: ten dollars was a standard rate in New York and Boston, and in 1898 the Michigan Board of Health estimated that one third of all pregnancies were artificially terminated." Contraceptives were available in the form of spermicidal douches, sheaths made from animal intestines, rubber condoms, patent medicines, and early types of diaphragms.[4] Discussions about birth control, childless marriage, and avoiding pregnancy surfaced early in medical self-help volumes, such as Dr. A. M. Mauriceau's *The Married Women's Private Medical Companion* (1855), and received widespread publicity with the jailing of Margaret Sanger for promoting such ideas in her book *Family Limitations,* published in 1915.

Many domestic advisers, physicians, ministers, and reformers fretted about the declining birthrate of white Anglo-Saxon families during the nineteenth century. For white women aged 15 to 44, the fertility rate dropped from 278 live births per 1,000 women in 1800 to 124 live births per 1,000 women in 1900. The average family size decreased from 7 (5 children) in 1800 to between 5 and 6 (3.42 children) in 1910. It should be noted that the decline in fertility did not apply equally to black, immigrant, and some rural women who continued to have large families. Figures for two ethnic groups in Philadelphia showed that German and Irish immigrants averaged, respectively, 7.22 and 7.34 children. Significant differences among different groups of white native-born women, for example, suggest that fertility control varied. Southern white farm women, for instance, continued to bear almost six children at the turn of the century.[5]

CHILD NURTURE

While breast-feeding prevailed as the accepted practice among American women of all classes, the nursing bottle had its users. By 1885 more than 1.5 million bottles were sold annually. An 1889 article in *Good Housekeeping* told mothers to place bottles in an oven for fifteen minutes, fill them with cow's milk, and steam them for a half hour to destroy "all germs."

Infancy ended when weaning commenced, usually around age one. *Diet After Weaning,* a 1905 publication of the Mellin's Food Company in Boston, recommended this transition date as the time to begin using their processed baby foods. Mellin's distributed free samples and promotional souvenirs door to door. Their advertising trade cards also gave advice on healthy eating habits for children. In offering both sustenance and suggestions, food processors like Mellin, Gerber, and Beechnut sought a place beside the doctor in the nurturance of children.

A century earlier most child rearing took place at home. Books and toys were minimal, as was schooling and organized play. The passage from childhood to adulthood occurred relatively quickly, families and their clergy exerting the major influence on child training. By 1915, middle-class children were the subject of compulsory school attendance, a consumer market directed at their interests, and a profusion of public and private institutions to promote their welfare. Family influence remained strong, but attitudes and behavior toward the young were now also shaped by teachers (who called themselves educators), progressive reformers, social scientists (especially psychologists), journalists, and corporate advertisers.[6]

This "discovery" or "invention" of American childhood as a distinct life stage (extending roughly from age two to fourteen for boys, and two to twelve for girls) manifested itself in various cultural forms: prescriptive literature like William J. Shearer's *The Management and Training of Children* (1904); special periodicals, such as *Youth's Companion* and *St. Nicholas;* and a plethora of manufactured toys, particularly "educational" toys, including "Crandall's Wide-Awake Alphabet" (1875) or Lloyd Wright's Lincoln Logs (1900).

Middle-class children by 1915 might awaken in a nursery (figure 8.3) with special furnishings and wallpaper and take meals at a set of dishes and utensils scaled to their physical size. Other than in some rural contexts, a set of earlier furniture forms—cradles and standing and walking stools—disappeared from general use, to be replaced by the baby crib, nursery swing, perambulator, and high chair. These new furnishings, especially the baby crib and pram, symbolized not only a consumerism of abundance and ostentatious display, but a child-rearing context that was both permissive and specialized.

PARENTAL ROLES

Mothers were responsible for caring for and, by 1915, usually for disciplining their children. Maternal primacy in childrearing received support from domestic advisers, such as Lydia Maria Child in *The Mother's Book* (1844); in periodicals *(Mother's Assistant)* from the National Congress of Mothers (with sixty thousand members in 1915), which later evolved into the modern Parent-Teacher Association; and, of course, in the enshrinement of American maternalism in the national holiday Mother's Day in 1912.

In the 1870s, many fathers still assumed a patriarchal stance in relation to their offspring, particularly their sons. By 1920 that role was changing. When the Lynds examined family patterns in Muncie, they claimed that a majority of Midwestern fathers saw themselves primarily as reliable providers. Even in some immigrant families, the father's traditional sources of authority was weakened. For example, in the voluminous first-generation Jewish-American literature, the mother, not the father, appears as the principal source of approval and emotional support for the child.[7]

Working-class and middle-class families evolved different strategies for functioning in urban-industrial America. These strategies can be summarized by two models: the cooperative family and the companionate family.[8] In the cooperative model (applicable to many immigrant, rural, minority, and American-born workers' families), individual members usually subordinated personal desires to larger family considerations. Major decisions—regarding emigration or relocation, whether or not wives and children should work, if, when, and where children should attend school, and when sons and daughters should marry—usually focused on collective family needs, rather than on individual preferences. All household members contributed to the material support of the family economy. Since family living costs exceeded the head of the household's wages, other sources of income, including the taking in of boarders, doing piecework in the home, and working as domestics, made up the difference.

On the other hand, a fall in the birthrate and the sharp increase in the number of women who continued their education or found employment outside the home (or did both) helped to create a new model for the middle-class family, one that later sociologists called "the companionate family."[9] Analyzed repeatedly by psychologists and educators, the companionate family rejected both patriarchal authority and the mother as the principal guardian of domestic morality, as well as the notion that marriage was the way to overcome "man's animal nature." In a companionate family, the husband and wife were friends and lovers. Their children did not work but went to school, from kindergarten to college. The parents were also urged to permit children greater freedom and an increased interaction of adolescents with their peer subculture. While companionate parents still assumed the responsibilities for their children's economic security, they relinquished some of their traditional parental prerogatives to a growing phalanx of experts, reformers, and institutions that controlled many aspects of childhood through recreational programs and social agencies.

Rites of Passage

DISCOVERY OF ADOLESCENCE

As reformers campaigned to disengage children from the factory, street, and tenement and to place them in schools and institutions, they discovered a new period in the life cycle, a special time of youth between childhood and adulthood. In 1904, G. Stanley Hall defined this special life stage, with its unique needs and developmental problems, in a book entitled, *Adolescence: Its Psychology and Its Relations to Physiology, Anthropology, Sociology, Sex, Crime, Religion and Education.* Drawing upon his earlier studies of the "juvenile" period of development (a stable time of growth from about eight to twelve), Hall contrasted it sharply with the adolescent stage, a turbulent period from twelve or thirteen through the early twenties. His thousand-page treatise surveyed the characteristics of this life stage: the rate of height, weight, and strength often doubled; self-consciousness increased, sexual identity surfaced; new "repulsions" were felt toward home and school; an interest in adult life and vocations emerged. Adolescents' needs, in Hall's analysis, were neither those of childhood nor of adulthood, but of a romantic limbo where they needed "repose, leisure, art, legends, romance, and idealization."[10] Booth Tarkington's 1915 novel, *Seventeen,* provided a popular expression of adolescence. In it, Tarkington portrayed his hero, William Baxter, as a teenager driven by his sexual and romantic instincts to acts of foolishness, poetry, and tenderness in a "time of life when one finds it unendurable not to seem perfect in all outward appearances."

Adolescence, as a seemingly new, scientifically sanctioned life stage, exerted widespread influence on educational, social, and recreational trends in the 1910s. For instance, it justified separating the upper years of the eight-grade common school and creating the American junior high school. It supported the vocational guidance movement and the development of guidance counselors as a new occupation in high schools. The differentiated curricula and extracurricular activities (as in figure 7.4) of the comprehensive high school, summarized in the 1918 report *Cardinal Principles of Secondary Education,* read like an abridgement of Hall's massive tome.

Beyond the school, as well as in concert with it, adults who hoped to direct the storm-and-stress teenage years toward desirable directions founded new institutions for adolescents (figure 8.4). These institutions included the Junior Departments (for ages twelve to eighteen) in the YMCA and YWCA; the Boys Clubs of America (1906), which catered to urban working-class youngsters; and the best-known character builders: the Boy Scouts of America (1910) and the Girl Scouts of America (1912).

Young men and women in their teens who were growing up in the teens encountered influences that were largely unknown to the two previous generations. One was the impact of the popular culture, particularly advertising, popular music, and the movies. A second was the emergence of a distinct youth subculture, outside the home, with its own argot, modes of dress, rituals, and status hierarchy. In comparing the Muncie high school yearbooks of 1894 and 1924, the Lynds found that by the later date, an identifiable peer group conditioned much adolescent behavior. They wrote: "The high school, with its athletics, clubs, sororities and fraternities, dances and parties, and other 'extra-curricular activities,' is a fairly complete cosmos in itself, and about this city within a city the social life of the intermediate generation centers."[11]

COURTING, MARRYING, DIVORCING

Courting practices varied widely according to class, religion, and ethnic group. Middle-class mothers marked their daughters' eligibility for courtship with a change in coiffure and corset. In her autobiography, *Glimpses of Fifty Years* (1889), Francis Willard vividly recalled this transition. Like most prepubescent girls, she wore her hair unpinned and her dresses loose and hemmed well above her ankles. All this changed at the outset of puberty: "Mother insists that at last I must have my hair 'done up woman-fashion.' My 'back' hair is twisted up like a corkscrew; I carry eighteen hair pins; my head aches miserably; my feet are entangled in the skirt of my hateful new gown."[12] Adolescent girls also exchanged their child's underwear for the more substantial whaleboned or steel-springed foundation garments that the era deemed essential to support a woman's back and to shape the fit of her clothing. Most Victorian women, from their teenage years to death, went about their daily activities in a corset that encompassed them from the hips to "within a hand's breath of the armpit." Even the rural poor, who, Thorstein Veblen observed, did not habitually use corsets donned them "as a holiday luxury."[13]

Girls, such as Willard, received possible suitors via the elaborate calling-card system described in chapter 3. Unless they had known each other since childhood, courting couples addressed each other as "Mister" and "Miss." Unlike various European traditions, less formally chaperoned social activity characterized American courtship. Young people attended outings—church suppers, county fairs, chautauqua lectures—with parents or young married friends, rather than with older women. If one generalization could be made about courting couples between 1876 and 1915, regardless of class, race, or ethnicity, it would be to note the shift from domestic, self-generated, social activities to public, commercial contexts. Whereas couples made much of the chance to walk home together from church or to join a backyard croquet match in the 1880s, they went together to vaudeville shows, amusement parks, and the movies by the 1910s.

While marriage manuals disagreed on the proper age to begin courtship (fourteen and sixteen were commonly proposed) or to enter into marriage (usually in the twenties but *before* the thirties), the average age of a woman who married for the first time in the 1890s was twenty-two; her counterpart for the 1790s had been twenty-seven. Working-class young men and women were often an exception to this trend; studies estimate that they worked several years before marrying in order to supplement their family's income.[14] Many times they did not establish households of their own until their early thirties.

Marriage within the ethnic group (figure 8.5) tended to decline after the first generation. Although only 3.5 percent of second-generation southern Italians and 8 percent of Jews married outside their group, 30 to 50 percent of northern Italians, Irish, Czechs, and Poles did so. Scandinavians and Germans had even higher rates of intermarriage.[15] Weddings usually entailed gifts, special dress, photographs, and perhaps a honeymoon or a shivaree. As early as the 1890s, department stores featured bride's registers indicating a woman's preference for patterns in silver, china, and crystal. A commercialized form of the traditional hope chest, the register encouraged a new form of consumerism. Although white, symbolizing purity and virginity, has become the usual color of the twentieth-century wedding dress, many Victorian women chose colored dresses. Grooms wore their best dark suits. Although wedding portraits were fashionable, they were often taken sometime after the ceremony and in the photographer's studio (figure 8.5). As William Dean Howells's novel, *Their Wedding Journey* (1888), suggests, the honeymoon, like the annual summer vacation, was primarily a middle-class phenomenon. Niagara Falls was the place to go.

While marriages continued to be as perennial as the spring in which they most often occurred, divorces increased fifteenfold in Victorian America, making the United States the country with the

highest divorce rate in the world in 1915. One out of seven marriages ended in divorce in the nation at large; in Los Angeles, the
rate was one in five and in San Francisco, one in four.

To counter this trend, various state legislatures passed laws to
raise the marital age of consent, to impose physical and mental
health requirements, and to prohibit common-law and interracial
marriages and polygamy. States established separate family
courts, specifically charged to deal with desertion, child abuse,
juvenile delinquency, and divorce. Many states, as Elaine Tyler
May has shown, strengthened their divorce legislation, requiring
longer residence requirements before petitioning for a divorce
and fewer grounds for granting a divorce.[16] New Mexico and
Oklahoma, however, for the first time allowed divorce on the
grounds of incompatibility.

Courts rarely dealt with alimony awards and the division of
property. Few spouses requested alimony (20.3 percent in 1916)
and even fewer were awarded such payments (15.4 percent in
1916). Contemporary observers and later scholars disagreed about
what caused the sudden jump in the divorce rate. Many, then as
now, argued that increased divorce resulted from a decline in
family values, increased pressures of the urban environment, the
liberation of women, or the chauvinism of men. William O'Neill
contended that divorce in the early twentieth century might also
be explained by the expectations of the white, Anglo-Saxon, Protestant family. He concluded that instead of reflecting a loosening
of family ties, more frequent divorce grew out of the tightening
demands of such bonds.[17]

ROUTINES OF SENESCENCE

Although adult Americans long recognized old age as the final
stage in the life course before death, only in Victorian America did
they begin to see it as a problem to be mitigated by the society at
large. Historian David Fischer traced this new awareness to the
1910s. It appeared in the appointment of the first public commission on aging (Massachusetts, 1909), in the first state old-age-
pension system (Arizona, 1915), and in the development of a new
science named geriatrics (1909). A bit later, G. Stanley Hall, who
coined the term *adolescence*, developed a parallel concept in his

book, *Senescence, The Last Half of Life* (1922).[18]

The aging of the American population from 1870 to 1920 can be charted in several ways. Simply put, the number of young people (aged 14 to 20) dropped, the portion of older people (aged 65 and over) rose, and the nation's median age increased (from 20.2 to 25.3). Another indicator of this trend was the acclaimed (figure 8.8) and actually increasing rate of life expectancy.

Most factories and firms did not impose a fixed retirement age on their workers. Only one-fourth of American men over sixty-five were not actively working in 1870; by 1920 that number had risen to one-third.[19] A few corporations like the Baltimore and Ohio Railroad, plus craft unions such as the United Brotherhood of Carpenters and Joiners, attempted to establish retirement plans on a typical formula that paid a pension roughly equal to 1 percent of a worker's wage multiplied by the number of his years of service. Most of these early plans, however, protected only a small minority. Management regarded a pension not as a contractual right, but as a paternal favor.

Since most workers received no pensions, few could afford not to work until death. As a consequence, many struggled to achieve ownership of some sort, preferably a home, to act as their social security. In many immigrant families, one daughter often remained unmarried to care for her elderly parents.

Women faced the possibility of being widowed more frequently than men did of becoming widowers. Since many married women depended upon their husbands for part or all their sustenance, widowhood meant economic as well as emotional loss. Moreover, whereas society expected a widower, young or old, to remarry, public opinion maligned the older women in quest of a spouse.[20]

Reformers pressed for a national system of compulsory old-age insurance comparable to those that many European countries had implemented by 1910. The proposal went nowhere. Capitalists thought the idea socialistic; labor leaders denounced it as deferred wages. Social scientists, politicians, and the clergy damned the concept as hostile to American individual liberty. Ironically, as this debate raged, the United States maintained the largest public pension system in the world for its Civil War veterans (figure 8.7). Between 1870 and 1920 the federal government spent more than

FIGURE 8.3. Joseph Byron, nursery in the home of A. C. Cronin (ca. 1915). Photograph courtesy of the Byron Collection, Museum of the City of New York.

FIGURE 8.4. Pathfinder Lodge, Girls' Camp, Otsego Lake, New York (ca. 1925). Dry plate photograph courtesy of the Smith and Telfer Collection, New York State Historical Association.

FIGURE 8.5. Phillip Dorsch and Mary Ida Schremmer wedding party (September 14, 1899), Pittsburgh, Pennsylvania. Commercial photograph, private collection.

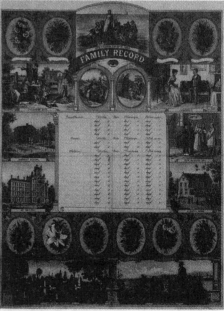

FIGURE 8.6. Family genealogical record (ca. 1880). Chromolithograph courtesy of the Library of Congress, Division of Prints and Photographs.

FIGURE 8.7. Battlefield Photo Company, *Grand Army of the Republic Veterans and Spouses, 143rd Pennsylvania Infantry,* Gettysburg National Battlefield (September 28, 1910). Photograph courtesy of the Library of Congress, Division of Prints and Photographs.

FIGURE 8.8. Advertisement, Insurance Medicine Company (ca. 1880s). Lithograph courtesy of the University of Notre Dame Archives.

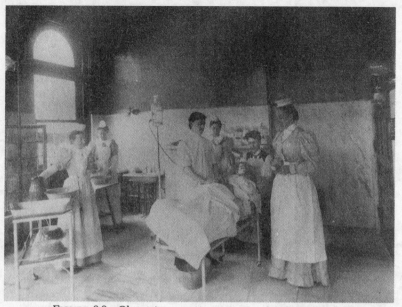

FIGURE 8.9. Obstetrics operating room, South Side Hospital, Pittsburgh, Pennsylvania (1905). Courtesy of the Historical Society of Western Pennsylvania.

FIGURE 8.10. Funeral of a Slovak miner, coal fields, Easton, Pennsylvania (ca. 1916). Photograph courtesy of Culver Pictures.

$5 billion in veterans benefits—an enormous sum in a period when its total budget for 1890 was only about $300 million. Federal military pensions rose from 127,000 immediately after the Civil War to nearly a million in 1905, not including Confederate veterans who drew pensions from southern state governments.[21]

Sickness and Death

SELF-DOSAGE: AT HOME AND OVER-THE-COUNTER

An honest doctor in Victorian America recognized the limited curative potential of medicine at the time. He or she would acknowledge that the improvement in human life expectancy from 1870 to 1920 probably resulted more from better sanitation and nutrition than from the direct intervention of medical therapies. Such a doctor would also admit that many Americans, when sick, first tried to cure themselves. Every region and subculture had its different home remedies. For example, in the Midwest the purge continued as a nineteenth-century remedy for various ailments, and such natural laxatives as bran, prunes, and sauerkraut were served with and for regularity. Native Americans knew that chewing parts of the meadowsweet plant or the willow tree (which contained a salicylic compound related to aspirin) ameliorated fevers, inflammations, and arthritic pain. Everyone knew that baking soda cured a stomachache, belladonna helped ease heart palpations, castor oil doubled as a laxative, and salt was used for brushing teeth and as a general disinfectant.

Patent medicines (figure 8.8) competed with folk medicines. Daily dosing with supposedly "scientifically prepared" oils, bitters, tonics, and balsams became common for people who were seeking to rid themselves of "brain fatigue," "torpid liver," or the "female complaint." Whatever affliction troubled the American man, woman, or child, patent medicines promised a cure for it. Many achieved national reputations: Fletcher's Castoria, Hall's Catarrh Cure, Pinkham's Vegetable Compound, and Doan's Liver Pills. All advertised constantly. Historian Daniel Pope estimated that of the 104 companies that spent more than $50,000 on national promotions in 1893, over half were manufacturers of patent medicines.[22]

Since content labeling was not required, numerous patent medicines contained opium and its derivatives (like codeine, paregoric, and laudanum) and, of course, alcohol.

In addition to prepackaged gargles, inhalations, enemas, poultices, tonics, elixirs, pills, lotions, syrups, and ointments, Americans bought home medical technology with equal enthusiasm. Galvanic belts, braces, and trusses applied electricity to self-healing. Special vibrators and massage devices came into vogue with the growth of osteopathy and chiropractics.

With the new technology and the discovery that organic chemical synthesis could create new drugs, a wide range of new analgesics appeared. One, acetylsalicylic acid, now known as aspirin, was first synthesized by chemists at the Bayer firm in Dusseldorf, Germany. Marketed first as a loose powder in 1899, it came in tablets by 1915. It quickly became the world's most prescribed drug both by doctors and home medicators. At the Treaty of Versailles in 1919, the Aspirin trademark became part of the Allies' war-reparation demands, forcing Germany to surrender the brand name to France, England, Russia, and the United States. Aspirin with a capital A became plain aspirin.

The Victorian fetish about body cleanliness, noted in chapter 4, had its analogs in popular medicine. Listerine, developed by a Missouri physician, Joseph Lawrence, and named in honor of the nineteenth-century British surgeon who pioneered sanitary operating-room procedures, became one of the country's most successful commercial mouthwashes and gargles. Deodorants, in the form of scented oils, powders, and perfumes, masked common body odors as they had for centuries. Once the physiology of the sweat glands was better understood in the nineteenth century, however, new products, antiperspirants, appeared. Early promoters of these products did so obliquely, well aware that personal sweat was a body function not spoken of in polite company—hence, the names of early creams and compounds: Mum (1888), Everdry (1902), and Hush (1908).

DOCTORING AND HOSPITAL LIFE

Sick Americans in the 1870s often saw a doctor only as a last resort and if they did, the doctor usually came to them. The reverse, as shall be shown, happened only to the urban poor, who had no alternative but to seek medical help at hospital clinics and dispensaries. Most doctors treated their patents at home, whether for a contagious disease such as tuberculosis or for a surgical amputation. They also tended to have family practices, caring for entire households; in rural areas they cared for farm animals as well. One or two dollars was the charge for a routine visit; babies were delivered in Illinois in 1902 for ten dollars.

A family doctor entering a home sick room had three resources: (1) his individual presence and the ability to inspire a patient or those attending the sick that something would be done; (2) his black medical bag containing drugs and instruments, all of which were portable; and (3) an increasing ability to make accurate diagnoses about a patient's sickness. In the last skill, a doctor had help from two medical advances—pathology, the study of diseased tissues, and the germ theory of disease. While a doctor could discover a patient's problem, often he could do little else. His power to cure often failed to match his ability to diagnose. In his medical bag he carried a number of drugs that he used to palliate insomnia (chloral hydrate), high blood pressure (barbiturates), angina (nitroglycerin), and pain of all types (morphine). He could not cure the era's killer diseases: influenza, tuberculosis, diphtheria, or yellow fever. In addition to limited curative powers, doctors in the early 1870s remained divided between the "regular" practitioners just described and several competing "sects." These sectarian practitioners, many of whom possessed M.D. degrees, offered a wide range of alternatives to regular medicine, from the infinitesimal doses of the homeopaths, to the botanical emetics of eclectics, to the water cures of the hydropaths.[23]

By 1915, regular physicians dominated health care in the United States. Through upgrading and winnowing in medical schools, forming state licensing boards, and reorganizing their national professional association (the American Medical Association), American doctors attempted to improve their image and status. In so doing, they competed with others—dentists, optometrists, pharmacists, and psychologists—who wished to have a slice of the health industry that emerged in Victorian America. More women practiced medicine by 1915 than they did earlier in the period, comprising approximately 6 percent of all American doctors in cities like Boston and Minneapolis and almost a fifth of the nation's total.[24] Two new specialties, obstetrics and pediatrics, reflected the culture's growing acceptance of birth as a medical condition and childhood as a life stage. Women and children dominated the rosters of patients of American doctors by 1920. By then, the average, middle-class woman saw a doctor 2.4 times a year, the average man 1.8 times. A child was visited by a doctor twice a year.[25]

In the last third of the nineteenth century, nursing schools were established (America's first was at New York's Bellevue Hospital in 1873), attracting middle-class women who desired to work at service for others. Between 1900 and 1910, the number of trained nurses multiplied sevenfold. Pioneer women physicians and some male physicians encouraged the upgrading of nurses' training, but the new nursing schools siphoned off some women who might have become midwives or gone to medical school and become doctors. Instead, the women were trained only to follow doctors' orders.[26]

In addition to increased contact with both nurses and doctors, patients more frequently saw their physicians in offices or in the hospitals with which the doctors had affiliated. Whereas doctors came to patients in the 1870s, by the 1920s, patients increasingly came to doctors. Over this time span, the American hospital changed in size and clientele. An 1873 survey counted 178 hospitals, about 50 of which were institutions for the mentally ill. A 1923 tabulation listed 6,830, or an increase of about 3,800 percent. This figure excluded institutions for chronic diseases, such as tuberculosis.[27] Even in smaller towns, local boosters and energetic doctors who wanted advanced medical facilities began to think of a community hospital as a necessary civic amenity. In the same way that early nineteenth-century towns built opera houses or colleges as testaments to their modernity, so communities and county seats in the late nineteenth century put up new hospitals.

General hospitals in the 1870s tended to be in large cities like Philadelphia, where the first one had opened in 1752. They were also likely to be public or private charities, linking the voluntary efforts of doctors and donors in providing inexpensive care for the indigent, the aged and dependent, single mothers, and itinerant workers. For the middle class, a bed "among strangers" in a hospital ward, as Charles Rosenberg suggested, was to be avoided at all costs.[28]

Hospital patients in the 1870s often stayed long, frequently over a month, in what were primarily custodial institutions. They were nursed by convalescing patients who had neither experience nor training for the task. Patients, as well as pregnant women awaiting delivery, often did hospital cleaning and maintenance work. In such conditions, time healed more people's afflictions than did hospital medicine.

Over the next two generations, the American hospital (figure 8.9) evolved from a private charity into a corporate institution. It increasingly became the locale for several momentous events in the life cycle (birth, sickness, and death), events that had previously taken place at home. What had earlier been a haven for the society's lowest-income outcasts became a gleaming white fortress of the middle class, who had come to look upon the hospital as a place of comfort and convenience, science and safety.

Childbirth now took place in delivery rooms, after which mothers recuperated in maternity wards while their children spent their first days in communal nurseries. Innovations in surgical anesthesia (the first major American contribution to medical science), coupled with Lister's antiseptic principles and Pasteur's germ theory, transformed surgical practices and hospitals themselves. By the turn of the century, Rosenberg noted, "the increasing complexity and effectiveness of aseptic surgery, the advantages of the x-ray and clinical laboratory, the convenience of twenty-four-hour nursing, and the house-staff attendants were making the hospital operating room the most plausible and convenient place to perform surgery."[29]

MORBIDITY AND MORTALITY

Despite advances in medical care, Victorian America remained an unhealthy and often deadly place. Life expectancy improved if one lived to middle age, but infancy and childhood remained dangerous life stages. Americans in rural environments lived longer than did those in urban settings, whites survived longer than did nonwhites, and women lived longer than did men.

Infant mortality, orphanhood, and early widowhood plagued a large portion of working-class families. In the coal districts of northeastern Pennsylvania, one in three newborns died before their first year. High rates of death among children, adolescents, and young adults also prevailed. One demographic estimate claims that early death would disrupt between 35 and 40 percent of all American families before all the children had left home.[30]

Death came in many ways, but the leading causes were infectious diseases that spread through the nation's growing population centers. Besides intermittent epidemics of yellow fever, cholera, and small pox, there was the ever-present influenza, pneumonia, typhus, scarlet fever, measles, whooping cough, and, above all, tuberculosis. Three enervating, so-called lazy diseases—malaria, hookworm, and pellagra—took a high toll among the southern poor. Few of their rural homes were well screened against malaria-carrying mosquitos; often they went barefoot, which made them prone to the hookworm parasite; and many had continual diets of corn, causing them to suffer from pellagra, a severe niacin deficiency. Deaths from diphtheria rose during the 1890s in the urban industrial centers of the Northeast. An affliction of the respiratory system exacerbated by air pollution, diphtheria was unknown before industrialization.

Tuberculosis—which dominated the later nineteenth century as cancer does the later twentieth century—touched many lives. This "white plague," also called consumption or "TB," was the country's greatest killer disease prior to 1915. Early in the nineteenth century, American doctors first tried to cure TB via the so-called heroic therapies—purging, vomiting, sweating, diuresis, and bleeding—but to no avail. More conservative approaches developed after the Civil War, a time when consumptives were often institutionalized in charity hospitals or private sanitoriums. In New Mexico the tuberculosis industry helped populate and develop the state's economy. New hospitals, hotels, and boarding-houses profited from the steady stream of tuberculars or "lungers," as the locals called them.[31] Other regions, like Colorado and California, touting clean air and sunshine, also attracted consumptives. Tuberculosis influenced local life in other ways. Municipal legislation by 1915 required certain individuals—schoolteachers, nurses, and public health officers—to submit to regular physical examinations. New laws prohibiting public spitting were enacted. States and cities also outlawed the public drinking "dipper," a tin vessel found in many railroad stations, schools, and offices, creating by 1908 a market for the glass-tank water cooler and the disposable paper cup.

The Victorian fascination with two "diseases"—dyspepsia and neurasthenia—deserves a brief review. Although neither had the fatal consequences of influenza or tuberculosis, each influenced middle-class ideas of health and identity.

"Who can expect greatness, wisdom, or honesty from a nation of moody dyspeptics?" asked the compiler of *The American Code of Manners,* a middle-class etiquette book of the 1880s. By that time, dyspepsia was a term that encompassed stomach pains, cramps, and intestinal disorders; it also was used, incorrectly, as a synonym for constipation. Although anyone might suffer it, middle-class men, if the numerous patented enemas, laxatives, diets, suppositories, and tonics marketed at them are to be believed, were most afflicted by it. Middle-class men did indeed cultivate their rotundity through heavy, multicourse meals. They prized their corpulence while touting their gastric distress. One suspects, however, it was fashionable to do so. A full belly and an expanded waistline may have signified to its male owner that he was the victim of achieving so much material abundance that dyspepsia was his class's curse.[32]

In 1881, Dr. George Bard, a neurologist in private practice in New York, published a medical analysis of *American Nervousness: Its Causes and Consequences* in which he described a new malady that he labeled "neurasthenia." The affliction had many possible symptoms: sick headache, atonic voice, insomnia, depression, fidgetiness, palpitations, neuralgia, spinal irritation, impotence, chills, morbid fears, hopelessness, and claustrophobia. In retrospect, medical historians now recognize what Beard called neurasthenia was actually a wide range of conditions that were later classified by psychiatrists as psychoneuroses.

In his time, however, neurasthenia provided a respectable covering term for many distressing, but not life-threatening, complaints. Beard also differentiated his formulation of American nervousness from hysteria (long the most frequent nervous disease attributed to women) and hypochondria (long the most frequent nervous disease attributed to men) and insanity. He ascribed neurasthenia as principally a disease of "the comfortable classes"; it was also "oftener met with in cities than in the country, more marked and frequently at the desk, the pulpit, and the counting-room than in the shop or on the farm."[33] Doctors treated neurasthenia with rest, tonics, and massage. Bromides, cannabis, and other drugs were also prescribed, in addition to patent medicines like Baker's Stomach Bitters (42.6 percent alcohol) and Warner's Safe Tonic Bitters (35.7 percent alcohol).

DYING, BURYING, MOURNING

Although most people died at home, institutions, such as hospitals, homes for the elderly, rest homes, and sanitoria, became the places of death for a growing number of Americans by 1915. Burial practices (figure 8.10) varied widely, but a few generalizations apply to the typical American experience. First, Victorians embraced death as a cause for elaborate ritual. Queen Victoria, after her consort Prince Albert died in 1859, became The Royal Widow of Windsor and set the century's Anglo-American standard by publicly mourning her husband for the rest of her long life. Second, the nineteenth century romanticized and domesticated earlier burial customs, incorporating them into its sentimental culture. Finally, while men participated in such rites, the advice literature and mourning manuals viewed funeral practices as primarily women's work.

The Victorian cult of death differed radically from that of colonial America. To New England Puritans, as David Stannard and others have described, death meant a final resolution of their quest for salvation.[34] To those who believed in predestination, it meant that most dying souls were damned to hell. When a death occurred in the seventeenth century, the family of the deceased, often assisted by women in the community, washed the body, wrapped it in a simple shroud, and prepared it for internment. The least elaborate burial found the family of the deceased following the coffin (borne by friends or a hearse if one was available) to the burying ground or graveyard. Funeral sermons were often given several days after the event. Tombstones, first of wood then of stone, frequently carried ominous symbols: death heads, skeletons, skulls and crossed bones, and the warnings—"Memento Mori" and "Fugit Hora." After the funeral, the family of the deceased sometimes invited the participants for hospitality in their home. They offered tokens as well, depending on their status and wealth. Mourning gloves, rings, pendants, and scarves were popular.

Death did not change in the nineteenth century, but as Martha Pike and Janice Armstrong suggested, American middle-class attitudes toward it did. New ideas about nature, family, and heaven prompted a different view. Heaven became a domesticated haven; it no longer held the terror of a dreadful last judgment. So complete was its domestic remodeling that novels, such as *Beyond The Gates* (1868) by Elizabeth Phelps Stuart, could describe heaven's roadways, life-styles, and occupations.[35]

Funerals now took place in churches or in new institutions— funeral homes or parlors—under the direction of a new professional: the funeral director or mortician. The funeral procession from the church or parlor to the cemetery evolved into an elaborate parade. The hearse, sometimes a wagon or a modest black carriage, gradually evolved into an imposing, heavily ornamented vehicle. Originally closed on all sides, it later had plate-glass sides so that mourners could view the casket. The coffin, previously a plain wooden, roughly human-shaped box was redefined as a "casket," a term whose original meaning described a container for precious objects. Women kept jewels in caskets, and *The Young People's Casket* was a popular children's periodical of short literary "gems."[36] Similarly the deceased body came to be regarded as precious, enshrined as it now was in an ornate, cushioned container. More opulent caskets also had plate-glass tops through which mourners could view the body. Metal caskets came guaranteed not to leak once sealed.

The decay of the corpse, which the seventeenth century accepted as natural and inevitable and which hastened burial soon after death, was arrested by new chemical procedures in the nineteenth century. First refrigeration was tried, as in the Frederick and Trump corpse cooler. Civil War undertakers with military contracts for burying the dead experimented with arterial embalming. By the 1880s, morticians had the necessary techniques and equipment to keep a corpse on view for several days. They had also perfected the public display of the body, clothed and seemingly asleep, by closing its eyes and mouth, inserting false teeth if necessary, sewing its lips shut, and tinting the face with cosmetics.[37]

Morticians often prepared a corpse for home display. Italian families laid out their dead in the home bedroom where the deceased once slept. Irish Catholics also preferred to have the life cycle's most final ritual begin and conclude in their residences. Laid in the casket, the corpse held a crucifix or rosary. As friends and family paid their respects, the tradition of "waking" began. Keening, drinking, mock marriages, and games took place in the home before the casket was escorted to the funeral Mass and burial. Merriment resumed after the mourners returned to the deceased's home.

Victorians lengthened the time span of mourning and expanded its accessories. By the 1880s, a rigorous and detailed system of rules governed proper mourning dress and behavior. Women in "full" or "deep" mourning wore dresses of black bombazine and mourning bonnets with long, thick, black crepe veils. Black gloves and handkerchiefs with a black border completed the costume. The most popular mourning jewelry was an oval brooch containing a lock of hair from the deceased.

New attitudes toward death also altered the landscape as sylvan cemeteries and memorial parks replaced crowded graveyards and burying grounds. The rural cemetery movement, launched in 1831 with the creation of Mt. Auburn cemetery in Cambridge, Massachusetts, reached its apex fifty years later in the curvilinear roads, picturesque plantings, and sepulchral art of the Victorian cemetery park. Many middle-class families, customarily on a Sunday afternoon, went to such cemeteries to "visit their dead," to stroll for exercise, or to have a discreet family picnic.

The Victorian way of death paralleled several of its ways of life (figure 8.6). For example, it contributed to the culture of professionalism as the mortician (a new term to ape the status of the physician) learned mortuary science in colleges and universities.

These "embalming surgeons" provided a consumer service that included all funeral arrangements, from the dead body's odorless, antiseptic display in a funeral parlor to its internment in a memorial cemetery, a site resembling other middle-class landscapes, such as the pleasure park and the romantic suburb. Finally, in addition to these technological manipulations of nature, the Victorian way of death fostered both sentimentality and science, emotion and expertise, as it transformed a traditionally brief, personal, private drama of the everyday life cycle into a prolonged, ceremonial, public ritual.

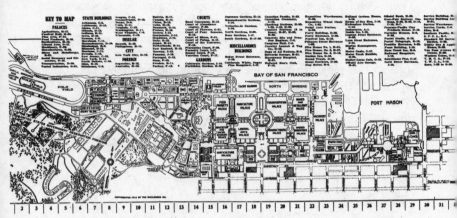

FIGURE E.1. Progressivism and the World's Fair design, plan of grounds, Panama-Pacific International Exposition, San Francisco (1915). Courtesy of the Bancroft Library, University of California.

FIGURE E.2. Procession of Maori warriors in front of Joy Zone Concession, U.S. Dollar Watch Company, Panama-Pacific International Exposition, San Francisco (1915). Courtesy of the Bancroft Library, University of California.

$\mathbf{A}$s 150,000 people waited in balmy San Francisco on February 20, 1915, President Woodrow Wilson, at his White House desk in Washington, signaled an aerial tower at Ruckerton, New Jersey, which, in turn, relayed a wireless radio message across the continent to an antenna atop a 435-foot Tower of Jewels at the entrance to the Panama-Pacific International Exposition. Within the fairgrounds, the wheels of a gigantic Busch-Sulzer Diesel engine began rotating. Overhead, aviator Lincoln Beachey circled the exposition, performing side-spirals in his Curtis biplane.

Although Portland (1904) and Seattle (1909) had staged earlier regional fairs, San Francisco's represented the Pacific Coast's first major international exposition. It signaled the increased role of the nation's western states (Arizona and New Mexico had joined the union in 1912) and its newly acquired Pacific territories: Alaska (1867) by purchase and Hawaii (1898) by conquest. Many Californians viewed the fair's landscaping and architecture as emblematic of a region often called the "American Mediterranean"; other residents considered its educational, medical, and welfare exhibits as an exemplar of their state's political and social Progressivism. San Franciscans saw it as a civic triumph over its devastating 1906 earthquake.

The opening salvos of the awesome Krupp guns in August 1914, not the British queen's death in 1901, ended the Victorian epoch. Similarly, although less violently, the Panama-Pacific Exposition concluded a major period in the common culture of the United

States. San Francisco's long summer simultaneously summed up two generations of past experience and manifested new trends in everyday life. Like the Centennial Exposition of 1876, it revealed that many Americans were mesmerized by movement, infatuated with consumer goods, and concerned to make it in (or into) the middle class. San Francisco in 1915, however, also suggested that Americans played more, put greater stock in education and engineering, and found themselves living in a culture more homogenous and urban, more incorporated and interdependent, than their counterparts who had visited Philadelphia in 1876.

The fair's walled city plan reinforced a sense of global intimacy and urban density. An inner core of eight main structures (figure E.1), tightly clustered around five courts, formed its nucleus. Vivid polychromy and brilliant illumination enthralled visitors. Unlike the cast-iron gray of the 1876 Centennial or the hygienic uniformity of the 1893 White City, the Jewel City of 1915 exuded the region's ultramarine blues, chaparral browns, and hibiscus reds. Jules Guerin, the director of color, splashed the four golds of California—wheat, oranges, gold, and wild poppies—over the entire landscape. Like a master chromolithographer or department store decorator, he color coordinated everything: attendants' uniforms, banners, admission tickets, and souvenir autochromes.

The fair's architects manipulated other materials and colors. Instead of Chicago's white plaster facades, the San Francisco exposition cladded its main buildings with base travertine, a chemical composition first used by architects McKim, Mead, and White in parts of their 1910 Pennsylvania Station in New York when true stone proved too expensive. Just as the artificial travertine faked marble's substance and antiquity's patina, another foreshadowing of the American fascination with synthetics could be seen in the Varied Industries Building, where Bakelite plastic was displayed in a rainbow of colors.

Appropriately, in the state that would become the world's cinema capital, the Panama-Pacific Exposition featured film as a medium for shaping cultural values. Lewis J. Selznick, vice-president of the World Film Corporation, distributed promotional films of the exposition to 3,500 theaters across North America. Seventy-seven movie theaters on the fairgrounds "bombarded fairgoers with films on topics ranging from immigration to city planning to state politics."[1] Newsreels reported the latest developments in the European war.

The Joy Zone (figure E.2) had twenty-five theaters offering light opera, vaudeville, and movies. Here many Americans first experienced cafeteria eating (in the YWCA Building), bought a dollar watch (from the U.S. Pocket Watch Company), or drank pineapple juice (at the Hawaiian Pavilion). Here they could ride the Universal Bus System (ten cents a ride) or the "Electriquette" battery-powered wicker chairs (one dollar an hour). Here, as spectators, they could pay to watch cars and motorcycles career around the open Autodrome or "Race for Life" at one hundred miles per hour or, as participants, ride the Auto Race at half the speed. (Sufficient visitors came to San Francisco in their own cars that the fair included four parking lots equipped with service stations operated by Shell Oil of California.) The ultimate in speed trials meant height: either a fifty-cent ride in the Zone's Strauss Aeroscope (a massive arm of a bascule bridge with propeller blades) or a brief— ten dollars for ten minutes—barnstorming flight in a Lockheed airplane.

The western railroads, each erecting a corporate pavilion, promoted vacation travel by re-creating American scenic wonders in the Zone: the Santa Fe miniaturized the Grand Canyon, the Union Pacific showed the Old Faithful Inn at Yellowstone, and the Great Northern reproduced Glacier National Park. One could also be conveyed, via a mobile platform capable of carrying 1,200 people, around a working model of the Panama Canal. An automated system of phonographs and telephones described the canal's operations.

Other displays in the Zone indulged the Victorians' persistent (but often prejudiced) interest in faraway places. As Native Americans and Afro-Americans had been caricatured in the 1876 and 1893 fairs, Asians received similar abuse in 1915. New imperial conquests, Filipinos and Samoans appeared as the nation's "little brown brothers," while the Zone represented older immigrants to America, the Chinese and the Japanese, with disgraceful displays, such as the Underground Chinatown and the Oriental Joy Garden. Racism surfaced elsewhere, for example, at the exhibits of the

Race Betterment Foundation. Here eugenicists, through the use of large plaster casts of Atlas, Venus, and Apollo and printed materials espousing IQ tests, advertised their "scientific judgement for the human race at its best." Pictures of the foundation's supporters—among them Harvard president Charles W. Eliot, conservationist Gifford Pinchot, and John H. Kellogg—attested to the movement's influence among Progressive reformers.[2]

In the Education Palace and its companion Liberal Arts Building, Americans saw two of Progressivism's most hallowed beliefs presented: (1) democratic education meant a reformed politics and (2) a reformed politics meant social improvements. In addition to kindergartens and common schools, the work of state agricultural colleges, industrial and vocational schools, and centralized urban high schools could be examined. Three model schools operated within the grounds: a commercial business college, the Palmer School of Penmanship, and Maria Montessori's preschool. Informal education also demonstrated the Victorian American's penchant for striving. Both the YMCA and the YWCA had separate buildings. The Chautauqua crusade and the social settlement movement were represented. Although there was no counterpart, at least in size, to the Columbian Exposition's World Parliament of Religions, a World Bible Congress and a Social Christianity Congress took place.

Within the Liberal Arts pavilion, the social sciences (particularly economics, political science, and anthropology) contended for a place in the academic curriculum and in national policy. The fair's congresses, a new world's record of 928, averaging 10 a day, pressed their causes (with ample supporting statistics) for public health, social welfare legislation, and federal income taxation. The world's first Insurance Congress, seen as the "era's latest combination of economics and social service," mirrored changes in American demography and health. The insurance industry also mounted a seventy-five-company collective exhibit, published a daily paper during the fair, and bombarded visitors with statistics on mortality related to gender, race, marital status, occupation, weight, disease, and seventy-seven other variables. Anthropometry, manifested in graphs, charts, maps, models, and diagrams ran riot. The Prudential Company, assuring visitors (via its trademarked slogan and

logo) that only it possessed the "strength of Gibraltar," also provided a calculus of statistics on living and dying that were specific
for the generation of 1886 to 1912; they likewise advertised the
benefits of life, home, and car insurance.[3]

Government bureaus, along with private reform groups, also
monitored the nation's cult of youth and health. The U.S. Children's Bureau and the displays of the Boy Scouts and Girl Scouts
documented the Victorian discovery of childhood and adolescence. Exhibits on hospital care, on the nation's chronic diseases,
and on new pharmaceuticals reflected the growing impact of institutional and prepackaged medical care.

American corporations mounted many major displays. Beginning in 1876 with separate pavilions by companies, such as Singer
and Goodyear, the corporate presence expanded at each subsequent American world's fair. Multinational firms, including Ford,
Heinz, and U.S. Steel, controlled a large portion of the economy
and the fairgrounds. So did the giants of the transportation industry. Visitors saw how Huntingon's railroads carried Rockefeller's
oil along Carnegie's steel tracks.

A quest for control, particularly through education, expertise,
and engineering, also characterized much of what Americans saw
at the San Francisco exposition. Not only did the engineering
triumph of the Panama Canal's completion occasion the celebration, but the nation's "new managers" administered the exposition's bureaucracy. For example, Charles C. Moore, president of
one of the nation's hydroelectrical engineering firms, chaired the
fair's board of directors, a group that included Herbert Hoover,
the first engineer to be president. As James Beniger argued in *The
Control Revolution* (1986), massive changes generated in manufacturing, transportation, and communications—evident at the
1915 fair in exhibits showing Ford's assembly line, wireless teleg-
raphy and radio, and displays of scientific management methods—
also heralded "a revolution in social control."[4]

Elsewhere, others questioned or confronted such control or
sought to impose their own hegemony. On November 19, 1915,
the state of Utah executed, by firing squad, IWW organizer Joe
Hill. Earlier that year, racial tensions flared over the showing of
D. W. Griffith's *The Birth of a Nation.* On Thanksgiving night atop

Stone Mountain near Atlanta, William Simmons revived the Ku Klux Klan, to promote "white supremacy." Labor strikes took place in Pittsburgh, Gary, and Seattle. The U.S. Senate passed legislation requiring literacy tests for all immigrants, while the House moved to adopt the Eighteenth Amendment prohibiting the manufacture, sale, import, or export of liquor in the United States.

The Panama-Pacific International Exposition epitomized American society at its first twentieth-century fault line. It revealed Americans in one of their typical Janus-like postures. "Conceived in optimism and carried through despite the outbreak of World War I," its palaces and "courts dripping with allegorical statues and murals,"[5] the exposition reflected a final sentimental, opulent display of American Victorianism. The fair also foreshadowed future modernity. It asserted the importance of California and the American West while turning national attention toward the Pacific and South America. It adumbrated the everyday life of the future in ways that were mundane, like processed Kraft cheese, Pyrex glass, and Carrier air-conditioning, and in ways that were typically middle class: white-collar work, wider leisure-time activities, consumerism, access to information, and social reform.

Anyone who had visited the Philadelphia Centennial in 1876 as a young adult and had later attended the Panama-Pacific Exposition in 1915 as an older person, would have readily acknowledged that fundamental changes had taken place in American everyday experience during his or her lifetime. Within that time span, what had been a fundamentally agrarian nation of 46,107,000 had more than doubled into a largely urban and industrial society of 100,549,000. Urbanization and industrialization, in turn, added to such trends as the increased homogenization and quantification of daily activities and a marked increase in money-oriented values. Amidst these demographic and economic changes, one also found a bifurcated culture, one shot through with numerous cultural contrasts.

No matter what the means—emigrant ship, transcontinental railroad, commuter train, suburban streetcar, or private auto—mobility had become a conscious part of the national self-definition. In addition to almost continuous immigration from abroad and high rates of natural increase in the population at home, a series of exceptional communication inventions (for example, the telephone and the typewriter) occurring almost yearly in the 1880s, coupled with new sources of energy (electricity and oil) contributed to the rapid movement of people, goods, services, and ideas.[6]

The heightened pace of this world was no longer linked to the cycle of the days and the passing of the seasons, but to the tempo of the timetable and the time clock. Americans, by 1915, also moved about on, inhabited, and continually manipulated a physical landscape that was transformed in scale and size. Bigness was everywhere: colossal suspension bridges, skyscrapers, railroad stations, department stores, apartment houses, traction systems, hotels, and interoceanic canals. Everyday life, particularly in the cities, became a vast metropolitan environment of modernity's materials—steel, glass, and concrete.

New mechanisms, often first displayed in the Machinery Halls of the era's world's fairs, nurtured speed and movement. Taken separately, innovations, such as the alarm clock, streetcar, cafeteria, elevator, gas furnace, or auto, may seem limited in their impact; viewed collectively, however, they (along with others) contributed to, in Siegfried Giedion's estimate, a cultural process wherein "mechanization takes command."[7]

More than ever before, the American workplace was a factory plant, powered by dynamos, connected to suppliers and distributors by telephone, administered by a hierarchial organization of clerical workers and white-collar managers, and owned by anonymous stockholders.[8] German, Irish, and Asian workers in industry, joined in large numbers by Slavs, Jews, Italians, Poles, and blacks after 1890, manned such enterprises. Despite temporary gains made by labor such organizations as the Knights of Labor in the 1880s and the American Federation of Labor in the 1910s, under 15 percent of this massive workforce belonged to a union. The majority knew daily toil without guarantees against wage cuts, accident insurance, sick leave, or a paid vacation. All knew frequent times of inflation, wage reductions, and unemployment, particularly during the era's six major recessions and depressions.[9]

An increasingly large segment of urban families lived in multi-occupancy housing, such as tenements, boarding- and lodging houses, and apartments. For most, however, home ownership remained the domestic ideal, a goal achieved by 10,866,960 American families in 1920.[10] Neighborhoods were more clearly demarcated by economic class than had been the residential patterns before the Civil War: the middle classes in sylvan suburbs, well-paid workers in contractors' subdivisions, and a multiracial, ethnic, urban proletariat scattered about a growing number of inner-city districts. Most everyday domestic life, no matter what its locale, changed significantly in its home financing, access to utilities, and greater use of prepackaged foods and consumer goods.

Consumer and communication interests promoted (and profited from) many of these changes in where and how Americans lived. Department and franchise stores, mail-order houses, metropolitan newspapers, and mass-circulation magazines projected an American cornucopia of material abundance in which workers and employers alike saw themselves as consumers as well as producers of life's necessities and luxuries, its daily bread and its creature comforts. For some the sheer excitement of expanded consumption, the new rituals of buying and selling—universalized by name brands, national trademarks, and chain stores—became characteristic of everyday life in which millions, regardless of place or position, shared.[11] Materialism became Americanism.

By 1915 Americans consumed leisure activities as well as material goods. Vaudeville, motion pictures, fraternal organizations, amusement parks, and professional sports enticed patrons from all segments of the population, providing another, albeit tenuous, cultural unity amidst growing pluralities of race, ethnicity, age, status, and gender. None of these commercial mass entertainments existed in the early 1870s.

Neither did a substantial professional class. Only a tiny minority of Americans (primarily Anglo-Saxon, Protestant, and male) attended college and practiced a profession before the Civil War. But, as demonstrated by the growing number of conventions assembled at every American world's fair (events organized and administered by the country's middle-class professionals and business leaders), thousands (including some women and men from non-WASP backgrounds) took their daily occupational identity from a variety of white-collar professional roles.[12] These "new" professionals (accountants, engineers, civil servants) often coming from families of modest means, faced considerable prejudice because of their class, gender, race, and religion, but they endured in sufficient numbers to become a major constituency of the era's expanded (and "new") middle class—a class with a "vertical vision," one that championed the rise of the expert in American life, whether in school administration, city planning, interior decoration, mortician services, certified public accounting, library science, physical education, child psychology, or mechanical engineering.[13] Many began their climb for economic and social status in the classrooms of the new American high schools. Many continued their ascent by participating in and paying for the period's agencies and activities of self-culture, such as public libraries and chautauquas.

The expanded middle-class promoted other new institutions of Victorian everyday life: the municipal hospital, university, life insurance company, and government bureau. It also played an important role in certain Progressive reforms like women's suffrage and a professional civil service and participated in conservative crusades, such as Prohibition and the restriction of immigration. In the name of imperial destiny, it made war on Spain, tolerated Jim Crow legislation and lynchings of black Americans, savaged Native Americans, and discriminated against Catholics, Jews, and Orientals. Yet it also sought to supplement private charity with public social services, settlement houses, and urban reforms and enacted public health legislation that helped drop the nation's death rate by a third and increase its life expectancy by six years. Finally, middle-class America also sought to impose a homogenized national unity on the country's public life through a ritualized civil religion that included the rites of a daily pledge of allegiance to the flag; almost yearly commemorative historical anniversaries; and a creed of classicism for its public buildings, civic art, world's fairs, military parks, and official monuments.[14]

Yet despite the fragile commonality of experiences promoted by patriotic classicism, nationwide consumption, an expanded communications network, compulsory school attendance, and new mass entertainments, American everyday life was still fraught with striking contrasts. Native critics and cassandras, such as Henry George, Walt Whitman, Mark Twain, Van Wyck Brooks, Henry Adams, and W. E. B. Dubois, recognized this contrariety.[15] So did foreign commentators, including James Bryce, George Santayana, and James Muirhead. Later historians, such as Michael Kammen, Neil Harris, Thomas Bender, and David Noble, have likewise argued that although Americans have always been a "people of paradox," their common culture perennially something of a "contrapuntal civilization," such especially was the case for those who lived between 1876 and 1915.[16]

It is appropriate, therefore, to conclude this overview of America from 1876 to 1915 by remembering how much of Victorian everyday life abounded in paradox. How America, in the words of James Muirhead's book title, was *The Land of Contrasts* (1898). For example, people bought traveler's checks for the first time in 1891, one indicator of the population's increased coming and going, only to need a few years later the first Traveler's Aid Society, which testified to some of the hazards of widespread mobility. Gross inequities existed between the bright world of gilded wealth and the gray facts of poverty because "the labor-capital question" was *the* social and economic issue of the day. In an increased discovery of their growing diversities—of class, age, nationality, gender, and race—many Americans made strident claims for a "100 percent Americanism." Similarly, as Sarah Orne Jewett, Joel Chandler Harris, Bret Harte, and Hamlin Garland described the regional peculiarities and local color of everyday life, others, such as Louis Sullivan, Daniel Burnham, Charles Dana Gibson, and Edward Bok searched for a uniquely American national style and aesthetic. Although numerous developments—Hollerith's electric punch card system, the social science survey and questionnaire, the IQ test, and the College Board examination—show the Victorian mania to rationalize and measure everyday experience, Americans were also fascinated with magic and fantasy. *The Wizard of Oz* (1896) was but one manifestation of the age's intrigue with children's literature, science fiction, and utopian novels.[17] Perhaps, most paradoxical of all was that in an era that often saw itself as composed of rugged individualists espousing traditional values, American everyday life became a more institutional, homogeneous, material, and urban experience.

NOTES

INTRODUCTION

1. Van Wyck Brooks, *The Confident Years, 1885–1915* (New York: E. P. Dutton, 1952); Walter Lord, *The Good Years: From 1900 to the First World War* (New York: Bantam Books, 1960); Irwin Unger, *The Vulnerable Years: The United States, 1896–1917* (New York: New York University Press, 1978); Ray Ginger, *An Age of Excess: The United States From 1877–1914* (New York: Macmillan, 1965); Howard Mumford Jones, *The Age of Energy: Varieties of American Experience, 1865–1915* (New York: Viking Press, 1971); Thomas Cochran and William Miller, *The Age of Enterprise: A Social History of Industrial America* (New York: Harper & Row, 1961); Lewis Mumford, *The Brown Decades: A Study of The Arts of America, 1865–1895* (New York: Beacon Press, 1931); and Thomas Beer, *The Mauve Decade: American Life at the End of the Nineteenth Century* (New York: Alfred A. Knopf, 1926).

2. Daniel Walker Howe, "Victorian Culture in America" in Howe, *Victorian America* (Philadelphia: University of Pennsylvania Press, 1976); John F. Kasson, *Amusing the Million: Coney Island at the Turn of the Century* (New York: Hill & Wang, 1978), 4–5; and Miles Orvell, *The Real Thing: Imitation and Authenticity in American Culture, 1880–1940* (Chapel Hill: University of North Carolina Press, 1989), 42–46.

3. In my thinking, the late Warren Susman's exploration of the idea of transformation proved particularly helpful. In *Culture as History: The Transformation of American Society in the Twentieth Century* (New York: Pantheon, 1984), Susman suggested that *transformation* acted "as a key word in the late nineteenth and early twentieth centuries, becoming significant not only in the worlds of physics and biology but also in the worlds of history and social science as well." For example, writing on

Victorian America, Susman stated: "History increasingly had to confront the changing of forms in which experience was expressed—often rapid change because of technological innovation. Such transformations created the need for still others" (page 234; see also pages xxv–xxvii). In the subsequent chapters of this book, I take Susman literally at his word. On other aspects of transformation as an interpretive model, see Lawrence A. Cremin, *The Transformation of the School: Progressivism in American Education, 1876–1957* (New York: Alfred A. Knopf, 1961); Richard D. Brown, *Modernization: The Transformation of American Life, 1600–1865* (New York: Hill & Wang, 1976); Robert Higgs, *The Transformation of American Economy, 1865–1914: An Essay in Interpretation* (New York: John Wiley & Sons, 1971); Karl Polyani, *The Great Transformation: The Political and Economic Origins of Our Times* (New York: Farrar & Rinehart, Inc., 1944); and Steven Hahn and Jonathan Prude, eds., *The Countryside in the Age of Transformation: Essays in the Social History of Rural America* (Chapel Hill: University of North Carolina Press, 1985).

4. When describing both change and continuity in cultural history, I follow James Axtell's definition of culture as "an idealized pattern of meanings, values, and norms differentially shared by the members of a society, which can be inferred by the noninstinctive behavior of the group and from the symbolic products of their actions including material artifacts, language, and social institutions." The historian who works from this premise, Axtell stated, should attempt to determine "just what the patterns are in a particular society over time and how the individual parts—whether actions, beliefs, or artifacts—together constitute the functional whole." Axtell, *The European and the Indian: Essays in the Ethnohistory of Colonial North America* (New York: Oxford University Press, 1981), 6.

5. George Pierson, "The M-Factor in American History" in Pierson, *The Moving American* (New York: Alfred A. Knopf, 1973), 229–258; Walter Nugent, "The Emergence of the Metropolitan Mode" in Nugent, *The Structures of American History* (Bloomington: Indiana University Press, 1981), 87–97; John Stilgoe, *The Metropolitan Corridor: The Railroad and the American Scene* (New Haven: Yale University Press, 1982); and Lawrence A. Cremin, *American Education: The Metropolitan Experience, 1876–1980* (New York: Harper & Row, 1988).

6. Richard D. Brown, *Modernization: The Transformation of American Life, 1600–1865* (New York: Hill & Wang, 1976), 3–22; and Herbert G. Gutman, "Work, Culture, and Society in Industrializing America, 1815–1919," *American Historical Review* 78 (June 1973): 531–587. Gutman saw the transformation of preindustrial America beginning in the 1850s and reaching maturity by the 1920s. Others, such as Alfred Chandler, in *The Visible Hand: The Managerial Revolution in American*

Business (Cambridge, Mass.: Harvard University Press, 1977), locate its origins in the 1870s, when entrepreneurial capitalism superceded mercantile capitalism, only to be challenged by managerial capitalism.

7. On these trends, see Robert Wiebe, *The Search for Order, 1877–1920* (New York: Hill & Wang, 1967); and Alan Trachtenberg, *The Incorporation of America: Culture and Society in the Gilded Age* (New York: Hill & Wang, 1982).

8. Studies of Victorian consumerism that I found useful included Daniel Horowitz, *The Morality of Spending: Attitudes Toward the Consumer Society in America, 1875–1970* (Baltimore: Johns Hopkins University Press, 1985); Simon Bronner, *Consuming Visions: Accumulation and Display in America, 1880–1920* (New York: W. W. Norton & Co., 1989); two doctoral studies: Peter E. Samson, "The Emergence of a Consumer Interest in America, 1870–1930" (University of Chicago, 1980) and John E. Hollitz, "The Challenge of Abundance: Reactions to the Development of a Consumer Economy, 1880–1920 (University of Wisconsin–Madison, 1981); and, of course, David Potter's seminal work, *A People of Plenty: Economic Abundance and the American Character* (Chicago: University of Chicago Press, 1954).

9. Here and elsewhere in this volume, I follow Daniel Horowitz (*The Morality of Spending,* page 68) and Nell Irvin Painter, (*Standing at Armageddon: The United States, 1877–1919* [New York: W. W. Norton & Co., 1987], xix–xxviii) and use the word *class* in a cultural sense, relying on occupational patterns, how contemporaries saw social differences, and on real and perceived group ways of living. As many historians are quick to point out, the differences between the working class and the middle class in Victorian America were complex and continually shifting. Both terms are problematic concepts because between 1870 and 1920 both groups underwent unprecedented statistical expansion, became more diverse with new occupations, and simultaneously contended with each other. See also Stuart Blumin, "The Hypothesis of Middle-Class Formation in Nineteenth-Century America: A Critique and Some Proposals," *American Historical Review* 90 (April 1985): 299–338; Arno J. Mayer, "The Lower Middle Class as a Historical Problem," *Journal of Modern History* 47 (September 1975): 409–36; Susman, *Culture as History,* xxi–xxiii; and Steven Mintz, Appendix, "A Note on the Use of the Term, 'Middle Class,' " in *A Prison of Expectations: The Family in Victorian Culture* (New York: New York University Press, 1983), 203–06.

10. Focused case studies on the expansion of the American middle class in the nineteenth century include Burton J. Bledstein, *The Culture of Professionalism: The Middle-Class and Development of Higher Education in America* (New York: W. W. Norton & Co., 1976); Cindy Sondik Aron, *Ladies and Gentlemen of the Civil Service: Middle-Class Workers*

in Victorian America (New York: Oxford University Press, 1987); John S. Gilkeson, Jr., *Middle-Class Providence* (Princeton: Princeton University Press, 1986); Karen Haltunnen, *Confidence Men and Painted Women: A Study of Middle Class Culture in America, 1830–1870* (New Haven: Yale University Press, 1983); Richard Sennett, *Families Against the City: Middle-Class Homes of Industrial Chicago, 1872–1890* (Cambridge: Harvard University Press, 1970); and Mary Ryan, *The Cradle of the Middle Class: The Family in Oneida County, New York, 1790–1865* (Cambridge: Cambridge University Press, 1981).

11. Nugent, *The Structures of American History,* 116; see also 115–118.

12. Kenneth L. Ames, "Meaning in Artifacts: Hall Furnishings in Victorian America," *Journal of Interdisciplinary History* 9 (Summer 1978): 21.

13. Lewis Mumford, *Technics and Civilization* (New York: Harcourt, Brace and Company 1934), 105.

14. Henry Adams, a frequent visitor to several of the century's expositions, recognized how they might be analyzed as bellwethers of American life. Writing in *The Education of Henry Adams,* (Boston: Houghton Mifflin Co., 1907, 1961), he "professed the religion of world's fairs, without which he held education to be a blind impossibility" (page 465). Modern historians agree. John Cawelti ("America on Display, 1876, 1893, 1933," in *America in the Age of Industrialism,* ed. Frederic C. Jaher [New York: Free Press, 1968], p. 317) wrote: "Because it brings together many different aspects of civilization under, so to speak, a single roof, a world's fair can give us much insight into how people view the unity of their culture, how they understand the structure of its means, achievements, and aspirations." In this volume, three American fairs—the 1876 Centennial, the 1893 Columbian, and the 1915 Panama-Pacific expositions—in addition to marking the country's geographic diversity, serve as vignettes summarizing changes in occupational trends, housing preferences, consumer choices, recreational developments, and demographic and social patterns.

15. On the paradoxical nature of American culture, see Michael Kammen, *The Contrapuntal Civilization: Essays Toward a New Understanding of the American Experience* (New York: Thomas Y. Crowell, 1971); and Kammen, *People of Paradox: An Inquiry Concerning the Origins of American Civilization* (New York: Alfred A. Knopf, 1973). Consult Neil Harris, ed., *The Land of Contrasts, 1880–1901* (New York: George Braziller, 1970) for the use of James Muirhead's theme of cultural contrast as an interpretive model.

PROLOGUE: *Americans at the 1876 Centennial*

1. Robert Rydell, *All the World's a Fair: Visions of Empire at American International Expositions, 1876–1916* (Chicago: University of Chicago Press, 1984), 32–33.

2. John Maass, "Who Invented Dewey's Classifications?" *Wilson Library Bulletin* 47 (December 1972): 335–41.

3. Robert Post, ed., *1876: A Centennial Exhibition* (Washington: D.C.: National Museum of History & Technology, Smithsonian Institution, 1976), 21.

CHAPTER 1: *Moving*

1. As quoted in Leslie Allen, *Liberty: The Statue and the American Dream* (New York: Summit Books, 1985), 90.

2. Robert Rydell, *All the World's a Fair: Visions of Empire at American International Expositions, 1876–1916* (Chicago: University of Chicago Press, 1984), 226.

3. John Bodnar, *The Transplanted: A History of Immigrants in Urban America* (Bloomington: Indiana University Press, 1985), 45–50, 54–56, 206–16; and Caroline Golab, *Immigrant Destinations* (Philadelphia: Temple University Press, 1977).

4. Philip Taylor, *The Distant Magnet: European Immigration to the U.S.A.* (New York: Harper & Row, 1971), 94–97, 150–51.

5. David Brody, *Steelworkers in America: The Nonunion Era* (Cambridge, Mass.: Harvard University Press, 1960), 106.

6. Taylor, *The Distant Magnet,* 105–106; Virginia Yans-McLaughlin, *Family and Community: Italian Immigrants in Buffalo, 1880–1930* (Ithaca, N.Y.: Cornell University Press, 1977), 34–36, 48–49; U.S. Department of Commerce, Bureau of the Census, *Historical Statistics of the United States,* I, Series C296-301 (Washington, D.C.: Government Printing Office, 1975) 119, hereafter cited as *Historical Statistics of the United States;* Alan M. Kraut, *The Huddled Masses: The Immigrant in American Society, 1880–1921* (Arlington Heights, Ill: Harlan Davidson, 1982), 17; and Stephen Thernstrom, ed., *Harvard Encyclopedia of American Ethnic Groups* (Cambridge, Mass.: Harvard University Press, 1981), 1036.

7. Howard Mumford Jones, *The Age of Energy: Varieties of American Experience, 1865–1915* (New York: Viking Press, 1971), 145–50.

8. *Historical Statistics of the United States,* I, Series C25-75, 93–95.

9. William L. Barney, *The Passage of the Republic: An Interdisciplinary History of Nineteenth-Century America* (Lexington, Mass.: D. C. Heath & Co., 1987), 270–71; and Everett S. Lee and Anne S. Lee, "Internal Migration Statistics for the U.S.," *Journal of the American Statistical Association* 56 (1960): 664–97.

10. Marion Tuttle Rock, *Illustrated History of Oklahoma* (Topeka, Kans.: Hamilton & Sons, 1890), 21; and H. Wayne Morgan, *Oklahoma, A Bicentennial History* (New York: W. W. Norton & Co., 1977) 52–53.

11. Angie Debo, *Prairie City: The Story of an American Community* (New York: Alfred A. Knopf, 1944), 47–48.

12. Nell Irvin Painter, *Exodusters: Black Migration to Kansas After Reconstruction* (New York: Alfred A. Knopf, 1977); Neil Fligstein, *Going North: Migration of Blacks and Whites from the South, 1900–1950* (New York: Academic Press, 1981); and Daniel M. Johnson and Rex R. Campbell, *Black Migration in America: A Social Demographic History* (Durham, N.C.: Duke University Press, 1981), 22, 72–76.

13. Peter J. Coleman, "Restless Grant County: Americans on the Move," *Wisconsin Magazine of History,* 46 (Autumn 1961), 16–20; Fred Shannon, *The Farmer's Last Frontier, 1865–1900* (New York: Holt, Rinehart & Winston, 1966), 357; and Frederick Jackson Turner, quoted in Walter Nugent, *The Structures of American Social History* (Bloomington: Indiana University Press, 1981), 113.

14. Howard P. Chudacoff, *Mobile Americans: Residential and Social Mobility in Omaha, 1880–1920* (New York: Oxford University Press, 1972), 122, 129, 150; Clyde Griffen and Sally Griffen, *Natives and Newcomers: The Ordering of Opportunity in Mid-Nineteenth-Century Poughkeepsie* (Cambridge, Mass.: Harvard University Press, 1978); Stephan Thernstrom, *Poverty and Progress: Social Mobility in a Nineteenth-Century City* (Cambridge, Mass.: Harvard University Press, 1964); Clifford E. Clark, *The American Family Home, 1800–1960* (Chapel Hill: University of North Carolina Press, 1986), 191; and Stephen Thernstrom and Peter R. Knight, "Men in Motion: Some Data and Speculations about Urban Population Mobility in Nineteenth-Century America," *Journal of Interdisciplinary History* 2 (Autumn 1970): 7–35.

15. David Montgomery, *The Fall of the House of Labor: The Workplace, the State, and American Labor Activism, 1865–1925* (Cambridge: Cambridge University Press, 1987), 76–78.

16. Kenneth L. Kusmer, "The Underclass in Historical Perspective: Tramps and Vagrants in Urban America, 1870–1930," in *On Being Homeless: Historical Perspectives,* ed. Rich Beard (New York: Museum of the City of New York, 1987), 21; and Eric Monkkonen, ed., *Walking to Work: Tramps in America, 1789–1935* (Lincoln: University of Nebraska Press, 1984), 161–65, 189–211.

17. David Corbin, *Life, Work, and Rebellion in the Coal Fields: The Southern West Virginia Miners, 1880–1922* (Urbana: University of Illinois Press, 1981), 40–42.

18. Kenneth T. Jackson, *Crabgrass Frontier: The Suburbanization*

of the United States (New York: Oxford University Press, 1985), 45–50, 54–61.

19. Mary Cable, *American Manners and Morals* (New York: American Heritage Press, 1969), 190.

20. Gustave Stickley, "Als IK Kan" and "The Motor Car and Country Life," *The Craftsman* 5 (November 1905): 278–79, and 20 (May 1911): 227; and Burton J. Bledstein, *The Culture of Professionalism: The Middle Class and Development of Higher Education in America* (New York: W. W. Norton & Co., 1976), 64.

21. Quoted in Lewis Atherton, *Main Street on The Middle Border* (Bloomington: Indiana University Press, 1954, reprint 1984), 37–40.

22. Alan Trachtenberg, *The Incorporation of America: Culture and Society in the Gilded Age* (New York: Hill & Wang, 1982), 57; see also Walter Licht, *Working for the Railroad: The Organization of Work in the Nineteenth Century* (Princeton: Princeton University Press, 1983), 31–36; and Taylor and Irene D. Neu, *The American Railroad Network* (Cambridge, Mass.: Harvard University Press, 1956).

23. John Stilgoe, *Metropolitan Corridor: Railroads and the American Scene* (New Haven: Yale University Press, 1983), 3.

24. R. Stuart, "People Act as If They Wanted to Be Killed," *American Magazine* 92 (September 1921): 38–39; "Grade-Cross Scandal," *Scientific American* 109 (July 26, 1913): 62–63; and Stilgoe, *Metropolitan Corridor*, 163–88.

25. Jackson, *Crabgrass Frontier*, 107–115.

26. William D. Middletown, *The Interurban Era* (Milwaukee: Kalmback, 1970); and Stilgoe, *Metropolitan Corridor*, 289–310.

27. J. Abbot, *Panama and the Canal in Picture and Prose* (New York: Syndicate Publishing Co., 1913); I. E. Bennett, *History of the Panama Canal: Its Construction and Builders,* builder's ed. (Washington, D.C.: Historical Publishing Co., 1915); *King's Views of the Panama Canal in the Course of Construction* (New York: Moses King, 1912); and *Panama Canal Pictures, Showing the Latest Photographs of the Progress of Construction* (Philadelphia: Wilmer Atkinson, 1913).

28. Alba M. Edwards, *Population: Comparative Occupation Statistics for the United States, 1870 to 1940: Sixteenth Census of the United States 1940* (Washington, D.C.: U.S. Government Printing Office, 1943), 101–2; Bledstein, *Culture of Professionalism*, 35–39, 45; and P. K. Whelpton, "Occupational Groups in the United States, 1820–1920," *Journal of the American Statistical Association* 21 (1926): 335–43.

29. Nell Irvin Painter, *Standing at Armageddon: The United States, 1877–1919* (New York: W. W. Norton & Co., 1987), xxiv. Painter also noted that "classes were not formed once and for all, in the sense that a middle-class family's antecedents might have been in other classes, and

its descendants, too, might belong to the working or lower classes." In addition to native-born white Protestant Americans, a small but influential group of blacks and immigrants belonged to the economic middle class. "These families achieved their upward mobility through education, the priesthood, entrepreneurship, and leadership in political, fraternal, or labor organizations" (page xxv).

30. Carlene E. Stephens, "Before Standard Time: Distributing Time in 19th-Century America," *Vistas in Astronomy* 28 (1985): 113–18; and Stephens, *Inventing Standard Time* (Washington, D.C.: National Museum of American History, 1983), 4–10.

CHAPTER 2: *Working*

1. David Montgomery, "Strikes in Nineteenth-Century America," *Social Science History* (February 1980): 81–104; Montgomery, *Worker's Control in America: Studies in the History of Work, Technology, and Labor Struggles* (Cambridge: Cambridge University Press, 1979); Sari Bennett and Carville Earle, "The Geography of Strikes in U.S., 1881–1914," *Journal of Interdisciplinary History* 13 (Summer 1982), 63–84.

2. On the distribution of wealth and income at the turn of the century, see Nell Irvin Painter, *Standing at Armageddon: The United States, 1877–1919* (New York: W. W. Norton & Co., 1987), xix–xxi; Steven Dubnoff, "A Method for Estimating the Economic Welfare of American Families of Any Composition: 1860–1901," *Historical Methods* 13:3 (Summer 1980): 176–77; Alan Trachtenberg, *The Incorporation of America: Culture and Society in the Gilded Age* (New York: Hill & Wang, 1982), 90–91; and the contemporary appraisal by Charles B. Spahr, *An Essay on the Present Distribution of Wealth in the United States* (New York: T. Y. Cromwell, 1896), 69, 128–130.

3. Alexander Keyssar, *Out of Work: The First Century of Unemployment in Massachusetts* (Cambridge: Cambridge University Press, 1986), 4–8, 300–07. For unemployment figures for specific depressions, such as 1893–97, see Carlos A. Schwantes, *Coxey's Army: An American Odyssey* (Lincoln: University of Nebraska Press, 1985), 13–14; Painter, *Standing at Armageddon*, 116–17, 295–96; and Paul T. Ringenbach, *Tramps and Reformers: The Discovery of Unemployment in New York City, 1873–1914* (Westport, Conn.: Greenwood Press, 1973).

4. Hal S. Barron, "Staying Down on the Farm: Social Processes of Settled Rural Life in the Nineteenth-Century North" in *The Countryside in the Age of Capitalist Transformation: Essays in the Social History of Rural America*, ed. Steven Hahn and Jonathan Prude (Chapel Hill: University of North Carolina Press, 1985), 335–38.

5. Pete Daniel, *Breaking the Land: The Transformation of Cotton,*

Tobacco, and Rice Cultures Since 1880 (Urbana: University of Illinois Press, 1985), 24–26; 202–12; and Sidney Nathans, *The Quest for Progress: The Way We Lived In North Carolina, 1870–1920* (Chapel Hill: University of North Carolina, 1983), 11–13.

6. Allan Bogue, *From Prairie to Corn Belt: Farming on the Illinois and Iowa Prairies* (Chicago: University of Chicago Press, 1963), 267–79, provides a detailed study of the Savage diary from which this overview has been extracted.

7. Gilbert C. Fite, *Cotton Fields No More, Southern Agriculture, 1865–1890* (Lexington: University of Kentucky Press, 1984), 35–36.

8. Theresa Singleton, ed., *The Archaeology of Slavery and Plantation Life* (Orlando, Fla.: Academic Press, 1985), 321.

9. M. A. Barber, "On Reflections of a Hired Man," in Thomas Nixon Carver, ed., *Selected Readings in Rural Economics* (Boston: Ginn & Co., 1916), 547–48.

10. Cletus E. Daniel, *Bitter Harvest: A History of California Farmworkers, 1870–1941* (Ithaca, N.Y.: Cornell University Press, 1981), 27–31, 46–50.

11. Kevin Starr, *Inventing the Dream: California Through the Progressive Era* (New York: Oxford University Press, 1985), 172.

12. Stanley N. Murray, *The Valley Comes of Age* (Fargo: North Dakota Institute for Regional Studies, 1967).

13. John Brinckerhoff Jackson, *American Space: The Centennial Years, 1865–1876* (New York: W. W. Norton & Co., 1972), 49–55, documents this overview of bonanza farming.

14. Quoted in Daniel Boorstin, *The Americans: The Democratic Experience* (New York: Vintage, 1974), 313.

15. Robert C. Alberts, *The Good Provider: H. J. Heinz and His 57 Varieties* (Boston: Houghton Mifflin Co., 1973), 136–48.

16. Nathans, *Quest for Progress,* 22–27; John H. Winkler, *Tobacco Tycoon: The Story of James Buchanan Duke* (New York: Random House, 1942), 47–88; Robert F. Durden, *The Dukes of Durham, 1865–1929* (Durham, N.C.: Duke University Press, 1975), 26–81; Nannie M. Tilley, *The Bright-Tobacco Industry, 1860–1929* (Chapel Hill: University of North Carolina Press, 1948), 545–632; and Susan Wagner, *Cigarette Country: Tobacco in American History and Politics* (New York: Praeger, 1971), 32–62.

17. This account of an anthracite miner's everyday life and the region's mortality statistics is based upon Donald L. Miller and Richard E. Sharpless, *The Kingdom of Coal: Work, Enterprise, and Ethnic Communities in the Mine Fields* (Philadelphia: University of Pennsylvania Press, 1985), 84–134.

18. Philadelphia's craft shops are described in Philip Scranton and

Walter Licht, *Worksights: Industrial Philadelphia, 1890–1950* (Philadelphia: Temple University Press, 1986), 16–47. I am also indebted to this study for its site typology of shops, mills, and plants.

19. Herbert G. Gutman, "Work, Culture and Society in Industrializing America, 1815–1919" *American Historical Review* 78 (June 1973): 546.

20. Richard P. Hunt, "The First Labor Day," *American Heritage* 133: 109–12; and Theodore F. Watts, *The First Labor Day Parade, Tuesday, September 5, 1882: Media Mirrors to Labor's Icons* (Silver Spring, Md: Phoenix Rising, 1983), 25–57.

21. Gutman, "Work, Culture, and Society": 540–41, 543; Kenneth L. Kusmer, "The Underclass in Historical Perspective: Tramps and Vagrants in Urban America, 1870–1930," in *Our Being Homeless: Historical Perspectives*, ed. Rick Beard (New York: Museum of the City of New York, 1987), 24; and Richard Edwards, *Contested Terrain: The Transformation of the Workplace in the Twentieth Century* (New York: Basic Books, 1979).

22. Quoted in Morris B. Schnapper, *American Labor, A Pictorial History* (Washington, D.C.: Public Affairs Press, 1972), 78.

23. Harry Braverman, *Labor and Monopoly Capital: The Degradation of Work in the Twentieth Century* (New York: Monthly Review Press, 1974), 166–67.

24. W. H. Orr in *Report of the Committee of the Senate Upon the Relations Between Labor and Capital* (1885), I, 219, quoted in Painter, *Standing at Armageddon*, xxv.

25. Alice Kessler-Harris, *Out to Work: A History of Wage-Earning Women in the United States* (New York: Oxford University Press, 1982), chapters 4 and 5; see also Barbara Mayer Wentheimer, *We Were There: The Story of Working Women in America* (New York: Pantheon, 1977); and Susan Estabrook Kennedy, *If All We Did Was Weep at Home: A History of White Working-Class Women in America* (Bloomington: Indiana University Press, 1979).

26. Schnapper, *American Labor,* 329.

27. David Hounshell, *From the American System to Mass Production, 1800–1930: The Development of Manufacturing Technology in the U.S.* (Baltimore: Johns Hopkins University Press, 1984), 247–59, describes the engineering of the first Ford assembly lines. My summary of this complicated development is indebted to this detailed account.

28. Trachtenberg, *Incorporation of America*, 89–90.

29. Robert M. Fogelson, *America's Armories: Architecture, Society, and Public Order* (Cambridge, Mass.: Harvard University Press, 1989); Eric H. Monkkonen, *Police in Urban America, 1860–1920* (Cambridge: Cambridge University Press, 1981); and Frank Morn, *"The Eye That*

Never Sleeps": A History of the Pinkerton National Detective Agency (Bloomington: Indiana University Press, 1982).

30. William L. Barney, *The Passage of the Republic: An Interdisciplinary History of Nineteenth-Century America* (Lexington, Mass.: D. C. Heath & Co., 1987), 309–10; Alfred D. Chandler, Jr., "The Railroads: Pioneers in Modern Corporate Management," *Business History Review* 39 (Spring 1965): 16–40

31. Jonathan Prude, "The Uniform of Labor: Some Thoughts on the Dress of Workers in the Nineteenth Century" (Paper presented at the Delaware Seminar in Material Culture Studies, University of Delaware, Fall 1984), 7.

32. Harold Williamson, *Winchester: The Gun That Won the West* (Washington, D.C.: Combat Forces Press, 1952), 87.

33. Daniel Nelson, *Managers and Workers: Origins of the Factory System in the United States, 1880–1920* (Madison: University of Wisconsin Press, 1975), 43–44.

34. David Noble, *America by Design: Science, Technology and the Rise of Corporate Capitalism* (New York: Oxford University Press, 1977), 38–39; Monte A. Calvert, *The Mechanical Engineer in America, 1830–1910: Professional Cultures in Conflict* (Baltimore: Johns Hopkins University Press, 1967), 277–82; and Cecelia Tichi, *Shifting Gears: Technology, Literature, and Culture in Modernist America* (Chapel Hill: University of North Carolina, 1987), chapter 3.

35. James H. Bridge, *The Inside History of the Carnegie Steel Company* (New York: The Aldine Book Company, 1903), 85. For other examples of the rationalization of industry from the workers' perspective, see David Montgomery, *Workers' Control in America: Studies in the History of Work, Technology, and Labor Struggles* (Cambridge: Cambridge University Press, 1979); and Richard Edwards, *Contested Terrain: The Transformation of the Workplace in the Twentieth Century* (New York: Basic Books, 1979).

36. David Montgomery, *The Fall of the House of Labor: The Workplace, the State, and American Labor Activism, 1865–1925* (Cambridge: Cambridge University Press, 1987), 215–16; see also Sanford M. Jacoby, *Employing Bureaucracy: Managers, Unions, and the Transformation of Work in American Industry, 1900–1945* (New York: Columbia University Press, 1985).

37. Gutman, "Work, Culture, and Society": 547, 554, 557–60, 565–66; Daniel T. Rodgers, *The Work Ethic in Industrial America, 1850–1920* (Chicago: University of Chicago Press, 1978), 162–65; Dan Clawson, *Bureaucracy and the Labor Process: The Transformation of U.S. Industry, 1860–1920* (New York: Monthly Review Press, 1980); and David M. Gordon, Richard Edwards, and Michael Reich, *Segmented Work, Divided*

Workers: The Historical Transformation of Labor in the United States (Cambridge: Cambridge University Press, 1982).

38. Daniel Nelson, *Frederick W. Taylor and the Rise of Scientific Management* (Madison: University of Wisconsin Press, 1980), 104–67; and Hugh Aitken, *Taylorism at the Watertown Arsenal: Scientific Management in Action 1908–1915* (Cambridge, Mass.: Harvard University Press, 1960).

39. Margary Davies, *A Woman's Place Is at the Typewriter: Office and Office Workers, 1870–1930* (Philadelphia: Temple University Press, 1982), 51–78, 97–128.

40. Joli Jensen, "Women as Typewriters" (Paper presented at the American Studies National Meeting, November 1987), 2–14; and Martha Vicinus, *Independent Women: Work and Community for Single Women, 1850–1920* (Chicago: University of Chicago Press, 1985); Carole Srole, "A Position That God Has Not Particularly Assigned to Men: The Feminization of Clerical Work, Boston, 1860–1915" (Ph.D. diss., University of California, Los Angeles, 1984); and Elyce J. Rotella, *From Home to Office: U.S. Women at Work, 1870–1930* (Ann Arbor: University of Michigan Research Press, 1981).

41. Adrian Forty, *Objects of Desire: Design and Society from Wedgewood to IBM* (New York: Pantheon, 1986), 124–28.

42. Carlene Stephens and Steven Lubar, "A Place for Public Business: The Material Culture of the Nineteenth-Century Federal Office," *Business and Economic History,* 2nd Series, 15 (1986): 165–79.

43. JoAnne Yates, "From Press Book and Pigeonhole to Vertical Filing: Revolution in Storage and Access Systems for Correspondence," *Journal of Business Communication* 1 (Summer 1982): 5–26; see also Yates, *Control Through Communication: The Rise of System in American Management* (Baltimore: Johns Hopkins University Press, 1989).

44. As quoted in Faye E. Dudden, *Serving Women: Household Service in Nineteenth Century America* (Middletown, Conn: Wesleyan University Press, 1983), 81; Daniel E. Sutherland, *Americans and Their Servants: Domestic Service in the United States from 1800 to 1920* (Baton Rouge: Louisiana University Press, 1981), 45–62.

45. Susan Strasser, *Never Done: A History of American Housework* (New York: Pantheon, 1982), 171; on Irish women servants, see Hasia R. Diner, *Erin's Daughters: Irish Immigrant Women in Nineteenth Century America* (Baltimore: Johns Hopkins Press, 1983), 79–81, 84–94.

46. Ruth Schwartz Cowan, *More Work for Mother* (New York: Basic Books, 1983), 126; and Sutherland, *Americans and Their Servants,* 51–53, 56–59.

47. Strasser, *Never Done,* 176; the Bridget-Beulah comparison is found on page 170; David M. Katzman, *Seven Days a Week: Women and*

Domestic Service in Industrializing America (Urbana: University of Illinois Press, 1978), 78–79; and Sutherland, *Americans and Their Servants,* 58–62.

48. On the important role of the stint in a salesclerk's work, see Susan Porter Benson, *Counter Cultures: Saleswomen, Managers and Customers in American Department Stores, 1890–1940* (Urbana: University of Illinois Press, 1986), 248–58.

49. Warren Susman, *Culture as History, The Transformation of American Society in the Twentieth Century* (New York: Pantheon, 1984), xxiii.

50. William Nesbit, "Making a Living in Wisconsin," *Wisconsin Magazine of History* 69 (Summer 1986): 267. See also *Historical Statistics of the United States,* vol. 1, series D, 85–86.

51. Clarence Long, *Wages and Earnings in the United States, 1860–1890* (Princeton: Princeton University Press, 1960), 61–68; John Modell, "Patterns of Consumption, Acculturation, and Family Income Strategy in Late-Nineteenth-Century America," in Tamara K. Hareven and Maris A. Vinovskis, eds., *Family and Population in Nineteenth-Century America* (Princeton: Princeton University Press, 1978), 212–14; James Leiby, *Carroll Wright and Labor Reform* (Cambridge, Mass.: Harvard University Press, 1960); and John F. McClymer, "Late Nineteenth-Century American Working Class Living Standards," *Journal of Interdisciplinary History* 17 (Autumn 1986): 379–98.

52. Long, *Wages and Earnings,* 94–108; for important exceptions to the slow rise of wages, see Melvyn Dubofsky, *Industrialism and the American Worker, 1865–1920,* 2d. ed. (Arlington Heights, Ill.: Harlan Davidson, 1985), 19–25.

53. On the analysis of middle-class budgets, see Daniel Horowitz, *The Morality of Spending: Attitudes Toward the Consumer Society in America, 1875–1940* (Baltimore: Johns Hopkins University Press, 1985), 90–94.

54. Edwin R. A. Seligman, *The Income Tax: A Study of the History, Theory and Practice of Income Tax at Home and Abroad* (New York: Macmillan, 1911); and Gerald Carson, *The Golden Egg: The Personal Income Tax: Where It Came From, How It Grew* (Boston: Houghton Mifflin Co., 1977), 70–87.

CHAPTER 3: *Housing*

1. John A. Jakle, Robert W. Bastian, and Douglas K. Meyer, *Common Houses in America's Small Towns: The Atlantic Seaboard to Mississippi Valley* (Athens: University of Georgia Press, 1989), 207–24; and Fred Peterson, "Vernacular Building and the Victorian Architecture of

Midwest American Farmhouses," *Journal of Interdisciplinary History* 12 (Winter 1982): 409–27.

2. Everett Dick, *The Sod-House Frontier* (New York: D. Appleton Century, 1937), 112.

3. Robert Barrows, "Beyond the Tenement: Patterns of American Urban Housing, 1870–1930," *Journal of Urban History* 9 (August 1983), 418.

4. Lawrence Veiller, *Housing Reform: Handbook for Practical Use in American Cities* (New York: Charities Publication Committee, 1910), as quoted in Roy Lubove, *The Urban Community: Housing and Planning in the Progressive Era* (Englewood Cliffs, N.J.: Prentice-Hall, 1967), 58.

5. James L. Garvin, "Mail-Order House Plans and American Victorian Architecture," *Winterthur Portfolio* 16 (Winter 1981): 309–34.

6. Katherine Cole Stevenson and H. Ward Jandl, *Houses By Mail: A Guide to Houses from Sears Roebuck and Company* (Washington: D.C.: Preservation Press, 1986), 20–23.

7. Don J. Hubbard, "Domestic Architecture in Boise, 1904–1912: A Study in Styles," *Idaho Yesterdays* 22 (1978): 2–18; Karl T. Haglund and Philip F. Notarianni, *The Avenues of Salt Lake City* (Salt Lake City: Utah State Historical Society, 1980), 14–17.

8. John R. Stilgoe, *Borderland: Origins of the American Suburb, 1820–1939* (New Haven: Yale University Press, 1988), 129–61; and Elizabeth K. Burns, "The Enduring Affluent Suburb," *Landscape* 24 (1980): 33–41. Kenneth T. Jackson, *Crabgrass Frontier: The Suburbanization of the United States* (New York: Oxford University Press, 1985), 344, identified the servants' housing in Brookline, Massachusetts.

9. Sam Bass Warner, Jr., first provided the typology for this suburban form in *Streetcar Suburbs: The Process of Growth in Boston, 1870–1900* (Cambridge, Mass.: Harvard University Press, 1969). See also Robert J. Jucha, "The Anatomy of a Streetcar Suburb: A Development History of Shadyside, 1852–1916," *Western Pennsylvania Historical Magazine,* 62 (October 1979): 301–19; Harry A. A. Jebsen, "Blue Island, Illinois: The History of a Working-Class Suburb" (Ph.D. diss., University of Cincinnati, 1971); Robert M. Fogelson, *The Fragmented Metropolis: Los Angeles, 1850–1930* (Cambridge, Mass.: Harvard University Press, 1967), 154–55, 185, 194, 273–76; and Jackson, *Crabgrass Frontier,* 119.

10. Alan Gowans, *The Comfortable House: North American Suburban Architecture 1890–1930* (Cambridge, Mass.: MIT Press, 1986), chapters 3 and 10. My label, the Eclectic Manse, serves as a covering term for much (but not all) American housing, 1860–1890; I think Gowans's term, the Comfortable House, aptly characterizes many residential trends, 1890–1930.

11. Clifford E. Clark, Jr., *The American Family Home, 1800–1960*

(Chapel Hill: University of North Carolina Press, 1986), 92; and Jackson, *Crabgrass Frontier,* 84–85.

12. Francis P. Prucha, *American Indian Policy in Crisis: Christian Reformers and the Indian, 1865–1900* (Norman: University of Oklahoma Press, 1976), 180–97, 217–21, 224–34; and Prucha, *Americanizing the American Indian: Writings of the "Friends of the Indian," 1880–1900* (Cambridge, Mass.: Harvard University Press, 1973).

13. Michael J. Doucet and John C. Weaver, "Material Culture and the North American House, The Era of the Common Man, 1870–1920," *Journal of American History* 72 (December 1985): 565–577.

14. Gwendolyn Wright, *Moralism and the Model Home: Domestic Architecture and Cultural Conflict in Chicago, 1873–1913* (Chicago: University of Chicago Press, 1980), 40–45, 83, 94.

15. *Historical Statistics of the United States,* Series N238–245, II, 646; Doucet and Weaver, "Material Culture and the North American House," 563–64; Clark, *The American Family Home,* 93–94; Barrows, "Beyond the Tenement," 414–15; Claudia Goldin, "Family Strategies and the Family Economy in the Late Nineteenth Century: The Role of Secondary Workers" in *Philadelphia: Work, Space, Family, and Group Experience in the Nineteenth Century: Essays Toward an Interdisciplinary History of the City,* ed. Theodore Hershberg (New York: Oxford University Press, 1981), 292; Howard P. Chudacoff, *Mobile Americans* (New York: Oxford University Press, 1972), 123–29; and Carolyn Tyirin Kirk and Gordon W. Kirk, "The Impact of the City on Home Ownership: A Comparison of Immigrants and Native Whites at the Turn of the Century," *Journal of Urban History* 7 (August 1981): 471–87. See also Angie Debo, *Prairie City: The Story of an American Community* (New York: Alfred A. Knopf, 1944).

16. Oliver Zunz, *The Changing Face of Inequality: Urbanization, Industrial Development, and Immigrants in Detroit, 1880–1920* (Chicago: University of Chicago Press, 1982), 152–56; John Bodnar, Roger Simon, and Michael P. Weber, *Lives of Their Own: Blacks, Italians, and Poles in Pittsburgh, 1900–1960* (Urbana: University of Illinois Press, 1982), 153–57; Roger Simon, *The City-Building Process: Housing and Services in New Milwaukee Neighborhoods, 1880–1910* (Philadelphia: American Philosophical Society, 1978), 5–58; Virginia Yans McLaughlin, "Patterns of Work and Family Organization: Buffalo's Italians," *Journal of Interdisciplinary History* 2 (1971): 299–314; and John Bodnar, *The Transplanted: A History of Immigrants in Urban America* (Bloomington: Indiana University Press, 1985), 127, 180–83.

17. Barbara M. Posadas, "A Home in the Country: Suburbanization in Jefferson Township, 1870–1889," *Chicago History* 7 (Fall 1978): 134–49; and Jackson, *Crabgrass Frontier,* 129.

18. James M. McKay, "The Building and Loan Movement in the United States," *Proceedings of the American Bankers Association* (1910): 539–45.

19. Clark, *American Family Home*, 87.

20. *Historical Statistics of the United States*, Series D-583, I, 144; John Modell and Tamara K. Hareven, "Urbanization and the Malleable Household: An Examination of Boarding and Lodging in American Families," *Journal of Marriage and the Family* 35 (1973): 470–76; and Susan Strasser, *Never Done: History of American Housework* (New York: Pantheon, 1982), 151–61.

21. Paul E. Groth, "Forbidden Housing: The Evolution and Exclusion of Hotels, Boarding Houses, Rooming Houses, and Lodging Houses in American Cities, 1880–1930," (Ph.D. diss., University of California, Berkeley, 1983), 79.

22. Edith Abbott, *The Tenements of Chicago, 1908–1935* (Chicago: University of Chicago Press, 1936).

23. Groth, "Forbidden Housing," 85–94; and Kenneth L. Kusmer, "The Underclass in Historical Perspective: Tramps and Vagrants in Urban America, 1870–1930," in *On Being Homeless: Historical Perspectives*, ed. Rick Beard (New York: Museum of the City of New York, 1987), 20–31.

24. James Borchert, *Alley Life in Washington, D.C.: Family Community, Religion and Folklore in the City, 1850–1970* (Urbana: University of Illinois, 1980), chapter 3.

25. Gwendolyn Wright, *Building the Dream: A Social History of Housing in America* (New York: Pantheon, 1981), 114–132.

26. John F. Sutherland, "Housing the Poor in the 'City of Homes' at the Turn of the Century," in *The Peoples of Philadelphia, 1790–1940*, ed. Allen Davis and Mark H. Haller (Philadelphia: Temple University Press, 1973), 176–79; 190–96.

27. Barrows, "Beyond the Tenement," 395–420; Jules Tygiel, "Housing in Late Nineteenth-Century American Cities: Suggestions for Research," *Historical Methods*, 12 (Spring 1979): 84–88.

28. Wright, *Building the Dream*, 136–37, 146–50; and Elizabeth Cromley, *Alone Together: A History of New York's Early Apartment Houses* (Ithaca, N. Y.: Cornell University Press, 1990).

29. Nelson M. Blake, *Water for the Cities* (Syracuse, N.Y.: University of Syracuse Press, 1956), 248–87; F. E. Turneature and H. L. Russell, *Public Water Supplies*, 3d. ed. (New York: John Wiley & Sons, 1924), 9.

30. Joel A. Tarr and Francis C. McMichael, "The Evolution of Wastewater Technology and the Development of State Regulation: A Retrospective Assessment," in *Retrospective Technology Assessment*, ed. Joel A. Tarr (San Francisco: San Francisco Press, 1977), 165–90.

31. Deborah J. Hoskins, "Brought, Bought, and Borrowed: Mate-

rial Culture on the Oklahoma Farming Frontier, 1889–1907" in *Home on the Range: Essays on the History of Western Social and Domestic Life,* ed. John R. Wunder (Westport, Conn.: Greenwood Press, 1985), 121–36; *Historical Statistics of the United States,* Series M1-2, I, 580.

32. Quoted in Tamara K. Hareven and Randolph Langenbach, *Amoskeag: Life and Work in an American Factory City* (New York: Pantheon, 1978), 258.

33. "A Literate Woman in the Mines: The Diary of Ruth Haskell," in *Let Them Speak for Themselves: Women in the American West, 1848–1900,* ed. Christine Fischer, (New York: E. P. Dutton, 1972), 65, 88; and Strasser, *Never Done,* 104–24.

34. Katherine C. Grier, *The Popular Illuminator: Domestic Lighting in the Kerosene Era, 1860–1900* (Rochester, N.Y.: The Strong Museum, 1986), 3–9; Harold F. Williamson and Arnold R. Daum, *The Age of Illumination, 1859–1899,* vol. 1 of *The American Petroleum Industry* (Westport, Conn. Greenwood Press, 1981), 55–60; 521–25; and Albert Eide Parr, "Heating, Lighting, Plumbing and Human Relations," *Landscape* 19 (Winter 1970): 28–29.

35. Thomas Parke Hughes, "Thomas Alva Edison and the Rise of Electricity," in *Technology in America,* ed. Carroll W. Pursell, Jr. (Cambridge, Mass.: MIT Press, 1981), 123–25. The industrial backdrop for this discussion can be found in Harold Passer, *The Electrical Manufacturers 1875–1900* (Cambridge, Mass.: Harvard University Press, 1953); and Thomas P. Hughes, *Networks of Power: Electrification in Western Society, 1880–1930* (Baltimore: Johns Hopkins University Press, 1983).

36. Fred E. H. Schroeder, "More Small Things Forgotten: Domestic Electric Plugs and Receptacles, 1881–1931," *Technology and Culture* 29 (July 1986): 525–43; and Bernard S. Finn and Robert Friedel, *Edison: Lighting a Revolution: The Beginning of Electric Power* (Washington, D.C.: Smithsonian Institution, 1979).

37. Kenneth L. Ames, "Meaning in Artifacts: Hall Furnishings in Victorian America, *Journal of Interdisciplinary History* 9 (Summer 1978): 19–46.

38. Katherine C. Grier, *Culture and Comfort: People, Parlors, and Upholstery* (Amherst: University of Massachusetts Press and The Strong Museum: 1988), 59–80; Angel Kwolek-Folland, "Domesticity and Moveable Culture in the United States, 1870–1900," *American Studies* 25 (Fall 1984): 21–37.

39. Harvey Green: *The Light of the Home: An Intimate View of the Lives of Women in Victorian America* (New York: Pantheon, 1983), 93–100.

40. Margaret Byington, *Homestead: The Households of a Mill Town* (New York: Russell Sage Foundation, 1910), 55; Robert Lynd and

Helen Lynd, *Middletown: A Study in Contemporary American Culture* (New York: Harcourt, Brace, 1929), 98–99; and Louise Bolard More, *Wage-Earner's Budgets: A Study of Standards and Cost of Living in New York City* (New York: Henry Holt & Co., 1907), 133–134, 146.

41. Mary Buell Sayles, "Housing and Social Conditions in a Slavic Neighborhood," *Charities and the Commons,* 13 (December 1904), 258.

42. Evan J. Jenkins, *The Northern Tier, or Life Among the Homestead Settlers* (Topeka, 1880), 150, 154.

43. Sally Ann McMurry, "American Farm Families and Their Houses: Vernacular Design and Social Change in the Rural North, 1830–1900" (Ph.D. diss., Cornell University, 1984), 203–256.

44. Warren Susman, *Culture as History: The Transformation of American Society in the Twentieth Century* (New York: Pantheon, 1984), 252–87.

45. Gwendolyn Wright, "Sweet and Clean: The Domestic Landscape in the Progressive Era," *Landscape* 20 (October 1975), 38–43; Wright, *Building the Dream,* 158–76; Clark, *American Family Home,* 131–70; and Lizabeth Cohen, "Embellishing a Life of Labor: An Interpretation of the Material Culture of American Working Class Homes, 1885–1915," in *Material Culture Studies in America,* ed. Thomas J. Schlereth (Nashville: American Association for State and Local History, 1982), 298–305.

46. Laura Shapiro, *Perfection Salad: Women and Cooking at the Turn of the Century* (New York: Farrar, Straus, & Giroux, 1986), 96–101; Susan Williams, *Savory Suppers and Fashionable Feasts: Dining in Victorian America* (New York: Pantheon Books, 1985), 91–140; and Harvey A. Levenstein, *Revolution at the Table: The Transformation of the American Diet* (New York: Oxford University Press, 1988), 23–29; 60–71.

47. Byington, *Homestead,* 56.

48. Mary Antin, *Promised Land* (Boston: Houghton Mifflin Co., 1912; Sentry ed., 1969), 337.

49. Jeanne Hunnicut Delgado, "Nellie Kedzie Jones's Advice to Farm Women: Letters From Wisconsin, 1912–1916" *Wisconsin Magazine of History* 57 (Autumn 1973): 7.

50. Phillip R. Seitz, "The Privy Problem: Rural Sanitation and Public Health, 1900–1925" (Paper presented at the American Studies Association National Meeting, San Diego, November 1985): 12–18.

51. Catharine Beecher and Harriet Beecher Stowe, *The American Women's Home, or Principles of Domestic Science* (1869; reprint, Hartford, Conn.: Stow-Day Foundation, 1975), 403–18; Greeley's remark is quoted in George E. Waring, *Earth Closets: How To Make Them and How To Use Them* (New York: Tribune Association, 1868).

52. David Handlin, *The American Home: Architecture and Society,*

1815–1915 (Boston: Little, Brown & Co., 1979), 455–63; and Martha Van Renssalaer, "Home Sanitation," *Chautauquan Magazine* 34 (November 1901): 183–91.

53. As quoted by Lizabeth Cohen, "Embellishing a Life of Labor," 302; and Wright, *Building the Dream,* 132.

54. Karin Calvert, "Cradle to Crib: The Revolution in Nineteenth-Century Children's Furniture" in *A Century of Childhood, 1820–1920* Mary Stevens Heininger, ed. (Rochester, N.Y.: The Strong Museum, 1984), 33–64.

55. Massachusetts Bureau of Statistics of Labor, *Comparison of the Cost of Home-Made and Prepared Food* (reprint from Massachusetts Labor Bulletin, no. 19, August 1901; Boston: Wright & Potter Printing Co., 1901), 11–12.

56. Ellen Richards, *The Cost of Cleanness* (New York, 1908), 8–10.

57. Strasser, *Never Done,* 61–64, 80; Green, *Light of The Home,* 75–78.

58. Handlin, *American Home,* 194; Jackson, *Crabgrass Frontier,* 54–61; J. Weidenmann, *Beautifying Country Homes: A Handbook of Landscape Gardening* (1870; facsimile ed. by David Schuyler, ed., *Victorian Landscape Gardening* [Watkins Glen, N.Y.: American Life Foundation, 1978]; Frank J. Scott, *Victorian Gardens,* (1870; reprint, Watkins Glen, N.Y.: American Life Foundation, 1982).

59. Patricia M. Tice, *Gardening in America, 1830–1910* (Rochester N.Y.: The Strong Museum, 1984), 37; and Ann Leighton, *American Gardens of the Nineteenth Century* (Amherst: University of Massachusetts Press, 1987), 228–248.

60. Charles Dudley Warner, *The Complete Writings of Charles Dudley Warner* (Hartford, Conn.: American Publishing Co., 1904), 111; and Tice, *Gardening in America,* 39–40.

61. Melvin G. Holli, *Reform in Detroit: Hazen S. Pingree and Urban Politics* (New York: Oxford University Press, 1969), 70–72; and Handlin, *American Home,* 198.

62. Handlin, *American Home,* 193–94.

CHAPTER 4: *Consuming*

1. Clarence D. Long, *Wages and Earnings in the United States, 1860–1890* (Princeton: Princeton University Press, 1960), 35–38, 72–73, 109; and Gwendolyn Wright, *Moralism and the Model Home: Domestic Architecture and Cultural Conflict in Chicago, 1873–1913* (Chicago: University of Chicago Press, 1980), 83.

2. Susan Strasser, *Never Done: A History of American Housework* (New York: Pantheon, 1982), 12, 18.

3. Thomas Clark, *Pills, Petticoats, and Plows: The Southern County Store* (Norman: University of Oklahoma Press, 1964), 98–113.

4. Robert Hendrickson, *The Grand Emporiums: The Illustrated History of America's Great Department Stores* (New York: Stein & Day), 234–35; and Clark, *Pills, Petticoats, and Plows,* 189–211; Gerald Carson, *The Old Country Store* (New York: E. P. Dutton, 1965), 267–70; and William Leach, "Strategists of Display and the Production of Desire," in *Consuming Visions: Accumulation and Display of Goods in America, 1880–1920,* ed. Simon J. Bronner (New York: W. W. Norton & Co., 1989), 99–132.

5. Alfred Chandler, *The Visible Hand: The Managerial Revolution in American Business* (Cambridge, Mass.: Harvard University Press, 1977), 334–35, 349; and William Cahn, *Out of the Cracker Barrel: The Nabisco Story from Animal Crackers to Zuzus* (New York: Simon & Schuster, 1969), 89–98.

6. John Wanamaker, *Golden Book of the Wanamaker Stores* (Philadelphia: John Wanamaker, 1911), 43–56, 61–68; and Herbert A. Gibbons, *John Wanamaker,* 2 vols. (New York: Harper & Row, 1926), 161–80.

7. Thomas S. Hines, *Burnham of Chicago: Architect and Planner* (New York: Oxford University Press, 1974), 302–07; and Neil Harris, "Shopping—Chicago Style," in *Chicago Architecture, 1872–1922,* ed. John Zukowsky (Munich: Prestel-Verlag, 1987), 137–55.

8. William R. Leach, "Transformations in a Culture of Consumption: Women and Department Stores," *Journal of American History* 71–72 (September 1984): 323.

9. Robert Grier Cooke, "Show Window Displays: The People's Picture Galleries," *American Magazine of the Fine Arts* 2 (April 1921): 115–117; and Leonard S. Marcus, *The American Store Window* (New York: Whitney Library of Design, 1978), 23, 54, 56–57.

10. Mary Antin, *The Promised Land* (Boston: Houghton Mifflin, 1912), 187, 260–63.

11. Neil Harris, "Museums, Merchandising, and Popular Taste: The Struggle for Influence" in *Material Culture and the Study of American Life,* ed. Ian M. G. Quimby (New York: W. W. Norton & Co., 1978), 140–74; and Hendrickson, *Grand Emporiums,* 58.

12. Claudia Kidwell and Margaret C. Christman, *Suiting Everyone: The Democratization of Clothing in America* (Washington, D.C.: Smithsonian Institution Press, 1974), 101–11; and Daniel Boorstin, *The Americans: The Democratic Experience* (New York: Random House, 1973), 97–100.

13. Mary H. Tolman, *Positions of Responsibility in Department Stores and Other Retail Selling Organizations: A Study of Opportunities for Women* (New York: Bureau of Vocational Information, 1917), 37;

Leach, "Transformations in a Culture of Consumption," 332; and Louise Robinson Blaisdell, "From Cash Girl to Buyer, *Business Woman's Magazine* 2 (April 1915): 50–52.

14. Godfrey M. Lebhar, *Chain Stores in America* (New York: Chain Store Publishing Co., 1952), 23–25, 29–30; M. M. Zimmerman, *The Supermarket: A Revolution in Distribution* (New York: McGraw-Hill Book Co., 1955), 2–4; and Boorstin, *The Americans: The Democratic Experience*, 109–10.

15. Susan Strasser, *Satisfaction Guaranteed: The Making of the American Mass Market* (New York: Pantheon, 1989), 248–50; Zimmerman, *Supermarket*, 21–24; and Boorstin, *The Americans: The Democratic Experience*, 115–16, 446.

16. John K. Winkler, *Five and Ten: The Fabulous Life of F. W. Woolworth* (New York: Robert McBridge, 1940), 42–60; and Boorstin, *The Americans: The Democratic Experience*, 113.

17. Hendrickson, *Grand Emporiums*, 115–23; Winkler, *Five and Ten*, 162–82.

18. Stan Luxenberg, *Roadside Empire: How the Chains Franchised America* (New York: Viking Press, 1985), 13–16.

19. Viola I. Paradise, "By Mail," *Scribner's* 4 (April 1921): 480.

20. Hendrickson, *Grand Emporiums*, 205.

21. Quoted in Stuart and Elizabeth Ewen, *Channels of Desire: Mass Images and Shaping of American Consciousness* (New York: McGraw-Hill Book Co., 1982), 65–66.

22. Gordon L. Weil, *Sears, Roebuck, U.S.A.: The Great American Catalog Store and How It Grew* (New York: Stein & Day, 1977), 25–27; and Ewen and Ewen, *Channels of Desire*, 66.

23. J. H. Kolb, *Service Relations of Town and Country* (Madison: Wisconsin Agricultural Experiment Station, Research Bulletin No. 58, 1923), 73; and *Congressional Record*, 68th Cong., 2nd sess., 349.

24. David W. Potter, *People of Plenty: Economic Abundance and the American Character* (Chicago: University of Chicago Press, 1954), 169.

25. A. W. Shaw, *Some Problems of Market Distribution* (Cambridge, Mass.: Harvard University Press, 1915), 43–44, 88–89.

26. Paul Cherington, *Advertising as a Business Force* (New York: Doubleday, Page, & Co., 1913), 93.

27. For this typology of advertising styles prior to 1920, I follow Stephen Fox, *The Mirror Markers: A History of American Advertising and Its Creators* (New York: Random House, 1984), 41–74.

28. E. L. Godkin, "The Advertiser," *Atlantic Monthly* (January 1898); and F. P. Dunne, "A Man Don't Want," *American Magazine* (October 1909).

29. Leach, "Transformations in a Culture of Consumption," 338.

30. Orson D. Munn, *Trade Marks, Trade Names, and Unfair Competition in Trade* (New York: Munn & Co., 1915), 31–46; and Strasser, *Satisfaction Guaranteed,* 44–48.

31. Frank Presbrey, *The History and Development of Advertising* (Garden City: N.Y.: Doubleday, Doran & Co., 1929), 378; and Strasser, *Satisfaction Guaranteed,* 91–93, 134–36.

32. Boorstin, *The Americans: The Democratic Experience,* 147.

33. Harvey A. Levenstein, *Revolution at the Table: The Transformation of the American Diet* (New York: Oxford University Press, 1988), 30–43.

34. Harold L. Platt, "Samuel Insull and the Electric City," *Chicago History* 15 (Summer 1986): 30.

35. Robert Atwan, Donald McQuade, and John W. Wright, *Edsels, Luckies, and Frigidaires: Advertising the American Way* (New York: Delta, 1979), 251–52.

36. Russell B. Adams, Jr., *King C. Gillette: The Man and His Wonderful Shaving Device* (Boston: Little, Brown & Co., 1978), 101–05.

37. Lois Banner, *American Beauty* (Chicago: Chicago University Press, 1983), 217.

38. Anzia Yezierska, *Bread Givers: A Struggle Between a Father of the Old World and a Daughter of the New World* (1925; reprint, New York: Perse Books, 1975), 28–29.

INTERLOGUE: *Americans at the 1893 Columbian Exposition*

1. Joseph W. Barnes, "How To Raise a Family on $500 A Year," *American Heritage,* 33 (December 1981): 91–95.

2. Burton Benedict, *The Anthropology of World's Fairs—San Francisco's Panama-Pacific International Exposition of 1915* (Berkeley: Scoler Press, 1983), 60.

3. David F. Burg, *Chicago's White City of 1893* (Lexington: University Press of Kentucky, 1976), chapter 6.

4. Robert Rydell, *All the World's a Fair: Visions of Empire at American International Expositions, 1876–1916* (Chicago: University of Chicago Press, 1984), 48–68.

5. "National School Celebration of Columbus Day: The Official Program," *Youth's Companion* 65 (8 September 1892): 446–47.

6. Charles Hoffman, "The Depression of the Nineties," *Journal of Economic History* 16 (June 1956): 137–64.

CHAPTER 5: *Communications*

1. Warren Susman, *Culture as History: The Transformation of American Society in the Twentieth Century* (New York: Pantheon, 1984), xx; Robert G. Albion, "The Communications Revolution," *American Historical Review* 37 (July 1932), 718–20; James R. Beniger, *The Control Revolution: Technological and Economic Origins of the Information Society* (Cambridge: Cambridge University Press, 1986), 6–10; Carolyn Marvin, *When Old Technologies Were New: Thinking About Electric Communication in the Late Nineteenth Century* (New York: Oxford University Press, 1988), 3–8; Burton J. Bledstein, *The Culture of Professionalism: The Middle-Class and Development of Higher Education in America* (New York: W. W. Norton & Co., 1976), 47–48, 65–79; and Neil Harris, ed., *Land of Contrasts, 1880–1901* (New York: George Braziller, 1970), 6–7.

2. Wayne E. Fuller, *RFD: The Changing Face of Rural America* (Bloomington: Indiana University Press, 1964), 38–39.

3. Ibid., 116–17, 134.

4. James H. Barnett, *The American Christmas: A Study in National Culture* (New York: Macmillan Co., 1954) 18–19, 28–29, 84–85, 91–95; and Daniel Boorstin, *The Americans: The Democratic Experience* (New York: Random House, 1973), 158–62.

5. Lewis Atherthon, *Main Street on the Middle Border* (Bloomington: Indiana University Press, 1954, reprint 1984), 161–68; *Historical Statistics of United States,* Series R 244–257, II, 810; Edgar Howe, *Plain People* (New York: Dodd, Mead & Co., 1929); and William Allen White, *The Autobiography of William Allen White* (New York: Macmillan Co., 1946), 126–27.

6. Gunther Barth, *City People: The Rise of Modern City Culture in Nineteenth-Century America* (New York: Oxford University Press, 1980), 80–83.

7. Ibid., 106.

8. Charles Fanning, *Finley Peter Dunne and Mr. Dooley: The Chicago Years* (Lexington: University Press of Kentucky, 1978), 37–67; and Lee Coyle, *George Ade* (New Haven, Conn.: College & University Press, 1964), 23–39.

9. Quoted in Sidney A. Sherman, "Advertising in the United States," *Publications of the American Statistical Association* 7 (December 1900), 4.

10. Salme Harju Steinberg, *Reformer in the Marketplace: Edward W. Bok and the Ladies' Home Journal* (Baton Rouge: Louisiana State University Press, 1979), 59–74; Jan Cohn, *Creating America: George Horace Lorimer and the Saturday Evening Post* (Pittsburgh: University of Pittsburgh Press, 1989), 30–33, 95, 243–46.

11. Frederick L. Rhodes, *Beginnings of Telephony* (New York: Harper & Row, 1929); and Robert V. Bruce, *Bell: Alexander Graham Bell and the Conquest of Solitude* (Boston: Little, Brown & Co., 1973).

12. "The Telephone's New Uses in Farm Life," *The World's Work* (April 1905).

13. *Telephones: 1907,* Special Report (Washington, D.C.: U.S. Department of Commerce & Labor, 1910), 76, 116; Robert H. Glauber, "The Necessary Toy: The Telephone Comes to Chicago," *Chicago History* 7 (Summer 1978), 79–83.

14. John Brooks, *Telephone: The First Hundred Years* (New York: Harper & Row, 1975), 102–26; Robert W. Garnet, *The Telephone Enterprise: The Evolution of the Bell System's Horizontal Structure, 1876–1909* (Baltimore, Md.: Johns Hopkins University Press, 1985), 128–54, 160–65; and Henry M. Boettinger, *The Telephone Book: Bell, Watson, Vail and American Life* (Croton-on-Hudson, N.Y.: Riverwood Publishers, 1977), 163–71.

15. Bruce, *Bell,* 493–97; Ithiel de Sola Pool, ed., *The Social Impact of the Telephone* (Cambridge, Mass.: MIT Press, 1977), 15–39, 159–97; and Brooks, *Telephone,* 108.

16. *The World's Work* (April 1905).

17. Roland Gelatt, *The Fabulous Phonograph, 1877–1977* (New York: Collier Macmillan, 1954; rev. ed., 1977), 21; see also Boorstin, *The Americans: The Democratic Experience,* 379.

18. Ibid., 46–56; and Boorstin, *The Americans: The Democratic Experience,* 379–82.

19. Gelatt, *Fabulous Phonograph,* 191–95.

20. Harris, *Land of Contrasts,* 7.

21. Peter C. Marzio, *The Democratic Art: Pictures for a 19th-Century America* (Boston: David R. Godine, 1979), 10.

22. Robert Taft, *Artists and Illustrators of the Old West, 1850–1900* (New York: Scribner, 1953), 142–48.

23. Edward W. Earle, ed., *Points of View: The Stereograph in America—A Cultural History* (Rochester, N.Y.: Visual Studies Workshop, 1979), 70.

24. Carl William Ackerman, *George Eastman* (Clifton, N.J.: A. M. Kelley, 1939, reprint 1973); 71–108; see also, Brian Coe and Paul Gates, *The Snapshot Photograph: The Rise of Popular Photography, 1888–1939* (London: Ash & Grant, 1977), 16–29.

25. Karin Becker Ohrn, "The Photoflow of Family Life: A Family's Photograph Collection," *Folklore Forum* 13, Bibliographic and Special Series (1975): 27–36; Judith Mara Gutman, "Family Photo Interpretation," in *Kin and Communities: Families in America,* ed. Allan J. Licht-

man and Joan R. Challinor (Washington, D.C.: Smithsonian Institution Press, 1979), 241–243.

26. Foster Rhea Dulles, *A History of Recreation: America Learns to Play* (New York: Appleton-Century-Crofts, 1965), 294.

27. Joseph H. North, *The Early Development of the Motion Picture, 1887–1909* (New York: Arno Press, 1973), 8–18.

28. Quoted in Robert Sklar, *Movie-Made America: A Social History of the American Movies* (New York: Random House, 1975), 13–14.

29. See also Barton W. Currie, "The Nickel Madness," *Harper's Weekly*, (August 24, 1907): 1246–47; Edward Wagenknecht, *The Movies in the Age of Innocence* (New York: Ballantine Books, 1971), 8–24; Sklar, *Movie-Made America*, 14–19.

30. Mark Sullivan, *Our Times, 1900–1925* (New York: Charles Scribner's Sons, 1946), vol. 3, 552–53.

31. Sklar, *Movie-Made America*, 16.

32. Early film censorship is traced by Garth Jovett, *Film: The Democratic Art, A Social History of American Film* (Boston: Little, Brown & Co., 1976), 108–35.

33. Sklar, *Movie-Made America*, 58, 71–72; Lary May, *Screening Out the Past: The Birth of Mass Culture and the Motion Picture Industry* (New York: Oxford University Press, 1980), 43–59.

34. Ben M. Hall, *The Best Remaining Seats* (New York: Bramhall House, 1961), 12–51.

35. Lewis Mumford, "The Architecture of Escape," *The New Republic* (August 12, 1952), 321–22; and May, *Screening Out the Past*, 158, 295.

CHAPTER 6: *Playing*

1. William Allen White, "A Typical Kansas Community" *Atlantic Monthly* 80 (1897): 171–77; and John W. Dodds, *Everyday Life in Twentieth Century America* (New York: G. P. Putnam & Sons, 1966), 155–60.

2. Russell Nye, *The Unembarrassed Muse: The Popular Arts in America* (New York: Dial Press, 1970), 9–59. A criteria for best-seller status is found in Frank Luther Mott, *Golden Multitudes; The Story of Best Sellers in the United States* (New York: Macmillan Co., 1947), 8, 204–06, 303–15, 329–31.

3. Quoted in Richard J. Hooker, *Food and Drink in American History* (Indianapolis, Ind.: Bobbs-Merrill, 1981), 269.

4. Hamlin Garland, *A Son of the Middle Border* (New York: Macmillan Co., 1917), 165–66; and Lewis Atherton, *Main Street on the Middle Border* (Bloomington: Indiana University Press, 1954, reprint 1984), 319–20.

5. Roy Rosenzweig, *Eight Hours for What We Will: Workers and Leisure in an Industrial City, 1870–1920* (Cambridge: Cambridge University Press, 1983), 74–81.

6. Ibid., 81–84; see also Raymond W. Smilor, "Creating a National Festival: The Campaign for a Safe and Sane 4th, 1903–1916," *Journal of American Culture* 2 (Winter 1980): 611–22.

7. Arthur M. Schlesinger, "Biography of a Nation of Joiners," *American Historical Review* 50 (October 1944), 1–25; Charles W. Ferguson, *Fifty Million Brothers* (New York: Farrar & Rinehart, Inc., 1937); B. H. Meyer, "Fraternal Beneficial Societies in America," *American Journal of Sociology* 6 (March 1901), 647, 649–50, 655; and Wallace E. Davies, *Patriotism on Parade: The Story of Veterans' and Hereditary Organizations in America, 1783–1900* (Cambridge, Mass.: Harvard University Press, 1955), 1–2, 142.

8. Foster Rhea Dulles, *A History of Recreation: America Learns to Play* (New York: Appleton-Century-Crofts, 1965), 255–56.

9. Neil Harris, "On Vacation" in *Resorts of the Catskills* ed. Alf Evers, et al. (New York: St. Martin's Press and the Gallery Association of New York State, 1979), 101–08; Hugh DeSantis, "The Democratization of Travel: The Travel Agent in American History," *Journal of American Culture* 1 (April 1978): 1–19; and Burton J. Bledstein, *The Culture of Professionalism: The Middle-Class and Development of Higher Education in America* (New York: W. W. Norton & Co., 1976), 64.

10. Betsy Blackwell and Elizabeth Cromley, "On the Veranda: Resorts of the Catskills," in *Victorian Resorts and Hotels,* Richard Guy Wilson, ed. (Philadelphia: Victorian Society in America, 1982), 49–58.

11. Ellen B. Weiss, *City in the Woods: The Life and Design of an American Camp Meeting on Martha's Vineyard* (New York: Oxford University Press, 1987), 137–158.

12. Harrison Rhodes, *In Vacation America* (New York: Harper & Bros., 1915), 10–12.

13. Charles E. Funnell, *By the Beautiful Sea: The Rise and High Times of That Great American Resort, Atlantic City* (New York: Alfred A. Knopf, 1975), 45; and George A. Birmingham, *Connaught to Chicago* (London: Nisbet, 1914), 89.

14. Peter J. Schmitt, *Back to Nature: The Arcadian Myth in Urban America* (New York: Oxford University Press, 1969), xvii–xviii; and Alfred Runte, *National Parks: The American Experience* (Lincoln: University of Nebraska Press, 1979), 65–105.

15. John Jakle, *The Tourist: Travel in Twentieth-Century North America* (Lincoln: University of Nebraska Press, 1985), 68–71; Schmitt, *Back to Nature,* 160–61; and Warren J. Belasco, *Americans on the Road:*

From Autocamp to Motel, 1910–1945 (Cambridge, Mass.: MIT Press, 1979), 93–94.

16. As quoted in Harvey Green, *Fit for America: Health, Fitness, Sport and American Society* (New York: Pantheon, 1986), 192–94; Green also provides an important interpretation of Lewis, 184–191.

17. Ibid., 201, 202–05, 213–14, 321–22; and James C. Whorton, *Crusaders for Fitness: The History of American Health Reformers* (Princeton: Princeton University Press, 1982), 270–303.

18. Richard D. Schwarz, *John Harvey Kellogg* (Nashville, Tenn.: Southern Publishing Co., 1970), 209–19; Harvey A. Levenstein, *Revolution at the Table: The Transformation of the American Diet* (New York: Oxford University Press, 1988), 33, 92–93; and Green, *Fit for America*, 304–13.

19. Gary A. Tobin, "The Bicycle Boom of the 1890s: The Development of Private Transportation and the Birth of the Modern Tourist," *Journal of Popular Culture* 7:4 (1974): 838–849; and Dale A. Somers, "The Leisure Revolution: Recreation in the American City, 1820–1920," *Journal of Popular Culture* 5 (1971): 125–47.

20. George D. Bushell, "When Chicago Was Wheel Crazy," *Chicago History* 4 (Fall 1975), 167–75; and Philip P. Mason, *The League of American Wheelman and the Good Roads Movement, 1880–1905* (Ann Arbor: University of Michigan Press, 1958).

21. Quoted in Jakle, *The Tourist*, 113; see also Belasco, *Americans on the Road*, 79–86, 113–18.

22. Allen Guttmann, *Sports Spectators* (New York: Columbia University Press, 1986), 83.

23. Elliott J. Gorn, *The Manly Art: Bare-Knuckle Prize Fighting in America* (Ithaca, N.Y.: Cornell University Press, 1986) 230–36; and Gunther Barth, *City People: The Rise of Modern City Culture in Nineteenth-Century America* (New York: Oxford University Press, 1980), 158.

24. Guttmann, *Sports Spectators*, 119; and Gorn, *The Manly Art*, 197.

25. Steven M. Gelber, "Working at Playing: The Culture of the Workplace and the Rise of Baseball," *Journal of Social History* 16 (Summer 1983); 3–22; and Barth, *City People*, 178–79.

26. Jon M. Kingsdale, "The 'Poor Man's Club': Social Functions of the Urban Working-Class Saloon," *American Quarterly* 25 (October 1973), 472–75, provides both statistics on saloons and the typology of workers' saloons.

27. Kingsdale, "Poor Man's Club," 474–75; and George Ade, *The Old-Time Saloon, Not Wet—Not Dry, Just History* (New York: R. Long & R. Smith, 1931).

28. Perry R. Duis, *The Saloon: Public Drinking in Chicago and Boston, 1880–1920* (Urbana: University of Illinois Press, 1983), 52, 55.

29. Rosenzweig, *Eight Hours,* 61.

30. Edwin Milton Royle, "The Vaudeville Theatre," *Scribner's Magazine* 26 (October 1899): 485–95. Barth, *City People,* 204–207, provides the insight of the vaudeville's "continuous show" as the theatrical analog to the rhythm of city life.

31. Albert F. McLean, *Vaudeville As Ritual* (Lexington: University of Kentucky Press, 1977), 77.

32. Barth, *City People,* 220–21.

33. Warren J. Gates, "Modernization as a Function of an Agricultural Fair: The Great Granger's Picnic Exhibition at Williams Grove, Pennsylvania," *Agricultural History* 58 (July 1984): 264–65, 270–71.

34. As quoted in J. B. Jackson, *American Space: The Centennial Years, 1865–1876* (New York: W. W. Norton & Co., 1972), 217; Bledstein, *Culture of Professionalism,* 57.

35. Galen Cranz, *The Politics of Park Design: A History of Urban Parks in America* (Cambridge, Mass.: MIT Press, 1982), compare chapters 1 and 2.

36. Dominick J. Cavallo, *Muscles and Morals: Organized Playgrounds and Urban Reform, 1880–1920* (Philadelphia: Temple University Press, 1981), 2, 36–40, 45–48, 102–03; and Rosenzweig, *Eight Hours,* 142.

37. Louise Bolard More, *Wage-Earners' Budgets: A Study of Standards and of Living in New York City;* (New York: Henry Holt & Co., 1907), 142; and Robert Coit Chapin, *The Standard of Living Among Workingmen's Families in New York City* (New York: Russell Sage Foundation, 1909), 211, 276.

38. Richard Snow, *Coney Island* (New York: Brightwaters Press, 1984) 86; John Kasson, *Amusing the Million: Coney Island and Turn of the Century America* (New York: Hill & Wang, 1977), 37–42, 47–50; and Kathy Lee Peiss, *Cheap Amusements: Working Women and Leisure in Turn-of-the-Century New York* (Philadelphia: Temple University Press, 1986), 123–29; 136–38.

39. Robert E. Snow and David E. Wright, "Coney Island: A Case Study in Popular Culture and Technical Change," *Journal of Popular Culture* 9 (Spring 1976): 960–75; and "The Mechanical Joys of Coney Island," *Scientific American* 99 (15 August 1908).

40. Kasson, *Amusing The Million,* 41.

41. Guy Wetmore Carryl, "Marvelous Coney Island," *Munsey's Magazine* 25 (September 1901): 814; and Kasson, *Amusing the Million,* 41–43.

CHAPTER 7: *Striving*

1. James A. Burns, *The Growth and Development of the Catholic School System in the United States* (New York: Benziger Bros., 1912), 197–249, 346–80; and John F. Ohles and Shirley M. Ohles, *Private Colleges and Universities,* vol. 2 (Westport, Conn.: Greenwood Press, 1988), 1450–63.

2. Alan Trachtenberg, " 'We Study the Word and Works of God': Chautauqua and the Sacralization of Culture in America," *Henry Ford Museum Herald* 13 (1984): 3–11.

3. Richard Mosier, *Making the American Mind: Social and Moral Ideas in the McGuffey Readers* (New York: King's Crown Press, 1947), 161.

4. Marvin Lazerson, *Origins of the Urban School: Public Education in Massachusetts, 1870–1915* (Cambridge, Mass.: Harvard University Press, 1971), ix–xviii, 241–57.

5. For discussions of the kindergarten, see Marvin Lazerson, "Urban Reform and the Schools: Kindergartens in Massachusetts, 1870–1915," in *Education in American History,* ed Michael B. Katz (New York: Harper & Row, 1973), 224–28; Evelyn Weber, *The Kindergarten: Its Encounter with Educational Thought in America* (New York: Teachers College Press, 1969); Dale Ross, *The Kindergarten Crusade* (Athens: Ohio University Press, 1976); and Karen Feinstein, "Kindergartens, Feminism, and the Professionalism of Motherhood," *Journal of Women's Studies* 3 (January–February 1980), 28–39.

6. Joel H. Spring, *Education and the Rise of the Corporate State* (Boston: Beacon Press, 1972), 36–43.

7. Edward A. Krug, *The Shaping of the American High School* (New York: Harper & Row, 1964), 439; and *Historical Statistics of the United States,* Series 598–601, I, 379.

8. David Nasaw, *Schooled to Order: A Social History of Public Schooling in the United States* (New York: Oxford University Press, 1979), p 89–91; see also Steven L. Schlossman, *Love and the American Delinquent: The Theory and Practice of "Progressive" Juvenile Justice, 1825–1910* (Chicago: University of Chicago Press, 1977); Anthony Platt, *The Childsavers: The Invention of Delinquency* (Chicago: University of Chicago Press, 1969), 137–145.

9. Reed Yeda, "The High School and Social Mobility in a Streetcar Suburb: Somerville, Mass., 1870–1910," *Journal of Interdisciplinary History* 14 (Spring 1984): 751–771; and Nasaw, *Schooled to Order,* 117–120.

10. Krug, *Shaping of the American High School,* 391–93, 443–444.

11. Seymour E. Harris, *A Statistical Portrait of Higher Education* (New York: McGraw-Hill Book Co., 1972); O. Edgar Reynolds, *The Social*

and Economic Status of College Students (New York: Bureau of Publications, Teachers College, Columbia University, 1927), as quoted in Lawrence A. Cremin, *American Education: The Metropolitan Experience, 1876–1980* (New York: Harper & Row, 1988), 556; Colin B. Burke, "The Expansion of American Higher Education," in Konrad H. Jarausch, ed., *The Transformation of Higher Learning 1860–1930: Expansion, Diversification, Social Opening, and Professionalization in England, Germany, Russia, and the United States* (Chicago: University of Chicago Press, 1983), 108–30.

12. Hugh Hawkins, *Between Harvard and America: The Educational Leadership of Charles W. Eliot* (New York: Oxford University Press, 1972), 80–119.

13. Helen Lefkowitz Horowitz, *Campus Life: Undergraduate Cultures from the End of the Eighteenth Century to the Present* (Chicago: University of Chicago Press, 1987), 3–22.

14. Ibid., 14–15, 56–81.

15. Ibid., 15–16, 82–97; and Henry May, *The End of American Innocence: A Study of the First Years of Our Own Time, 1912–1917* (New York: Alfred A. Knopf, 1959), 121–218.

16. Burton J. Bledstein, *The Culture of Professionalism: The Middle-Class and Development of Higher Education in America* (New York: W. W. Norton & Co., 1976), ix–xi, 159–202; Bailey B. Burritt, *Professional Distribution of College and University Graduates,* U.S. Bureau of Education Bulletin No. 19 (Washington, D.C.: U.S. Government Printing Office, 1912); Horowitz, *Campus Life,* 6, 9; and Joseph F. Kett, *Rites of Passage: Adolesence in America, 1790 to the Present* (New York: Basic Books, 1977), 151.

17. Bledstein, *Culture of Professionalism,* 44–45, 56; Randall Collins, *The Credential Society: An Historical Sociology of Education and Stratification* (New York: Academic Press, 1979).

18. Bruce Sinclair, "Episodes in the History of the American Engineering Profession," and Harold C. Livesay, "The Profession of Management in the United States," in *The Professions in American History,* ed. Nathan O. Hatch (Notre Dame, Ind.: University of Notre Dame Press, 1988), 127–144, 199–220; Cremin, *American Education: The Metropolitan Experience,* 493; and Neil Harris, *The Land of Contrasts, 1880–1900* (New York: George Braziller, 1970), 16–17.

19. John Vincent, *The Chautauqua Movement* (Boston: Chautauqua Press, 1886), 75; Arthur Eugene Bestor, Jr., *Chautauqua Publications: An Historical and Bibliographical Guide* (Chautauqua, N.Y.: Chautauqua Press, 1934); Leon H. Vincent, *John Heyl Vincent, A Biographical Sketch* (New York: Macmillan Co., 1925).

20. John S. Noffsinger, *Correspondence Schools, Lyceums,*

Chautauquas (New York: Macmillan Co., 1926), 109; and Theodore Morrison, *Chautauqua: A Center for Education, Religion, and the Arts in America* (Chicago: University of Chicago, 1974).

21. M. Sandra Manderson, "The Redpath Lyceum Bureau" (Unpublished Ph.D. diss., University of Iowa, 1981); Harry P. Harrison, *Culture Under Canvas* (New York: Hastings House, 1958); Gay MacLaren, *Morally We Roll Along* (Boston: Little, Brown & Co., 1938); and David W. Noble, *The Paradox of Progressive Thought* (Minneapolis: University of Minnesota Press, 1958).

22. David M. Maxfield, "Santa Carnegie Packs Bag with 1,679 Public Libraries," *Michiana Magazine*, (8 December 1985): 4; see also George S. Bobinski, *Carnegie Libraries: Their History and Impact on American Public Library Development* (Chicago: American Library Association, 1969); Helen Lefkowitz Horowitz, *Culture and the City: Cultural Philanthrophy in Chicago from the 1880s to 1917* (Lexington: University Press of Kentucky, 1976), 20–21.

23. Jane Addams, *Twenty Years at Hull House* (1910; reprint, New York: Signet, 1960), 98.

24. Allen F. Davis, *Spearheads for Reform: The Social Settlements and the Progressive Movement, 1890–1914* (New Brunswick, N.J.: Rutgers University Press, 1984), 68, 85, 96–8, 124, 133, 171–73.

25. Robert Hunter, *Poverty* (New York: Macmillan, 1904), 3–10; Daniel Boorstin, *The Americans: The Democratic Experience* (New York: Random House, 1973), 215–16. The label "factual generation" comes from Robert H. Bremner, *From the Depths: The Discovery of Poverty in the United States* (New York: New York University Press, 1956), 140–65.

26. On the discovery of poverty, see Bremner, *From the Depths;* and for the asylum, see David J. Rothman, *The Discovery of the Asylum: Social Order and Disorder in the New Republic* (Boston: Little, Brown & Co., 1971), and its sequel, *Conscience and Convenience* (Boston: Little, Brown & Co., 1980).

27. *National Prison Statistics,* Series H1135-1140 (Washington, D.C.: U.S. Bureau of Prisons, Bulletin 47, April 1972); and Rothman, *Conscience and Convenience,* 34–36, 342–43, 391–98.

28. Davis, *Spearheads for Reform,* 33–39.

29. Martin Marty, *The Righteous Empire: The Protestant Experience in America* (New York: Dial Press, 1970), 147, 169.

30. Sidney E. Ahlstrom, *A Religious History of the American People* (New Haven: Yale University Press, 1972), 1025; and Stephen Gottschatt, *The Emergence of Christian Science in American Religious Life* (Berkeley: University of California Press, 1973).

31. George T. Bushnell, "The Place of Religion in Modern Life," *American Journal of Theology* 17 (October 1913): 530.

32. George Marsden, "The Era of Crisis: From Christendom to Pluralism," in Marsden, *Christianity in America* (Grand Rapids, Mich.: Eerdmans Publishing Co., 1983), 297–98.

33. Robert Handy, *A Christian America: Protestant Hopes and Historical Realities* (New York: Oxford University Press, 1971, reprint 1984), 101–33.

34. Colleen McDannell, *The Christian Home in Victorian America* (Bloomington: Indiana University Press, 1988), 85–91, 96–98, 101–05.

35. John Higham, *Strangers in the Land: Patterns of American Nativism, 1860–1925* (New York: Atheneum, 1965), 80–871; *Historical Statistics of the United States,* Series H 1168–70, I, 422; and Ida B. Wells, *A Red Record: Tabulated Statistics and Alleged Causes of Lynchings in the United States, 1892–1893–1894* (Chicago: Donohue & Henneberry, 1895), 9–15, 45–48.

36. W. E. B. DuBois, *Souls of Black Folk* (New York: Fawcett Reprint, 1961), 142; Booker T. Washington, *The Story of the Negro* (New York: Doubleday, 1909) vol. 1, 278.

37. DuBois, *Souls,* 143.

38. Irving Howe, *World of Our Fathers* (New York: Simon & Schuster, 1976), 190–95.

39. Donald K. Gorrell, *The Age of Social Responsibility: The Social Gospel in the Progressive Era, 1900–1920* (Macon, Ga.: Mercer University Press, 1988), 117–276; and Janet F. Fishburn, *The Fatherhood of God and the Social Gospel in America* (Philadelphia: Fortress Press, 1982), 67–129.

CHAPTER 8: *Living and Dying*

1. Carroll Smith-Rosenberg and Charles E. Rosenberg, "The Female Animal: Medical and Biological Views of Woman and Her Role in 19th-Century America." *Journal of American History* 60 (September 1973): 332–356; see also Judy Litoff, *American Midwives, 1860 to the Present* (Westport, Conn.: Greenwood Press, 1978).

2. Judith Walzer Leavitt, *Brought to Bed, A History of Childbearing in America* (New York: Oxford University Press, 1986), chapters 5 through 8; and Dorothy C. and Richard Wertz, *Lying-In: A History of Childbirth in America* (New York: Free Press, 1977), 109–73.

3. Grace Meigs, *Maternal Mortality from All Conditions Connected with Childbirth in the U.S.* (Washington, D.C.: U.S. Government Printing Office, 1917), 7; Peter R. Uhlenberg, "A Study of Cohort Life Cycles: Cohorts of Native-Born Massachusetts Women, 1830–1920," *Population Studies* 23 (1969): 410, 412–15; and Uhlenberg, "Changing Configurations of the Life Course," in *Transitions: The Family and the Life*

Course in Historical Perspective ed. Tamara K. Hareven (New York: Academic Press, 1978), 94–95.

4. Harvey Green, *The Light of the Home: An Intimate View of the Lives of Women in Victorian America* (New York: Pantheon, 1983), 30–33; and James Reed, *From Private Vice to Public Virtue: The Birth Control Movement and American Society Since 1830* (New York: Basic Books, 1978), 3–54.

5. Steven Mintz and Susan Kellogg, *Domestic Revolutions: A Social History of American Family Life* (New York: Free Press, 1988), 109–10; and Robert V. Wells, *Uncle Sam's Family: Issues in and Perspectives on American Demographic History* (Albany: State University of New York Press, 1985), 28–56.

6. Mary Stevens Heininger, "Children, Childhood, and Change in America, 1820–1920," in Heininger, *A Century of Childhood, 1820–1920* (Rochester, N.Y.: The Strong Museum, 1984), 1–2; and Burton J. Bledstein, *The Culture of Professionalism: The Middle-Class and Development of Higher Education in America* (New York: W. W. Norton & Co., 1976), 68.

7. Steven Mintz, *A Prison of Expectations: The Family in Victorian Culture* (New York: New York University Press, 1983), chapter 4. Robert Lynd and Helen Lynd, *Middletown: A Study in Contemporary American Culture* (New York: Harcourt, Brace, 1929) 148–49; Theodore Caplow et al., *Middle Town Families: Fifty Years of Change and Continuity* (Minneapolis: University of Minnesota Press, 1982), 18–19, 148–49; on causes of the shift in the role of the father, see John Higham, "Reorientation of American Culture in the 1890s," in *Origins of Modern Consciousness,* ed. Horace John Weiss (Detroit: Wayne State University Press, 1960), 25–32.

8. Mintz and Kellogg compare these two models in Mintz and Kellogg *Domestic Revolutions,* chapters 5 and 6.

9. The phrase first achieved public notice in Ben J. Lindsay and Wainright Evans, *Revolt of Modern Youth* (New York: Boni & Liveright, 1925); also see Charles Larson, "Introduction" in Lindsay and Evans *The Companionate Marriage* ed. Charles Larson (New York: Bonit & Liveright, 1927; reprint, New York: Arno Press, 1977).

10. Hall as quoted in Joseph Kett, *Rites of Passage: Adolescence in America, 1790 to the Present* (New York: Basic Books, 1977), 62–67, 204–39.

11. Lynd and Lynd, *Middletown,* 211; and Kett, *Rites of Passage,* 252, 257–58, 260.

12. Francis E. Willard, *Glimpses of Fifty Years: The Autobiography of an American Woman* (Chicago: H. J. Smith & Co., 1889), as quoted in *The Female Experience: An American Documentary,* ed. Gerda Lerner (Indianapolis: Bobbs-Merrill, 1977), 36.

13. Veblen as quoted in Claudia Kidwell and Margaret C. Christ-

man, *Suiting Everyone: The Democratization of Clothing in America* (Washington, D.C.: Smithsonian Institution Press, 1974), 148.

14. Claudia Goldin, "Family Strategies and the Family Economy in the Late Nineteenth-Century: The Role of Secondary Workers" in *Philadelphia: Work, Space, Family, and Group Experience in the Nineteenth Century,* ed. Theodore Herschberg (New York: Oxford University Press, 1981), 277–305; and Leslie Woodcock Tentler, *Wage-Earning Women: Industrial Work and Family Life in the United States, 1900–1930* (New York: Oxford University Press, 1979), 89–93.

15. Philip A. M. Taylor, *The Distant Magnet: European Migration to the U.S.A.* (New York: Harper & Row, 1971), 210–11, 232; Mintz and Kellogg, *Domestic Revolutions,* 94; Ellen K. Rothman, *Hands and Hearts: A History of Courtship in America* (Cambridge, Mass.: Harvard University Press, 1987), 179–284.

16. For statistics quoted here and legislation regarding Victorian marriage, see Elaine Tyler May, *Great Expectations: Marriage and Divorce in Post-Victorian America* (Chicago: University of Chicago Press, 1980), 167–81.

17. William O'Neill, *Divorce in the Progressive Era* (New Haven: Yale University Press, 1967), chapters 1 and 2.

18. David Hackett Fischer, *Growing Old in America* (New York: Oxford University Press, 1978), 146.

19. Mintz and Kellogg, *Domestic Revolutions,* 97, 275.

20. Fischer, *Growing Old in America,* 62–63, 147; and Michel Dahlin, "The Problem of Old Age, 1890–1929" (Unpublished Ph.D. diss., Stanford University, 1978).

21. John W. Oliver, *History of Civil War Military Pensions, 1861–1885* Bulletin of the University of Wisconsin History Series 844 (Madison, Wisc. 1917); Fischer, *Growing Old in America,* 169–71; and Wallace Evan Davies, *Patriotism on Parade: The Story of Veterans and Hereditary Organizations in America, 1783–1900* (Cambridge, Mass.: Harvard University Press, 1955), 181–88.

22. Daniel Pope, *The Making of Modern Advertising* (New York: Basic Books, 1983), 45–46; and James H. Young, *The Toadstool Millionaires: A Social History of Patent Medicines in America before Federal Regulation* (Princeton: Princeton University Press, 1961).

23. Harris L. Coulter, *Science and Ethics in American Medicine, 1800–1914* (Washington, D.C.: McGrath Publishing Co., 1973); Martin Kaufman, *Homeopathy in America: The Rise and Fall of a Medical Heresy* (Baltimore: Johns Hopkins University Press, 1971), chapters 3, 8, 11; Susan E. Cayleff, *Wash and Be Healed: The Water-Cure Movement and Women's Health* (Philadelphia: Temple University Press, 1987); William G. Rothstein, *American Physicians in the Nineteenth-Century* (Balti-

more: Johns Hopkins University Press, 1972); and Jane B. Donegan, *"Hydropathic Highway to Health": Women and Water-Cure in Antebellum America* (Westport, Conn.: Greenwood Press, 1986).

24. Mary Roth Walsh, *"Doctors Wanted: No Women Need Apply": Sexual Barriers in the Medical Profession, 1835–1975* (New Haven: Yale University Press, 1977), 183, 244–67.

25. Edwarter Shorter, *Bedside Manners: The Troubled History of Doctors and Patients* (New York: Simon & Schuster, 1985), 110.

26. Barbara Melosh, *"The Physician's Hand": Work, Culture and Conflict in American Nursing* (Philadelphia: Temple University Press, 1982), 15–35.

27. Charles E. Rosenberg, *The Care of Strangers: The Rise of America's Hospital System* (New York: Basic Books, 1987), 6. For the type of institutions dealing with tuberculosis, see Mark Caldwell, *The Last Crusade: The War on Consumption, 1862–1954* (New York: Atheneum, 1988).

28. Rosenberg, *The Care of Strangers,* 4–5.

29. Ibid., 149, 147–48.

30. Mintz and Kellogg, *Domestic Revolutions,* 104.

31. Jake W. Spide, Jr., "An Army of Tubercular Invalids': New Mexico and the Birth of a Tuberculosis Industry," *New Mexico Historical Review* 61 (July 1986): 179–201.

32. Harvey A. Levenstein, *Revolution at the Table: The Transformation of the American Diet* (New York: Oxford University Press, 1988), 22.

33. George Beard, *American Nervousness: Its Causes and Consequences* (New York: G. P. Putnam's Sons, 1881), 26, 126, 131; and Barbara Sicherman, "The Uses of a Diagnosis: Doctors, Patients, and Neurasthenia," in *Sickness and Health in America,* ed. Judith Leavitt and Ronald Numbers (Madison: University of Wisconsin Press, 1985), 22–35.

34. David E. Stannard, *The Puritan Way of Death: A Study in Religion, Culture, and Social Change* (New York: Oxford University Press, 1977), 72–95; and Martha V. Pike and Janice Gray Armstrong, "Custom and Change," in Pike and Armstrong, *A Time to Mourn: Expressions of Grief in Nineteenth Century America* (Stony Brook, N.Y.: Museums at Stony Brook, 1980), 15–18.

35. Pike and Armstrong, *A Time to Mourn,* 16–17.

36. Green, *Light of the Home,* 179; Charles O. Jackson, *Passing: The Vision of Death in America* (Westport, Conn: Greenwood Press, 1977), 91–146; and James J. Farrell, *Inventing the American Way of Death, 1830–1920* (Philadelphia: Temple University Press, 1980).

37. Karen Halttunen, "Death and Mourning in the Victorian Era," *Henry Ford Museum and Greenfield Village Herald,* 12 (1984): 124–31;

and Charles R. Wilson, "The Southern Funeral Director: Managing Death in the New South," *Georgia Historical Quarterly* 67 (Spring 1983): 49–69.

EPILOGUE: *Americans at the 1915 Panama-Pacific Exposition*

1. Robert Rydell, *All the World's a Fair: Visions of Empire at American International Expositions,* (Chicago: University of Chicago Press, 1984), 231.

2. Burton Benedict, *The Anthropology of World's Fairs—San Francisco's Panama-Pacific International Exhibition of 1915* (Berkeley: Scolar Press, 1983), 43–45, 49–52; Rydell, *All the World's a Fair,* 221–29; and Donald K. Pickens, *Eugenics and the Progressives* (Nashville: Vanderbilt University Press, 1968).

3. Frank Morton Todd, *The Story of the Exposition* (New York: G. P. Putnam's Sons, 1921), vol. 5, 90–97.

4. James R. Beniger, *The Control Revolution: Technological and Economic Origins of the Information Society* (Cambridge, Mass.: Harvard University Press, 1986).

5. Burton Benedict, *The Anthropology of World's Fairs—San Francisco's Panama-Pacific International Exposition of 1915* (Berkeley: Scoler Press, 1983), 60.

6. Carolyn Marvin, *When Old Technologies Were New: Thinking About Communications in the Late Nineteenth Century* (New York: Oxford University Press, 1988), 3–8; and Howard Mumford Jones, *The Age of Energy: Varieties of American Experience, 1865–1915* (New York: Viking Press, 1971), 145, 149.

Siegfried Giedion, *Mechanization Takes Command: A Contribution to Anonymous History* (New York: W. W. Norton & Co., 1969), 5–10; and Alan Trachtenberg, *The Incorporation of America: Culture and Society in the Gilded Age* (New York: Hill & Wang, 1982), 41–43, 45–47.

8. Nell Irvin Painter, *Standing at Armageddon: The United States, 1877–1919* (New York: W. W. Norton & Co., 1987), 385.

9. Daniel T. Rodgers, *The Work Ethic in Industrial America, 1850–1920* (Chicago: University of Chicago Press, 1978), 155; Trachtenberg, *Incorporation of America,* 94–95; and Walter Licht, *Working on the Railroad: The Organization of Work in the Nineteenth Century* (Princeton: Princeton University Press, 1983), 164–213.

10. Michael J. Doucet and John C. Weaver, "Material Culture and the North American House, The Era of the Common Man, 1870–1920," *Journal of American History* 72 (December 1985): 560–61; and John Bodnar, *The Transplanted: A History of Immigrants in Urban America* (Bloomington: Indiana University Press, 1985), 127, 180–83.

11. Simon Bronner, "Reading Consumer Culture," in *Consuming*

Visions: Accumulation and Display of Goods in America, 1880–1920, ed. Bronner (New York: W. W. Norton & Co., 1989), 13–54.

12. Stuart M. Blumin, *The Emergence of the Middle Class: Social Experience in the American City, 1790–1900* (Cambridge: Cambridge University Press, 1990), 258–97; Burton J. Bledstein, *The Culture of Professionalism: The Middle-Class and Development of Higher Education in America* (New York: W. W. Norton & Co., 1976), 37–38; Daniel Horowitz, *Mortality of Spending: Attitudes Toward the Consumer Society in America, 1875–1940* (Baltimore, Md.: Johns Hopkins University Press, 1985), 151; and Painter, *Standing at Armageddon,* 386.

13. Loren Baritz, *The Good Life: The Meaning of Success for the American Middle Class* (New York: Alfred A. Knopf, 1989), 3–55; Robert Wiebe, *Search for Order, 1877–1920* (New York: Hill & Wang, 1967), 111–132; Bledstein, *Culture of Professionalism,* 34–40; and Bailey B. Burritt, *Professional Distribution of College and University Graduates,* U.S. Bureau of Education Bulletin No. 19, Whole Number 491 (Washington, D.C.: U.S. Government Printing Office, 1912).

14. Richard Guy Wilson, *The American Renaissance* (New York: Pantheon, 1979), 11–74; and Wilbur Zelinsky, *Nation into State: The Shifting Symbolic Foundations of American Nationalism* (Chapel Hill: University of North Carolina Press, 1988), 71, 150.

15. John L. Thomas, *Alternative America: Henry George, Edward Bellamy, Henry Demarst Lloyd and the Adversary Tradition* (Cambridge, Mass.: Harvard University Press, 1983); Alan Trachtenberg, *Critics of Culture: Literature and Society in the Early Twentieth Century* (New York: John Wiley & Sons, 1976), 3–13, 99–107.

16. See Introduction, page vi and note 15.

17. Warren Susman, *Culture as History, The Transformation of American Society in the Twentieth Century* (New York: Pantheon, 1984), xxvi–xxvii.